KT-418-636

THE 24 HOUR BUSINESS PLAN

WITHDRAWN

NAPIER UNIVERSITY LIBRARY

THE
24 HOUR BUSINESS PLAN

*A Step-by-Step Guide to Producing
a Tailor-Made Business Plan in
24 Working Hours*

RON JOHNSON

CENTURY
BUSINESS

S 658. 4012 JOH

© Ron Johnson 1990, 1997

All rights reserved

Ron Johnson has asserted his rights under the Copyright, Designs and Patents Act, 1988, to be identified as the author of this work.

This edition first published in the United Kingdom by Century Ltd
Random House, 20 Vauxhall Bridge Road, London SW1V 2SA

Random House Australia (Pty) Limited
20 Alfred Street, Milsons Point
Sydney, New South Wales 2061, Australia

Random House New Zealand Limited
18 Poland Road, Glenfield
Auckland 10, New Zealand

Random House South Africa (Pty) Limited
Endulini, 5a Jubilee Road, Parktown 2193, South Africa

Random House UK Limited Reg. No. 954009

Papers used by Random House UK Limited are natural, recyclable products made from wood grown in sustainable forests. The manufacturing processes conform to the environmental regulations of the country of origin.

ISBN 0 7126 7779 8

Typeset by SX Composing DTP, Rayleigh, Essex
Printed and bound in Great Britain by Butler & Tanner Ltd, Frome, Somerset

Companies, institutions and other organizations wishing to make bulk purchases of any business books published by Random House should contact their local bookstore or Random House direct:

Special Sales Director
Random House, 20 Vauxhall Bridge Road, London SW1V 2SA

Tel 0171 840 8470   Fax 0171 828 6681

Contents

Part Five

FINANCIAL STRATEGY

Part Six

PUTTING IT TOGETHER

Part Seven

THE BUSINESS PLAN

FOREWORD

This book takes you step by step through the complex process of drawing up a credible business plan for a three-year period. Some firms plan five, seven or even more years ahead, but many firms do little serious forward planning and if you are new to this activity, three years is not a bad start.

The book does *not* set out to teach you how to run your business, or manage your accounts, sales, production or distribution. It assumes you can do that already. However, many managers are not all that familiar with the financial terms used in a business plan and I have attempted to explain most of these, when they occur, in simple terms.

If you have all the information at your fingertips, it really does take only about 24 hours to write a business plan for a simple business. However, if you have to get information - for example, if you have to study the market and collect cost data - it can take longer. If your first estimates prove to be wildly out, then revising the plan and re-working the sums will take time.

I am afraid there are a lot of questions to answer, and a lot of sums to do. The arithmetic is not really difficult. If you can add, subtract, multiply and divide, that's about all you need. But you must do the sums. Be careful and methodical. You must get a feel for the figures. You must form your estimates, however difficult it may be.

You must be clear about one thing. A business plan is *not* a blueprint to be followed meticulously through, as if you were making an aeroplane out of a kit. A business plan is a means of mapping out the scene so that you (and others) can make better decisions today in the light of what might happen tomorrow. So you do *not* have to get it right - only as good as you can in the light of the information you have. Better information should make it better, but never perfect. Once you have the plan, use it as the basis of your management systems, updating your estimates and forecasts in the light of actual figures that emerge as you trade.

Business planning is hard work - but fun. Have fun.

Ron Johnson

Guildford
May 1990

Note for the Second Edition

Much has happened in the six years since I wrote the original text. The Internet has appeared on the scene and many people in business now make regular use of its facilities. I find that the book has been used by organizations wishing to apply for grants from public bodies. It is also used by Consultants helping businesses to develop in the UK and in the newly democratic countries in eastern Europe. The text has been expanded to take these developments into account, but I trust you will still find it easy to read and to follow.

I am indebted to Martin L. Smith, FCA, FILog, FCIT.FIstD (Business Consultant) and Mark L. Johnson, BSc, ACA (Financial Planning Manager, BOC Process Plants) for helpful comments.

Ron Johnson
Guildford
January 1997

PLANNING TO PLAN

> **OBJECTIVE:** to review the process of planning and the elements of a business plan, and on that basis, to prepare a programme of work to complete the business plan.

- **How to get started**

- **What information you need to assemble**

- **The initial decisions you need to make**

- **The sales and marketing decisions you must face**

- **How to plan your financial strategy**

- **Putting it all together**

- **Making up a planning timetable**

This chapter deals with how to get the planning process started. It will help you draw up a programme of action to prepare your business plan. We shall examine the make-up of a plan and the steps you must take. You must then consider the people involved and the work required, and on this basis, set yourself targets and a timetable. This timetable should be written down and talked through with the people whose support you will need (see Figure 1).

If you have already been trading you may find it easier to answer many of the questions. But it is very important in planning to *look at everything afresh*, to question every assumption and to build up the plan from scratch.

A business plan is typically for three to five years. Since planning involves to some extent trying to predict the future, the longer the plan the more speculative it becomes. But business plans of less than two years are scarcely worth the effort.

1

Figure 1 Planning Timetable

ACTION	PEOPLE & METHODS	TARGET DATE	DONE BY
1. Plan the plan			
2. Decide the purpose			
3. Enlist support			
4. Define the business			
5. People profile			
6. Scan the market			
7. Scan the environment			
8. Identify your 'niche'			
9. Pricing policy			
10. Location and address			
11. Forecast sales			
12. Marketing strategy			
13. Forecast expenditure			
14. Capital expenditure			
15. Forecast profit/loss			
16. Turnover and stocks			
17. Forecast cash flow			
18. Review funding			

19. Revise business plan

20. Information systems

21. Complete plan

22. Check viability

23. Implement plan

24. Update the plan

Note All the activities on this checklist must be completed, but since each decision has implications for others, every early decision must be kept under review as the plan develops. In many cases more than one activity can be carried out at the same time.

GETTING STARTED

You will need to spend time deciding who will use the plan and why ('The Purpose of Your Plan' - Chapter 1). Decisions about this will enable you to decide on who will be involved, how much detail you need and how the plan should be put together and presented.

Consider the people who will help you to draw up the plan ('Enlisting Support' - Chapter 2). There are two aspects to this. The people whose support you will need to put the plan into effect (your colleagues and senior managers, and those who will lend money or invest in the venture), and those whose expertise you may need to assemble information and to put the plan together (for example, coping with specialist topics, such as market intelligence, taxation, property, contracts).

To 'Define Your Business' (Chapter 3) can be one of the most difficult problems. It is not good enough to make bland statements about the kind of business you are conducting. This lack of clarity can lead to the dissipation of managerial effort over several different market segments, covering several types of products or services, using a variety of techniques. For small to medium-sized companies, this generally leads to disaster.

Success lies in making a very clear and crisp statement about what the firm aims to sell, and to whom and at what price/quality mix, and by what means, and in following these through with vigour. If the aims are based on a sound

THE 24 HOUR BUSINESS PLAN

analysis of the market and of the firm's strengths and weaknesses, there is a good chance of success.

The definition you produce becomes the starting point for considering the people you need and the market-place you need to scan; but you may need to review this definition of your firm's aims, and perhaps even revise it dramatically, when you have completed the market analysis.

This also has a bearing on the location of your business. In some businesses, the actual location where customers will visit or the address from which you trade will be of crucial importance. The location you choose will also have an important bearing on its cost to your business.

ASSEMBLING DATA

You and the people you gather around you to run the business are crucial to its success ('People Profile' – Chapter 4). You need to take a good hard look at your knowledge and abilities. Together, do you have what it takes to tackle each aspect of your chosen business? If not, what are you going to do about it?

Once you have decided, provisionally at this stage, what business you want to be in, you will need to consider:

• Your potential customers
• Your competitors
• The environment in which you, your customers and your competitors are working

('Scanning the Market' – Chapter 5 and 'Scanning the Environment' – Chapter 6.) Experience has shown that an effective way to get to grips with the complexities of the environment is to consider, in turn, the political, economic, technical and social situation.

INITIAL DECISIONS

In the light of the information gathered in your market scan, you may need to review your definition of the business, identifying more precisely the segment of the market you plan to serve ('Identify Your Niche' – Chapter 7). This will enable you to estimate what products and services you propose to sell, what prices you will charge and what methods you will choose to reach your potential customers.

Fixing the prices for your goods and services is no easy matter ('Pricing Policy and Profit' – Chapter 8). Make them too high and nobody will buy them. Make them too low and you will lose money. But there is more to it than that. You need to fix the price and quality according to where you have decided to be in the market-place. You can buy a pen for 20p or £10: Different pens, different parts of the market-place.

Where is your business located in the market-place? Making inexpensive items and selling them in large quantities? Or making a few and charging a great deal of money for them because people value them and are prepared to pay?

Many new companies start by identifying a 'gap' in the market-place, a need that nobody else is meeting, a market 'niche'. But to do this successfully means identifying precisely what to offer, and at what price.

Rarely does it make sense to work out the cost per unit and then add the required profit to fix the price. This may be necessary in some kinds of business, but it is in most cases approaching the business backwards. Having identified the product or service, and the right price, you must work out a way to provide it – and make a profit!

Before you can make any final decisions about pricing policy, you will need to consider the financial information about costs and profitability factors (Chapters 12 to 16).

As part of your planning activity, you may wish to review the legal form of your business: will it be best as a sole tradership, a partnership, a co-operative, a limited company; or are you aiming to trade in its shares? You must have expert advice on such a decision. The key factors include the extent of business risk, the sharing of authority, responsibility and risk, the disclosure of information, freedom of manoeuvre, and financial, especially taxation matters.

You will need to consider afresh where you will site your business in the light of your decisions about the market ('Location and Address' – Chapter 9). You may decide to operate from one site, which may involve design, manufacture, storage, trading, demonstration, distribution, servicing, and so forth. Your business may not involve all of these functions, but as the business grows, it may be wise to consider the location for each function.

As mentioned previously, there are two aspects to the location decision. One aspect is concerned with the image and trading situation, and the other with the costs involved. Availability of suitable employees is another factor.

SALES AND MARKETING DECISIONS

A knowledge of your market-place, the customers, their requirements, your competitors and their particular strengths, coupled with your decisions about what to sell and how, will enable you to estimate what you will sell, and what income will be generated from sales ('Sales Forecasting' – Chapter 10).

If we assume that you have already decided in broad outline what your marketing strategy will be, you will now need to put a lot more flesh on the bones ('Marketing Strategy' – Chapter 11). You will need to specify in more detail how you intend to inform and reach your customers, how you expect them to respond, how you will react to their response, make a sale, provide the goods or services and collect the revenue.

According to the nature of your business, you will need to consider advertising, exhibitions, sales promotions, telephone selling, sales representatives, distribution systems, invoicing and customer record systems, credit facilities, and so forth.

You will also need to consider your 'corporate identity'. In what light do you wish to be seen by your customers and the public? Do you wish to be firmly associated with one kind of business? Do you wish to appear substantial and respectable? Do you want to appear prestigious and exclusive – or inexpensive? This will have an important effect on your company or business name and how you want this represented.

FINANCIAL STRATEGY

Now that you have some idea about how the business will operate you can start to write down in detail the costs involved in running the business ('Expenditure Forecast' – Chapter 12). For the run up to the beginning of trading and for the first year of the plan you will need a month-by-month forecast of what you will spend, and when payments will become due. For the second and subsequent years a quarterly forecast will suffice.

Your business is likely to involve expenditure on capital items, for example, cars, premises and equipment ('Capital Expenditure and Liquidity' – Chapter 13). You will need to identify these capital items separately, to specify when you will need to acquire them, how you will finance them and how long you consider they will perform effectively – before they become unreliable or obsolete. Remember that there may well be advantages in leasing capital equipment.

Armed with a knowledge of what you expect to earn in each year, and what costs can be attributed to the provision of the goods and services concerned, you can calculate the anticipated profit or loss ('Profit Forecast' – Chapter 14).

Beware. This is not a simple calculation. Be careful to ensure that you understand the methods you must use. You may find it useful to calculate the profit and loss on a monthly basis, but *do not confuse* this with the cash flow forecast. These two calculations give you quite different information, and they are used for two different reasons.

Do not be surprised if you find that the business is not making a profit to begin with. This often happens. The key questions are (a) how long will it take to achieve profitability and (b) taken over the first two or three years, will the business be worth running? If you find that the business is not reaching the desired profitability levels, you may need to do some radical re-thinking about your market niche, and the definition of your business.

If you are involved with products or services that require you to hold materials in stock, whether they be finished goods for sale, raw materials, components or spare parts, it is important to consider the quantities you will store ('Turnover and Stocks' – Chapter 15).

The temptation is to keep plenty of materials around you to deal with any situation that may arise. But there are several reasons for looking at this in more detail. Goods in store take up space, and you have to pay rent and rates on that space – money that could otherwise be earning interest. Goods in store might become obsolete or deteriorate and hence lose value.

The level at which you keep stocks must be considered carefully, taking full account of the cost implications, delivery times from suppliers, rate of use and the importance to the business of adequate stocks.

From your forecasts of sales and estimates about when payments will be received, together with your estimates of when bills must be paid, you can draw up a forecast of the cash flowing into and out of the business ('Forecast Cash Flow' – Chapter 16).

This forecast is a vital management tool. It must be prepared on a month-by-month basis for the first year, and quarterly for the second and subsequent years of the plan. On this basis the firm's requirements for cash will be known. Once the basic business plan is clear, you will need to set up systems for monitoring the actual cash flow (Chapter 19) in comparison with what you have predicted, so that you can anticipate and deal with a shortage of ready cash to pay bills.

If you do not update your cash flow predictions, there is a very real danger of running out of money and becoming, in effect, bankrupt and unable to pay bills. It is quite possible to be making adequate profits but become bankrupt in this way, and for the business to fail when it appears to be successful.

In the light of the cash flow forecasts the financial underpinning which the firm requires can be determined, taking into account the anticipated investment by the owners, sources of loans and judicious use of leasing methods ('Funding Review' – Chapter 17).

PUTTING IT TOGETHER

With most of the pieces of the plan gathered, they must now be put together ('Revise Your Plan' – Chapter 18). A typical outline for a business plan is provided in Figure 2. You may wish to vary this outline in the light of your own particular business, but you should consider carefully each of the headings and ensure that the answers to key questions are covered in each case.

Figure 2 Outline of Business Plan

Name of the business

Address of the business

Nature of the business

People in the business

Marketing and sales strategy

Profit and loss forecasts

Cash flow forecasts

Capital expenditure plans

Stock purchasing policy

Funds required – financial base

Book-keeping – management information systems

Special factors and risk assessment

Action plan – key decisions – target dates

Before you put the plan into effect you should consider carefully how you will keep track of your firm's performance ('Management Information' – Chapter 19). How will you monitor sales? How will you keep up to date on receipts and payments, and update your cash flow forecasts? How will you control your stock levels?

In effect you will be building up the plan section by section as you proceed

('Complete Your Plan' – Chapter 20). Now is the time to pull all the sections together and check for internal consistency.

There are no 'sure-fire' ways to predict whether a business will succeed or fail, but there are some pretty useful indicators ('Check for Viability' – Chapter 21). When the chips are down, there are three types of factors to consider: the men and women who will run the business; the market-place and practicality of the business idea; and the management of money.

To put your plan into effect, you will need to work out a simple 'critical path' ('Implement' – Chapter 22). The order in which actions are taken can materially affect the speed with which you can make progress and get your business or your new initiative off the ground.

Almost as soon as the ink is dry on the plan some new factor is likely to arise ('Updating the Plan' – Chapter 23). It might be a change in the cost of fuel or a major component of your product, or the appearance of a new competitor. Refer to your plan and you will soon see whether any major changes are needed.

The very existence of your plan, the information you have assembled and the thought you have given to your business will enable you quickly to take account of the new factor, consider the implications and decide on what action to take.

Apart from these responsive modifications to your plan, you should get into the habit of updating the business plan on an annual basis, rolling it forward one year and firming up the first year on a month-by-month basis in the light of your experience and the current situation.

PLANNING TIMETABLE

As you can see, many of the decisions cannot be taken until quite a bit of the information has been assembled. Thus, in drawing up your timetable for planning, the essential steps are:

- Decide why you want the plan
- Become familiar with what a plan looks like
- Decide who will help you draw up the plan
- Describe the kind of business you want to run
- Gather information about the market and the environment
- Gather information about costs
- Make some forecasts and do your sums
- Revise your business ideas
- Check for viability
- Revise monitoring procedures
- Work out your 'critical path'
- Pull it together and go for it

Part One

GETTING STARTED

Chapter 1

THE PURPOSE OF YOUR PLAN

OBJECTIVE: to decide on why you are writing the plan before you start detailed work. This chapter will help you to make this key decision and to consider how it affects the way you will work.

- **Be clear about why you are preparing a plan**

- **Identify those who will make decisions based on your plan**

- **Itemize the factors which investors and lenders will look for**

- **Consider the management decisions involved**

- **List the people who will help you draw up the plan**

- **Recognize the value of planning and give it some priority**

- **Compile your own checklist of key factors**

The first step in the planning process is to decide just why you are undertaking the exercise. Business planning is *not* about producing a blueprint to be slavishly followed through, line by line. It is about pulling together all the information you can in a sensible way to *enable people to make better, more informed decisions today*, not to make tomorrow's decisions.

In general, businesspeople prepare business plans:

• When they start out
• When they see a need for a change in direction
• As part of an ongoing review process

This book assumes that you are not simply rolling forward a five-year plan, but that you have decided to take a long, hard, deep look at what you want to do over the next five years, and that you want to plan properly for this.

Careful planning will help you to make better decisions and avoid costly mistakes.

PEOPLE INTERESTED IN YOUR PLAN

Three groups of people make decisions based on your plan:

- The people who will invest in the business, the equity shareholders if you have a limited company
- The people who will lend money to the business
- The people who will run the business on a day-to-day basis

You may be applying for a grant from a public body (for example an agency or department of a Government agency or of the European Commission). In this case the officials of the body concerned will be a further group of people with a keen interest in your business plan.

Those who will give credit terms on supplies are also, in effect, lending money to the business and will need to be satisfied that it is credit-worthy. Such people do not usually study the business plan, but establishing your credit-worthiness with such people must be included as part of your plan.

In Figure 3, list the people who you expect to read the plan and make decisions based on it – including yourself (as investor as well as manager?). If you have senior managers, the list should also include them: they will each have a particular interest according to their specialism, for example, marketing, production, engineering, or whatever.

From time to time, as the planning process proceeds, you will need to check that each of these groups of people will gain what they need from the final document. What will each group of decision-makers look for in the plan?

Investors and lenders
The people who invest in the business or lend it money are looking basically at two factors: first, at whether or not, within a reasonable period, the business will earn more money than it costs to run; second, whether the rate at which cash will flow into the business will enable it to meet each demand for payment as it arrives. In other words, they are looking for profitability and cash flow.

Figure 3 People Interested in the Business Plan

On the left hand side, list all the people who will make decisions based on the plan. Remember that it is the people who make decisions, not companies, banks or public bodies. Be careful to specify in each case the individuals who will play a key part in the decision.

On the right hand side, write down what you consider they would wish to see in the plan: in other words, the basis for their decisions.

DECISION-MAKERS   **DECISION FACTORS**
(Investors)

(Lenders)

(Managers – make a note of
their specialist interest)

(Officials in Grant-awarding bodies)

Investors and lenders will ask a number of 'what if' type questions: for example, they might look to see whether the business has the financial resources to fund any expansion plans, or to weather the effect of higher-than-forecasted sales. High sales figures may appear superficially attractive, but they could lead to cash flow problems: for example, when your company is required to pay for more raw materials and equipment to fund production, whilst income from sales is taking longer to arrive.

Alongside these factors they will be making judgements about whether their investments or loans are secure, and taking into account the relative proportions of loan money to investor's money supporting the business and whether or not any of this investment is related to tangible assets such as land, buildings or saleable plant and machinery.

Investors and lenders will look behind the figures at what assumptions have been made about costs, sales, and so forth, and above all at the competence of the people who will be running the business. It is helpful to include a curriculum vitae for each key manager, showing his or her unique contribution to the future business.

Thus the written document must be designed to enable people to make these judgements and this can be used as a kind of yardstick against which to assess the quality of the business plan.

Grant-Awarding Bodies

If you wish to apply for a grant from a public body you must consider the concerns of the officials with whom you will be dealing. It is likely that they will have two overriding concerns:

1. The objectives of the grant. Generally speaking when a public body offers a grant, the scheme forms a part of an overall strategy to bring about a change of some sort. The strategy may be, for example, to improve the prosperity of a geographical area, to encourage a particular type of trade, to generate employment, or to accelerate the introduction of new technology.
2. The viability of the organization to whom the grant is given. It will bring no credit to the officials or the public body if they give a grant only to find that the organization fails to deliver.

It follows that when you are preparing your business plan and engaging in discussions with these officials you must clearly demonstrate how the activities of your organization will help to further the strategic aims of the public body. This factor is over and above the requirements of an ordinary business plan, but essential if you are dealing with a grant-awarding body. Study carefully the aims and objectives of the public body as well as the criteria for the award of a grant. From these studies you will be able to see how to draw up a plan that meets business objectives and also contributes to public policy development. It will also help you in the way you write the plan and present its key features. If, for example, the grant is associated with employment generation you will need to estimate the number of jobs the business will generate and when. Hopefully these will be new jobs, that is not jobs effectively transferred to you from another local employer because you take away his or her business. Public officials tend to judge viability on the quality of the people who will manage the operation as well as the validity of the written plan. It is vital to include a detailed curriculum vitae for each of the key managers who will be involved in running the business when applying for public funds. This section should show the expertise and experience that they will bring to the operation to make it a success. Public officials are also likely to be interested in the extent to which these managers have been forged into a team who are dedicated to the organization's goals.

Managers and planning decisions

Those who will manage the business on a day-to-day basis will need to be assured of its financial viability – the same basic data as that required by investor and lenders. They will also need to know, from the plan, what are the key indicators of performance, which expenditure figures to monitor closely, how to judge sales performance, which targets are crucial to success, and so forth. They will need to know how sensitive the business is to fluctuations in the price of fuel, raw materials, labour costs, and what policy it is sensible to adopt on discounts to customers.

If you and your colleagues who manage the business are closely involved in drawing up the plan, you will find the process valuable in itself in highlighting the key assumptions and factors that influence success or failure. As the situation changes, you will also find that the information you have assembled for the plan and the insights you have gained will improve the quality of your decisions and those of your senior people on a day-to-day basis.

You will not need higher mathematics to deal with the financial side of the plan. The basic work can be done with a pencil and paper, provided you can add, subtract, multiply and divide, although it speeds things up to use a calculator, or better still if you know how to use it, a computer. If you use a calculator, I recommend the use of a printing calculator because it makes it easier to trace arithmetical errors. An accountant will help you to deal with some of the more sophisticated aspects of financial planning.

The manager in charge of each function or activity in the business will learn from the planning process the key parameters of his or her function. The manager will appreciate in particular:

• Where costs arise
• Where and how the activity contributes to business success
• How the function relates to other parts of the business
• What relationship should be developed with other key people in the business
• What areas of the activity need to be monitored closely, what figures need to be collected and compared with the planned performance

Consider Figure 4 overleaf and for each activity seek to establish likely performance measures that should be monitored closely. Some examples are given below, but these serve only to illustrate the point. You must work out the measures which are relevant to your particular business.

Figure 4 Key Decisions and Performance Monitors

ACTIVITY

Advertising

Sales

Manufacture

Distribution

Financial control

Purchasing and stores

Field service engineers

Examples of decision areas and measures of performance

Advertising

• Budget for advertising
• How the money will be spent
• Number of enquiries generated
• Cost per enquiry generated, preferably attributed to each medium as far as this is possible, for example, by coding
• Advertising cost per completed sale

Sales

• Methods used for interfacing with customers and closing sales
• Sales mix (where there are different kinds of products/services)
• Number of sales
• Cost of sales department per sale
• Time taken to respond to enquiries

Manufacture

- Methods of manufacture to be used
- Cost per item produced
- Labour cost per item produced
- Cost of raw material per item produced
- Levels of work in progress
- Wastage of raw materials
- Other associated costs

Distribution

- Warehouse size/location
- Cost per pack/carton moved
- Cost per vehicle mile
- Picking accuracy
- On time deliveries
- Productivity – cartons per hour work
    – cartons per trip

Financial control

- Terms of trade
- Invoicing, statements, debt collection methods
- Cost per invoice
- Amount of creditors due
- Number of invoices unpaid
- Other associated costs

Purchasing and stores

- Cost per order placed
- Levels of stocks maintained (raw materials, finished goods, spare parts)
- Storage costs

Field service engineers

- Number and geographical distribution
- Cost per service call
- Time taken to respond to request for service
- Customer satisfaction

For each significant activity in the company you will need to set out how it will be done and targets for performance. Where possible, financial figures for budgets and targets should be derived from zero-based budgeting: in other words, building up from basic factors, such as on the anticipated consumption and costs of raw materials, the time taken to perform various functions, the anticipated use of services, the power consumption of key equipment, and so forth.

In any organization, it is all too easy to build in 'fat' over the years, and re-examining these figures from scratch will cause managers to justify each item of expenditure and the use of time. Early attempts at estimating may prove difficult, and you may need the help of experts.

Don't spend time calculating figures very precisely, but work hard to ensure that your estimates are realistic. Spend time on the crucial figures, and use rough estimates where the costs are relatively minor.

COSTS AND BENEFITS FROM PLANNING

The main cost in business planning is undoubtedly the time of directors and senior managers. The difficulty in persuading busy directors and managers from the hurly-burly to spend time in planning is one of the reasons why some firms use management consultants. Quite apart from any expertise they bring, they stimulate managers and help them to gain the collective will and discipline to plan.

The benefits from a properly conducted corporate strategy review and business planning exercise involving the board of directors and key senior managers can be summarized as follows:

- The managing director, other board members and senior managers gain a thorough understanding of the business, its environment, its strengths and weaknesses, its opportunities and threats: in other words, they have a *realistic overview* of the business
- The managing director, other board members and senior managers gain a shared vision of where the company is going, what its goals are and how they will be achieved: in other words, they gain a *sense of direction* and purpose
- The managing director, other board members and senior managers gain an understanding of the key decisions in the business and the part which each department will play in achieving results: in other words, they are well placed to co-operate and *work as a team*
- The managing director, other board members and senior managers will have reviewed each key contact, for example, with their customers,

suppliers and investors, and will know what to look for to help the business prosper: in other words, they will know how best *to deal with customers, suppliers and investors*
- The written plan can form the basis of a system of objective-setting, enabling each section of the company to set goals which demonstrably *contribute to business success*
- Because of their deeper understanding of the business, the managing director, other board members and senior managers will be better placed *to respond quickly, intelligently and effectively* to new situations that arise
- Because of the detailed analysis and data gathering that have been undertaken, the board will be well-placed *to secure the financial backing* required to implement its plans

You will notice that the major gains are for the management team of the company. The written document itself does not provide evidence to investors and lenders, but it does provide a starting point for a penetrating conversation with the board and senior managers of the company. If the management team can explain the plan, defend the data and the conclusions drawn from it, and convince the investors and lenders that the proposals are viable, and that the team of people who will lead the enterprise have the ability to succeed – the plan will have served a valuable purpose.

PEOPLE INVOLVED IN PLANNING

Ideally, everyone involved in the company should be involved in the planning at some level. This is not always possible in practice, but the important thing to remember is that you must consider every facet of the business as the plan is drawn up. In a small business, as each section of the plan is prepared, care will be needed to ensure that the correct research and investigation has been conducted and the appropriate advice has been taken. It is crucial for you to ask the right questions, and general guidance is given in later chapters; specialist advice, however, may be needed in relation to the nature of the business.

If you have some managers or people with specialist knowledge of the business, their advice and views should be sought and, where appropriate, they could join the planning team. There will be some areas where outside specialist advice may be required, in, for example, taxation planning and insurance matters, and in areas such as employment legislation, health and safety matters.

If your firm needs to enter into formal business contracts or agency agreements, legal advice is desirable. Specialist advice will be needed if the firm is

Figure 5 People Involved in Planning

On the left hand side, list the key factors you can identify which will impact on the business plan. As your work proceeds you may find that you must add further factors, so you will need to keep this list updated.

In the second column, list the people who will help you with this aspect of the plan, and in the third column, indicate whether they are to be included in the planning team (put 'T') or to be consulted (put 'C') as required.

A few headings have been included to get you started, but you can cross these out if you find that they do not apply to your business.

			Date consultation	
FACTOR	**PERSON**	**INVOLVEMENT**	**PLANNED**	**OCCURRED**
Sales forecast				
Production				
Promotion				
Purchasing				
Delivery				
Sales and invoicing				
Pricing policy				
Tax planning				
VAT				
Employing people				
Health & safety				
Contracts				
Computers				

concerned with patents, trade or service marks.

Thus, apart from board members, there may be people within the firm who should be involved in the planning process, and there are people outside who will need to be consulted. Use Figure 5 to prepare a checklist of the areas which will need to be covered in preparing your plan, and the way you will gain the help and advice you need.

Remember that by involving key people in the planning process, you will help them to gain insights into the reasons for your decisions and to be committed to making it work out in practice. A business plan has many parts that need to fit together and talking it over with other people involved will help you see the plan from several angles.

There may be occasions when you and some members of your management team will need to visit investors, lenders or public officials. On such occasions the people who have been involved in the business planning process are likely to be more convincing – both as team players and as people who are committed to the plan and believe in it. This belief is not based on blind trust, but on working through the detail of how the thing will work.

In my experience managers who have worked together on a business plan (or indeed any kind of plan) are likely to display their familiarity with the plan and faith in its execution in discussion. It is more difficult for people who have not been involved in the plan's creation to demonstrate that they are convinced of its viability.

Chapter 2

ENLISTING SUPPORT

OBJECTIVE: to decide on the expertise and assistance you will need to prepare your plan and to harness these resources effectively.

- **Assess your own expertise**

- **Bring together your 'planning team'**

- **Start to gather data and write drafts of key sections**

- **Be prepared to modify your ideas as information is gathered**

- **Be prepared to deal carefully with sensitive issues**

- **Consider a 'mission statement' when business aims become clearer**

In the Introduction, you were encouraged to make a start by writing down some first thoughts on the nature of the business, introduced to the component parts of the plan, and encouraged to draw up a programme to prepare your plan.

In Chapter 1, we looked at the people who will need to make decisions based on the plan and through the planning process itself. As you get down to the planning process in earnest, however, you should consider who would actually be involved in the planning process, and what part each person should play. If you are setting up a one-person business then clearly you must write all of the plan yourself, but with help from the many advisory services available.

YOUR EXPERTISE

You must be able to see the business as a whole, to see how the parts fit together and to understand enough about each aspect of the business to ask the right questions and to seek the help of experts where necessary. Be honest with yourself and check out the areas of your knowledge and assess your skills. Use Figure 6 as a starting point.

If you have the time for a course in business planning, you are strongly advised to take one. If you want to set up a very small business, you may find a relevant short course helpful. Try to ensure that the tutors involved are experienced in the management of small businesses, and have the time to provide personal counselling and advice on the programme. You will find that having someone with experience with whom you can talk over your ideas is invaluable.

If you are already in business, attendance at a course may be difficult, in which case you may like to use the help of a management consultant. Do not, however, ask someone else to write the plan for you. The greatest value of a business plan is the understanding that you (and your managers if they are

---

Figure 6 Your Expertise

Below are some of the areas of knowledge and skills you will need in order to take charge of a business and to draw up a credible plan. The detail may vary according to the business, but this list should provide an initial prompt for your personal 'stock-taking'. Note on the right hand side the state of your knowledge and skills in this area and any steps you intend to take to improve it, if necessary.

TYPICAL KNOWLEDGE AND SKILLS NEEDED FOR SUCCESS	YOUR KNOWLEDGE AND SKILLS

1. The technology of the kind of business you intend to run, the tools of the trade, the methods used, the skills involved.

2. The business parameters of the kind of business you intend to run: for example, typical cost factors, turnover, profit margins, typical contractual arrangements, typical credit terms (buying and selling).

---

3. Marketing and sales methods: for example, how to research the need for the products or services, how to estimate demand, how to determine the price and quality, how to identify your market segment, how to reach your customers, the selection of advertising medium, writing advertising copy, technical brochures, selling methods, negotiating with customers, managing a sales force, merchandising methods.

4. Managing money: for example, estimating costs, forecasting and managing cash flow, calculating profit and loss, reading a balance sheet, assessing alternative financial strategies and making decisions about the source and application of funds.

5. Dealing with people: for example, recruiting and selecting the right staff, choosing and working effectively with associates, collaborators, partners or co-directors, managing a team of people, motivating and developing people, gaining the commitment of your staff and colleagues, maintaining effective relationships with customers, suppliers and others crucial to business success – including investors and lenders.

involved) derive from the thought and work put into it. If someone else writes it, they will get this benefit.

The kind of consultant you want is the one who will take you (and your managers perhaps) through the planning process step by step, so that you learn the key points and can draw up subsequent plans yourself.

You may have sufficient confidence to tackle the exercise without taking a course or hiring a consultant, but be careful to recognize where your knowledge is not good enough, and seek specialist help as required.

At an appropriate stage you will want to talk over your business plan with an accountant and probably with your bank manager, too. It is worthwhile asking other businesspeople in your locality to check out which of the accountants and bank officials are sympathetic towards the smaller enterprise and known to be helpful to people starting out or seeking to impart a fresh impetus to the business. You need enough knowledge to conduct an effective business discussion with these people.

You must recognize that a business plan should cover at least three years, even for the very smallest enterprise. At first sight this seems daunting, as many people find it hard to see even a few months ahead. But a few months is not good enough for business planning. It would be all too easy to set up an enterprise that might survive for a few months, for example, by selling home-made craft items to sympathetic friends and relatives, or setting up a service to meet an evident, but perhaps short-lived demand, only to find that other customers are more distant or more discerning, or that the needs of the iden-tified customers are soon fulfilled or that competitors quickly enter the scene, so that the business fizzles out.

There are other types of business which take time to become established so that the first few months, maybe even the whole of the first year, produce a loss, which must be compensated by adequate profits in the second and third years. If the prospects of profits in subsequent years are not presented in the plan, why would any sane person invest or lend money to the venture?

As a rule of thumb, smaller enterprises should plan to be making a profit by the second year, and this should be clearly indicated in the financial forecasts in the three-year business plan. You must acquire sufficient expertise to draw up a plan which will demonstrate the viability of the business, and which you can present to potential investors or lenders.

THE PLANNING GROUP

If you decide to prepare your plan without involving colleagues, you will need to go through the same steps, but seeking professional help as and when required. Use the checklist in Figure 7 to help you choose when to seek help.

If you are already in business with a small management team, or you intend to start off with some other experienced colleagues, then you should engage in this planning process together. You must discuss each part of the plan between you, although particular sections may be allocated to different mem-bers of the team to prepare in draft form.

If you have been running your business for some time and now wish to do some serious planning, you should attempt to draw up a five-year plan, although the last few years will be speculative. The discipline of looking five

Figure 7 Specialist Help

Here is a list of some of the areas of expertise and specialists that you may need to call on, and some of the areas they cover which may be important for your business.

Accountant — for advice on financial matters, including taxation, social security payments, customs and excise, the effect of different forms of business and financing, dealing with company matters such as annual returns and audited accounts. Do not ignore free advice from the authorities: they will generally answer questions, but not offer suggestions!

Advertising — for advice on the best medium to use, and the preparation of copy and illustrations.

Export/Import — for advice on markets, sources of supply, documentation and rules. Do not ignore official sources of information and advice: public authorities and your local Chamber of Commerce may be able to help.

Insurance — (a) general insurance advice on property, equipment, third party, employer's liability, etc., and (b) specialist on keyman insurances, life insurances and pension matters.

Lawyer — help with partnership agreements, property matters and business contracts (but be sure that these are matters the individual specializes in, as there are several different areas of law).

Marketing — for advice on methods of gathering and interpreting data about the market-place, customers and their needs. You may get a lot of help from the public library and government survey data, but this needs to be interpreted.

Information Technologist — for advice on the use of computers in the business and, if appropriate, access to the Internet and the creation of a Web Site for the operation.

Patent Agent	will generally be able to advise on patents, trade marks, etc.
Property	advice on available property suitable for your business and, in particular, on the conditions of leases, rent reviews, and the like.
Recruitment	advice on the availability of labour, labour costs, cost-effective methods of recruitment for particular kinds of staff you may need. Do not forget the public employment services.
Technical Author	for help in drafting technical literature: for example, manuals and brochures.

years ahead will require you to look more widely at the changes taking place around you, and will also enable you to take a longer term view of any major changes or investments you might decide upon: for example, major investments in plant, a relocation to a new geographical area or expansion into new markets.

When companies outgrow their premises or the capacity of their equipment, or find that they must update their methods and approaches to stay in the market, then longer term business planning becomes a necessity and not a luxury. The same is true if the market for the business is changing and competitors pose a very real threat.

Thus in a medium-sized firm, you will need to involve in the planning process all the senior people who you want to be committed to putting the plan into action. We will call this the 'Planning Group'. You may need to call on the advice of other experts in the company as well, if they have specific knowledge, insights or judgements to contribute.

You may need some specific help from outside the firm, for example, from a management or business planning consultant, accountant, marketing specialist, insurance broker or on the technical side of your business. Sound advice is rarely free, although there may be subsidized advisory services or consultancy services available.

Once you start to pay for this help, you will need to be very specific in the questions you ask and the results you expect from this involvement. You have the right to expect an initial discussion (for say an hour) free of charge, and you should use this to see whether you can have confidence in the ability of the adviser and whether you consider that he or she will relate well to you, to your Planning Group and to your business. A professional consultant will want to discuss your needs and relate these to his or her own expertise before discussing fees. But following this a reputable consultant will not object to discussing fee rates and what you will get for your money.

Planning group meetings

The first meeting of the Planning Group should consider:

- Why the business plan is being drawn up
- The structure of a business plan
- What they see as the future of the business (what they consider it should be making, selling or providing, and to whom, and how)
- What information is needed to draw up the business plan
- How this information will be obtained and who will get it
- When to meet next to consider progress and to move the planning programme forward

The information you will need includes data about the *environment* of the business, especially the characteristics of potential *customers* and their numbers, the types of products and services the potential customers need (maybe the state of the technology in their sector of industry, for example, in terms of machinery, methods and materials used), the activities of *competitors* or potential competitors, at home and from abroad, the availability of skilled *labour*, the key costs, for example, of buildings and equipment, raw materials, *sources* of supply. If your business is up and running, you will need to pull together key facts – your existing customer base, pattern of sales to your customers, key costs and ratios, potential areas for development, and so forth.

Experience indicates that the Planning Group should meet often, with intervals no longer than three to four weeks between meetings. Any slower progress will result in waning enthusiasm, and information collected for early meetings will be out of date at later meetings.

Aim to complete the planning process within, say, two to four months. This should be achievable even in businesses that are up and running with all the senior people busily engaged in day-to-day management activity. An existing management group will have a sound basis of knowledge and understanding to build on in the planning process – but they must be prepared to open their minds to new situations and new possibilities, and where appropriate, to go back to basics and prepare and justify zero-based budgets.

A Planning Group brought together to plan a new business may well have a good deal of investigative work to do: if this is done properly it will take time, but it is vital if the plan is to be of real value to the business, not only in the pre-start period, but when the business has to be steered through its initial stages.

In the vital matter of identifying potential customers and their needs, you cannot rely on impressions, uninformed opinions and anecdotes. This would mean building a plan on shifting sands. You must, somehow, get out there and find out what people want.

As information is brought together, you may well find that you must refine your ideas about who will be your key customers in the future, just what you will be providing, the best way to reach them, the best way to provide the goods and services, the best location for your business, and so forth.

Sensitive issues

As these ideas develop, you may well find that some controversial suggestions arise that could easily unsettle some of your key staff. You may find it necessary to keep some of these suggestions confidential within the group at the early stages. There is no point in upsetting staff over something that may never happen.

However, if such a suggestion becomes a real possibility, you will need to think through how you will deal with the people concerned as a responsible employer, and then inform them of the possibilities you are considering, how it will change their situations and what provision you intend to make.

As an example, suppose that you consider moving your manufacturing plant from Sussex to Cumbria. Will you want to take some key staff with you? Will they be prepared to go? What help will you give them? What about the people you do not wish to take? Do you want them to work with you up to the last minute? What compensation will you offer them? What help will you give those that are left behind in finding new employment?

These factors must form a part of your plan, but there is also the important issue of how and when information about your plan is communicated to individuals. You should seek to speak to them before these ideas leak out through the local grapevine where people will get a garbled version of what will happen, making them feel insecure, uninformed and unhappy with the management.

Mission statement

It has become fashionable in recent years for companies to draw up a statement encapsulating what they are about: in other words, what their business aims are, who their customers are, what their products and services are, and what distinguishes their business in terms of cost, quality, reliability, value for money or whatever.

At an appropriate stage the Planning Group should set about producing this, but only when they have developed and explored their ideas about what is possible in the market-place and coupled these with the strengths of the business and where they feel they will gain satisfaction and be able to do a job well.

Chapter 3

DEFINE YOUR BUSINESS

OBJECTIVE: to examine critically the business idea and to check this against your initial perception of the market-place so that you may write a first draft 'nature of the business' statement on which market investigations and calculations can be based.

■ Sketch out the key features of your business

■ Question the nature of your business

■ Do a 'quick check' on the feasibility of your business idea

■ Write your first draft of the 'nature of the business'

Refer to the 'Outline Business Plan' (Figure 2 in the Introduction). It is important to recognize that you do not write such a plan by starting at the beginning. In your final document the name of the business will appear on the front page, but it will probably be one of the very *last* things you decide. The plan will, of course, give the address from which the business will operate initially, if this is known.

The first step is to write down in simple terms what the business is about, what products and services it intends to provide, who will be its customers, and so on. This part may seem easy, but in a new business, people tend to be far too woolly in thinking about this, and existing businesses tend to assume, without thinking, that the customers they have now and the goods and services they provide should be the pattern for the future.

These assumptions have to be challenged throughout the planning process. They cannot be challenged if they have not been articulated clearly in the first place.

QUESTION THE NATURE OF THE BUSINESS

You will will need to produce a rough draft of the nature of the business, but as the planning process proceeds you may well find that this needs to be modified.

Make a start by referring to Figure 8 and write down what it is that you intend to sell, to whom you intend to sell it and what methods you will use. Discussion of a few examples of different types of business may help you to think along the right lines. It is not possible to cover every type of business, but if you grasp the basic ideas from these examples you should be able to work out how to describe your own business.

Figure 8 Key Features of the Business

Below are listed some of the questions you will need to consider as you refine your ideas on the nature of your business. Make a note of your answers to relevant questions and draw these answers together into a succinct statement.

What do you intend to sell?
• Products? How many different types, ranges?
• Services? How would you define these?

Where will be your 'position' in the market?
• High quality and price?
• High volume, low price?

Who will be your customers?
• Individual members of the public? What social class, geographical area, particular interests?
• Manufacturing companies? What size, nature, area? Which managers will make or influence crucially the decision to buy?
• Shops or chains of shops? What kind of shops? What locations (high street, out of town, clustered)?

How will you reach your customers?
• Passing trade?
• Press advertisements? Direct mail?
• Representatives in your employ?
• Advertising on radio or television?
• Advertising on a Web Site on the Internet?

How will you obtain products?
• Manufacture from raw materials?
• Assemble from intermediates?
• Purchase from manufacturer?

How will you provide services?
• Yourself? Plus partners or fellow directors?
• Employees?
• Sub-contractors or franchisees?
• Is your business selling information, for example through the Internet? You may need to advertise a Web Site through other media if you wish to reach customers.

How will you sell?
• Direct to the public? To manufacturers?
• Through your shop(s)? To shops, individually or by chain?
• By mail order?
• Through a distributor?
• Through the Internet or via cable television?
• Telephone sales?

How will you support your sales?
• What delivery will you provide?
• What geographical area?
• What after-sales service?
• What trade terms? What financial help, for example, leasing or loans?

The examples are drawn from manufacture, distribution and sales, and from the service industries, and as you read, look for similar problems and how you will overcome them.

Manufacturing examples

Suppose you want to manufacture articles, for example. Your first thoughts may be: 'The business will comprise the manufacture of metal ashtrays for sale to the general public'; 'The business will be concerned with the manufacture of hand-carved wooden objects for tourists'; or 'The business will consist of the manufacture of high pressure pumps for engineering companies'. But these statements will not do. They leave too many questions unanswered.

How do you intend to manufacture the ashtrays? Where do you intend to manufacture them? How do you intend to sell them? By mail order? If so, you need to state that. (I would not recommend that option in this case!)

Do you intend to sell them to shops, for sale to the public? What kind of shops? Where? Why should these shops buy them?

If you intend to manufacture on a small scale at first, you may well start by selling such articles in shops near to your place of manufacture – if you have reason to believe that you can sell enough to make a profit. As you grow, you may find it better to have a distributor or a sales agent. If you decide to export, particular care will be needed in the choice of people and firms to do business with, and this will involve research.

Thus, although the ultimate customers may be members of the general public, the nature of your business may mean that you are making articles for sale to the general public through distributors or agents, through certain kinds of shops, in certain geographical areas.

Clearly, if you are manufacturing for the tourist trade, you must again decide the way in which you will distribute and sell your goods and the geographical areas where you will work.

Consider the sale of high pressure pumps for engineering companies. Once more you must specify the type of company: for example, size, type of engineering operation, geographical situation, and so forth. In this case, geography is an issue because of the need to transport goods and possibly to provide back-up services, such as maintenance and spare parts.

How will you sell these pumps? Will you sell them by mail order, through distributors, through a network of specially trained salespeople or through engineering craftspeople trained to act as sales representatives, installers and maintenance engineers?

How will you reach key people in such companies? Which people in the companies do you expect to make the purchasing decision? In what way will your particular product appeal to them? How will you present its special properties? Will there be only one pump, or a range of pumps of different sizes and applications?

Distribution and sales examples

Your initial sentences might read: 'The business will consist of a craft shop selling hand-crafted articles and also the materials, tools and equipment used by craftspeople'; or 'The business will involve operating a warehouse where groceries and related goods will be collected together and distributed to grocery shops in the locality'; or 'The business consists of the sale by mail order of a range of household goods'.

The statement about the craft shop business should mention the site of the shop (for example, high street of a well-known and busy town, or in a shopping precinct, or on the sea front of a popular resort), and will hopefully indicate whether you intend to build up a number of regular repeat customers or rely mainly on passing trade.

Will the warehouse distribute to independent grocery shops or a chain? (If a chain is involved, what makes you think the stores will buy from your warehouse? Or do you anticipate having a contract with the chain?)

If you are intending to sell household goods by mail order, what socio-economic groups do you intend to sell to and how will you build up your mailing list? Will you buy lists or advertise in particular magazines? What will these alternatives cost?

Service sector examples

This is often the most difficult area of all to define. Many people have a skill or service to offer, but find it a hard discipline to look at this expertise from the customer's point of view. But a successful business is concerned first and foremost with meeting a customer's need.

Thus, identifying precisely who the likely customers are and what you can provide to meet their needs must be done before you start the business in earnest.

For example you might start by writing: 'The business will consist of the provision of typing services'; or 'The business will be contract cleaning'; or 'The business will consist of hiring out and servicing building equipment'; or 'The business will consist of the provision of consultancy services concerned with garden design and maintenance'.

But the question is, Who will buy your typing services? Householders (unlikely), large companies (who probably have their own staff, or will hire in temps, rather than contract out typing) or small businesspeople who need occasional typing services? But is that all the office services support they will need? How will the business be operated? Will clients bring their work to you – or will you take it to them?

Who will pay for your contract cleaning? Occupiers of small houses? Large houses? Shops? Offices? Factories? Warehouses? Hospitals? Local authorities? How will you reach the category of customer you seek to serve? If you are proposing to deal with companies or public bodies (for example, hospitals, local authorities), how will you reach the decision-makers and how will you persuade them to award you the contract? In other words, what are the attractive features of your service?

What kind of premises will you cover? How high will you go – the first floor or 20 storeys up? What equipment will you use? How will you ensure quality? How will you recruit, train and monitor your staff? How far will you go, geographically, to get the contract?

If you are in the equipment hire business, will you hire your gear out for long periods (years or months) or for short periods (days or weeks)? Are your customers small builders, middle-sized builders or large companies? How large a range of equipment will you hold in stock? Will you deliver and collect the equipment? Over what geographical areas? Will you own, lease or hire as required the heavy goods vehicles you will need to transport the equipment?

If you propose to offer consultancy services in garden design and maintenance, what size of garden or estate will you deal with? How will your customers come to know of your existence? What will convince them that you know enough about design, plants, the construction of garden features, and so forth? How will you establish your fee rates?

QUICK CHECK ON FEASIBILITY

Whatever your business, you need to start off with a draft statement of precisely what you are selling and to whom. It is often helpful to state in this section of your plan how you propose to reach your customers and maintain contact with them, too.

It is important to remember, however, that as we move on to the other stages of planning, especially the marketing and financial sections, this original draft may need to be changed as your ideas are subject to financial analysis.

At the outset, check your statement about the nature of the business against the questions listed in Figure 9. Repeat this process from time to time as your planning proceeds. Ultimately every business involves risk. The idea is not to eliminate risk, but to reduce it to an acceptable level. Generally speaking, without risk there is not much chance of real profit.

You *must* be honest with yourself. If there is a weakness in your business idea, you must work through this, modify it if necessary and satisfy yourself and your business colleagues that the risks are acceptable.

Figure 9 Quick Check on Feasibility

Success in business depends crucially on three things:

• Management
• Marketing
• Money

Work through these checklists from time to time as you plan, until you are satisfied.

MANAGEMENT

▶ Do you and your management team have the motivation and the technical skills to make the products or services you envisage?
▶ Do you and your management team have all the skills needed to look after the administrative side of the business, including all the money matters?
▶ Has your organization the ability to sell your goods or services to the potential customers you have identified?
▶ Are you prepared to modify your business plans in the light of what people will want to buy?
▶ Are you confident that you and your key managers will be able to manage skills and time to full effect?
▶ Do you have access to the information technology skills you need?
▶ Have you and your management team developed the approach needed to deal with the officials of public funding bodies – if that is required?
▶ Does your management team have the ability to cope with the multitude of demands for compliance with the law, for example in terms of taxation, employment, contracts and environmental issues?

MARKETING

▶ What is so special about the products that you intend to sell or the services that you intend to provide?
▶ How do you know that anyone will want to buy them?
▶ How much will you charge for your products or services? Will people be prepared to pay those prices?
▶ Are you sure that you can provide those goods or services at these prices, make a profit and manage cash flow?
▶ Why should anyone buy your goods or services rather than others on the market? Is this the right time to start providing the goods or services that you have in mind? Is this the moment when people will want them?

► Will you be able to develop your products or develop new products as your market develops?

► Have you considered how you will advertise or promote your products and how much this will cost?

► Do you know who your competitors are and what products they are selling?

► Have you spoken to any potential customers about the products or services that you intend to provide?

MONEY

► Will your business make a profit?

► Will you be able to pay each bill when it arrives?

► What financial resources will you need to be successful, especially over the initial trading period?

► Are you fully prepared to make your share of this financial commitment?

► Do you need – can you obtain – a loan at a reasonable rate of interest?

► Are you confident that you can pay back any loans over a reasonable period, and pay the interest?

► Have you researched, listed and costed the expenditures that you will incur, and when income will start to flow?

► Have you analysed the risks – for example of low sales, late payments, scarce raw materials, currency fluctuations – and how you will cope?

► Have you considered your insurance needs and any licences and permits that will be required?

► What sources of information, help and advice do you need? Do you know where these can be obtained?

► Have you discovered any problems that you have never had to deal with before?

► Have you developed financial management systems that will satisfy public funding bodies – if that is required?

Part Two

ASSEMBLING DATA

Chapter 4

PEOPLE PROFILE

OBJECTIVE: to review the skills and knowledge needed to run the business, to plan to succeed through ensuring that the business has these available and to encapsulate this information in a 'people statement'.

- **Recognize the importance of people in your plan**

- **Itemize the key tasks and areas for decision**

- **Identify the people concerned and the skills needed**

- **Decide what option to take to meet the need in each case**

- **Summarize your decisions in a 'people statement'**

THE PEOPLE YOU NEED TO SUCCEED

Having identified the core of your business, you must now decide what skills you and your key people will need to make the business a success.

Use Figure 10 to identify these needs. In some cases you or one of your senior people will possess these skills. In the areas where you are weak, it may be worthwhile updating your skills.

Since the success of your business depends on the skills of the people in charge, this step is vital. People who invest in your business or lend you money will want to know how you intend to cope, and the only way you can convince people is to spell out the key tasks and decisions and state why you think the people you have, or will have, can together deliver the goods.

Figure 10 Skills for Success

First list the skills required (column 1), then the people who should have the skills (column 2). Under the 'action' heading, place a tick if the people concerned have the skills. Otherwise indicate how these skills will be made available to the firm.

SKILLS REQUIRED	PEOPLE INVOLVED	ACTION
Technical skills		
Marketing skills		
Selling skills		
Negotiating skills		
Planning skills		
Costing skills		
Money management		
Quality assurance		
Transport and distribution		
Health and safety		
Information systems		

ITEMIZE YOUR NEEDS

The following checklist should be used in conjunction with Figure 10 to start you thinking about each aspect of the business. There are many tasks to be performed and you need to list the ones which are crucial to your success, and identify the people who will make the key decisions and who will perform these tasks.

Technical skills

- What knowledge and skills do you need in connection with your particular trade?
- What machinery will you use and who will run it and maintain it?
- What procedures and documentation will be used?
- Who will ensure that your firm complies with all the laws and regulations relevant to your trade?

Marketing skills

- What do you need to know about the market-place, the sources of information?
- Who will interpret the data about your potential customers, your competitors and the shifts in demand?
- Who will identify your potential customers?
- Who will ensure that your products and services match the needs of the market-place?
- Who will set the sales targets?

Selling skills

- What methods will you use to reach people and to close the sale?
- What will you need to know about advertising, mailshots, mailing lists, etc?
- To what extent will you need to use cold calls or telesales methods?
- Who will converse with your customers, demonstrate products, describe services, establish customers' needs and desires, deal with objections and close the sales?
- Who will ensure that your sales and marketing efforts are matched by prompt delivery and adequate after-sales service?
- Who can affect the way your firm appears to the potential customer (the 'image' of the firm)? Who will train them and monitor their performance?

Negotiating skills

- What skills and abilities will you need in presenting your case and negotiating with customers, suppliers, backers and officials of public bodies?

Planning skills

- What knowledge and skills will you need in forecasting, costing, budgeting, route planning, critical path analysis?

Costing skills

- What do you need to know about costing your anticipated expenses, costing your overheads, costing your products and services?

Money management

- How will you manage money, monitor your cash flow and profitability, control expenditure, ensure payment for goods and services provided?

Quality assurance

- How will you monitor quality? Who will do it?
- Will you seek official recognition for your quality assurance methods?
- How will you train your people to maintain quality?

Storage, transport and distribution

- Who will manage the storage of goods?
- Are you aware of any special conditions required or particular precautions to be taken in your industry?
- How will you ensure proper stock rotation?
- Will you need a licence to manage heavy goods vehicles? Who is qualified to do this?
- How will you optimize your vehicle routing?
- How will you manage distribution costs?

Health and safety

- How will you ensure compliance with the demands of the law and take all reasonable precautions?
- Will you need a first-aider?

Information management

- How will you set up your management information systems?
- Who will maintain these systems and alert management when necessary?
- What do you know about information storage and retrieval?
- Will you need computer systems? Databases? Spreadsheets? Financial management software?
- How will you choose your systems? Who will use them? Who will interpret the data generated?
- Will you need to acccss the Internet for information? Will you want to use the Internet for advertising, for selling or to provide a service?

CONSIDER YOUR OPTIONS

Where none of your key staff have these skills you have a number of alternatives: for example, you can plan to recruit someone, or to train someone, or to buy in the expertise as you need it. Indicate in the final column of Figure 10 how you intend to achieve this.

If you intend to recruit someone, you will need to work up a job specification to see how the time of this individual will be spent and the contribution he or she will make to the business. Then you will need a person specification for recruitment purposes. You will need to research the market to find how much you will need to pay, how long it might take to find the right person and what the recruitment costs will be.

If you opt to develop your own skills or one of your colleague's, think through how this will be achieved and what it will cost.

If you decide to use external expertise from time to time, it is worthwhile to identify the people you would use, and to estimate how much of their time you will employ, what it will cost, and when you will use them – for your expenditure forecast.

The book *Profits through People* by Ron Johnson (Hutchinson Business Books 1990) explains in more detail how to do this analysis and how to develop the skills of people in your business.

YOUR PEOPLE STATEMENT

Just as you encapsulated the essence of your business idea in a statement, so you must now pull the important points from this analysis into a statement explaining, in relation to the nature of your business:

• What areas of knowledge and skill are crucial to its success
• What you and your management team have to offer against this
• How you intend to cope with any shortfall

Some backers may want more details about yourself and other key people in your organization. In such cases you may need to draw up and present a curriculum vitae for each key person. This should focus on the individual's qualifications and experience, and indicate how these relate to the needs of the business.

Chapter 5

SCANNING THE MARKET

> **OBJECTIVE: to review the market for your goods and services, the competition you face, and the decisions you need to take to ensure success.**

- **Use market segmentation to identify your potential customers**

- **Assess the impact of your competitors**

- **Use market survey methods to characterize your potential customers and their needs**

In your draft statement on the nature of the business, you described your customers and the goods and services you will provide. Your next step is to study your potential customers thoroughly using every method at your disposal.

Information may be available in written form, for example reference books on specific types of companies, published household expenditure surveys or marketing company reports. Lists of potential customers can be purchased. Useful information about customers may also be available through the Internet. There are now books that list Web Sites of interest to business people.

Finally, you can go and talk to people. If your potential customers are too numerous to tackle in this way you may need to commission a market survey. You need to consider very carefully what information you need and how much it will cost. In many cases you can't beat the 'feel' of talking to potential customers yourself.

SEGMENT THE MARKET

The ultimate aim is to specify your customers as accurately as possible, as this is the information your advertising and sales activities will be based on. There

---

Figure 11 Market Segmentation

1. List the geographical areas in which you will trade with customers.

Indicate briefly how you intend to service these areas if they are widespread.

2. List the characteristics of the people most likely to buy your goods or services (if you sell to the public).

Indicate any special seasons or purchasing times and places where purchases are more likely to occur.

3. List the characteristics and likely requirements of the intermediaries you hope to do business with.

Indicate the particular types of intermediaries who would favour your products and services.

4. List the characteristics of the kind of organizations you want to do business with.

Within these organizations, identify the people (by job title) that you will need to convince of the value of your goods and services to gain sales.

---

are millions of people and companies in the world and it is folly for a modest-size company to try to sell to everybody. There are a number of ways of narrowing down the list of your potential customers. Refer to Figure 11 as you work through this section.

You can narrow the list down by geography. Do you intend to offer your goods and services worldwide, or just in Europe, or just in England, or just in Yorkshire, or just in Harrogate? If the worldwide market is represented as a circle, segments of the circle can represent sections of the market. Thus we call this process of identifying groups of customers 'market segmentation'.

List the geographical areas where you intend to start trading. You can base your planned marketing and sales activity on these areas, and calculate costs accordingly. There is nothing to stop you from moving into other areas as the opportunity arises – but you will probably incur extra costs and will need to change your financial calculations.

But you can segment the market in other ways. For example, if you are selling to the public, are your products and services of universal appeal or are they likely to be particularly attractive to:

- Young people, middle-aged people, older people?
- Men, women, young men, young women?
- Mums, dads, uncles, aunts, children (for example, Mothers' Day)?
- Fit people, people with a medical complaint or disability?
- Rich people, poor people?
- People with a particular sporting interest?
- People with a particular cultural interest?
- People who want to learn a subject, skill or trade?
- People who work in a particular type of business?
- People keen on DIY activities?
- People keen on travel?

The list is endless, and many of these items combine to narrow down the kind of person to whom you are most likely to sell.

When and where are these people most likely to want to buy your products? When they see a need? When they are gearing up for a sports season or preparing for a holiday? When they are on holiday? At particular seasons or religious festivals? Will they go to a shop in the high street, or to a specialist shop, or buy it by mail through a magazine? Will they surf the Internet?

If you sell through intermediaries like chain stores, agents or wholesalers, are there particular requirements they might want? What types of intermediaries will most likely be happy to deal with your products? Will you deal with supermarkets, grocery chains, department stores? Do they prefer particular sizes, shapes, types of packaging, delivery schedules?

If you sell your products or services to manufacturers, commercial firms, public bodies, and so forth, what sizes of organization do you have in mind? Are you interested in the large international bodies and international companies, or government departments, large local authorities and national companies, or smaller firms and smaller local authorities? What do you know about their purchasing procedures and requirements? How will you decide which organizations are most likely to buy your wares?

If you are looking at large organizations, are there particular sections or activities with which you are concerned? Do you want to provide raw materials for the manufacturing section, the garden and parks section, the hygiene and cleansing department, the engineering maintenance department or the training department?

Can you identify in each case the key decision-makers when it comes to purchasing your kind of products and services? In large organizations it is often necessary to convince two or three different people that what you have to offer is worth considering. The purchasing department will have its own priorities, as well as the section that will actually use your materials.

If you are selling capital items, or a part of a contract to a main contractor (for example, in a building project), then you will frequently be helping somebody else to make out a case, and you will have to appreciate not only what your client wants, but what help he or she needs in making out a case that includes your part of the action.

These questions are fundamental to the identification of your particular set of prospective clients or customers – the market segment in which you will operate. Your choice will depend on relating your goods and services, and the particular strengths of your business, to the particular requirements of customers in each segment.

CHARACTERIZE THE CUSTOMERS

At the outset you may have identified a range of goods and services to offer and many groups of potential customers. It is unwise to attempt too wide a range of goods or services, or too many different kinds of customers. Each variation adds to the burden on management. A modest range targeted at a well-defined group of customers is a better way to start.

We have discussed above how to identify the particular group of customers most likely to be responsive to your approach. Now you need to use a variety of means to answer the following key questions. Within the chosen segment you will need to determine:

- How many potential customers you have
- Where they are to be found
- Exactly what they are likely to buy (in terms of quality, size, colour, packaging, delivery, financial terms)
- How much they will buy (quantity to be purchased and frequency)

A detailed discussion of methods for studying the market is beyond this text, but somehow you need to get a 'feel' for your customers. There may be a wealth of information about your potential customers from household expenditure surveys, sector reports on industry and commerce, trade directories, and so forth. Much of this can be accessed through the larger public libraries. Some of this data (for example, about the people who live in different neighbourhoods) may well be on computer files which you can buy into.

Wherever possible, the best way is to go and talk to potential customers about their needs and concerns. The key questions you need to ask in such interviews include:

(a)　What kind of business are you in?
(b)　What need do you have (for the kind of goods and services concerned)?
(c)　How is this need currently being met?
(d)　How does this contribute to your business success?
(e)　What characteristics do you like about the goods and services you are getting now?
(f)　In what ways do you consider that these products and services could be improved?
(g)　How are your activities likely to develop in this area over the next year or so?
(h)　How do you consider this will alter your demands for the goods or services?
(i)　What kind of prices would you be prepared to pay for improved goods and services that met your needs more closely?

Naturally, you must be subtle in the way you ask these kinds of questions, and the phrasing will vary with the kind of products and services you are discussing.

If you are hoping to provide goods and/or services which are quite novel, potential customers may not be able to relate to these until you have demonstrated or explained them. But do not launch into any explanations or demonstrations until you have established answers to questions (a) to (i).

You will also need to make an estimate of the market share you expect to attain – and explain how and why. Remember that if your market share is modest, your competitors may not be too concerned; but as this share grows, you can expect an aggressive response.

EVALUATE THE COMPETITION

Now that you have a clear idea of your potential customers and their needs as they relate to your proposed business, you need to identify the companies that are currently meeting these needs.

Study the size of their operations, the nature and quality of their products, the characteristics of the service they offer, before, during and after the sale. Study the image they present, and see if you can infer, from their advertising, what they consider their advantage to be in the market-place.

Is their strength in dependability? Do they build good rugged machines that go on and on, year in year out, without giving trouble? Do they have a range of goods that just slot into their customers' requirements? Are they up-to-the-minute in sensing their customers' needs and responding; or does it take them quite a while to change in response to a changing market need?

It is by studying factors like these that you will be able to see where you can be different, but in a way that will please prospective customers. There is little point in trying to compete with an established competitor in features where he is strong. You may need to match these – or deliberately take a different line. For example, if your competitor's reliability is dependent on heavily constructed machinery that is difficult to move about, you may decide to make a machine that uses modern materials and design to give strength without excessive weight, and make a virtue out of the portability of the equipment – if your customers will see that as a benefit.

Chapter 6

SCANNING THE ENVIRONMENT

> **OBJECTIVE: to review the environment in which your business is operating as the basis for strategic decisions.**

- **Look for the trends in the environment that can affect your business**

- **Examine the political, economic, social and technical issues**

- **Make full use of your managerial talent in identifying the issues**

- **Evaluate the impact and take this into account in your plan**

IDENTIFYING THE TRENDS

In any business you need to look at the environment – the current situation and current developments – and to assess the likely impact of impending changes on your business. Foretelling the future is always a doubtful activity. The best we can do is to look around at trends and new ideas and try to estimate which ones are likely to continue, and what impact these are likely to have on each aspect of the business.

Although one is tempted to consider one's own town and country, it is nowadays vital to consider the European scene and, indeed, in some industries the world scene. This is often not as difficult as it seems because if you know your business, you should be able to focus your attention on those aspects which are likely to affect you.

In respect of each development you identify, you will need to consider:

• Whether it will last
• Whether it will grow, decline or change suddenly
• What effect it will have on your industry and on your business

Your business may be affected because the change influences:

- The people who work for you or those you seek to recruit, their aspirations, their expectations, their skills and knowledge: for example, through changes in family structures, housing costs, educational provisions
- The organizations or people you serve, through shifting fashions, changing priorities (for example, a reduction in international tensions, shifts in the spending power of different groups of customers), and hence, the nature of the goods and services you provide
- The way you manufacture, distribute or provide your services as technology transforms working methods and relative costs (for example, between fuel, capital investment, labour) change
- The way you structure your workforce and the pattern of communications: for example, as technology impacts on internal communications and decision-making.

AREAS OF CHANGE

Use this prompt list to stimulate your thinking about the areas which are relevant in your business and complete Figure 12 for yourself. It is not possible to cover every eventuality, but the list should help you to do your own analysis.

Political pressures

- What is the current government posture towards business? Is it on being competitive, getting results, cutting costs, removing barriers to innovation and growth?
- What will be the impact of health and safety legislation, environmental protection and consumer protection?
- What effect do you anticipate in the area of legislation related to portable pensions, transport policy, fuel prices, etc?
- What about employment legislation? Where is the balance of industrial relations? Is it in favour of employers, against closed shops and restrictive practices?
- What is the current policy on training for employment, for young people, for skills and for adults?
- What is the impact of regional imbalances and the response of the national government and the European Community authorities?
- How does the pressure for equality of opportunity and the elimination of discrimination manifest itself?

Figure 12 Environmental Impact

FACTORS	LIKELY IMPACT	RESPONSE
Political		
Economic		
Social		
Technological		

- What is the influence of European Community institutions on national practice?
- What government departments are particularly relevant to your business? In what areas are they developing policies that should be of interest to your firm? What sections of the Commission of the European Community are active in your industry?

If you are unaware of some of the answers to these questions, you should consult your trade or professional bodies, or the government departments concerned.

Economic pressures

- What do the key economic indicators mean for your industry and your company? What about interest rates and inflation?
- What about the exchange rate? Do any of these factors impact on your customers, your competitors, your suppliers?

- What are the unemployment levels like, nationally, in your area, in relation to the skilled people you need in your industry?
- Is your industry growing or declining in employment terms? Is your growth likely to be retarded by a shortage of skilled people?
- Does the movement of workers geographically between employers give rise to implications for housing, pensions, and so forth?
- Who has the spending power now? Older people? Younger people? Private companies? Public institutions? Which government departments have big budgets?

The economic scene is volatile and needs to be constantly monitored. In your planning, you may need to consider how you will deal with alternative economic scenarios. One method of doing this is to put alternative figures (for example, for inflation, interest rates, exchange rates) into your calculations and see what effect they have on, say, cash flow or profitability. This simple technique is sometimes called 'sensitivity analysis' as it enables you to see how 'sensitive' your business is to such variations.

Social pressures

- Do people expect to be involved in decisions which affect their lives? What impact does this have on company communications, negotiations and possible management structures?
- Do people expect an improving quality of life – at work, at home and in the general environment? How will you take this into account?
- How will changing family patterns (for example, higher proportion of divorces and one-parent families, and families where both husband and wife are employed) influence your decisions?
- Will part-time working, short-term contracts, sub-contracting become increasingly important?
- Are people reluctant to move home geographically, and if so, how might this affect your business?

As you can see from this brief list of possible issues, social pressures can influence your business in several ways: the availability and cost of labour, the way you deal with staff, the spending habits and priorities of different customer groups, and so forth.

Technological pressures

- How will the increasingly dramatic improvements in communication methods and systems change the way you work and interact with your customers, suppliers and field staff?

- Consider the all-pervasive impact of new technology: for example, in the home, the factory, the office, the warehouse, the hospital and the retail check-out.
- What will be the effect of improvements in information handling within your firm? What will be the impact on the jobs people do, and perhaps the training they will require?
- How can the dramatic improvements in technological aids for design and control systems be used to your advantage?
- Will developments in biotechnology impact on your business?
- Will methods for improving the efficient use of fuel have a significant effect on your business?

IDENTIFYING THE KEY ISSUES

It is doubtful whether one person can do such an analysis well. If you and a few of your senior managers really know your business, your market-place and what is happening in the world outside, you should be able to do this analysis between you. Do not be afraid to seek information – from your trade body, from the public library, from the relevant government departments.

A good way to gather and sift information is to get each member of the management team to complete a copy of Figure 13 and then to bring all this information together in one document.

This summary document is then circulated to the managers, but with the last column left blank. The managers are then asked whether they agree with the analysis, and if not, to explain why in the comments column.

Bringing this information together in this manner before having a detailed discussion in the management group is much richer and more effective than launching straight into it. An unprepared discussion is less effective, and some people feel inhibited from contributing.

If you intend to apply for financial assistance from a public body you will need to gather background information on its aims and objectives. Normally the assistance will be granted within an operational programme of the body concerned. You will need to find out the objectives of the particular programme as well as the rules governing financial assistance. Will your application go to the management board? If so, it is as well to find out about the background of the members so that you can assess how they are likely to view and judge your proposal.

Most of your contact will be with officials. As they are accountable for public funds you should expect them to be particularly careful about how the funds will be applied and how expenditure will be recorded.

Figure 13 Environmental Scanning

FACTORS	LIKELY IMPACT	COMMENT
Political		
Economic		
Social		
Technological		

EVALUATING THE IMPACT

There are clearly too many topics to consider in depth, but you and your colleagues must identify those areas of prime concern to you. You need, therefore, to consider what are the *major* external influences on your industry, and then what are the *main* implications for:

• Your customers and hence your products and services
• Your technology and the way you will work
• The way you will organize your staff and manage your communications and decision-making
• The way you will recruit, train and remunerate your staff

Part Three

INITIAL DECISIONS

Chapter 7

IDENTIFY YOUR NICHE

OBJECTIVE: to refine your definition of the business
in the light of the scanning exercise so that detailed
calculations can begin.

- **List the features of your products and services**

- **Identify the advantages of your products and services**

- **Specify the benefits offered to each group of customers**

- **Consider the ease of serving your customers in each group**

- **Identify your 'USP', your 'unique selling point'**

FEATURES

Having scanned the market-place and identified the particular kind of customers you intend to serve, you must now specify in detail the kind of products and services you propose to provide. In Figure 14 there is a framework to enable you to consider each group of customers. Where will you be 'positioned' in the quality/price spectrum? The price aspect of positioning is covered in more detail in Chapter 8. Here we are concerned with the nature and quality of the goods and services you intend to provide.

If you are talking about a product, what is its size, shape, purpose, power, quality? What power consumption does it require and what plumbing? What floor-space or desk-space does it take up? What size of materials will it take to process? How many items at a time? How automatic will it be? How fast will it go? How much information can it store? Get the idea? List the features of your product.

Figure 14 Market Niche

What is your chosen market niche? Where will you 'position' your goods and services? (Price positioning is covered in the next chapter.)

	LOW QUALITY **LOW PRICE** **HIGH VOLUME**	**MEDIUM QUALITY** **MODEST PRICE** **MODERATE VOLUME**	**HIGH QUALITY** **HIGH PRICE** **LOW VOLUME**
CUSTOMER GROUP A What can you provide? What do your competitors provide? What is your competitive edge – your USP?			
CUSTOMER GROUP B What can you provide? What do your competitors provide? What is your competitive edge – your USP?			

If you are making and selling a product, what are the features of the services you provide alongside? What about delivery times? What about minor changes to suit the customer, for example, different colours or minor changes in specification? Can you produce a specially made article to the customer's requirements, or must he or she have a black one, two metres long – or else!

How reliable is your machine? How durable? What about installation, maintenance and after-sales service, spare parts, and so forth? Can it be repaired on site, or be taken away, or must the customer bring it to your plant in the Outer Hebrides? How quickly can you get a service engineer to call? The same day? Next day? Next week – but not on Saturdays or Sundays or after 4.30 p.m.?

Suppose you are offering a service. What are the features of the service? What precisely will you (or your representatives) do? How comprehensive is the service, or are you prepared to do only certain kinds of work? (For example, if you are offering secretarial services, does this include photocopying, word-processing, book-keeping, desk-top publishing, telephone answering?) At what times is the service available? Where can the service be obtained? If you are providing an information service, is this available in written form, with regular updates, on the telephone, with 24-hour availability, via the Internet, interactively?

Is there a feature which is inherent in the company, rather than the product? For example, does your company already have a reputation for reliability, quality or personal service? That should be listed as a feature, and moreover, one that might distinguish your products and services from those of your competitors.

Now compare these features with those of the competitors' products and/ or services. In what ways do you consider yours is superior, inferior or just plain 'different'? How many of these features will be significant to your customers? How do you know?

ADVANTAGES

Having compared your products and services with those of your main competitors, list what you see as key features of your wares and tick off those which seem to you to offer an advantage (see Figure 15).

You can do this in general terms to begin with. Space is provided for just ten features, but you may draw up your own table and list as many as you wish. Think of your customers as a whole as you do this. Will they like the compact size, the availability of the service at weekends, the rugged construction, the personal touch, the low power consumption, the fast response time? How do you know? This information may come from your own impressions or those of your managers, but are these impressions reliable? Often they are NOT.

Figure 15 Benefits

FEATURES	ADVANTAGES	BENEFITS – CUSTOMER GROUP
List the main features	Tick off the features which offer an advantage	Specify the benefits which you can see for this group of customers
1.		
2.		
3.		
4.		
5.		
6.		
7.		
8.		
9.		
10.		

Information of this kind can only be gained by talking to customers – by customer research. If you have not done this research properly, you are building on shifting sand.

BENEFITS

So, you have identified the advantages of your products and services. But do they actually matter to each of your customer groups? What is the benefit to Group A of Advantage 1? If the customers in Group A have plenty of space, a compact design has no particular merit.

What about Advantage 2? If Group B customers do not open at weekends, it is of no consequence. In other words, you need to consider now the requirements of each group of customers and what benefits they can gain by using the products and services you offer. Remember that a benefit is when the customer's life is made easier, or his or her profits increased or reputation enhanced.

SERVING THE CUSTOMER

You must now consider rather carefully just how easy it will be to provide the appropriate level of service to each group of customers. The problem is that each group will have to be reached through relevant advertising media and be serviced according to its own requirements.

You may be tempted to plan for diversification. Be careful. Companies can diversify by increasing the number of product lines or the range of services offered. It is also possible to diversify by increasing the number of customer groups targetted.

Diversification in one or the other direction will add considerably to the burden on management. Can your management team cope? Can your sales team cope? Diversification in both directions is generally a recipe for disaster unless you have more than one self-contained management team.

In recent years formal systems of quality assurance have assumed increasing importance. The international standard (ISO 9000) has been widely adopted by companies who wish to assure their customers that every effort is taken to ensure conformity of criteria for product quality and service levels. Indeed in some markets this accolade is essential for companies wishing to trade. Closely allied to this is the concept of the customer code adopted by organizations that serve the general public.

UNIQUE SELLING POINT

On the basis of all this analysis, you should now be able to come up with what is special about your products and services. What marks you out from the crowd? What are you uniquely offering to your chosen customers?

What is your unique selling point? What is your market niche?

Chapter 8

PRICING POLICY AND PROFIT

> **OBJECTIVE: to review the factors that govern your pricing policy and to determine provisional prices for your products and services as a basis for further calculations.**

- **Calculate your cost – price – profit relationship and risk**

- **Decide how to take competitor prices into account**

- **Decide how and when to apply the cost-plus method**

- **Decide on your market price**

How will you set about setting the prices you charge for your goods and services? The basis of your prices can be:

- What it will cost to produce the goods or to provide the services
- What your competitors are charging
- What the market will bear

For the purpose of discussion, let us call these the 'cost-plus price', the 'competitors' price' and the 'market price' respectively. You will need to use the cost-plus pricing method if you are tendering for a contract against other suppliers, but otherwise it is generally better to offer your goods and services at the market price.

In order to determine the market price you will need to take careful note of your competitors' price, but you do not need to follow their example. If you draw up a price/quality table (Figure 16) you will need to 'position' your goods and services on this table in relationship to your competitors.

Although your prices may not be based on the cost-plus approach, the

---

Figure 16 Positioning

Where will you 'position' your goods and services? Where are your competitors?

QUALITY =	LOW	MEDIUM	HIGH
PRICE			
HIGH			High quality goods and services can command high prices and good profit margins
MODERATE		Goods and services of moderate quality in the middle price range can generate healthy profits	
LOW	Inexpensive goods and services have a place in the market-place – but profit margins are generally low		

---

quantity of goods and services you sell at the prices you charge must, of course, cover your total costs and provide you with a profit – a return on the investment in the business.

COST–PRICE RELATIONSHIPS

At first sight this seems quite straightforward. In practice it is not straightforward at all, because the cost of your goods and services depends on how much you actually sell.

There are a number of costs that you incur however much you make and sell up to a certain level. Calculations of costs will be covered more thoroughly later. For now, suppose you are running a bookshop: you must pay rent and rates, heating, lighting, basic wages, the interest on any loans, and so on. You must also take into account the 'depreciation' on any capital items. All these costs are effectively fixed and independent of how much you sell. They are called your 'fixed costs'.

Each book you sell has cost you money to buy. When you sell goods, you must buy more to replace them. The price which you charge the customer for

---

Figure 17 Risk Table

First, estimate the quantity you expect to sell – in the worst possible case you can envisage, what you think is entirely feasible, what you can hope for if all goes well, and a figure which means that the sales are appreciably better than you anticipate – and put these figures in line A.

Next, take your chosen price and multiply up to get the income generated from sales in each case, in line B. Now multiply up your quantity of sales by cost per item to yield the variable cost (line C) and subtract these figures from those in line B to yield the gross profit (line D).

Finally, deduct the fixed cost (line E) from the gross profit to yield the net profit (line F).

A: QUANTITY SOLD	lowest estimate	reasonable estimate	optimistic estimate	highly optimistic estimate
B: PRICE CHARGED × QUANTITY SOLD (INCOME GENERATED)				
C: COST PER ITEM × NUMBER SOLD (VARIABLE COSTS)				
D: GROSS PROFIT				
E: FIXED COSTS				
F: NET PROFIT				

a book, less the cost you paid for it, represents what is called the 'gross profit'. The more books you sell, the more costs you incur in buying them, so that the costs of purchasing items for sale is variable (it varies with the 'volume of sales'). We call it 'variable cost'.

Every business will have its fixed and variable costs, and there will be some grey areas of 'semi-variable costs' as well. It is important to think this through, as one man's fixed cost may be another man's variable cost. If you are in the publishing business, your fixed costs will be the cost of actually printing and binding an initial print run and advertising the book. In this case, the cost of the books is fixed whether you sell one book or the whole of the 10,000 in your initial print run. The price of each one is a fixed cost – in contrast to the bookseller.

These two examples show that the calculation of costs and profit can be done over a period of time (for example, a month, a quarter or a year of trading in a shop) or on the basis of a specific project, such as the publication of a book. If you are a book publisher, you will need a number of titles to publish over a period of time and you will need to estimate when books will be ready for publication, advertising and selling to estimate what will happen over each period of time.

To see the relationship between the price, costs and profit, draw up your own 'risk table'. Think through your fixed and variable costs and insert these into the table in Figure 17. The table can be used to calculate the risks involved over a period of time or in mounting a project.

Highly simplified examples are provided in Figure 18 to illustrate the principle of the risk table. We noted above that some costs are fixed 'up to a certain level'. This is because a point will be reached where the volume of sales requires extra fixed costs: for example, the shop is too small and needs to be extended, or the number of books sold by the publisher exceeds the first print run and so a decision has to be made whether or not to print more. The shop extension or the extra print run will increase the fixed costs in each case. The effect of this is illustrated in Figure 19.

A brief study of the examples will show that, in theory, a point is reached where the fixed costs must be increased to handle the extra sales. The point at which the gross income is equivalent to the variable costs plus the fixed costs is called the 'breakeven' point. Above this level of sales your business is making a profit: below this point it is making a loss. In Figure 19, the figures in brackets at the bottom of the first column indicate that the business will make a loss at this level of sales.

In this way the risk table will enable you to estimate profit and loss at various sales volumes and price levels. For these initial calculations precise figures are not necessary, but later you will need to do your costing thoroughly to check out this vital equation.

Figure 18 Example Risk Table (Fixed cost unchanged)

A: QUANTITY SOLD	lowest estimate	reasonable estimate	optimistic estimate	highly optimistic estimate
	500	2000	3000	5000
B: PRICE CHARGED × QUANTITY SOLD (INCOME GENERATED) say average £12	6000	24000	36000	60000
C: COST PER ITEM × NUMBER SOLD (VARIABLE COSTS) say average £5	2500	10000	15000	25000
D: GROSS PROFIT	3500	14000	21000	35000
E: FIXED COSTS	14000	14000	14000	14000
F: NET PROFIT/(LOSS)	(10500)	BREAKEVEN	7000	21000

The table is over-simplified, but it does show the basic principles and you should make sure you understand them. Complications include:

- The possibility of getting better discounts from suppliers as your volumes of sales increase, hence improving your profit
- The possibility of offering a variety of products at different prices: you will then need to decide how to allocate fixed costs to different products
- The need to assess at which point your volume of sales will require you to increase your overhead costs
- The need to take into account the taxation implications as they apply to your business
- The possibility of selling your goods in different ways which would make the variable costs more difficult to calculate.

Figure 19 Example Risk Table (Change in fixed cost)

A: QUANTITY SOLD	lowest estimate	reasonable estimate	optimistic estimate	highly optimistic estimate
	500	2000	3000	5000
B: PRICE CHARGED × QUANTITY SOLD (INCOME GENERATED) say average £12	6000	24000	36000	60000
C: COST PER ITEM × NUMBER SOLD (VARIABLE COSTS) say average £5	2500	10000	15000	25000
D: GROSS PROFIT	3500	14000	21000	35000
E: FIXED COSTS	14000	14000	14000	21000
F: NET PROFIT/(LOSS)	(10500)	BREAKEVEN	7000	14000

Bearing all these factors in mind, complete your own 'risk table'.

COST–PLUS CALCULATIONS

From the previous section you can see that fixing price on the basis of cost plus a figure for profit is not that easy in most businesses. It means knowing in advance the volume of sales. Where the technique does come into its own, however, is when you are asked to undertake a particular assignment, whether it be making a product or undertaking a task (for example, contract cleaning or a market survey).

If you find yourself in a tendering situation, you must carefully think through each step of the work you will be offering to do, estimating the cost of the materials, the time taken to do each part, the extent to which you will be dependent on deliveries or work done by other people (including the employees of the customer!), the precise sequence in which tasks will be done and the effect of any possible delays, however caused, on your costs.

You will then need to bear in mind the fact that most jobs can be undertaken at different quality levels. Once you know the cost, you need to add your required profit margin. You will need to determine the quality levels required and then pitch your tender on that basis, hoping that the customer will be prepared to pay your price for the quality you specify, and that this quality/price mix is better than anyone else's. You should endeavour to find

---

Figure 20 Contract Costing (Key Questions)

1. What does the customer want, precisely?

2. On what criteria will the customer decide which tender to accept?

3. What level of quality will you aim at? What delivery time or completion time will you quote?

4. What materials will you need? Where will you get them? What will they cost? How reliable are the deliveries? What are the cost implications of delays here?

5. How long will each step, or each task involved, take to complete? How many hours of work will be involved, and what level of staff will be employed?

6. To what extent will you use sub-contractors? What will they cost? How reliable will they be? What will be the cost implications of delays here?

7. What margin of profit will you require?

---

out the criteria for the award of the contract and to work within those parameters.

But what has this got to do with planning? When you come to write your plan for an operation of this kind you need to forecast, as best you can, the number and kinds of contracts you expect to win, so that you can work out your cash flow and profit and loss.

Use Figure 20 to stimulate your thinking on typical contracts that will form the core of your business. Make some rough estimates of the costs involved, add in your profit requirement and compare these figures with what customers will be prepared to pay.

COMPETITOR PRICES

As part of your initial survey of the market-place, you should have identified your major competitors, the products and services they offer and the prices they charge. You now need to examine the data more carefully, and to fit them into the price/quality table. Do not be tempted to compete on price alone. This is generally a recipe for disaster, especially for the smaller or medium-sized business.

Large firms have many ways of reducing costs, for example, large runs to reduce the ratio of fixed to variable costs, bulk buying to reduce the variable costs, the use of sophisticated machinery to speed manufacture which can only make sense with large volumes. Furthermore, large firms can sustain particular product lines or services at an unprofitable level to gain a foothold in the market, or to squeeze a competitor – making up for the loss on other product lines or services.

For these reasons you need to be careful in interpreting the data on customer prices, but they are a key factor in the market-place. In general, it is better to compete on some parameter other than cost, for example:

• Quality
• Delivery
• Uniqueness
• Packaging and presentation
• Personal service, tailor made to the customer's need
• After-sales service

Occasionally, a businessperson will consider that his or her product or service is unique and that he or she does not have a competitor. This is very rarely true. If you make an absolutely unique object, it has some purpose. It might be a talking point, a work of art, an implement or a machine. But right now, the likelihood is that your potential customers are living their lives without it! They have other ways to stimulate conversation, other works of art to view, other ways of achieving what your implement or machine will do, although not perhaps so cleanly, or efficiently, or effectively.

But these artefacts are the competition. If your goods and services will do these jobs better, then hopefully people will be prepared to pay. But you may be asking people to move to a different part of the price/quality spectrum, to purchase something in a different 'position' (Figure 16) in the market-place. You need to recognize that, and to overcome people's inertia in accepting new ideas.

MARKET PRICE

By market price we mean the price the customer is willing to pay for the goods and services you are offering, including the quality, frequency, packaging and presentation, after-sales service, financial deal, and so forth. It is for you to determine this, and you should make it as high as the market will bear.

Clearly if the price the market will bear does not give you a profitable return on your investment, you will need to go back to the drawing-board and re-define your business. There is no point in adding a profit figure to your cost and calling this the price when nobody will pay it.

You can only determine this price by a careful study of your potential customers, their needs and their priorities. You must consider how the products and services you are providing meet their needs and respond to their priorities.

Once you have decided on the quality/price position, you must gear your advertising and selling methods to this 'image'. In simple terms, you must manufacture and sell goods and provide services which people feel meets a need which they perceive, in a pleasant, cost-effective manner.

The word 'people' is used deliberately, as it will be people (not 'organizations' or 'companies') that decide whether to buy or not. We return to this question in the sales and marketing sections. Remember that people buy from people they like and to meet a need they perceive.

Your price, therefore, must reflect the benefit that the decision-maker will gain, and be sold on that basis. If your product is for sale direct to the public, for example, will it provide for the purchaser a status symbol to make him or her feel wealthy and successful, or will it help the purchaser to do some tasks that are important (for example, enhancing his or her home, increasing his or her business success) or interesting (enhancing his or her leisure), or will it improve his or her health or appearance?

If not, why should he or she buy it?

Figure 21 Market Price/Quality Factors

Are you selling direct to members of the public?

• Will your products and services enhance their wealth, their self-image, their health, their pleasure . . . or what?

Are you selling to the public through intermediaries?

• Will your products and services fit with their existing ranges?
• Will you provide help with merchandising and advertising as part of the deal?
• If appropriate, will you provide installation and after-sales service as part of the deal?
• Are your trading terms acceptable?

Are you selling to industrial, commercial or public bodies?

• Who will make the decision to buy?
• What will be the appeal to the people who will actually use the goods and services?
• What will be the appeal to the purchasing manager of the concern?

Where does your product sit in the positioning table?

What are your competitors charging?

• How do your products and services compare price for price, when you take the overall package into account?

If you are selling your products to a company, the decision-makers will often include the people who will use the materials and services plus the people responsible for actually placing and processing the orders. Here the price/quality position must satisfy both parties.

If you are selling to the public through intermediaries like shops, distributors or agents, then your price/quality position will need to reflect the needs of the public purchaser, but also be acceptable to the intermediaries. Use Figure 21 to summarize your conclusions on the factors influencing price in your particular business.

If you are tendering for a contract you may have a difficult decision to make regarding the price/quality package that will give you the business. Wherever possible you should speak to officers of the company or public authority to determine the actual objectives of the project as well as studying the invitation to tender documentation. This will enable you to make a judgement on the extent to which it is necessary to pare costs to the bone. The alternative is to put forward a realistic proposal that will not only meet the conditions of the 'invitation' but also provide a quality service that will take forward the objectives of the purchaser. It is rarely the best plan to compete on price alone.

Chapter 9

LOCATION AND ADDRESS

> **OBJECTIVE: to review the factors influencing your choice of location, and to decide how many sites you will operate from, what you will do at each site, and list the cost factors.**

- **Define what you will use your premises for**

- **Draw up a specification for your premises**

- **Consider your travel needs and labour requirements**

- **Make decisions about the financial implications**

In deciding just where you will locate your business there are a number of factors to consider (see Figure 22). As you work through this chapter you will be making decisions about the location of the property and its physical condition. Be careful at the same time to make a note of the various costs that are indicated, so that these may be incorporated into the expenses section of your business plan.

PURPOSE

What kind of operation will you be running on your premises? Will there be a retail sales outlet? Sales only to wholesalers or tradespeople? Manufacture? Office work? Bulk storage? Distribution? Will it involve food preparation or the use of dangerous substances?

Where will you site your main office and what will you do there? Will this be a purely administrative centre or will you also conduct your main activities there? Most smaller firms find it better to have their main activities and their 'head office' under one roof. More sites mean more communications by letter

Figure 22 Location

Refer to the text for guidance on completing this schedule.

PURPOSE
- Where will you site your main office?
- What activities will you conduct from this site?
- Will you have any other sites for the business?

(*Note* Complete the next three sections for each site.)

PROXIMITY
- Will your proposed site be near to your customers, or your suppliers?
- What will be the availability of suitable labour at your chosen site?
- Will the location prove acceptable to the managers and skilled people you wish to employ?
- Will your proposed site be near public transport or public roads?

REQUIREMENTS
- Can you obtain planning permission to use the site for the intended purpose?
- How much space will you require?
- How much of this will need to be at ground floor level?
- What services will you require: for example, gas, electricity, water, drainage, telephone, air venting?
- What size vehicles will be visiting your premises?
- What access and egress will you require?
- What parking and vehicle manoeuvring space will you require?

• Will you need to modify the premises in any way, and will your alterations be approved by the local authority and, if necessary, by the landlord?
• Will the premises comply with any legislation relevant to its uses: for example, related to health and safety or to the employment of people there?

FINANCE
• Will the premises be rented, leased or purchased?
• How will you raise the cash needed for the purchase price or premium?
• What will it cost to have the premises properly surveyed?
• What kind of maintenance payments and insurances will you be required to sustain?
• When will the rent and rates be reviewed, and how much should you allow for this in your business plan?

or telephone line (speech, fax or computer network) with the risks of delays and misunderstandings, or movement of people to and fro taking up valuable time.

A head office can be sited virtually anywhere that key people are prepared to work. But will you or some of your managers need to visit people (customers, suppliers)? Will you expect to receive customers? If you are running a retail outlet, will you depend on passing trade, or will you expect people to make a conscious effort to visit your store? If you need passing trade, then your premises probably needs to include a ground floor site with a display area fronting on to a high street in a reasonable-sized town. This is expensive, and you must ensure that your turnover and profit levels can sustain the cost.

If yours is a specialist shop, antiques, for example, it might be better sited with other similar shops, as people keen on these objects will usually prefer to come and visit several dealers.

If you want to manufacture or to operate a distribution centre, you will find places (generally out of town and in certain geographical areas) where the costs are relatively modest and where planning permission can be readily obtained.

If you are involved in both manufacture and retail, you may find it necessary to operate from two sites. The questions that follow should be addressed to each of your sites.

You may run a very small business from home, provided that you have the permission of the owner, or the lender if your house is mortgaged. If you do work from home, you must ensure that your business causes no disturbances to the neighbourhood: for example, from extra traffic (deliveries, customers or excessive mail deliveries), noise, dirt, smell or unsightly materials or machinery on public view.

If you have salespeople who operate over areas distant from your main office, you may ask them to operate from home.

PROXIMITY

If you or your senior managers expect to travel a lot, or if you expect many people to visit your premises, then the availability of good road and rail links becomes important. In many businesses the ability to get to your customers quickly is a distinct advantage.

You must also take into account the labour market and amenities in the area where you will locate your premises. Will you be able to recruit and retain good quality staff? If necessary, will you be able to persuade key people to relocate to your chosen area?

Ambitious and able people are no longer content with just a job. They want to live in an area which is pleasant, clean and has amenities for themselves and their families (for example, schools, shops, sports and leisure facilities).

REQUIREMENTS

Once you have decided on the approximate location, you will need to look for a specific site or building, and you will need to draw up a list of your requirements – a *specification*. In the area you have chosen, can you obtain planning permission to use the site for the intended purpose? Does it fit into the structure plan for the area? It might be worth discussing this with a local planning officer and a surveyor.

You will need to assess the amount of space you will require for, for example, the storage of raw materials, the manufacturing operation, the storage of finished goods, the office, toilet facilities, maintenance areas, display areas, and so forth. Analyze your operation and estimate your own requirements.

How much space will need to be at ground floor level, for example, as a display area, a sales area, an area where heavy machinery will be sited or stored, where goods will be outloaded?

What services will your operation require (for example, gas, electricity, water, telephone)? Remember that whilst it is not difficult to install gas, electricity and telephones, extra drainage or air extraction systems (for example, for welding operations) may well involve extra expense and time. Will you need higher voltages than the normal mains supply for special machinery, for example?

You will need to consider carefully what vehicles will be visiting your premises. How large will they be? You may use only small vans, but your suppliers may use big vehicles which will need to be able to get close to your loading bay. What access and egress will you require? Will you need to provide parking and vehicle manoeuvring space?

The building you find may not be entirely suitable for your use. Will you need to modify the premises in any way, and will your alterations be approved by the local authority? If the property is rented or leased, will the landlord agree?

If you will be using the premises for certain purposes, for example, food preparation or dangerous operations, or if your work entails the use of dangerous machinery or materials, there may well be special requirements with which you must comply. As people will work there, you will have another set of regulations to consider.

FINANCE

You must decide whether to rent, lease or purchase the property. On the one hand, purchasing a property ties up capital; on the other hand, it might be an investment. That is a matter for judgement, and it is by no means straightforward. Purchasing property will mean that you will not have a landlord to worry about when you make modifications to the premises. In leasehold property, there are restrictions on alterations, and the landlord's consent is generally required.

Whether you lease or purchase you will need to raise funds, and you will need to consider carefully how to do this. In the case of the purchase, the property will often be accepted as collateral for a loan, but not to cover the whole cost.

It is a wise precaution to have the property properly surveyed whether you lease or purchase, even if you intend to occupy only a part of the building.

There are a number of factors to be taken into account when you lease property, and you will need to get sound professional advice on this subject.

You will need to take into account, in your planning, such factors as repair obligations, maintenance charges, user clauses, planning permission, conditions of termination, sub-lets, assignment of lease, security of tenure, the schedule of delapidations, the schedule of condition of the property at the outset, and so on.

You will now have some clear ideas about the location of your premises and the costs. These may include structural survey fees, search fees, premiums for the lease or the purchase price/loan interest, maintenance charges, charges for repairs, insurances, re-instatement at the conclusion of the lease, rent (which may rise substantially on review), rates and the cost of installing services and many structural alterations. All this is quite separate from any furniture, equipment and fittings required.

Part Four

SALES AND MARKETING
DECISIONS

Chapter 10

SALES FORECASTING

> **OBJECTIVE: to make a realistic estimate of your sales over the plan period, to forecast receipts from sales and to set working targets.**

- **You *must* attempt to forecast sales and revenue**

- **Take into account any published sales figures**

- **Take full account of your firm's experience**

- **Make full use of market survey data**

- **Contracts require special treatment**

- **Convert your forecasts into targets**

- **Use sales forecasts to calculate anticipated revenue**

You may consider that it is impossible to forecast your sales accurately. That is probably true, but you *must* try. Your business depends on selling goods and services, and you cannot plan without some idea of how much you will sell, month by month for the first year of your plan, and quarter by quarter for the next two years.

What basis have you got for your sales forecasts?

First, there may be published data on sales for your kind of goods and services. Second, there are the results of your own efforts in the past – if you are already in business. Third, there are the results from your own market studies.

Now use the information from your environmental scan to see what changes are likely to influence this market. Has peace broken out, reducing the market for cables for warships and warplanes? Are there new regulations that make the machines produced by your competitors less attractive? Is there going to be a financial squeeze, reducing housebuilding and the sales figures for 'white' goods? You will know what issues are important to your trade. Now is the time to take these into account.

You must now draw on your own judgement and that of your colleagues in using this data and deciding how much of the market you consider you can penetrate, and how quickly. This depends in part on:

- How well you have identified your market niche, and pitched your prices
- How good you are at reaching your customers and convincing them of the benefits they will gain from your unique selling point
- How much you are blown off course by unexpected activity from competitors or by other factors

Special considerations apply to businesses that operate largely through a limited number of large contracts.

PUBLISHED DATA

In many cases, you can obtain total sales figures for particular types of products: for example, washing machines, video recorders, knitting wool, foodstuff products. It is more difficult to get such data for services, although even here you may be able to find out, for example, the number of television sets or sunbeds hired out.

Even more valuable, if you can get it, is data on sales by particular groups of people (for example, by socio-economic groups). You can obtain data on how many people, in different socio-economic groups, live in particular neighbourhoods; this can prove a valuable guide in, for example, calculating potential sales in a given area for a local shop.

The way you can use data varies according to the business. In siting a shop, for example, you can obtain figures for the turnover for different types of shop in different locations. You can then make a judgement on the likely turnover in the location you have chosen – taking into account such factors as other similar shops, the pattern of local transport and the shopping in the area. In choosing a location, it is not a bad idea to observe the movement of people going past the shop at various times of day and days of the week.

If you are selling products nationwide, then you can often obtain information about total sales, and your work on competitors will tell you who the key players are, and what chances you have of gaining a modest market share. These figures will give you an idea of the volume of sales you might achieve.

If you are opening a restaurant, you need information about how many people eat out, what they spend and what types of establishment they use. You also need some local intelligence about other restaurants in the locality and how well they do. Your sales figures are limited by the facilities (how many 'covers' you have), how much use can be made of them and what hours you propose to open.

In estimating sales in a restaurant, given the above data, there is not really much substitute for actually thinking about how many people you expect to attract into the restaurant, and how much they will buy, each morning, afternoon and evening, each day of the week, each week of the year.

The methods we have described so far are the kind you can use for estimating sales to the public. But if your business is selling machinery or services to business, then you have a different kind of problem. You may be selling only to local firms (for example, secretarial or employment services), or nationally (for example, specialized telephone equipment). Here you need data about the types of firm (in your locality or nationally), and the extent to which they buy your kind of goods or services.

If your business is concerned mainly with gaining a relatively few large contracts, then you need to know how many such contracts are awarded and how large they are.

EXPERIENCE

If you are already in business, then your starting point for estimating sales is clearly what you have achieved hitherto. For the first year of your new plan, write down the sales for each product line month by month that you achieved last year. Note any seasonal variation. Now, based on the kind of arguments used above, anticipate whether your sales of particular products and services will be higher or lower than before. Some people just add ten per cent to last year's figures, but few businesses can ignore changes in fashion and the activities of competitors.

Presumably you are introducing some modified or new products or services. Knowledge of your present customers, their likes and dislikes and future requirements should be a guide to future sales. Ask your salespeople for their views. They should be closest to your customers. If they are not already gathering such information, you should get them to do so in future – in spite of what some marketing experts say!

If you are introducing a completely new group of products or services, but to the same kind of customers, your knowledge of their needs should still be the prime source of the information you use. Here you are probably going to compete with other people who are already established in the market-place, and you will need to undertake your work on the unique selling point and the price positioning very carefully indeed.

MARKET SURVEY

The data referred to in the previous section will have come from your market investigation. But this investigation should also have gathered some data on the kind of customers you seek to serve and the potential sales for your kind of products or services.

If you included these points in your market survey, it should have revealed the extent to which customers would be prepared to use the services you propose to offer. Much of this may not materialize. Competitors may have become more active. In the light of your decisions about your market niche and your price positioning, you should now be able to make some estimates of likely sales. You must now make a judgement on how much you will be able to sell, and how quickly this will build up.

If you are selling nationwide, you will need to assess how effective your advertising will be and what response it will produce. Again, you must anticipate the level of sales you will be able to reach and how fast these sales will build up.

CONTRACTS

If your business is concerned with getting a series of large contracts (for example, for double-glazing new buildings as they are built, designing and managing an advertising campaign or acting as a distributor for a manufacturer), then many of the methods mentioned above will be of limited application.

What you need to know here is how many such contracts are awarded and on what basis. You need to estimate how long it will take you to get your first contract, and how large it will be, then your second and third, and so forth. In this way you can build up a sales projection chart.

If you are selling research services or management consultancy services to public bodies you will generally need to tender for the business. Each body will have its own procedures for processing tenders and you will need to assess your chances of gaining each contract you seek.

SALES TARGETS

Once you have identified what is feasible in terms of sales, these should be written into your plan, not just as forecasts, but as targets for your firm to achieve. If your managers and salespeople have been involved in drawing up these estimates and targets, they will be all the better motivated to achieve them.

Break down your targets by customer profile, by product line or service type, by geographical area and month by month, so that you can see just where you expect the sales to be achieved.

Set out your forecasts month by month for the first year, and quarter by quarter for the next two years, using Figure 23 to record your estimates.

Figure 23 Sales Projection for a Month

You will need a section on each area, for example, North, South, East and West.

AREA N					**AREA S**				
PRODUCTS	1	2	3	4	**PRODUCTS**	1	2	3	4
Sales to Customer					**Sales to Customer**				
Type A	—	—	—	—	Type A	—	—	—	—
Type B	—	—	—	—	Type B	—	—	—	—
Type C	—	—	—	—	Type C	—	—	—	—

FORECASTING REVENUE

Making a sale is good. Receiving the money from the sale is even better! From your knowledge of current practice in the industry, you must now estimate not only when the sales will be made, but also when the bills will actually be paid. In some trades payment is immediate, but in most cases you may have to wait a month, two months or even three months for your cash! Use the method presented in Figure 24 to record when you anticipate making sales, and when you anticipate receiving the cash in your bank account.

Each type of contracting business has its own way of staging payments. Some pay a portion at the outset, then portions as each stage is completed, holding back a portion until the whole work is approved. The staging of the payments must be built into your projection of the revenue to be received.

Naturally if you decide to offer discounts of any kind this must be taken into account in your revenue forecasts. Whichever method you use you should now enter the results in Figure 25 which will provide an essential part of your business plan.

Clearly where you expect cash on the nail, the receipts – in other words, the revenue (for a 'cash sale') – appears in the month when the sale is made; but when payment is expected one, two or three months later, or in stage payments, this must be reflected in the 'credit sales' receipts figures.

Figure 24 Anticipating Revenue

This demonstrates how to anticipate the revenue from sales based on sales forecasts, where payment is expected within one month.

	Month 1			Month 2		
	Sales Volume	Income Earned	Cash Due	Sales Volume	Income Earned	Cash Due
SALES						
Number of units sold (Price per unit = p)	n1			n2		
Income earned		n1 x p			n2 x p	
Cash received			NIL			£n1 x p

This calculation must be completed for each product or service sold to build up the anticipated revenue expected, month by month for the first year, and quarter by quarter for the second and third years of the plan.

Figure 25 Sales and Revenue Forecast

Month	1	2	3	4	5	6	7	8	9	10	11	12	TOTAL

SALES

Number of Units A
(price of A)
Income from A

Number of Units B
(price of B)
Income from B

Number of Units C
(price of C)
Income from C

Gross Income

RECEIPTS

Cash Sales

Credit Sales

TOTAL SALES

RECEIPTS

Chapter 11

MARKETING STRATEGY

> **OBJECTIVE: to decide on how to reach customers, maintain intelligence about the market-place, secure sales and generate revenue.**

- **Decide on how you will attract the attention of potential customers**

- **Design the message and the medium you need to evoke a response**

- **Prepare your staff and materials to secure sales**

- **Prepare to close sales and to follow through**

Successful marketing and sales depends on knowing who your customers are – from your previous analysis – and how to reach and influence them. In order to make a sale you must, in simple terms, (a) attract the attention of potential customers, (b) gain their interest in your wares and evoke a response, (c) foster, create if need be, a desire, and focus this desire on the purchase of your particular products and services and then (d) persuade the potential customer to act, in placing an order for which they have the desire, ability and intention of paying! In summary, you need a plan to:

- Attract customers
- Evoke a response
- Focus desire
- Secure action

In order to make a sale you will generally need to start off by reaching a large number of potential customers. As you move from stage to stage in the process, the number of customers often diminishes quite dramatically. Your marketing strategy must take this into account. The drop-out rates from stage to stage depend on:

- Your particular kind of business
- How well you have identified your particular customers
- How well you have adjusted your actions to these customers at each stage

In many instances you will need to reach from 200 to 500 customers to gain a response; of those who respond probably no more than one in ten is really serious, and of those who are serious you will do well to persuade one in three to place an order with you. These are very broad generalizations, but they do represent realistic orders of magnitude in terms of the advertising and sales methods used in all kinds of businesses.

If you can do no better than this, it means that you must reach 10,000 potential customers to make one sale. Have you ever tried to sell an unwanted item of furniture through advertising in a local newspaper? If it has a circulation of 10,000 or more, you stand a chance!

How can you reduce the odds in your favour? The answer is to target your advertising and promotional methods accurately and to streamline the way your firm deals with enquiries.

ATTRACTING CUSTOMERS

It is easy to spend a fortune on advertising which has little impact. List the methods you propose to use to reach your customers. This must be based on a thorough analysis of, for example, what newspapers, magazines and journals they read, what sections of these periodicals they study, what shopping areas they frequent, what exhibitions and conferences they attend, what radio programmes they listen to and (if you can afford this in relation to your products) what television stations they watch. The methods you can use include:

- Paid advertising (newspapers, magazines, journals, radio, TV)
- Press releases, sometimes alongside paid advertising
- Telephone or trade directories
- Mailshots (using your own lists, bought-in lists or agencies)
- Telephone sales calls (your own salespeople or agencies initially)
- Personal sales calls (your sales representatives or agents)
- Displays (for example, a shop or at exhibitions)
- Sales promotions
- Personal contact (for example, at conferences and other events organized by professional and trade bodies)
- Web Site on the Internet

Whatever method you use, try to build into your plan ways to evaluate its effectiveness: for example, by coding advertisement reply addresses or building a bit of simple research into the questions you ask people who respond and those who ultimately purchase your goods and services.

Use Figure 26 to list the methods you will use, how often you will use them and the costs incurred. Include in this figure any costs incurred in drawing up or purchasing lists of potential customers. Bear in mind that the cost of a good list may be worthwhile if it enables you to target your customers more precisely and to reduce your advertising budget. In the last column, make an estimate of the response you expect to get from each method.

Figure 26 Attracting Customers

In the first column, list the methods you propose to use to reach your customers. Indicate the frequency, for example, of your advertisement or exhibitions (second column), and the cost per month (third column). If this is phased irregularly, make a separate note of the expenditure each month through the first year and quarterly for the next two years. Write down what response (for example, in terms of numbers of enquiries) you anticipate in the final column.

METHODS TO BE USED	FREQUENCY	COST PER MONTH	ANTICIPATED RESPONSE

In some cases, your advertisement or promotion may not, in itself, produce direct responses, but may create an awareness of your products and services, and your existence in the market-place which will make it easier to sell when the time comes. For example, as a builder or a funeral director you may place a regular advertisement in a local paper so that when someone needs your services they are aware of your firm.

EVOKING RESPONSE

The key to evoking a response is to appeal to the vanity or the needs of your potential customer. Do they want to impress the neighbours or get relief for their sore feet? Do they need to create impressive sales documents or get their word-processing done efficiently? Your impact depends on reaching people who feel a need – or who could feel a need if you convey the right message. Only if your firm is well known and has a good reputation among your customers will using its name attract attention.

You need, therefore, a well-designed message and method for prompting a reaction on the part of your potential customers. Why should they stop, as they skim the pages of the magazine, at your advertisement? It is not the aim of this book to go into detail on this subject, but you will need to plan and budget for good design, decide how this will be achieved and what manner of response you will generate (for example, a written reply, a telephone call, a personal call).

The key questions you will need to address to complete this part of your plan are listed in Figure 27. The more specific you are in evoking a response only from the people who are likely to buy, the less time you will have to spend later in weeding out people who will simply waste your time.

FOCUSING DESIRE

The way you react to the customer's response is crucial. Many sales may be lost when someone in your firm answers the telephone in a negative and unconstructive manner. Plan to train all of your people who will have any contact at all with the customers or potential customers. Include the telephonist and the invoicing clerk, not just the telesales people and the sales representatives.

Train your people to ask questions, to take an interest in the enquirer, to seek to help and to meet needs. Where the need can be met by your own products and services, train your people to promote them. Otherwise, your firm should earn a reputation for helping people. Someone once said, 'People buy from people they like'. There is a lot of truth in that. Helping people, even if they do not buy your goods on that occasion, can be very good for business.

Figure 27 Evoking Response

1. What will be the basis of your appeal to the customer?

2. How will this message be put across?

3. What help will you need in designing the advertising and promotional material? How much will this cost?

4. How often will you need to review and revise your design and what will this cost – and when?

5. In what ways do you expect the potential customers to respond?

It is also important at this stage to have a procedure for ensuring that the customer has a genuine desire for the product or services, and the authority or means to pay. If you are selling, for example, machinery or raw materials to a company, you may need to convince two or three different people, so that your strategy must take this into account both in terms of the time your salespeople will need to secure sales, and also the costs involved.

Your plan (see Figure 28) must include a procedure for dealing with enquiries, and for training your people to do this really well. If you are expecting a written response (for example, a completed coupon from a newspaper, or a written request for information or a catalogue), will you send back literature (and if so, what kind?), or will you telephone, or ask a representative to call?

If you expect people to telephone, you will need to train the telephone operator to channel this call quickly to the right person, and that person must be trained to answer the call in a positive, constructive manner, to make a note of all the relevant information, and to arrange for prompt follow-up.

If you are expecting personal callers (for example, at a shop or warehouse, or at an exhibition), you will need literature, and probably samples or materials to exhibit, as well as well-trained sales assistants or consultants on hand.

If you expect a response via the Internet, how do you propose to deal with it? Will you have an automatic reaction to an enquiry, or have an operator available at all times, or expect the enquirer to leave a message by E-mail?

Figure 28 Focusing Desire

When your advertising and promotional methods produce a response, how will you deal with it? Do you expect a written, telephone or personal response? What materials will you need to provide (for example, written materials, display materials, specimen products)? What training will your people need? List these below.

RESPONSE ANTICIPATED	MATERIALS REQUIRED	YOUR PEOPLE INVOLVED	TRAINING REQUIRED	COSTS

SECURING ACTION

Sales may be achieved by face-to-face contact, by telephone or simply on the basis of written materials (for example, catalogues and order forms). In each case you need to question why people should buy your products and services rather than those of your competitors.

This means that all your sales and technical literature must stress the help

---

Figure 29 Closing the Sale

1. Will you expect to close the sale by face-to-face contact, by telephone or by written orders?

2. What materials will you need to support salespeople (for example, promotional literature, technical literature, samples, exhibits)?

3. What training will you give to your sales-people?

4. What procedures and documentation will you adopt for recording and progressing orders?

5. How will these procedures be followed through to check on customer satisfaction and invoicing?

6. What information will you collect from potential and actual customers about your advertising and promotion, and about positive and negative responses to your products and services?

7. If you are selling through intermediaries, how will you monitor customer reaction?

---

your customers will receive through purchasing your particular products and services, and your salespeople must be trained to listen to the customer and to respond accordingly.

You will need to plan out the means of recording and processing orders, and ensuring that each customer's needs are met, invoices issued and payment received.

The point of sale contact is ideal for collecting information about how people heard about your products and services, what they found attractive about your advertising and what prompted them to respond. It also provides an opportunity to probe their needs in more depth, providing you with information on which to base the further development of your products and services, as well as clues about how to promote them more effectively. Plan to collect and collate this information.

If you are selling to the public through intermediaries, you will need to work closely with them to ensure that your wares are presented properly. You may need to find alternative means of collecting information about how customers rate your particular products and services, and how they found out about them.

Use the checklist in Figure 29 to record the actions you propose to take.

Part Five

FINANCIAL STRATEGY

Chapter 12

EXPENDITURE
FORECAST

> **OBJECTIVE: to estimate the expenditure that will be
> incurred in running the business as a basis for
> calculating cash flow and profit forecasts.**

- **Calculate what your
  expenditure will be over
  three years**

- **Calculate variable costs
  on the basis of projected
  sales**

- **Identify and estimate
  your fixed costs, item by
  item**

Each possible item of expenditure must now be considered, and in each case
you will need to estimate:

- How much it will cost in the first year, the second year and the third year
- When you will be called upon to pay, on a month-by-month basis for the
  first year, and quarterly for the second and third years

If you feel a need to calculate profit and loss on a monthly basis, you will also
need to estimate the cost of the item on a month-by-month basis. Remember
that cost is incurred when an item is used or discarded, but expenditure is
involved when the cost of the item has to be paid.

It is very important at the outset to recognize the key difference between
cash flow (when cash actually comes into the business or out of it – receipts
and expenditures) and profit/loss calculations (which are based on the
income generated and the costs incurred over a given period or in connection
with a particular business activity).

For example, you must pay for raw materials even if you have not used
them, but they appear in your profit and loss calculation when they are used,

or when they are discarded. In the meantime, if you have borrowed money to pay for the raw materials, then you are incurring the cost of the loan all the time it is outstanding. Any costs associated with the storage of the materials are also ongoing.

When the cost of an item, for example, electricity, is incurred before the bill arrives, the cost is said to be accrued. It is included in the profit and loss, but only appears in the cash flow statement when the bill is paid. The same applies (in reverse) to your pre-payments.

Costs can be broadly divided into:

- Fixed costs, that remain virtually unaltered whatever volume of goods and services you sell
- Variable costs, that actually vary according to the volume of your sales

In some simple businesses the distinction is clear-cut, and the variable costs are directly proportional to the volume of sales. This is generally not the case, however, and there are some items of expenditure which are semi-variable.

Another factor to bear in mind is that fixed costs may change significantly when a particular volume of sales is reached: for example, because you need to employ more staff or purchase more machinery to service the orders. Fixed costs are often called the 'overheads' of a business.

Use Figure 30 as a checklist to prompt you to think about your fixed costs, about every single item of expenditure your business will incur at every stage.

A thorny question is how to deal with inflation. One method is to calculate all the figures at 'today's prices', and expect that as your costs increase so you can increase your prices. The problem is that this will not apply properly to items like depreciation or loan interest payments. If you are dealing with organizations in overseas countries you may need to take into account possible currency fluctuations. (See the section on risk assessment in Chapter 14.)

An alternative method – and one which has considerable merit – is to make a realistic estimate of increases in costs on a year-by-year basis and to estimate how much you will need to increase your prices to cover it.

In preparing these figures it is rarely worthwhile to attempt excessive accuracy. In most cases, figures to the nearest £1 or even £10 will probably be near enough. It is wise to overestimate a little – but not too much – when calculating expenditure.

Figure 30 Fixed Costs – Overheads – For Profit/Loss Calculation

	Year 1	Year 2	Year 3
Employees' wages	_____	_____	_____
Employers' National Insurance	_____	_____	_____
Training of staff	_____	_____	_____
Rent (rented premises)	_____	_____	_____
Rates and water rates	_____	_____	_____
Fuel (gas, electricity, etc.)	_____	_____	_____
Telecommunications	_____	_____	_____
Computer running costs	_____	_____	_____
Postage	_____	_____	_____
Printing and stationery	_____	_____	_____
Subscriptions and periodicals	_____	_____	_____
Advertising and promotions	_____	_____	_____
Repairs and maintenance	_____	_____	_____
Insurances	_____	_____	_____
Professional fees	_____	_____	_____
Interest payments	_____	_____	_____
Bank charges	_____	_____	_____
Vehicle and travel costs (other than depreciation)	_____	_____	_____
Depreciation – vehicle	_____	_____	_____
Depreciation – other assets	_____	_____	_____
Other expenses (specify)	_____	_____	_____
TOTAL OVERHEADS	======	======	======

FIXED COSTS

Wages

If you employ people on a regular basis, without taking account of the usual fluctuations in sales, the basic wages of such people (including yourself and your managers) represent fixed costs. If you employ people only when there is work to do, these costs are effectively variable. Furthermore, if any of your employees, for example, sales staff, are paid a commission on sales, that is strictly speaking a variable cost.

Once you have staff, of course, you become liable for their national insurance contributions and to administer their income tax related to their employment with you. In a monthly accounting system the cost will be shown in the month where the employee is employed, but strictly speaking the expenditure should be shown when the employee is paid (net of tax and employee's national insurance), with the related income tax and national insurance normally paid a month later.

List the kinds of people that you intend to employ (Figure 31) during the first, second and third year, and give details of the total number of hours, days or weeks of their employment during each year. This total multiplied by the expected gross rate of pay will give the total wage bill for the year. Ignore employees' PAYE and NI contributions for the calculation of profit/loss. An approximate figure for the employer's national insurance contributions can be calculated on this basis.

Figure 31 Wage Costs

Calculate these figures for each of the first three years.

TYPE OF EMPLOYEE	ANNUAL PERIOD OF EMPLOYMENT	RATE OF PAY	TOTAL WAGES	EMPLOYER'S NATIONAL INSURANCE

Training of staff

Whether you are starting out on a new business or embarking on a new phase in your business, the need to train your staff is paramount. This must not be neglected in your plan. Insert here any course costs and extra travel and subsistence involved – provided this has not been included in the vehicle and travel section.

Rent and rates

On the basis of the property you intend to occupy, estimate the annual rent (if any), business rates and water rates payable. Figure 32 indicates the key questions. Amortization of a lease premium should be included in 'other expenses' (see page 112).

Fuel

On the basis of the property you will occupy and the use you will make of it, estimate the amount of gas, electricity, heating oil, and so forth that you will consume in your business. Ignore fuel for vehicles as this comes under a different heading. Estimate how much you will use each year and the cost incurred for your profit/loss calculation, and note when this expenditure will be incurred.

Do you have any machinery or equipment that has a high rate of fuel consumption? If so, estimate the anticipated total hours of use in one year; and from the fuel consumption per hour and the unit cost of fuel, calculate the total estimated annual fuel cost and when this payment will be due.

Telecommunications and postage

You may well find this very difficult to quantify at first. If you are already in business, you will have past records to guide you, and you will then need to judge whether expenditure is going to be greater or smaller than in the past.

If either the telephone or the postal services are used extensively in your business, then you will need to make these estimates based on your best judgement as to the amounts involved. How many business calls will you expect your firm to make? Over what distance will the calls be made: locally, nationally, in Europe or further afield? What will be the average duration of the calls and at what time of day and rate of charge? From this information, a rough estimate can be made of the annual telephone costs incurred. What use will you make of Facsimile transmissions? Will there be any other telecommunication charges, such as for the Internet, including Web Site?

Computer running costs

Estimate the consumable materials you expect to use over the plan period and when payments fall due. This will normally cover software costs (includ-

Figure 32 Rent, Rates and Water Rates

1. Do you anticipate that leased or rented premises will be required?

2. When will rents be payable (in advance or in arrears, monthly, quarterly or annually)

3. What will be the annual rent payable? Insert this figure in your fixed costs.

4. How long is the contract?

5. When is a rent increase negotiable? If this falls in your first three years it must be reflected in your figures. Seek advice on the likely increase.

6. Will a premium be required? The cost of this must be spread over the contract period and included in the overhead figure for the profit/loss calculation.

7. The time at which the premium must be paid and when the rent payments fall due should be noted for the cash flow in the following chapter.

8. What are the anticipated annual business rate charges? How can payment be phased? How do you intend to pay?

9. What will be the annual water rate charges? How can payment be phased? How do you intend to pay?

ing support costs), maintenance contracts, floppy disks and items for peripheral equipment, for example printer cartridges and inkjet refills. Items such as on-line database subscriptions, computer equipment depreciation and insurance will be covered elsewhere.

Printing and stationery

If this is a minor item, make a rough estimate, based on previous experience if possible. But if this will be a major item of expenditure, you will need to estimate your requirements, including initial stationery supply, letterheads, business cards, complimentary slips, invoices, and so forth, including cost of design and artwork of any logo or heading. Include such items as record books, computer paper and any other special needs.

Subscriptions and periodicals

You will need to include here any subscriptions to trade associations, employers' organizations, professional bodies, and so forth which are important to your business. List any specialist journals, magazines or publications you will require and the cost involved. If you plan to subscribe to an on-line database, include the annual subscription here.

Advertising and promotions

From your marketing plan, you can now estimate the costs of all your advertising and promotional activities, including design and artwork, printing, postage, envelopes, distribution, and so forth. Include any technical leaflets and catalogues under this heading.

Repairs and maintenance

List any machinery and equipment that will require repairs and maintenance. Include also any buildings for which the business is responsible, and any fixtures and fittings. Where you decide to have a maintenance contract, insert this figure in the annual costs, and make a note of when payment will be due.

Where a maintenance contract does not exist, you will need to make sensible provision for repairs and maintenance in your costings and budget. If you have a lease that requires you to reinstate the premises when you vacate it, you may consider it wise to make provision for this cost over the life of the lease.

Insurance

List all of the insurance you will need for your particular business, stating the total amount of cover required and the annual premium. Note whether this will be paid annually or monthly, and during which months. Use Figure 33 to record your estimates.

Figure 33 Insurances

Type of Insurance	Cover Required	Annual Premium	Payment Dates

Professional fees

Decide what professional assistance you will require from a solicitor, accountant, bookkeeper, marketing expert or other kinds of consultant. List the fees you anticipate paying each year in each case.

Interest payments

This heading covers all interest payable on all loans and finance obtained for business purposes: for example, property mortgage, bank loans, hire purchase of equipment and overdrafts (but excluding vehicle finance which is included elsewhere).

In calculating the financing of interest, it is necessary to separate loan payments into (a) repayment of capital and (b) interest. If this is not yet known, then for the first three years calculate interest at the full expected annual rate (APR) on the full amount of the loan: this will be an overestimate, but corrected figures may be substituted when these are known.

It is not possible to include a figure for the interest payable on any expected

Figure 34 Interest Payments

TYPE OF LOAN	AMOUNT	PERIOD	INTEREST ON LOAN	ANNUAL REPAYMENT		PAYABLE INTEREST	(MONTHLY/ QUARTERLY)
				Rate (%)	Capital		

TOTAL ANNUAL PAYMENTS, CAPITAL AND INTEREST £_____ £_____

overdraft until calculations have been completed on the cash flow. If an over-draft is anticipated, include an estimate at this stage and correct it later. Record your estimates in Figure 34.

Bank charges

These are subject to wide variation and you should check on both the basis of charging and the rates to be charged on your bank account. Based on this and your anticipated use of the account, estimate the annual charge.

Vehicle and travel

Estimate the cost of running each vehicle which you will use in the business. The fixed cost will include depreciation (but see below), road fund tax, insurance, subscriptions to motoring organizations like the AA or RAC, interest on the loan to purchase the vehicles or leasing costs and incidental expenses. The variable costs will include petrol and oil, servicing, tyres, repairs, car-parking fees.

Where the use of the vehicle is not related to the volume of sales, the total annual costs, based on your anticipated mileage, less depreciation costs should be written into the vehicle expenses part of the profit/loss statement, together with any other travel costs, such as air or train fares, hotels, meals whilst on business or mileage allowances.

Figure 35 Capital Expenditure and Depreciation

Prepare a list of all the capital items costing more than £250 that you will need in the first three years. Include buildings but not vehicles.

CAPITAL ITEM	INITIAL COST	ANTICIPATED PURCHASE DATE	EXPECTED LIFE IN YEARS	DEPRECIATION PER ANNUM

Depreciation

The depreciation on vehicles is often accounted for using the 'reducing balance method': in other words, taking a percentage of the net book value at the commencement of the period. Thus the value of a car costing £20,000 would generally be written down at a rate of 25 per cent per annum, giving a depreciation of £5,000 in the first year, £3,750 (25 per cent of £15,000) in the second year, then £2,812 (25 per cent of £11,250) in the third year.

The depreciation on other capital items must be calculated, and also the date on which these capital items will be purchased. Use Figure 35 to record your calculations. If your requirements are complex, you may need to work through Chapter 13 before finalizing this section.

If you purchase and install equipment but cannot use it immediately, for example if you are building up a new plant, you may need to defer the depreciation on these items. Depreciation can start when the plant becomes operational. The funding costs incurred must be accounted for separately.

Other expenses

Include here items such as licence fees and the amortization of a lease premium, together with any other expenses which may be specific to your particular business. Give details in each case.

VARIABLE COSTS

The variable costs will depend very much on your kind of business. We have seen earlier that a fixed cost in one business can be a variable in another. What you must identify is where the cost varies with the volume of sales.

If you are running a road haulage company, for example, your fuel and oil costs will be variable, depending on the loads you carry for your customers. If you are running a retail shop, then the cost of the goods you have *sold* (not the cost of the goods you have bought) represents your variable costs.

Thus, you will need your sales projections to calculate your variable costs. You should estimate total costs for each year. In addition, you will need to think through when you will actually have to pay for these variable items. This is explained in Chapter 14.

Chapter 13

CAPITAL EXPENDITURE AND LIQUIDITY

> **OBJECTIVE: to review the capital expenditure needs of the business and alternative ways of meeting this expenditure whilst retaining adequate liquidity.**

■ Review the capital items you require

■ Review key financial ratios as you plan

■ Recognize the need for liquidity

■ On this basis, plan your investment strategy

■ Itemize the sources of cash available

REVIEWING REQUIREMENTS

You have already drawn up a preliminary list of the capital expenditure requirements of the business in Chapter 12, in Figure 35. We now need to examine this list in more depth and to decide how these capital items should be funded.

List separately:

• Property
• General plant, equipment and machinery
• Fixtures and fittings
• High-tech equipment that quickly becomes obsolete
• Motor vehicles

Figure 36 Financing of Capital Items

Prepare a list of all the capital items costing more than £250 that you will need in the first three years. Include buildings and vehicles.

Indicate in each case whether the article will be purchased outright or subject to a loan, rented or leased.

CAPITAL ITEM	INITIAL COST	ANTICIPATED PURCHASE DATE	METHOD OF PAYMENT	COMPLETION OF LOAN OR END OF LEASE

Your major investment will probably be in buildings and in complex machinery. You may also need to invest in a variety of furnishings and fittings and maybe in vehicles. In drawing up the profit and loss reports for limited companies the accountants use some well tested methods for assessing depreciation.

However, when you are assessing the viability of your business, you are not limited to these conventions. If you recognize that a computer will need to be replaced very quickly or become obsolete, you can write it down more quickly in calculating your business viability.

It is a matter for judgement and discussion with your accountant whether you use the 'straight line' or the 'reducing balance' method for calculating depreciation.

If you have a lot of spare cash available, you may wish to use this for capital items to reduce your need for borrowing cash, particularly during periods when interest rates are high or uncertain. However, as we shall see in later chapters, there are occasions when a business needs to raise ready cash and it is very unwise to tie up all your funds in capital items which cannot readily be converted to cash.

You should keep a proper record of capital items purchased. You will need this to keep track of depreciation costs and to deal with the tax authorities. Each year you will need to compile a statement of the current book value of your assets by category, clearly showing the depreciation you have allowed in each case. If these assets are likely to change significantly during the year it may be advisable to produce a summary statement or schedule of assets by categories on a quarterly basis. If for example, you expect to purchase additional vehicles during the year, the value of this asset category will change significantly.

LIQUIDITY

This need for ready cash is referred to as 'liquidity'. Cash in your hand or in the current account at the bank is 'liquid' – it can flow quickly. If your money is on deposit, it may not flow quickly, except at an unacceptable price. Such funds are less liquid.

Funds which are tied up in buildings, plant and equipment cannot usually be released quickly. Funds used to purchase stock items, or tied up in work in progress, can only be realized quickly if the items in question are highly saleable.

Finished goods can often be turned quickly into cash – unless the market has become saturated or the fashion has changed. Often, however, finished goods sold quickly do not fetch a good price.

SOURCES OF FUNDS

In essence, there are three ways to secure funds in a company for use in current expenditure or in capital items, and you will probably end up with a combination of all three methods. These ways are:

- To use money which belongs to the *owners* of the business (equity funding), which may come from original investments by the owners, or from profits generated by the business and retained in the firm rather than being distributed to the owners
- To use money which is effectively *loaned* to the company, whether this is in the form of a formal loan (for example, a mortgage, hire purchase agreement, bank loan or overdraft) or as goods which have been delivered to the company, but where a period of time elapses before payment falls due (in other words, credit from suppliers)
- To lease, hire or rent, for example, machinery, vehicles, property

You may be able to apply for a grant for public funds, for example from a government department or agency, or from an international body. There are a number of grants available through directorates or agencies of the European Union.

It is important to distinguish between these sources of funds. The owner invests in a business to gain a return on that investment, to make a profit which can be used either to develop the business or to be taken out as dividends or bonuses. The business could, however, make a loss, so that the owners are worse off, financially, than they were before. The owners have the last call on any money in a business (the government, lenders and employees all come earlier in the queue), and so can face a loss as well as a gain. They have taken a calculated business risk.

A lender expects to be paid interest, and to receive back the amount loaned (the 'principal' or capital originally loaned) in due course. The lender expects to be paid, in full, on time, whenever a payment falls due, and certainly takes precedence over the owners if funds are in short supply.

The ratio of *lenders' money* to *owners' money* in a business is crucial, and as a rule of thumb it should rarely exceed one. This ratio is known as the 'gearing' of a company. A highly geared company, where the ratio is much higher than one, is regarded by many people as potentially insecure.

When a firm borrows money from the bank there are a number of different mechanisms that can be employed, but two common methods are the term loan and the overdraft. Generally speaking, the term loans are used for capital items, whereas the overdrafts are used to cover current expenditure (in other words, to help with the 'buffer'). Banks can generally call in overdrafts if they wish, and it is unwise to become overly dependent on this method of funding.

If you consider that your company can apply for a publicly financed grant there are three things to consider.

1. Can you conduct your business in a way that enables you to meet the criteria for receiving grant aid?
2. Will the way you use the funds help the granting body to meet its objectives? Meeting the grant criteria may enable you to receive the award in the short term, but helping the grant-awarding body to achieve its goals may help to secure ongoing support.
3. Are you prepared to pay the price that may be involved? This could include the time taken to negotiate for the grant (in duration and management effort), the possible restriction to your freedom of manoeuvre (you must continue to conform to the grant criteria), and the need to keep detailed financial records that enable you to account to the awarding body and organizations that regulate public funds.

Often there are limits on your ability to move cash between budget sub-headings. The technical term for this movement is 'virement'. This may mean that you cannot move public funds from, say, administration to travel costs, or capital items to expenditure, without specific permission. Capital assets purchased from public funds frequently remain the property of the grant-awarding body. This may mean, for example, that you cannot sell a building or change its use. Funding you receive from a European body may be channelled through your own government. That means that technically your accounts will be subject to inspection by the national auditing body as well as by the European auditing body and the grant-awarding body. (This is, of course, in addition to your responsibilities to the taxation, customs and national insurance collection agencies. You must also ensure that you conform to government accountancy and reporting regulations.)

Cash is needed in a business to purchase capital items, but it is also required to act as a 'buffer' between payments which are due to the company and payments which are due from the company. A study of your trading cycle throughout the first few years could reveal a need for substantial cash for this 'buffer', and without it, you could technically become bankrupt. Indeed, you are more likely to fail in business through a shortage of cash than through low profitability.

At this stage, complete Figure 37 so that you have a clear picture, in a very simplified way, of where the money in the business has come from, and how it is being used. From these figures you can calculate the gearing ratio.

KEY FINANCIAL RATIOS

There are three other factors to consider. What is the ratio of the money you owe to the money which is owed to you? If your debts are much greater than the money owing to you, this is helping to fund the business – but may be damaging your reputation! On the other hand, if you are owed much more than your debts, you are effectively funding someone else's business.

The second factor, and one which is very important for planning purposes, is the amount of stock you hold, whether this is in the form of raw materials, work in progress or finished goods. Keeping a lot of stock means using storage spaces, tying up capital and, if for any reason it becomes obsolete or unfashionable, entailing problems.

For these reasons you need to plan for the minimum stock levels which will enable you to run your business effectively (Chapter 15). The manufacturing method known as 'Just in Time' has been adopted by a number of companies as a way of minimizing stock and work in progress.

The third factor is the liquidity ratio. What proportion of the funds can be

---

Figure 37 Sources of Funds

On the left hand side, list the funds being used in the business. As this will vary from time to time choose a particular date. For example, if you are in business it could be the end of your financial year. If you are starting a business this should be the day on which you propose to start trading, and the position you anticipate at the end of the first year.

On the right hand side, indicate how your total funds have been used under various headings.

Owners' money originally invested.	Tangible assets, property, plant and machinery, vehicles.
Loans from various sources.	Raw materials, work in progress. unsold finished goods.
Profits from previous years (if any).	Money owed by debtors.
Money owed to creditors.	Cash in hand or in the bank.
Grants from external bodies, if any.	

These two sides should balance, indicating how the business is funded and enabling you to calculate the gearing ratio (lenders' money divided by owners' money). If you have purchased capital items out of grant you need to be clear about whether these items belong to the company or whether the grant conditions mean that these are technically the property of the awarding body.

---

readily converted into cash to pay bills? This has been discussed above, but now is the time to do some sums and ensure that you are planning for a stable business.

FURTHER FUNDING

If further funds are needed, there are three avenues to explore:

• To invite others to invest in the business; to become joint owners with

you and to join in the venture, putting their own money at risk alongside yours, providing you do not mind losing a share of the business
- To raise a loan or overdraft facility, providing you retain a healthy liquidity and gearing ratio
- To sell capital items you own, if this is possible at a reasonable price, and to lease them instead

You can now choose between these alternatives in the light of your needs for liquidity, for appropriate gearing and the debt to creditor ratio you are aiming for in your business.

If you plan to run a tight ship, you will need to plan in firm controls and sound information systems (Chapter 19).

Chapter 14

PROFIT FORECAST AND RISK

> **OBJECTIVE: to calculate the level of profit (or loss) anticipated on the basis of the assumptions made so far about the business, and to apply sensitivity analysis to the data as a basis for refining decisions.**

- Calculate anticipated gross and net profit (or loss)

- Calculate the 'risk' involved if your sales volumes are low

- Consider alternative scenarios as you prepare your plan

- Use sensitivity analysis to assess alternatives and make decisions

When preparing the financial estimates for the profit/loss calculation, it is important not to lose sight of the ultimate objective: to produce realistic figures which can be used as the basis of decision-making now. Although one must estimate the expenses under the various headings as carefully as possible, it is often impossible to be really accurate.

It is time consuming to complicate the planning exercise by trying to be too precise. For most planning purposes, it is preferable to work in round pounds (ignoring the pence) for the figures inserted into the list of expenses and the projected sales income, otherwise you might fail to see the wood for the trees. It is, therefore, recommended that to maintain clarity pence are not entered, and that figures should at least be rounded off to the nearest pound, and in many cases, to the nearest five or ten pounds is often sufficient.

If you are able to use a computer to prepare your estimates, you may do so; but if the figures are not too complicated, it is better to use a pencil and paper. It is all too easy to get the computer to do sums for you without realizing the full significance of what is happening, and sometimes this causes you to forget the assumptions that are inherent in your figures (and hence the areas of doubt).

Many people find that actually writing down some of the key numbers and where they come from gives them a 'feel' for the figures and how they relate to one another – a 'feel' that few people get from computer print-outs. If you can use a calculator, you will find this a great help – especially the kind that prints out all the numbers you have entered in and adds up the number of entries.

If there is some doubt about the total amount that may be anticipated under any heading, it is preferable to err on the higher side rather than the lower. Do not grossly overestimate as this could mislead you into a wrong decision.

CALCULATING PROFIT – OR LOSS

In a straightforward business the 'gross profit' is calculated by taking the income generated by sales from the variable cost associated with these sales. Multiplying the sales forecast figure in units (say SF1 units for year 1) by the price charged (say PC1) gives the forecast of income generated from sales (SF1 × PC1). Multiplying the same sales forecast figure by the unit variable cost (VC1) of sales yields the variable costs (SF1 × VC1) associated with this sales volume.

Variable costs are discussed in Chapter 12. These are costs which relate directly to the volume of goods sold and generally this relationship is direct proportionally. Thus in this simple case, doubling the sales volume will double the variable costs.

However, we have the fixed costs to take into account. These were calculated in some detail in Chapter 12 and you can take the estimate prepared in Figure 30 for this, and calculate the total profit as shown in Figure 38.

When the gross profit is equal to the fixed costs the business has made neither a profit nor a loss. This volume of sales is called the 'breakeven point'. Clearly, below this volume of sales the business makes a loss, and above it the business is making a profit. Strictly speaking, we should also take into account any other income which the company has received, as shown in Figure 39.

Taxation rules change from time to time and you will need to take professional advice on the effect of National Insurance and Value Added Tax on your level of profit. You will also have to pay tax on profit, and this tax will be calculated according to the rules prevailing at the time. The Inland Revenue has its own method for calculating the profit on which tax should be levied.

There are some other terms and concepts you may find useful. The term 'markup', commonly used in the retail trade, denotes the amount of gross profit that is added to the cost of the goods to arrive at the selling price, often

---

Figure 38 Profit and Loss Forecast

	Year I	Year 2	Year 3
SALES FORECAST: units sold @ price per unit of P1...	═══	═══	═══
GROSS TURNOVER (quantity × price)	───	───	───
Less: variable costs	───	───	───
Gives GROSS PROFIT	═══	═══	═══
Less: OVERHEADS from Figure 30	───	───	───
NET PROFIT/(LOSS)	═══	═══	═══

This ignores any income from other sources, for example, interest from bank deposits or from the sale of assets at prices above their 'book' value. No account is taken of tax on profit.

---

expressed as a percentage. Thus, the cost of goods purchased plus percentage markup = selling price.

Another term which is used is the 'gross profit percentage', which is the amount of gross profit expressed as a percentage of the selling price. Thus, the gross profit on an item divided by selling price × 100 = gross profit percentage.

For example, a product with a selling price of £100, which costs £70, gives a gross profit of £30 (i.e. 30 per cent), but a markup of 42.9 per cent.

RISK ASSESSMENT

The element of risk can arise in a number of ways and in your plan you will need to identify possible risks and how you intend to deal with them. After reading this section, make a list of the kinds of risk relevant to your business. Against each item indicate, in general terms, what action you propose to take at the outset, if any, and what you can do if the unwelcome event occurs.

Figure 39 Profit and Loss Forecast

	Year 1	Year 2	Year 3
SALES FORECAST: units sold @ price per unit of P1...			
GROSS TURNOVER (quantity × price)			
Less: variable costs			
Gives GROSS PROFIT			
Plus other business income			
TOTAL			
Less: OVERHEADS from Figure 30			
PROFIT/(LOSS) (before tax)			

Remember that tax on profit will be deducted according to the Inland Revenue rules.

Some risks are insurable. For example, at the outset you might take out an insurance policy against a fire in your warehouse. Bad debt risks can be reduced by investigating the credit-worthiness of your key customers. However you may not be able to take action at the outset to deal with eventualities such as difficulties in securing raw materials or severe unexpected transportation problems. If you have taken out loans you must consider the way that interest rate changes might affect your business. Changes in the law may affect your business, especially if you are trading overseas. Trading with overseas customers or suppliers also means that currency fluctuations must be taken into account. Nevertheless, it is necessary to try to foresee such eventualities and to indicate in your plan how you would cope if these things were to happen. One way of getting a good list might be to involve your key managers in a 'brainstorming' session. When you have finished this exercise it can form a section in the 'special factors and risk assessment' part of your plan.

Risks associated with late payments will be dealt with in the next chapter, but you must face the possibility that some customers may never pay up.

Although you have done your best to forecast your sales figures, it is rare for these to be totally reliable. We need to be able to assess what will happen if you fail to achieve these targets. One way to get a grip on this problem is to calculate profit or loss based on more than one sales figure. You might, for example, calculate these figures on the basis of the worst sales you can imagine, the sales you consider you should reach reasonably easily, an optimistic figure and sales that were exceptionally good (see Chapter 8).

If we ignore other sources of income for a moment, we can see that the relationship between these key figures (volumes of sales, selling price, variable unit costs and overheads) can help us in our planning. Consider the information in Figure 40 where we are choosing to take four possible sales figures. By inspection you can see the breakeven point and the effect of sales volumes above and below this figure. You should now be able to substitute your own figures, estimating your worst possible sales figures for the first year, the most likely figure, an optimistic figure and a wildly enthusiastic overestimate!

Figure 40 Risk Calculation

Sales volume	50 Units	100 Units	200 Units	500 Units
@ £25 each sales income	£1,250	£2,500	£5,000	£12,500
Variable cost @ £5 each	£250	£500	£1,000	£2,500
GROSS PROFIT	£1,000	£2,000	£4,000	£10,000
Less the fixed cost	£2,000	£2,000	£2,000	£2,000
NET PROFIT/(LOSS)	(£1,000)	BREAKEVEN	£2,000	£8,000

You will now be able to assess the business risk inherent in your plan. You can now see the full implications of your decisions about the fixed costs you plan to incur, the sales volumes you anticipate, the cost of your materials and the chosen selling prices for your wares. Are you satisfied with the level of profit anticipated? Is it really worth investing that much money (the owners'

Figure 41 Sensitivity Analysis (Reduced overhead)

These figures illustrate what happens when the overhead is reduced by 25 per cent.

Sales volume	50 Units	100 Units	200 Units	500 Units
@ £25 each sales income	£1,250	£2,500	£5,000	£12,500
Variable cost @ £5 each	£250	£500	£1,000	£2,500
GROSS PROFIT	£1,000	£2,000	£4,000	£10,000
Less the fixed cost	£1,500	£1,500	£1,500	£1,500
NET PROFIT/(LOSS)	(£500)	£500	£2,500	£8,500

The breakeven point is reached with only 75 units sold and the loss at 50 units sold is much reduced when the overhead is reduced by 25 per cent.

---

money, as originally invested, plus retained profits – Figure 37) to earn that level of profit?

An external investor would compare the return on capital employed in your business with the figures other firms achieve. How will you stack up? Another ratio to look at is the net profit in relation to turnover. Is that good enough?

In the first year of trading you may not be able to reach an adequate level of profit, but you then have to look at the second and third years (and beyond if necessary) to see when reasonable levels of profitability will be attained, and make your decisions on that basis.

It is on this basis that potential investors or lenders will look at the business plan, and the senior people you can trust in your firm should understand the issues involved.

Quite often when this point is reached, you may conclude that the profit level and risk is unacceptable, and the next step in planning is to consider your options. What are they?

Figure 42 Sensitivity Analysis (Reduced variable costs)

These figures illustrate what happens when the variable unit costs are reduced by 20 per cent.

Sales volume	50 Units	100 Units	200 Units	500 Units
@ £25 each sales income	£1,250	£2,500	£5,000	£12,500
Variable cost @ £4 each	£200	£400	£800	£2,000
GROSS PROFIT	£1,050	£2,100	£4,200	£10,500
Less the fixed cost	£2,000	£2,000	£2,000	£2,000
NET PROFIT/(LOSS)	(£950)	£100	£2,200	£8,500

The breakeven point is reached with 96 units sold and the loss at 50 units sold is slightly reduced when the overhead is reduced by 20 per cent.

ALTERNATIVE SCENARIOS

You can look first at the overhead figures. Are there any areas where savings can be made without serious loss to the business? Could you manage with less expensive furniture and fittings for the first few years? Could you do with fewer telephones, less space, or storing your goods in a less expensive location? You may have to look more carefully at your advertising budget. Does it relate realistically to your sales volume and the income you expect to generate?

A second area for examination is the variable cost per unit of sale. Can you find a cheaper source of supply? Is there a less expensive method of distribution (if this is part of your variable cost)?

Finally, are you sure you have fixed your price realistically? If you are determined to produce good quality goods and services, you will want to buy in

Figure 43 Sensitivity Analysis (Increased price)

These figures illustrate what happens when the selling price is increased by ten per cent.

Sales volume	50 Units	100 Units	200 Units	500 Units
@ £27.50 each sales income	£1,375	£2,750	£5,500	£13,750
Variable cost @ £5 each	£250	£500	£1,000	£2,500
GROSS PROFIT	£1,125	£2,250	£4,500	£11,250
Less the fixed cost	£2,000	£2,000	£2,000	£2,000
NET PROFIT/(LOSS)	(£875)	£250	£2,500	£9,250

The breakeven point is reached with only 89 units sold and the loss at 50 units sold is materially reduced when the selling price is increased by 10 per cent.

good raw materials and do the job properly. If so, then are you still trying to compete on price? Or can you realistically increase your price a little?

SENSITIVITY ANALYSIS

With the information at hand you can readily calculate what happens in each case. Using our simple example (Figure 41), reducing the overhead by 25 per cent will mean that we reach the breakeven point more quickly (at 75 units of sale) and our risk of losing money is considerably reduced.

By reducing the variable unit costs by 20 per cent (Figure 42), the breakeven point is reached with 96 units sold and the loss at 50 units sold is slightly reduced. When the selling price is increased by ten per cent, the breakeven point is reached with only 89 units sold and the loss at 50 units sold is materially reduced (Figure 43).

Now it is your turn to assess the effects of variations in either your overhead expenses, your unit variable costs or your selling prices.

You will need to consider carefully the way in which costs vary with volume. For example you may find that at a certain point you can buy raw materials at a lower cost, decreasing your unit costs. On the other hand you may reach a point where you need to invest in new plant and equipment and your overheads increase. In both cases this will influence the breakeven point and you will need to take such factors into account.

Once you have finalized your decision, these are the figures to put into the final plan.

Chapter 15

TURNOVER AND STOCKS

OBJECTIVE: to determine the stock levels to be maintained in the company in the light of the anticipated turnover levels, so that you can assess the impact on requirements for capital employed in the business and cash flow.

- **Determine the levels of raw materials you intend to hold**

- **Decide on the levels of finished goods you need to have**

- **Plan for the level of work in progress**

- **Estimate the total capital employed, on average, in maintaining stocks**

If you are a manufacturing company, the likelihood is that you will need to buy and store raw materials and partially made-up goods for use in the factory. You also have plant and equipment and you will wish to carry some essential spares.

If your manufacturing process involves a number of steps, you will need to produce partially-made items and some of this 'work in progress' will be stored, albeit temporarily. Finally, you may have a modest store of finished goods ready to supply to your customer. Retailers and wholesalers also hold stocks of finished goods bought in and ready for sale.

If machinery spares form a significant proportion of your stockholding, prepare a similar chart to that in Figure 44 so that you can estimate the costs involved. If you are running, for example, a farm machinery maintenance business, the cost of holding spares can be quite high.

The costs associated with all this storage includes the cost of the capital tied up in the business (and this can materially reduce your profits) and also the cost of the storage space. If some of your goods are perishable or sensitive, you may need to control the environment in the store, for example, in respect of temperature, humidity or atmospheric gases – a further cost factor. Pest control can be a problem in some trades. If stocks are high, you also run the risk of having the goods left on your hands if the lines become unpopular for any reason, or if the goods deteriorate.

You will need to examine the level of stocks required at each stage, taking into account: the need to maintain a range of goods for sale; the speed at which you can make the goods; and the speed and reliability of deliveries. In the case of bought-in goods, you will need to specify how often you will order new supplies. (You may find that bulk orders give you a better discount, but do not be tempted to plan to do this if this causes you to hold unacceptable levels of stock.)

Record your decisions in Figure 44 and use the figures to calculate the capital to be employed in the business to maintain these stock levels. Is this acceptable? Have you allowed for this level of storage capacity? Will you need to revise your capital plans?

Relevant figures will also be used for the profit/loss calculation. For cash flow purposes you will also need to determine the amount of stocks you intend to secure at the outset, and how these are to be built up during the first year of trading, on a month-by-month basis, reflecting your sales projections.

Figure 44 Levels of Stock

RAW MATERIALS

ITEM	STOCK LEVELS (minimum)		STOCK LEVELS (average)		RE-ORDER		
	Quantity	Value (£)	Quantity	Value (£)	Frequency	Quantity	Value (£)

TOTAL AVERAGE VALUE OF RAW MATERIAL STOCKS HELD £_____

133

WORK IN PROGRESS

ITEM	STOCK LEVELS (minimum)		STOCK LEVELS (average)	
	Quantity	Value (£)	Quantity	Value (£)

TOTAL AVERAGE VALUE OF WORK IN PROGRESS HELD   £_____

FINISHED GOODS

ITEM	STOCK LEVELS (minimum)		STOCK LEVELS (average)		RE-ORDER (if this is appropriate)		
	Quantity	Value (£)	Quantity	Value (£)	Frequency	Quantity	Value (£)

TOTAL AVERAGE VALUE OF FINISHED GOODS STOCKS HELD   £_____

If your business is in retail you have a slightly different problem. In some cases the public will be willing to inspect samples and wait for products to be made to order. Generally, however, in the retail business you need to purchase and have in stock products that you believe you can sell to the public. Selling space is expensive and you may need an off-site storage warehouse for goods you wish to bring into the shop quickly. You will have the added problem of seasonal variation in sales. You may find it helpful to draw up a table of goods you intend to hold in the retail outlet and goods you intend to have in a warehouse. Once again you will need to take into account lead times for obtaining goods. In your accounting procedures and estimates you will need to allow for a proportion of goods that you may need to write off or sell at a knock-down price.

Chapter 16

FORECAST CASH FLOW

> **OBJECTIVE: to forecast when money will flow into and out of the business so that the firm will always be in a position to pay its bills and manage its cash flow efficiently.**

- Note the structure of the cash flow forecast sheets

- Estimate your receipts

- Estimate your payments

- Calculate your requirements for cash and make adequate provision

You forecast your firm's expenditure in working through Chapter 12 and the anticipated income from sales of your goods and services by the methods indicated in Chapter 10. As we have seen (Chapter 13) there are also other sources of income to the business (for example, owners' investments, loans, asset sales, interest on bank deposits).

A major planning and management tool is a sheet which shows, month by month, how much money is flowing into the business, and how much is flowing out. Note that we are dealing here with the actual movement of money, not placing or receiving orders, moving goods or using fuel.

If we compare these headings with the profit/loss forecast, we will find important differences which we need to examine and understand. These arise because the profit/loss calculation is concerned with linking income from sales with the expenditure incurred in providing them, whereas the cash flow is concerned with movements of money which will not be 'in phase' with sales or the consumption of supplies, and so forth.

STRUCTURE

You will notice from Figure 45 that down the left hand side we have first of all the opening balance and list of sources of income, followed by expenditure headings.

Figure 45 Headings in the Cash Flow Forecast

MONTH	0	1	2	3	4	5	6 ... 12	TOTAL

RECEIPTS

Opening balance (B)

Owners' investment
Loans from . . .
Cash sales
Credit sales
Asset disposals
Interest received

TOTAL RECEIPTS (R)

PAYMENTS

Premium on lease
Purchase of property
Purchase of plant,
   furniture and fittings
Purchase of vehicles

Raw materials
Goods for sale
Employees' net wages
Income tax and NI
Training expenses

Rent (rented premises)
Rates and water rates
Fuel (gas, electricity, etc.)
Telecommunications
Computer running costs
Postage

Printing and stationery
Subscriptions and periodicals
Advertising and promotions
Repairs and maintenance
Vehicle and travel costs
   (exclude vehicle purchases)

Insurances
Professional fees
Loan repayments
Bank charges
Bank interest
Value Added Tax
Other expenses (specify)

TOTAL PAYMENTS (P)

RECEIPTS LESS PAYMENTS
FOR THE MONTH (M)

**CASH REMAINING IN
THE BUSINESS (C)**

If this is a plan for a new business, you may well require some cash transactions before you actually start to trade. If so, the state of play anticipated before trading should be summarized in the column for Month '0'. Ignore the opening balance for Month 0, and insert, as appropriate under receipts, how much money you expect to be paid into the business up to that date, for example, by the owners or from loans.

Under the payments heading, indicate any items you want to purchase before trading commences (for example, property, plant and equipment, stationery, raw materials) or bills you expect to pay (for example, telephone installation, insurances). For the new business, subtract the payments from the receipts for the pre-trading period to give the opening balance for Month 1.

If your business is already trading, ignore the Month 0 column and carry forward the opening balance (in other words, what you expect to achieve by the starting date of the planning period) to the top of Month 1.

In Month 1, make a note of any further receipts you expect to receive, for example, from cash sales. Then work carefully through each item of expenditure and predict the level of payments you anticipate for that month.

The receipts less payments for the month will yield the net income for the month ($M = R - P$). If you add the opening balance, this will indicate how much cash is left in the company at the month's end ($C = B + M$). This figure C for Month 1 becomes the opening balance for Month 2, and the process is repeated.

In the final column (headed 'total') you may care to add together the rows and subtract payments from receipts as a cross-check on the arithmetic. It will also help in the preparation of your budgets as it will indicate what you expect to spend on each item of expenditure during the year, and how much income you actually expect to receive during the period (as opposed to the income you have earned).

If you are operating as a limited company you will need to make provision for the payment of corporation tax and you will need to add a column for this. The law on advanced corporation tax is particularly complicated and you may need to take special advice on the dates when payment will be required.

If you are trading as partnership or as a sole trader you will need to account for tax (and national insurance) on profits personally. This may be paid from the business account provided it is clearly shown as 'drawings'.

If you are trading in more than one currency you may need (a) to maintain your main records in one currency, and (b) to add one or more columns where you record the value of relevant items in the 'trading' currency for that item. You will generally be required to express your official accounts in the normal national currency and to use specified rates for reporting purposes.

RECEIPTS

You will need to consider carefully at what stage it is necessary to call on the owners' money and loans. If your business has any surplus assets (for example, equipment) these can be sold to generate cash. Although in the profit and loss account such a transaction will appear as the difference between the sale price and the 'book' value, in the cash flow forecast you will record *all* the cash you expect to receive.

Month by month, for each of the 12 months of the first year of the plan, insert the cash you expect to receive from sales and interest on deposits, and any other sources of income.

Later we shall examine whether this will be enough, and if not, study the options available.

PAYMENTS

Estimate payments, in the month they will fall due, for any purchases or services used: for example, for plant, equipment, raw materials, goods for sale, rent, rates, water rates, gas, electricity, telephone, printing and stationery, subscriptions, periodicals, advertising and promotion expenses, repairs, maintenance contracts, vehicle costs, travel and subsistence costs, insurances, professional fees, loan repayments, bank charges and bank interest payments (where these are not part of a loan repayment).

You will note that in the cash flow forecast, payments for raw materials and other variable costs are shown when they are made, not when the materials are bought, or used, or sold as part of the finished article.

Note that employees' wages are paid net of tax and insurance: the employees' tax and National Insurance, plus the employer's National Insurance contributions are paid in the following month. If you intend to make a contribution to the employees' pension fund, make allowances for this.

In dealing with loans, it is necessary to distinguish between the interest payments and repayment of capital; but in the cash flow forecast, all we are concerned with is the amount of money actually paid out, on a month-by-month basis.

How you deal with postage is a matter for you to decide. You can record what you expect to spend on postage or, as many firms do, you can use an 'imprest' system for postage (and also for minor items of expenditure). If you use an imprest system, you can record the cash you will use to initiate and to top up the imprest.

Under the heading of training expenses you can record either the course costs, or the course costs plus the participants' travel and subsistence costs.

The list of headings may not quite fit your business, although it should cover most eventualities. If you do not require some of these headings, leave them out. You may need more: for example, if you employ any subcontractors, you will require an extra line to make a note of what payments will be due to them, and when.

IMPLICATIONS AND DECISIONS

When you have completed the first year, study carefully the bottom line, and make a note if the figures drop below zero (in other words, if the receipts plus opening balance expected in the month is less than the payments due). We sometimes call this a 'negative cash flow'. Such figures often appear in the forecast for the first year of trading when the initial calculation of the cash flow is completed.

You cannot leave the plan in that state as it implies that when that month is reached the firm will be unable to pay its bills. You must review your funding structure to ensure that, by one means or another, you will be able to meet your commitments.

If, on the other hand, the bottom line is always in surplus, and a substantial surplus for some time, you need to plan to use this cash in some way, even if you simply put a proportion of the sum into a high interest account.

A negative cash flow can become serious very quickly if, for example, your debtors pay you very slowly but your creditors demand payment promptly. If you anticipate this, you must make provisions for dealing with it. You may be able to accelerate payments by offering discounts for prompt settlement of bills, or through factoring – provided your business can bear the costs.

ALTERNATIVE PRESENTATION OF DATA

Some funding organizations require a summary of balance sheet movements on a quarterly basis. This presentation (referred to by some people as a type of cash flow forecast) will show how the firm's sources and application of funds have changed with respect to a specified reference date. This will quickly indicate, for example, how the firm's capital is tied up in plant and machinery, or work in progress has changed during the period. It will also indicate the cash available. See the section on liquidity in Chapter 13, and the discussion of the balance sheet in Chapter 17. See Figure 46 for a typical format for this method of presentation. For the larger operating company this is particularly useful for senior managers: it presents a view of cash resource movements uncluttered with detail.

If this is a new company, the reference date may be taken as the day on which trading begins. For an existing company the date will normally be the beginning of a particular accounting period. These figures will then correlate with the balance sheet for the end of the previous trading period.

In this presentation account is taken of the depreciation of capital items, making clear the basis used for depreciation (Chapter 12). The value of stock, raw materials and work in progress is normally taken as the lowest of (a) the cost and (b) the current market value. Care must be taken in drawing up and interpreting this table. A higher debtors figure, for example, could be due to slower payments or increased sales. A higher figure for finished goods could be a reflection of higher production or lower sales. A transfer between stock and sales will incur no actual cash transfer until the relevant invoice is paid.

Figure 46 Quarterly Summary of Balance Sheet Movements

	1st Quarter	2nd Quarter	3rd Quarter	4th Quarter
FIXED ASSETS				
Buildings				
Plant				
Furniture				
Vehicles				
Computers				
Other				
CURRENT ASSETS				
Raw materials				
Work in progress				
Finished goods				
Debtors and prepayments				
LIABILITIES CAPITAL				
Equity (Owners)				
Retained profit				
OTHER LIABILITIES				
Loans				
Tax				
Creditors and accruals				
NET CASH				

Note: The figures represent the difference between the current values and the values at the 'reference date'. Bad debts are taken into account in the Debtors and prepayments. See text for interpretation.

Chapter 17

FUNDING REVIEW

> **OBJECTIVE: to review funding provisions for the business in the light of the capital and cash flow requirements estimated.**

- ■ **List the assets and liabilities of the firm**

- ■ **Review your capital requirements**

- ■ **Draw up balance sheets based on your forecasts**

ASSETS AND LIABILITIES

From the information you have gathered to underpin your plan, you are now in a position to draw up a balance sheet at the outset of the first year and at the end of the first, second and third years. The balance sheet at the end of the first year is, of course, the opening balance sheet for the second year. See Figure 47 for a simplified balance sheet: as you will see it is closely related to the source of funds work sheet (Figure 37) we saw earlier.

A balance sheet is a list of all the assets (what the firm owns) and liabilities (what the firm owes). These assets may be:

- Fixed ('permanent' assets like land, buildings, plant, machinery, furniture, fixtures and fittings)
- Current ('short-term' assets like stocks, debtors, cash and petty cash)
- Intangible (assets like customer relationships, patents, know-how which have a value but no physical existence)

On the liabilities side we have the investors' capital, because the firm owes it to the investor! Similarly, the business is, in effect, being funded by money owed by the firm to Her Majesty's Inspector of Taxes and other creditors, as well as money owed to the bank (term loan or overdraft).

Figure 47 Simplified Balance Sheet

LIABILITIES			ASSETS		
Capital (owners' money)			**Fixed assets**		
Owners' investment	£60,000		Buildings	£95,000	
Retained profit	£90,000		Plant	£50,000	
		£150,000	Furniture	£25,000	
					£170,000
Deferred liability			**Current assets**		
Term loan		£50,000	Stocks	£45,000	
			Debtors	£30,000	
			Cash	£5,000	
					£80,000
Current liabilities					
Creditors	£20,000				
Tax liability	£5,000				
Bank overdraft	£25,000				
		£50,000			
		£250,000			£250,000

If you expect to receive funds from a public body, study the conditions of the grant carefully. You may find that capital items purchased with this money become the property of the awarding body. In this situation make this clear in your accounts and maintain a separate asset list.

You will need to take care in the way you present receipts from grant-awarding bodies. A grant for a building may be shown as a reduced cost and this will have an effect on your depreciation. A grant towards labour costs will effectively reduce the revenue costs of wages.

PREPARE BALANCE SHEETS

From your previous work you will now know what funds are required for buildings, plant and equipment, furniture, fixtures and fittings and also the

Figure 48 Balance Sheet (Commencement of year)

LIABILITIES	ASSETS
Capital (owners' money)	**Fixed assets**
Owners' investment	Buildings
Retained profit	Plant
	Furniture
	Vehicles
	Computers
	_____ _____
Deferred liability	**Current assets**
Term loan _____	Raw materials
	Finished goods
	Debtors
	Cash
	_____
Current liabilities	
Creditors	
Tax liability	
Bank overdraft	
_____ _____	_____ _____
══════	══════
_____	_____

cash required to pay bills (from the cash flow forecast).

Complete Figure 48 based on your previous work in Chapter 13 (for capital items, especially Figure 36) and in Chapter 16 (for cash injected into the company and items purchased which become assets). Assets purchased at the outset of the year depreciate as described in Chapter 13, so that they have lower 'book values' at the end of the year. Complete a similar balance sheet for the end of the year.

Examine these balance sheets, and take careful note of the key figures and ratios. Consider, for example, the following questions:

- Are the firm's assets planned to grow or decline?
- Is the firm soundly geared or is the ratio of other people's money to the owners' money too high?
- Is the ratio of debtors to creditors reasonable?
- Are the stock levels approximately right for this operation?
- Is the level of 'working capital' high enough?

The 'working capital' in a business is calculated by subtracting the current liabilities from the current assets. The composition of the working capital will fluctuate between the different items, notably between stock and cash, but the level must be high enough to cope with these fluctuations. An indication of the level required will be given by the cash flow forecast.

REVIEW CAPITAL REQUIREMENTS

This is a suitable point at which to review the consistency of your overall financial strategy. The opening and closing balance sheets must be consistent with the anticipated profit/loss and the cash flow. Take some time to check out some of the key items (see Figure 49). Capital assets such as buildings, plant, furniture, vehicles and computer equipment do not give rise to cash flow movements during the year unless they are bought or sold. Related costs, for example for maintenance or related loans, are accounted for elsewhere. These items will reduce the profit level by depreciation during the period and hence also reduce the final balance sheet figures. Items such as raw materials will be bought during the year. The profit is reduced by costs incurred in ordering these, but the cash flow occurs when payment is made for them. Similarly a profit is generated when an item of finished goods is sold, but cash flows only when you receive payment. A series of simple sums should enable you to ensure that for each balance sheet item the opening and closing balances are consistent with the cash flow forecasts and profit/loss calculations.

In the light of this information, you may wish to review the way your firm is to be funded. If you decide you may have insufficient cash, you can:

- Seek more investment from owners
- Take out a further term loan
- Ask for an overdraft facility from the bank
- Consider leasing, renting or factoring
- Review your expenditure plans

Figure 49 Financial Consistency

Initial Balance Sheet	Effect on Cash Flow during period	Effect on Profit/Loss during period	Effect on Final Balance Sheet
Assets			
Buildings			
Plant			
Furniture			
Vehicles			
Computers			
Raw materials			
Work in progress			
Finished goods			
Debtors			
Liabilities			
Owners' investment			
Retained profit			
Term loan			
Creditors			
Tax liability			
Bank overdraft			
Cash available			

Part Six

PUTTING IT TOGETHER

Chapter 18

REVISE YOUR PLAN

> **OBJECTIVE: to bring together the various elements of the plan and to combine these into a coherent whole.**

- Decide on your business name, address and mission statement

- Ensure cohesion between the various financial elements of the plan

- Review the 'people plan' and your marketing strategy

- Satisfy yourself that it is realistic and practical

Name of the business

What thought have you given to the name you will use to describe your business? It is often very difficult to decide, and you need, of course, to check that someone else is not already using the one you want. You will probably need to talk to people with ideas and with people in your firm – the working group you set up at the outset.

Does the name that you have decided upon sit well with your kind of business? Will it help to create the right 'image' – or be misunderstood or a hindrance?

Address of the business

The location of your business has been explored in Chapter 9. Presumably you will trade from your premises and this will be your 'business address'. In most cases this will present no problems. The only question to ask is whether this address itself creates the right 'image', but that will not be an issue in most kinds of business.

You can, of course, use a Post Office Box Number, and this is often employed by mail order companies who wish to discourage personal callers.

Nature of the business – mission statement

Your original draft from the work on Chapter 3 now needs to be brought out, examined and discussed by your working group. In the light of revisions to your plan, for example, in respect of the customers you hope to serve or the goods and services you propose to offer, does this need to be revised?

At this time you may be in a position to take this statement and, with the support of your key people, rephrase it as a 'mission statement', worded in a manner calculated to inspire confidence in your customers, ambition in your staff and managers – and fear among your competitors.

If you are hoping to receive financial support from public funds it might be worthwhile making sure that your business name sounds respectable and sound. It might be worth checking this out in any of the languages spoken in the countries where you wish to trade. When your name appears in the annual report of the granting body it should not look unduly out of place!

People in the business

As your business idea has been refined, you may have cause to revise your assessment of the skills you will need to succeed (Chapter 4). This may mean that you have to look again at the people in your business, their strengths and weaknesses, and any further training they may require.

Are there any special requirements for qualified staff to run your particular business? You should check this out and ensure that you have staff with the requisite qualifications if any of the occupations relevant to your business are regulated: for example, in travel agency management, civil aviation, taxi services or transport management.

Now is the time to look again at your recruitment policy. If you will need more employees, spell out the people you will need, how you will recruit, select and train them. You may also need to reassess what help you will need from external experts.

Marketing and sales strategy

Work on the profit/loss projections and on the cash flow forecasts may have led you to revise your sales forecasts, or your advertising and promotion methods, or even your pricing policy and market niche.

If so, you must re-visit your marketing and sales strategy (Chapters 10 and 11) and make the necessary revisions now. You must also ensure that your plans for marketing and selling are consistent with your mission statement (your revitalized statement about the 'nature of the business').

Profit/loss forecasts

Were your initial calculations satisfactory, or did they lead you to make adjustments in your business plan? You should, at this stage, bring together on one set of papers all the information about the profit/loss forecasts for the three years, as in Figure 50.

Are these current figures final, and do they reflect a potentially healthy trading position? Are the assumptions realistic and achievable?

Figure 50 Summary Profit and Loss Forecasts

	Year I	Year 2	Year 3
SALES FORECAST: units sold	═══	═══	═══
@ price per unit of P1 . . .			
GROSS TURNOVER (quantity × price)	───	───	───
Less: variable costs	───	───	───
Gives GROSS PROFIT	───	───	───
Plus other business income	───	───	───
TOTAL	───	───	───
Less: OVERHEADS from below	───	───	───
PROFIT/(LOSS)			
(before tax)	═══	═══	═══

OVERHEADS/FIXED COSTS

	Year I	Year 2	Year 3
Employees' wages	───	───	───
Employers' National Insurance	───	───	───
Training of staff	───	───	───
Rent (rented premises)	───	───	───
Rates and water rates	───	───	───
Fuel (gas, electricity, etc.)	───	───	───
Telecommunications	───	───	───
Computer running costs	───	───	───
Postage	───	───	───
Printing and stationery	───	───	───
Subscriptions and periodicals	───	───	───
Advertising and promotions	───	───	───
Repairs and maintenance	───	───	───
Insurances	───	───	───
Professional fees	───	───	───
Interest payments	───	───	───
Bank charges	───	───	───

Vehicle and travel costs (other than depreciation)	_____	_____	_____
Depreciation – vehicle	_____	_____	_____
Depreciation – other assets	_____	_____	_____
Other expenses (specify)	_____	_____	_____
TOTAL OVERHEADS	══════	══════	══════

Cash flow forecasts

In Chapter 16 the method for drawing up the cash flow forecast for the first year was explained. You should now complete this exercise by working out a cash flow forecast for years two and three in your plan, but on a quarterly basis (see Figure 51 for guidance).

Figure 51 Cash Flow Forecasts (Second and third years)

	SECOND YEAR				THIRD YEAR			
QUARTERS:	1st	2nd	3rd	4th	1st	2nd	3rd	4th
RECEIPTS								
Opening balance (B)								
Owners' investment								
Loans from . . .								
Cash Sales								
Credit Sales								
Asset Disposals								
Interest received								
TOTAL RECEIPTS (R)								
PAYMENTS								
Premium on lease								
Purchase of property								

Purchase of plant,
   furniture and fittings
Purchase of vehicles
Raw materials
Goods for sale
Employees' net wages
Income tax and NI
Training expenses

Rent (rented premises)
Rates and water rates
Fuel (gas, electricity, etc.)
Telecommunications
Computer running costs
Postage

Printing and stationery
Subscriptions and periodicals
Advertising and promotions
Repairs and maintenance
Vehicle and travel costs
   (exclude vehicle purchases)

Insurances
Professional fees
Loan repayments
Bank charges
Bank interest
Value Added Tax
Other expenses (specify)

TOTAL PAYMENTS (P)   _____

RECEIPTS LESS PAYMENTS
FOR THE MONTH (M)   _____

**CASH REMAINING IN
THE BUSINESS (C)**   _____

Are you confident that you have identified all sources of income and when the cash will flow, and all items of expenditure and when they are due for payment? Have you made adequate provision to cover your cash needs throughout the plan period? You may find it useful to prepare a quarterly summary of balance sheet movements (see Chapter 16).

Capital expenditure plans

Are you satisfied that you have correctly identified all items of capital expenditure? Have you decided, in the light of your work on cash flow forecasts and the funds available, when each item will be purchased? Have you decided upon the method you will use for calculating depreciation?

Stock purchasing policy

Have you carefully considered your stockholding policy in relation to raw materials, work in progress and finished goods? Have you determined your purchasing policy and the quantity of goods you will order at a time?

Figure 52 Outline Business Plan (Key questions)

NAME OF THE BUSINESS
Does this now fit the nature of the business?

ADDRESS OF THE BUSINESS
Is this location suitable?

NATURE OF THE BUSINESS
Does this statement match with your current thinking?

PEOPLE IN THE BUSINESS
Have you identified the key skills needed for success and how you will ensure these are available to the business?

MARKETING AND SALES STRATEGY
Is this consistent with your 'nature of the business' statement? Will it work?

PROFIT AND LOSS FORECASTS
Are these healthy, based on your current assumptions?

CASH FLOW FORECASTS
Have you identified all sources of income and items of expenditure, and when they will occur? Have you made sure that you can cover your needs?

CAPITAL EXPENDITURE PLANS
Have you identified all items of capital expenditure and how you will fund them?

STOCK PURCHASING POLICY
Have you decided upon the level of stock to keep, how much you will start with, and in what quantities you will re-order?

FUNDS REQUIRED – FINANCIAL BASE
Have you satisfied yourself that you have a firm financial base?

BOOKKEEPING – MANAGEMENT INFORMATION SYSTEMS

SPECIAL FACTORS AND RISK ASSESSMENT

ACTION PLAN – KEY DECISIONS – TARGET DATES

Are all these decisions correctly reflected in your profit/loss projections and in your cash flow forecasts? Have these levels been taken into account in your work on 'working capital', and on the level of capital employed in the business?

Funds required – financial base
Have you identified the sources of funds available to the business and the use

to which these funds will be put? Have you properly considered renting or leasing where appropriate? Have you determined your anticipated gearing? Are you satisfied with the financial base of the firm and with projected balance sheets through the period?

Other factors

We shall be considering the methods you will use for bookkeeping and managing information in Chapter 19. You will need to consider now whether there are any special factors which relate to your business (for example, licences, patents, copyright) and what actions you will need to take to ensure that these are put in hand. (See also the section on 'People in the Business' above.)

MANAGEMENT INFORMATION

> **OBJECTIVE: to decide, in broad outline, the information systems you will use to manage the business, including your bookkeeping system.**

- Identify your needs for management information

- Plan to monitor sales and keep in touch with your market

- Plan to manage your money

- Plan to manage your people

In any business you need to manage your marketing, your money and your people. This means putting in place sensible means of setting targets and collecting and collating data to enable you to keep track of progress.

This book is not a treatise on management or on management information systems, but at the planning stage much of the information you produce can, with a little thought, be used as the basis of management control systems and incorporated into the plan.

MARKETING AND SALES DATA

The sales forecasts you have prepared and decided to include in your plan (Chapter 10) must now be turned into targets. You will need to divide up the year into months, and set out what you hope to achieve by way of sales of each product or service you provide. A simplified chart is provided in Figure 53 to illustrate the kind of documentation you can use, based on the sales forecasts.

You will notice that the price is also mentioned alongside each product. If you find it necessary to offer any discounts, it is important to record this information alongside each product line or type of service. The effect of discounts should be included in your plan.

Figure 53 Monitoring Sales

SALES	MONTH = 1 Forecast	Actual	MONTH = 2 Forecast	Actual	...
Number of units A					
Price					
Income from A					
Number of units B					
Price					
Income from B					
Number of units C					
Price					
Income from C					
Gross income					
RECEIPTS					
Cash sales					
Credit sales					
TOTAL SALES					
RECEIPTS					

If you have a number of lines, you should work out the monthly gross profit per item of each line, and from this, the contribution to the overhead made by sales of each product line. You will recall that the firm only moves into profit when the total gross profit exceeds the overhead. Thus, in each month you can calculate the total gross profit by adding the figures for each line.

Then you will need to plan a system to record the orders placed, goods and services delivered, invoices issued, payment received, and so forth. Thus,

---

Figure 54 Monthly Contribution to Profit

Table I Use to calculate the contribution to profit from each line

MONTH =	1		2	
SALES	Forecast	Actual	Forecast	Actual
Number of Units A Price				
Income from A Less variable cost				
CONTRIBUTION TO PROFIT (A)				

Table II Add up the contribution to profit from each line

MONTH =	1		2	
GROSS PROFIT	Forecast	Actual	Forecast	Actual
Line A Line B Line C				
TOTAL				

---

your monitoring system will be an extension of your sales forecast documentation.

At the same time you should plan to collect information about the marketplace. This should certainly involve collecting information about your customers, who they are, what they buy from you, how often and in what quantities, what they like about your products and services, what related goods and services they are interested in having, how their own businesses are developing, and so on. You should be able to collect much of this data through your sales force. Where this information is not readily available, plan to collect it and add the costs to your plan.

If you have a significant proportion of repeat business, you will need to set up a system for recording your dealings with each customer. From your financial systems (see below) you should be able to keep your actual dealings on file, but your recording system should also contain 'soft' information about each customer as described above, and a record of any comments made, significant telephone conversations and visits.

If you expect to receive grant aid you should monitor the 'political' situation, the environment within which the grant-aiding body operates. A change of government or a change in policy could influence the aims and objectives of the grant body. You may need to take this into account to secure ongoing support.

FINANCIAL INFORMATION

The financial information you will need depends on the nature of the business; but two crucial factors which are common to all types of firm are *cash flow* and *profitability*.

The cash flow forecast sheets you have prepared provide a simple, but effective, monitoring tool by providing two columns for each month (as in Figure 55). The first column will contain your forecast figures, and the second the actual receipts and payments made. You will need to customize this table to meet the needs of your own organization. The kind of detail provided in Figure 55 provides a useful basis for preparing departmental budgets. Heads of departments should draw up their own budgets from a zero base (see Chapter 1), listing in each case the assumptions they have made in building up the figures. As time passes each head of department should be able to account for differences between the forecast and the actual figures on the basis of the changing situation. This data will point up areas for improvement.

For planning purposes cash flow forecasts are produced on a monthly basis, but if your cash flow is precarious you may need to monitor this on a week-to-week, or even day-to-day, basis.

It may be useful to compile a summary of balance sheet movements on a quarterly basis (see Chapters 16 and 18). For senior managers this data provides valuable indicators of the state of the business – especially the way capital is being used in respect of raw material, work in progress, finished goods, and the figures for debtors and creditors.

As you manage the business you will find it useful to update the forecasts from time to time. Some organizations undertake this task on a quarterly basis, and where they have the computing power, the cash flow forecasts are updated monthly. This is particularly valuable if the trading pattern renders the firm vulnerable to a cash shortfall, for example if large amounts of cash flow frequently into and out of the business.

As mentioned above you will need a sound system for following up orders to ensure completion, invoicing and follow-up to ensure payment.

Taken together, this information will provide the basis for drawing up a bookkeeping system that will keep track of your income and expenditure, allocate each item to appropriate subheads that can be used for cash flow and profit monitoring, budget control and management information. Many computer-based systems exist and it should not be too difficult for you to find one appropriate to your needs. Make sure that you, and your key people, understand the system, and that it provides you with what you want: (a) to manage the business, and (b) to account for your activities in financial terms.

Figure 55 Monitoring Cash Flow

MONTH =	1		2	
SALES	Forecast	Actual	Forecast	Actual
Opening balance (B)				
Owners' investment				
Loans from . . .				
Cash sales				
Credit sales				
Asset disposals				
Interest received				
TOTAL RECEIPTS (R)				

PAYMENTS

Premium on lease
Purchase of property
Purchase of plant,
   furniture and fittings
Purchase of vehicles

Raw materials
Goods for sale
Employees' net wages
Income tax and NI
Training expenses

Rent (rented premises)
Rates and water rates
Fuel (gas, electricity, etc.)
Telecommunications
Computer running costs
Postage

Printing and stationery
Subscriptions and periodicals
Advertising and promotions
Repairs and maintenance
Vehicle and travel costs
   (exclude vehicle purchases)

Insurances
Professional fees
Loan repayments
Bank charges
Bank interest
Value Added Tax
Other expenses (specify)

TOTAL PAYMENTS (P)

**RECEIPTS LESS PAYMENTS
FOR THE MONTH (M)**

**CASH REMAINING IN
THE BUSINESS (C)**

PEOPLE INFORMATION

If you employ people, you will need to keep appropriate personnel records; but managing people involves much more than that. It involves ensuring that they are aware of their responsibilities and resources, that they are trained and guided in carrying out their duties, that they have clear aims and objectives.

It also involves letting people know how they are doing, giving praise and rewards as appropriate and keeping them informed and consulted on matters which affect them. Your key group of managers should be involved, as far as possible, in drawing up your plan, in formulating the assumptions on which it is based, and in making the crucial decisions.

Be careful, in managing people, to select measures of performance which go beyond what can be measured in figures. A full discussion about managing people is outside the scope of this book, but is covered by other books by the same author, including *How to Manage People* (Hutchinson Business Books, 1984), *Profits Through People* (Hutchinson Business Books, 1990) and *Perfect Teamwork* (Arrow Business Books, 1995).

OTHER DATA

According to the nature of your business you will need to establish monitoring systems, for example, for your stores, capital items, and so forth. In each case bear in mind the purpose of the record.

On the one hand, you have responsibilities to keep records so that you may deal with the authorities (for example, income tax, National Insurance, customs and excise, health and safety matters, licensing bodies). If you expect to receive a grant from a public body, make sure that your accounts will enable you to satisfy the requirements of the funding body and the organizations that regulate or audit the finances of that body. But for the day-to-day management of the business you need to provide information for your managers and your staff which will help them to make better decisions.

Chapter 20

COMPLETE YOUR PLAN

OBJECTIVE: to prepare the written document known as the business plan, setting out the relevant parts in order.

- Assemble your working papers ready for the final task

- Collate sections on the business name, address and mission statement

- Pull together sections on people, marketing and sales

- Check that the financial sections are consistent and clear

- Set out your 'critical path analysis' as a guide to decision-making

ASSEMBLE YOUR DATA

If you have worked carefully through the chapters, you will have far more information than you need to include in the formal plan. This information was needed to prepare the plan, and will be valuable as you put the plan into effect, and as you seek to explain it to, for example, senior staff, investors or lenders.

The work you and your colleagues have put into the plan will also be of enormous value if any unforeseen factors arise. The knowledge you now have will enable you to recognize the implications of the new situation and help you to make your decisions.

However, it is not wise to clutter up the written plan with too much detail. What is wanted in most cases is the summary sheets of key data with text to explain how it all fits together. All the supporting information should be carefully filed away. If you have to answer questions, for example, from investors, lenders or senior staff, you may well need to refer back to these supporting papers.

In this chapter we shall review what should be included in your formal written plan. In most cases, the text and financial tables can be simply assembled from the work you have done.

Name of the business
Address of the business
Nature of the business – mission statement

These sections are straightforward and have been discussed in detail in earlier chapters, especially Chapter 3 (Figure 8) and Chapter 18.

People in the business

- Describe the key people in the business and explain how, between them, they have the necessary skills to ensure success
- Describe any steps you propose to take to enhance the skills of your key people
- Describe any recruitment you propose to undertake, and why you consider the people you need will be available in the labour market
- List any outside expertise you require and how you propose to meet that need

Marketing and sales strategy

This should set out:

- Your customers, and what evidence you have about them
- What products and services you will offer
- How you will reach your customers, your advertising and promotion
- How you will engage with your customers and secure orders
- How you will maintain market intelligence

Profit and loss forecasts

Forecasts of the profits for each of the three years must be presented with full supporting information about income and expenditure, and explanations of all assumptions made. Figure 50 provides a model for presenting this financial data.

Cash flow forecasts

Full month-by-month forecasts of receipts and payments should be presented for the first year, and quarterly forecasts for the second and third years. Provide notes to explain each key section, and any arrangements that have been or will be made for, for example, loans, overdraft facilities or leases. A model format is provided in Figure 45.

Capital expenditure plans
A copy of Figure 36 with accompanying notes is required.

Stock purchasing policy
An account of your plans based on Figure 44 with explanatory notes should suffice.

Funds required – financial base
You will need to list here the sources of cash in the business and how these will be used to fund capital items and working capital. This is explored in Chapter 18.

Bookkeeping – management information systems
All that is required is a note outlining the key areas you propose to monitor, and the methods you will use, as discussed in Chapter 20.

Special factors and risk assessment
List here any special requirements (for example, licences, approval of premises, planning applications, qualified people) and the steps you plan to take to meet them. Outline the key risks and how you would expect to deal with them.

Action plan – key decisions – target dates
Set out here the timetable for action. Consider every action you need to take. Make a special note of actions which must occur in a particular sequence: for example, you need to refurbish a building before you can furnish it and occupy it.

Make an estimate of how long each step in the process will take. Figure 56 is an illustration of one way to plan ahead. The example, highly simplified, assumes that you have found a suitable shop and know that it is in a sound condition. You plan to open the shop.

Figure 56 Critical Path Analysis (Simplified form)

Note Activities which lie on a vertical line can all start at the same time. The next decision cannot be taken until the action which takes the longest has been completed.

For example, after the 'START', arranging finance takes only four weeks, but obtaining planning permission takes ten, so that the premises cannot be purchased until the ten weeks have expired

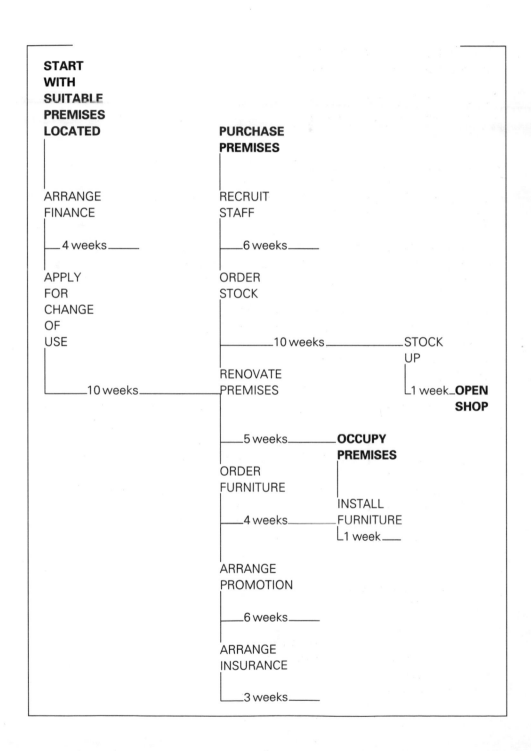

**START
WITH
SUITABLE
PREMISES
LOCATED**

**PURCHASE
PREMISES**

ARRANGE
FINANCE

RECRUIT
STAFF

└─ 4 weeks ─────

└─ 6 weeks ────

APPLY
FOR
CHANGE
OF
USE

ORDER
STOCK

STOCK
UP

└──────── 10 weeks ────────

└───────── 10 weeks ──────────

└1 week **OPEN
SHOP**

RENOVATE
PREMISES

└─ 5 weeks ──── **OCCUPY
PREMISES**

ORDER
FURNITURE

INSTALL
FURNITURE

└─ 4 weeks ────

└1 week ──

ARRANGE
PROMOTION

└─ 6 weeks ─────

ARRANGE
INSURANCE

└─ 3 weeks ─────

You will notice, in heavy type, some of the key decision points in the chart: the point at which you actually purchase the premises, occupy the shop and open the shop respectively. In each case there are actions which precede these key decision points.

You cannot purchase the premises until you have cleared the finance required and obtained permission to use the shop for your purpose. As you can see, we have estimated that obtaining permission takes longer.

Once the purchase has been secured many other actions can be initiated: recruitment of staff, renovation, ordering stock, ordering furniture and arranging advertising. Furniture cannot be installed until the building is ready. Stock cannot be installed on the shelves and displayed until it arrives.

Look on each of these various activities as 'paths' towards your goal. You cannot get there any quicker than the longest path! We call this the 'critical path' because it not only determines how long the exercise takes, but any delay in *this* path slows up the process, whereas minor delays in other paths may not make any difference.

Draw up a simple 'critical path analysis' chart for your own plans so that you may be able to make decisions and take actions in the most effective manner, and concentrate your energies on the critical areas.

You can then take the data from the chart and draw up a timetable for action with target dates.

Chapter 21

CHECK FOR VIABILITY

> **OBJECTIVE: to assess the plan that you have written and check that it is viable.**

- **Are you and your people up to it?**

- **Are you sure you have a market for your goods and services?**

- **Are you confident that you can manage the money side?**

- **Have you taken full account of all other factors?**

The viability of your business plan depends crucially on:

- The men and women who will put it into effect
- The market for your goods and services
- The management of money

Some of these questions were mentioned in Chapter 3, but this is a more complete list for you to tackle now that you have completed your plans.

Men and women involved

- Do you and your management team have the motivation to see you through the hard times, the long hours and the frustrations of running this business?
- Do you and your management team have the technical skills to make the products and to provide the services you envisage?
- Do you and your management team have all the skills needed to look after the administrative side of the business, including all the money matters?
- Has your organization the ability to sell your goods or services to the potential customers you have identified?

- Are you prepared to modify your business plans in the light of what people will want to buy?
- Are you confident that you and your key managers will be able to manage skills and time to full effect?
- Have you made arrangements to plug any gaps in the expertise of your team? How do you plan to ensure that they are kept up to date?
- Will you be able to get all the skilled workers you need in the location(s) you have chosen for your business?
- Are working conditions, wages and other rewards adequate to attract and retain the staff you will need?
- Is there adequate transport available to enable your workforce to attend work regularly and punctually?
- Are there any special requirements related to qualified people (for example, divers, HGV drivers, transport managers, registered traders) in your business, and are you sure you can attract and retain such people?
- Have you decided what arrangements to make, if any, concerning pensions for your staff?

The market

- What is so special about the products that you intend to sell or the services that you intend to provide?
- How do you know that anyone will want to buy them?
- How much will you charge for your products or services? Will people be prepared to pay those prices?
- Are you sure that you can provide those goods or services at these prices, make a profit and manage cash flow?
- Why should anyone buy your goods or services rather than others on the market?
- Is this the right time to start providing the goods or services that you have in mind? Is this the moment when people will want them?
- Will you be able to develop your products or develop new products as your market develops?
- Have you considered how you will advertise or promote your products and how much this will cost?
- Do you know who your competitors are and what products they are selling?
- Have you spoken to any potential customers about the products or services that you intend to provide?
- Have you planned to make adequate provision for the follow-up of all enquiries from potential customers?

- Have you planned to institute a method of keeping abreast of the needs of your customers and the situation in the market-place?
- If you intend to use intermediaries (for example, wholesalers, distributors or agents), are you confident that they will promote your products and services?

Money management

- Will your business make a profit?
- Will you be able to pay each bill as it arrives?
- What financial resources will you need to enable you to be successful, especially over the initial trading period?
- Are you fully prepared to put up your share of this financial commitment?
- Do you need – can you obtain – a loan at a reasonable rate of interest?
- Are you confident that you can pay back any loans over a reasonable period, and pay the interest?
- Have you researched, listed and costed the expenditures that you will incur, and when these expenditures will be incurred?
- In particular, have you adequately researched your capital requirements and needs for 'working capital'?
- Have you a clear idea of when income will start to flow?
- Have you considered your insurance needs and any licences and permits that will be required?
- What sources of information, help and advice do you need? Do you know where these can be obtained?
- Have you discovered any problems that you have never had to deal with before?
- Have you made adequate provision for depreciation and for the rapid obsolescence of some kinds of equipment?
- Have you taken into account the sudden and dramatic rise in rent that might occur at the time of rent review?
- Have you built a sound relationship with your accountant and bank manager?

Other factors

- Are your chosen locations and buildings suitable for your purpose?
- Do your premises have all the services you require, including any special drainage, air extraction or high voltages?
- Are your facilities for manufacture, storage, sales and offices adequate?

- Will your suppliers, customers and delivery vehicles be able to get into and out of your premises, and manoeuvre adequately?
- Are you confident that you have made adequate arrangements for the maintenance of any crucial plant and equipment?
- Are you sure that you can obtain adequate supplies of raw materials from reliable sources?
- Can you get planning permission as required?

Chapter 22

I M P L E M E N T

> **OBJECTIVE: to take action to implement the business plan.**

- **Form an 'implementation group'**

- **Allocate responsibilities, set targets with performance indicators**

- **Monitor and discuss progress in your group**

- **Prepare to cope with change constructively**

As we have noted, the effective implementation of your plan requires action by a number of people, and the support of a number of people. In Chapter 2 we spoke of enlisting support for the production of the plan. It becomes even more important to consider the people who are involved now in its implementation.

IMPLEMENTATION GROUP

You will need to bring together the managers concerned: any who have not been involved in the build-up to the plan must now be taken through the main points and the implications for their particular departments.

For each area of the business clear goals need to be set, based on the plan, with a requirement to report back to the group on progress from time to time. The plan provides the basis for reporting back against unequivocal performance indices: for example, for sales, income and expenditure, advertising and promotion activities, manufacturing targets, quality factors, and so forth.

Many firms find it useful to prepare a monthly summary of the key performance indicators, say, within a week or so of the end of the month, and this data provides a sensible basis for reviewing progress and planning for the short term.

If each department has its own budget, with carefully selected subheads of expenditure, the monthly results can be shown against the anticipated figures, with a running total alongside.

Most companies find that such review meetings should be held at least once a month; probably once a week at the outset. There should be a clear agenda and a business-like discussion of the key performance indices.

COPING WITH CHANGE

Inevitably there will be deviations from the plan: sales are lower than expected, or higher; raw materials become expensive; a new competitor appears on the horizon.

Clearly one cannot just grind on as if nothing has happened. You will need to revise the plan, in particular, your sales projections, cashflow predictions and profit forecasts. In the light of these figures and your knowledge of the business, you must decide on what action to take.

If you have a computer with a spreadsheet, it takes only moments to estimate the effect of different scenarios when the basic business data is recorded on file; but the sums may take longer by hand.

There is always a temptation, when faced with adverse trading conditions, to attack expenditure, to reduce costs and to draw back. Before reacting in this way it is worth examining the figures and the situation carefully. Are there possibilities of sales in some areas or lines, even if not in others? Can you change track quickly to take advantage of changes in the market-place? Cutting costs is not always the best way.

Your detailed knowledge of the business, the environment and the market-place (if you have done your homework properly) should help you to make constructive decisions at such a time.

Chapter 23

UPDATING THE PLAN

> **OBJECTIVE: to decide on the optimum intervals at which to update the plan and how this should be done.**

- **Short-term problems may require revisions**

- **A year-end review of results will help you to plan for the future**

- **The discipline of zero-based budgeting has its place**

- **Scanning the environment and the market must not be neglected**

This book has been concerned with helping you to prepare a three-year business plan for your firm, with a specified starting date. The plan is comparatively detailed for the first year and less so for the second and third years.

Short-term problems
You may find that some factor deflects you from carrying out the plan as you had envisaged during the first year. In the light of the new situation, revise your existing data and use this to review the plan and make any necessary changes.

Rolling forward
Failing this, assuming that the deviations are not too large, you should be in a position towards the end of the first year to take stock of the company position, note where you had under- or over-estimated and to understand why this happened.

Your next step is to 'roll the plan forward'. By this we mean taking the second year of your original plan and making it the first year of a new business plan. In the light of your experience you should be able to plan more accurately than before.

Once again, prepare a month-by-month plan for the first year of the new plan, and quarterly for a further two years.

Zero based budget

You will need to make due allowances for inflation, but do not make the mistake of simply adding another ten per cent to everything and calling this a revised plan.

Take each item, one by one, and consider what adjustments to make. In some cases it will be quite satisfactory to take last year's figure and to add some. But if you do this for all items, the business will, over the years, start to build 'fat' into the system.

Going back to basics and working out what each item should cost, or what price should be charged from first principles (what we call 'zero-based budgeting') is a healthy exercise that should not be shirked.

Scanning

The environmental scan (Chapter 6) and the market scan (Chapter 5) should also be repeated at decent intervals, say, once a year. Although one can get useful information from salespeople and senior managers if they keep their ears to the ground, this data is not 100 per cent reliable. If you are in receipt of public funds make an effort to keep in touch with the appropriate officials in the funding body. React to their concerns in a constructive manner.

Such scanning will inform your decisions for the updated plan.

Above all, *keep close to your customers*.

Part Seven

THE BUSINESS PLAN

This part contains an outline of a 'blank' business plan which can be copied and completed to form a presentation of your business plan. However, each business has its own characteristics and you may have to modify this plan to suit your own particular business.

You may wish to add a quarterly summary of balance sheet movements as described in Chapter 16, or a quarterly schedule of assets by category as described in Chapter 13. If you consider the document is becoming too cumbersome it may be helpful to present some tables in appendices, for example, the sales and revenue forecasts, profit and loss forecasts, cash flow forecasts and balance sheets.

Business Plan

_____
(name of business)

_____

_____
(address of business)

Nature of the Business

(A description of the nature of the products and services to be provided and an outline of the customers and mode of promotion and delivery)

Key People

(The names of the key people who will work in the business and an outline of the knowledge, skills and experience they will contribute to the success of the enterprise. Also, an indication of staff recruitment – how many and with what skills)

(Areas of skill and knowledge which are needed in addition to those mentioned above and how these will be dealt with)

Sales Plan

CUSTOMERS

(A precise description of the key decision-makers involved in purchasing the products and services)

PATTERN OF DEMAND

(An outline of anticipated sales over the first year, including any anticipated seasonal variation in sales)

Sales Plan – Continued

PRICING POLICY
(An outline of the prices to be charged and how these were determined)

REACHING CUSTOMERS
(An outline of how potential customers will be informed about the products and services, attracted to make enquiries, and encouraged to make purchases)

Sales and Revenue Forecast

Month   1   2   3   4   5   6   7   8   9   10   11   12   TOTAL

SALES

Number of Units A
(prioc of A)
Income from A

Number of Units B
(price of B)
Income from B

Number of Units C
(price of C)
Income from C

Gross Income
_____

RECEIPTS

Cash Sales

Credit Sales
_____

TOTAL SALES

RECEIPTS
_____

Profit and Loss Forecast

	Year 1	Year 2	Year 3
SALES FORECAST: units sold @ price per unit of P1 . . .			
GROSS TURNOVER (quantity x price)			
Less: Variable costs			
Gives GROSS PROFIT			
Plus other business income			
TOTAL INCOME			
Less: OVERHEADS from BELOW			
PROFIT/(LOSS) (before tax)			

OVERHEADS

	Year 1	Year 2	Year 3
Employees' wages			
Employers' National Insurance			
Training of staff			
Rent (rented premises)			
Rates and water rates			
Fuel (gas, electricity, etc.)			
Telecommunications			
Computer running costs			
Postage			
Printing and stationery			
Subscriptions and periodicals			
Advertising and promotions			
Repairs and maintenance			
Insurances			
Professional fees			
Interest payments			
Bank charges			
Vehicle and travel costs (other than depreciation)			
Depreciation – vehicle			
Depreciation – other assets			
Other expenses (specify)			
TOTAL OVERHEADS			

Note: tax on profit will be deducted according to the Inland Revenue rules.

Cash Flow Forecast (First Year)

MONTH	0	1	2	3	4	5	6	7	8	9	10	11	12	TOTAL

RECEIPTS

OPENING BALANCE (B)

Owners' investment
Loans from . . .
Cash sales
Credit sales
Asset disposals
Interest received

TOTAL RECEIPTS (R)

PAYMENTS

Premium on lease
Purchase of property
Purchase of plant,
   furniture and fittings

Purchase of vehicles
Raw materials
Goods for sale
Employees' net wages
Income tax and NI
Training expenses

Rent (rented premises)
Rates and water rates
Fuel (gas, electricity, etc.)
Telecommunications
Computer running costs
Postage

Printing and stationery
Subscriptions and periodicals
Advertising and promotions
Repairs and maintenance
Vehicle and travel costs
   (exclude vehicle purchases)

Insurances
Professional fees
Loan repayments
Bank charges
Bank interest
Value Added Tax
Other expenses (specify)

TOTAL PAYMENTS (P)

RECEIPTS LESS PAYMENTS
FOR THE MONTH (M)

**CASH REMAINING IN
THE BUSINESS (C)**

Cash Flow Forecast (Years 2 and 3)

YEAR/QUARTER	2/1	2/2	2/3	2/4	3/1	3/2	3/3	3/4
RECEIPTS								
OPENING BALANCE (B)								
Owners' investment								
Loans from . . .								
Cash sales								
Credit sales								
Asset disposals								
Interest received								
TOTAL RECEIPTS (R)								
PAYMENTS								
Premium on lease								
Purchase of property								
Purchase of plant, furniture and fittings								
Purchase of vehicles								
Raw materials								
Goods for sale								
Employees' net wages								
Income tax and NI								
Training expenses								
Rent (rented premises)								
Rates and water rates								
Fuel (gas, electricity, etc.)								
Telecommunications								
Computer running costs								
Postage								
Printing and stationery								
Subscriptions and periodicals								
Advertising and promotions								
Repairs and maintenance								
Vehicle and travel costs (exclude vehicle purchases)								
Insurances								
Professional fees								
Loan repayments								
Bank charges								
Bank interest								
Value Added Tax								
Other expenses (specify)								
TOTAL PAYMENTS (P)								
RECEIPTS LESS PAYMENTS FOR THE MONTH (M)								
CASH REMAINING IN THE BUSINESS (C)								

Capital Expenditure

(A list of all the capital items (including buildings and vehicles) costing more than £250 required in the first three years, including an indication in each case as to whether the article will be purchased outright or subject to a loan, rented or leased)

CAPITAL ITEM	INITIAL COST	ANTICIPATED PURCHASE DATE	METHOD OF PAYMENT	COMPLETION OF LOAN OR END OF LEASE

Stock Levels

RAW MATERIALS

ITEM	STOCK LEVELS (minimum)		STOCK LEVELS (average)		RE-ORDER		
	Quantity	Value (£)	Quantity	Value (£)	Frequency	Quantity	Value (£)

TOTAL AVERAGE VALUE OF RAW MATERIAL STOCKS HELD £_____

WORK IN PROGRESS

ITEM	STOCK LEVELS (minimum)		STOCK LEVELS (average)	
	Quantity	Value (£)	Quantity	Value (£)

TOTAL AVERAGE VALUE OF WORK IN PROGRESS HELD £_____

FINISHED GOODS

ITEM	STOCK LEVELS (minimum)		STOCK LEVELS (average)		RE-ORDER (if this is appropriate)		
	Quantity	Value (£)	Quantity	Value (£)	Frequency	Quantity	Value (£)

TOTAL AVERAGE VALUE OF FINISHED GOODS STOCKS HELD £_____

Financial Base

(How the company will be funded, including any loans or overdrafts that may be required)

Management Information Systems

(An outline of how financial and other quantitative records will be maintained)

Opening Balance Sheet
(Commencement of year)

LIABILITIES		ASSETS	
Capital (owners' money)		**Fixed assets**	
Owners' investment		Buildings	
Retained profit		Plant	
		Furniture	
		Vehicles	
		Computers	
	————		————
Deferred liability		**Current assets**	
Term loan	————	Raw materials	
		Finished goods	
		Debtors	
		Cash	
			————
Current liabilities			
Creditors			
Tax liability			
Bank overdraft			
	═══		═══

Closing Balance Sheet
(end of the year)

LIABILITIES   **ASSETS**

Capital (owners' money)   **Fixed assets**

Owners' investment   Buildings
Retained profit   Plant
                                                   Furniture
                                                   Vehicles
                                                   Computers
_____   _____

Deferred liability   **Current assets**

Term loan   _____   Raw materials
                                                   Finished goods
                                                   Debtors
                                                   Cash
                                                                    _____

Current liabilities

Creditors
Tax liability
Bank overdraft

_____   _____

_____   _____

Special Factors and Risk Assessment

Action Plan

(The dates intended for fresh initiatives to be taken based on the plan; the key decisions/actions that need to be taken; and any instance where more information is required and how this will be obtained)

DECISION/ ACTION	TARGET DATE	INFORMATION NEEDED?

INDEX

THE PAGAN LORD

PLACE NAMES

The spelling of place names in Anglo-Saxon England was an uncertain business, with no consistency and no agreement even about the name itself. Thus London was variously rendered as Lundonia, Lundenberg, Lundenne, Lundene, Lundenwic, Lundenceaster and Lundres. Doubtless some readers will prefer other versions of the names listed below, but I have usually employed whichever spelling is cited in either the *Oxford Dictionary of English Place-Names* or the *Cambridge Dictionary of English Place-Names* for the years nearest or contained within Alfred's reign, AD 871–899, but even that solution is not foolproof. Hayling Island, in 956, was written as both Heilincigae and Hæglingaiggæ. Nor have I been consistent myself; I should spell England as Englaland, and have preferred the modern form Northumbria to Norðhymbralond to avoid the suggestion that the boundaries of the ancient kingdom coincide with those of the modern county. So this list, like the spellings themselves, is capricious.

Æsc's Hill	Ashdown, Berkshire
Afen	River Avon, Wiltshire
Beamfleot	Benfleet, Essex
Bearddan Igge	Bardney, Lincolnshire
Bebbanburg	Bamburgh Castle, Northumberland
Bedehal	Beadnell, Northumberland
Beorgford	Burford, Oxfordshire
Botulfstan	Boston, Lincolnshire
Buchestanes	Buxton, Derbyshire
Ceaster	Chester, Cheshire
Ceodre	Cheddar, Somerset
Cesterfelda	Chesterfield, Derbyshire
Cirrenceastre	Cirencester, Gloucestershire

Coddeswold Hills	The Cotswolds, Gloucestershire
Cornwalum	Cornwall
Cumbraland	Cumbria
Dunholm	Durham, County Durham
Dyflin	Dublin, Eire
Eoferwic	York, Yorkshire
Ethandun	Edington, Wiltshire
Exanceaster	Exeter, Devon
Fagranforda	Fairford, Gloucestershire
Farnea Islands	Farne Islands, Northumberland
Flaneburg	Flamborough, Yorkshire
Foirthe	River Forth, Scotland
The Gewæsc	The Wash
Gleawecestre	Gloucester, Gloucestershire
Grimesbi	Grimsby, Lincolnshire
Haithabu	Hedeby, Denmark
Humbre	River Humber
Liccelfeld	Lichfield, Staffordshire
Lindcolne	Lincoln, Lincolnshire
Lindisfarena	Lindisfarne (Holy Island), Northumberland
Lundene	London
Mærse	River Mersey
Pencric	Penkridge, Staffordshire
Sæfern	River Severn
Sceapig	Isle of Sheppey, Kent
Snotengaham	Nottingham, Nottinghamshire
Tameworþig	Tamworth, Staffordshire
Temes	River Thames
Teotanheale	Tettenhall, West Midlands
Tofeceaster	Towcester, Northamptonshire
Uisc	River Exe
Wiltunscir	Wiltshire
Wodnesfeld	Wednesbury, West Midlands
Wintanceaster	Winchester, Hampshire
Wodnesfeld	Wednesbury, West Midlands

THE PAGAN LORD

BERNARD CORNWELL

HarperCollins*Publishers*

HarperCollins*Publishers*
77–85 Fulham Palace Road,
Hammersmith, London W6 8JB

www.harpercollins.co.uk

Published by HarperCollins*Publishers* 2013
1

Copyright © Bernard Cornwell 2013

Map © John Gilkes 2013

Photograph of silver penny of Alfred the Great © The Trustees
of the British Museum

Family tree © Colin Hall 2009

Bernard Cornwell asserts the moral right to
be identified as the author of this work

A catalogue record for this book
is available from the British Library

ISBN: 978 0 00 733190 1

This novel is entirely a work of fiction.
The names, characters and incidents portrayed in it while
at times based on historical figures, are the work of the author's imagination.

Set in Meridien by Palimpsest Book Production Limited,
Falkirk, Stirlingshire

Printed and bound in Great Britain by
Clays Ltd, St Ives plc

All rights reserved. No part of this publication may be
reproduced, stored in a retrieval system, or transmitted,
in any form or by any means, electronic, mechanical,
photocopying, recording or otherwise, without the prior
permission of the publishers.

MIX
Paper from
responsible sources
FSC **FSC˚ C007454**
www.fsc.org

FSC™ is a non-profit international organisation established to promote
the responsible management of the world's forests. Products carrying the
FSC label are independently certified to assure consumers that they come
from forests that are managed to meet the social, economic and
ecological needs of present and future generations,
and other controlled sources.

Find out more about HarperCollins and the environment at
www.harpercollins.co.uk/green

For Tom and Dana

Go raibh mile maith agat

Contents

N

Bebbanburg

*North
Sea*

NORTHUMBRIA

Eoferwic

Humbre

*Irish
Sea*

Grimsbi

Ceaster

Buchestanes

Lincolne

Snotengaham

Liccelfeld

Tameworþig

Teatanheale

EAST
ANGLIA

Eleg

Use

MERCIA

Tofeceaster

Dee

Sæfern

Gleawecestre

Fagranforda

Cirrenceastre

Temes

Lundene

WESSEX

Wintanceaster

Exeanceaster

0   20   40   60   80 miles

The Royal Family of Wessex

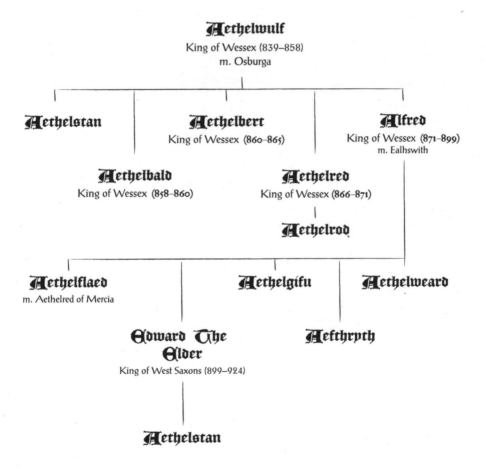

Aethelwulf
King of Wessex (839–858)
m. Osburga

Aethelstan

Aethelbert
King of Wessex (860–865)

Alfred
King of Wessex (871–899)
m. Ealhswith

Aethelbald
King of Wessex (858–860)

Aethelred
King of Wessex (866–871)

Aethelrod

Aethelflaed
m. Aethelred of Mercia

Aethelgifu

Aethelweard

**Edward The
Elder**
King of West Saxons (899–924)

Aefthryth

Aethelstan

PART ONE

The Abbot

One

A dark sky.

The gods make the sky; it reflects their moods and they were dark that day. It was high summer and a bitter rain was spitting from the east. It felt like winter.

I was mounted on Lightning, my best horse. He was a stallion, black as night, but with a slash of grey pelt running down his hindquarters. He was named for a great hound I had once sacrificed to Thor. I hated killing that dog, but the gods are hard on us; they demand sacrifice and then ignore us. This Lightning was a huge beast, powerful and sullen, a warhorse, and I was in my war-glory on that dark day. I was dressed in mail and clad in steel and leather. Serpent-Breath, best of swords, hung at my left side, though for the enemy I faced that day I needed no sword, no shield, no axe. But I wore her anyway because Serpent-Breath was my companion. I still own her. When I die, and that must be soon, someone will close my fingers around the leather-bindings of her worn hilt and she will carry me to Valhalla, to the corpse-hall of the high gods, and we shall feast there.

But not that day.

That dark summer day I sat in the saddle in the middle of a muddy street, facing the enemy. I could hear them, but could not see them. They knew I was there.

The street was just wide enough for two wagons to pass each other. The houses either side were mud and wattle, thatched with reeds that had blackened with rain and grown thick with lichen.

The mud in the street was fetlock deep, rutted by carts and fouled by dogs and by the swine that roamed free. The spiteful wind rippled the puddles in the ruts and whipped smoke from a roof-hole, bringing the scent of burning wood.

I had two companions. I had ridden from Lundene with twenty-two men, but my mission in this shit-smelling, rain-spitted village was private and so I had left most of my men a mile away. Yet Osbert, my youngest son, was behind me, mounted on a grey stallion. He was nineteen years old, he wore a suit of mail and had a sword at his side. He was a man now, though I thought of him as a boy. I frightened him, just as my father had frightened me. Some mothers soften their sons, but Osbert was motherless and I had raised him hard because a man must be hard. The world is filled with enemies. The Christians tell us to love our enemies and to turn the other cheek. The Christians are fools.

Next to Osbert was Æthelstan, bastard eldest son of King Edward of Wessex. He was just eight years old, yet like Osbert he wore mail. Æthelstan was not frightened of me. I tried to frighten him, but he just looked at me with his cold blue eyes, then grinned. I loved that boy, just as I loved Osbert.

Both were Christians. I fight a losing battle. In a world of death, betrayal and misery, the Christians win. The old gods are still worshipped, of course, but they're being driven back into the high valleys, into the lost places, to the cold northern edges of the world, and the Christians spread like a plague. Their nailed god is powerful. I accept that. I have always known their god has great power and I don't understand why my gods let the bastard win, but they do. He cheats. That's the only explanation I can find. The nailed god lies and cheats, and liars and cheaters always win.

So I waited in the wet street, and Lightning scraped a heavy hoof in a puddle. Above my leather and mail I wore a cloak of dark blue wool, edged with stoat fur. The hammer of Thor hung at my throat, while on my head was my wolf-crested helmet. The cheek-pieces were open. Rain dripped from the helmet rim. I wore long leather boots, their tops stuffed with rags to keep the rain from trickling down inside. I wore gauntlets, and on my arms were

4

the rings of gold and rings of silver, the rings a warlord earns by killing his enemies. I was in my glory, though the enemy I faced did not deserve that respect.

'Father,' Osbert began, 'what if . . .'

'Did I speak to you?'

'No.'

'Then be quiet,' I snarled.

I had not meant to sound so angry, but I was angry. It was an anger that had no place to go, just anger at the world, at the miserable dull grey world, an impotent anger. The enemy was behind closed doors and they were singing. I could hear their voices, though I could not distinguish their words. They had seen me, I was certain, and they had seen that the street was otherwise empty. The folk who lived in this town wanted no part of what was about to happen.

Though what was about to happen I did not know myself, even though I would cause it. Or perhaps the doors would stay shut and the enemy would cower inside their stout timber building? Doubtless that was the question Osbert had wanted to ask. What if the enemy stayed indoors? He probably would not have called them the enemy. He would have asked what if 'they' stay indoors.

'If they stay indoors,' I said, 'I'll beat their damned door down, go in and pull the bastard out. And if I do that then the two of you will stay here to hold Lightning.'

'Yes, Father.'

'I'll come with you,' Æthelstan said.

'You'll do as you're damned well told.'

'Yes, Lord Uhtred,' he said respectfully, but I knew he was grinning. I did not need to turn around to see that insolent grin, but I would not have turned because at that moment the singing stopped. I waited. A moment passed and then the doors opened.

And out they came. Half a dozen older men first, then the young ones, and I saw those younger ones look at me, but even the sight of Uhtred, warlord draped in anger and glory, could not stifle their joy. They looked so happy. They were smiling, slapping each other's backs, embracing and laughing.

5

The six older men were not laughing. They walked towards me and I did not move. 'I am told you are Lord Uhtred,' one of them said. He wore a grubby white robe belted with rope, was white-haired and grey-bearded and had a narrow, sun-darkened face with deep lines carved round his mouth and eyes. His hair fell past his shoulders, while his beard reached to his waist. He had a sly face, I thought, but not without authority, and he had to be a churchman of some importance because he carried a heavy staff topped with an ornate silver cross.

I said nothing to him. I was watching the younger men. They were boys mostly, or boys just turned to men. Their scalps, where their hair had been shaved back from their foreheads, gleamed pale in the grey daylight. Some older folk were coming from the doors now. I assumed they were the parents of these boy-men.

'Lord Uhtred.' The man spoke again.

'I'll speak to you when I'm ready to speak,' I growled.

'This is not seemly,' he said, holding the cross towards me as if it might frighten me.

'Clean your rancid mouth out with goat piss,' I said. I had seen the young man I had come to find and I kicked Lightning forward. Two of the older men tried to stop me, but Lightning snapped with his big teeth and they staggered back, desperate to escape. Spear-Danes had fled from Lightning, and the six older men scattered like chaff.

I drove the stallion into the press of younger men, leaned down from the saddle and grasped the man-child's black gown. I hauled him upwards, thrust him belly-down over the pommel and turned Lightning with my knees.

And that was when the trouble started.

Two or three of the younger men tried to stop me. One reached for Lightning's bridle and that was a mistake, a bad mistake. The teeth snapped, the boy-man screamed, and I let Lightning rear up and flail with his front hooves. I heard the crash of one heavy hoof into bone, saw blood bright and sudden. Lightning, trained to keep moving lest an enemy try to hamstring a back leg, lurched forward. I spurred him, glimpsing a fallen man with a bloody skull.

Another fool grasped my right boot, trying to haul me from the saddle, and I slammed my hand down and felt the grip vanish. Then the man with long white hair challenged me. He had followed me into the crowd and he shouted that I was to let my captive go, and then, like a fool, he swung the heavy silver cross on its long shaft at Lightning's head. But Lightning had been trained to battle and he twisted lithely, and I leaned down and seized the staff and ripped it from the man's grasp. Still he did not give up. He was spitting curses at me as he seized Lightning's bridle and tried to drag the horse back into the crowd of youths, presumably so I would be overwhelmed by numbers.

I raised the staff and slammed it down hard. I used the butt end of the staff as if it were a spear, and did not see it was tipped with a metal spike, presumably so the cross could be rammed into the earth. I had just meant to stun the ranting fool, but instead the staff buried itself in his head. It pierced his skull. It brightened that dull gloomy day with blood. It caused screams to sound to the Christian heaven, and I let the staff go and the white-robed man, now dressed in a robe dappled with red, stood swaying, mouth opening and closing, eyes glazing, with a Christian cross jutting skywards from his head. His long white hair turned red, and then he fell. He just fell, dead as a bone. 'The abbot!' someone shouted, and I spurred Lightning and he leaped forward, scattering the last of the boy-men and leaving their mothers screaming. The man draped over my saddle struggled and I hit him hard on the back of his skull as we burst from the press of people back into the open street.

The man on my saddle was my son. My eldest son. He was Uhtred, son of Uhtred, and I had ridden from Lundene too late to stop him becoming a priest. A wandering preacher, one of those long-haired, wild-bearded, mad-eyed priests who gull the stupid into giving them silver in return for a blessing, had told me of my son's decision. 'All Christendom rejoices,' he had said, watching me slyly.

'Rejoices in what?' I had asked.

'That your son is to be a priest! Two days from now, I hear, in Tofeceaster.'

And that was what the Christians had been doing in their church, consecrating their wizards by making boys into black-clothed priests who would spread their filth further, and my son, my eldest son, was now a damned Christian priest and I hit him again. 'You bastard,' I growled, 'you lily-livered bastard. You traitorous little cretin.'

'Father . . .' he began.

'I'm not your father,' I snarled. I had taken Uhtred down the street to where a particularly malodorous dung-heap lay wetly against a hovel wall. I tossed him into it. 'You are not my son, I said, 'and your name is not Uhtred.'

'Father . . .'

'You want Serpent-Breath down your throat?' I shouted. 'If you want to be my son you take off that damned black frock, put on mail and do what I tell you.'

'I serve God.'

'Then choose your own damned name. You are not Uhtred Uhtredson.' I twisted in the saddle. 'Osbert!'

My younger son kicked his stallion towards me. He looked nervous. 'Father?'

'From this day on your name is Uhtred.'

He glanced at his brother, then back to me. He nodded reluctantly.

'What is your name?' I demanded.

He still hesitated, but saw my anger and nodded again. 'My name is Uhtred, Father.'

'You are Uhtred Uhtredson,' I said, 'my only son.'

It had happened to me once, long ago. I had been named Osbert by my father, who was called Uhtred, but when my elder brother, also Uhtred, was slaughtered by the Danes my father had renamed me. It is always thus in our family. The eldest son carries on the name. My stepmother, a foolish woman, even had me baptised a second time because, she said, the angels who guard the gates of heaven would not know me by my new name, and so I was dipped in the water barrel, but Christianity washed off me, thank Christ, and I discovered the old gods and have worshipped them ever since.

The five older priests caught up with me. I knew two of them, the twins Ceolnoth and Ceolberht who, some thirty years before, had been hostages with me in Mercia. We had been boys captured by the Danes, a fate I had welcomed and the twins had hated. They were old now, two identical priests with stocky builds, greying beards and anger livid on their round faces. 'You've killed the Abbot Wihtred!' one of the twins challenged me. He was furious, shocked, almost incoherent with rage. I had no idea which twin he was because I could never tell them apart.

'And Father Burgred's face is ruined!' the other twin said. He moved as if to take Lightning's bridle and I turned the horse fast, letting him threaten the twins with the big yellow teeth that had bitten off the newly ordained priest's face. The twins stepped back.

'The Abbot Wihtred!' the first twin repeated the name. 'A saint-lier man never lived!'

'He attacked me,' I said. In truth I had not meant to kill the old man, but there was small point in telling that to the twins.

'You'll suffer!' one of the twins yelped. 'You will be cursed for all time!'

The other held a hand towards the wretched boy in the dung-heap. 'Father Uhtred,' he said.

'His name is not Uhtred,' I snarled, 'and if he dares call himself Uhtred,' I looked at him as I spoke, 'then I will find him and I will cut his belly to the bone and I will feed his lily-livered guts to my swine. He is not my son. He's not worthy to be my son.'

The man who was not worthy to be my son clambered wetly from the dung-heap, dripping filth. He looked up at me. 'Then what am I called?' he asked.

'Judas,' I said mockingly. I was raised as a Christian and had been forced to hear all their stories, and I recalled that a man named Judas had betrayed the nailed god. That never made any sense to me. The god had to be nailed to a cross if he was to become their saviour, and then the Christians blame the man who made that death possible. I thought they should worship him as a saint, but instead they revile him as a betrayer. 'Judas,' I said again, pleased I had remembered the name.

The boy who had been my son hesitated, then nodded. 'From now on,' he said to the twins, 'I am to be called Father Judas.'

'You cannot call yourself . . .' either Ceolnoth or Ceolberht began.

'I am Father Judas,' he said harshly.

'You will be Father Uhtred!' one of the twins shouted at him, then pointed at me. 'He has no authority here! He is a pagan, an outcast, loathed of God!' He was shaking with anger, hardly able to speak, but he took a deep breath, closed his eyes and raised both hands towards that dark sky. 'O God,' he shouted, 'bring down your wrath on this sinner! Punish him! Blight his crops and strike him with sickness! Show your power, O Lord!' His voice rose to a shriek. 'In the name of the Father, and of the Son and of the Holy Spirit, I curse this man and all his kin.'

He took a breath and I pressed my knee on Lightning's flank and the great horse moved a pace closer to the ranting fool. I was as angry as the twins.

'Curse him, O Lord,' he shouted, 'and in thy great mercy bring him low! Curse him and his kin, may they never know grace! Smite him, O Lord, with filth and pain and misery!'

'Father!' the man who had been my son shouted.

Æthelstan chuckled. Uhtred, my only son, gasped.

Because I had kicked the ranting fool. I had pulled my right foot from the stirrup and lashed out with the heavy boot and his words stopped abruptly, replaced by blood on his lips. He staggered backwards, his right hand pawing at his shattered mouth. 'Spit out your teeth,' I ordered him, and when he disobeyed I half drew Serpent-Breath.

He spat out a mix of blood, spittle and broken teeth. 'Which one are you?' I asked the other twin.

He gaped at me, then recovered his wits. 'Ceolnoth,' he said.

'At least I can tell the two of you apart now,' I said.

I did not look at Father Judas. I just rode away.

I rode home.

*   *   *

Perhaps Ceolberht's curse had worked, because I came home to death, smoke and ruin.

Cnut Ranulfson had raided my hall. He had burned it. He had killed. He had taken Sigunn captive.

None of it made sense, not then. My estate was close to Cirrenceastre, which was deep inside Mercia. A band of horse Danes had ridden far, risking battle and capture, to attack my hall. I could understand that. A victory over Uhtred would give a man reputation, it would spur the poets to taunting songs of victory, but they had attacked while the hall was almost empty. They would surely have sent scouts? They would have suborned folk to be spies for them, to discover when I was there and when I was likely to be absent, and such spies would surely have told them that I had been summoned to Lundene to advise King Edward's men on that city's defences. Yet they had risked disaster to attack an almost empty hall? It made no sense.

And they had taken Sigunn.

She was my woman. Not my wife. Since Gisela died I had not taken another wife, though I had lovers in those days. Æthelflaed was my lover, but Æthelflaed was another man's wife and the daughter of the dead King Alfred, and we could not live together as man and wife. Sigunn lived with me instead, and Æthelflaed knew it. 'If it wasn't Sigunn,' she had told me one day, 'it would be another.'

'Maybe a dozen others.'

'Maybe.'

I had captured Sigunn at Beamfleot. She was a Dane, a slender, pale, pretty Dane who had been weeping for her slaughtered husband when she was dragged out of a sea-ditch running with blood. We had lived together almost ten years now and she was treated with honour and hung with gold. She was the lady of my hall and now she was gone. She had been taken by Cnut Ranulfson, Cnut Longsword.

'It was three mornings ago,' Osferth told me. He was the bastard son of King Alfred, who had tried to turn him into a priest, but Osferth, even though he had the face and mind of a cleric, preferred to be a warrior. He was careful, precise, intelligent, reliable and rarely impassioned. He resembled his father, and the older he got the more like his father he looked.

'So it was Sunday morning,' I said bleakly.

'Everyone was in the church, lord,' Osferth explained.

'Except Sigunn.'

'Who is no Christian, lord,' he said, sounding disapproving.

Finan, who was my companion and the man who commanded my troops if I was absent, had taken twenty men to reinforce Æthelflaed's bodyguard as she toured Mercia. She had been inspecting the burhs that guarded Mercia from the Danes, and doubtless worshipping in churches across the land. Her husband, Æthelred, was reluctant to leave the sanctuary of Gleawecestre and so Æthelflaed did his duty. She had her own warriors who guarded her, but I still feared for her safety, not from the Mercians, who loved her, but from her husband's followers, and so I had insisted she take Finan and twenty men and, in the Irishman's absence, Osferth had been in charge of the men guarding Fagranforda. He had left six men to watch over the hall, barns, stables and mill, and six men should have been more than enough because my estate lay a long way from the northern lands where the Danes ruled. 'I blame myself, lord,' Osferth said.

'Six was enough,' I said. And the six were all dead, as was Herric, my crippled steward, and three other servants. Some forty or fifty horses were gone, while the hall was burned. Some of the walls still stood, gaunt scorched trunks, but the hall's centre was just a heap of smoking ash. The Danes had arrived fast, broken down the hall door, slaughtered Herric and anyone else who tried to oppose them, then had taken Sigunn and left. 'They knew you'd all be in the church,' I said.

'Which is why they came on Sunday,' Sihtric, another of my men, finished the thought.

'And they would have known you wouldn't be worshipping,' Osferth said.

'How many were there?' I asked Osferth.

'Forty or fifty,' he replied patiently. I had asked him the question a dozen times already.

Danes do not make a raid like this for pleasure. There were plenty of Saxon halls and steadings within easy reach of their lands, but these men had risked riding deep into Mercia. For Sigunn? She was nothing to them.

'They came to kill you, lord,' Osferth suggested.

Yet the Danes would have scouted the land first, they would have talked to travellers, they would know that I always had at least twenty men with me. I had chosen not to take those twenty into Tofeceaster to punish the man who had been my son because a warrior does not need twenty men to deal with a pack of priests. My son and a boy had been company enough. But the Danes could not have known I was at Tofeceaster, even I had not known I was going there till I heard the news that my damned son was becoming a Christian wizard. Yet Cnut Ranulfson had risked his men in a long, pointless raid, despite the danger of meeting my men. He would have outnumbered me, but he would have taken casualties that he could ill afford, and Cnut Longsword was a calculating man, not given to idiotic risks. None of it made sense. 'You're sure it was Cnut Ranulfson?' I asked Osferth.

'They carried his banner, lord.'

'The axe and broken cross?'

'Yes, lord.'

'And where's Father Cuthbert?' I asked. I keep priests. I am no Christian, but such is the reach of the nailed god that most of my men are, and in those days Cuthbert was my priest. I liked him. He was the son of a stonemason, gangly and clumsy, married to a freed slave with the strange name of Mehrasa. She was a dark-skinned beauty captured in some weird land far to the south and brought to Britain by a slave-trader who had died on the blade of my sword, and Mehrasa was now wailing and screaming that her husband was gone. 'Why wasn't he in church?' I asked Osferth, to which his only answer was a shrug. 'He was humping Mehrasa?' I asked sourly.

'Isn't he always?' Osferth sounded disapproving again.

'So where is he?' I asked again.

'Perhaps they took him?' Sihtric suggested.

13

'They'd rather kill a priest than capture one,' I said. I walked towards the burned hall. Men were raking at the ashes, dragging charred and smoking timbers aside. Perhaps Cuthbert's body was there, shrivelled and black. 'Tell me what you saw,' I demanded of Osferth again.

He repeated it all patiently. He had been in Fagranforda's church when he heard shouting coming from my hall, which lay not too far away. He left the church to see the first smoke drifting in the summer sky, but by the time he had summoned his men and mounted his horse the raiders were gone. He had followed them and had caught a glimpse of them and was certain he had seen Sigunn among the dark-mailed horsemen. 'She was wearing the white dress, lord, the one you like.'

'But you didn't see Father Cuthbert?'

'He was wearing black, lord, but so were most of the raiders, so I might not have noticed him. We never got close. They were riding like the wind.'

Bones appeared among the ash. I walked through the old hall door, which was marked by burned posts, and smelt the stench of roasted flesh. I kicked a charred beam aside and saw a harp in the ashes. Why had that not burned? The strings had shrivelled to black stubs, but the harp frame looked undamaged. I bent to pick it up and the warm wood just crumbled in my hand. 'What happened to Oslic?' I asked. He had been the harpist, a poet who chanted war-songs in the hall.

'They killed him, lord,' Osferth said.

Mehrasa began wailing louder. She was staring at the bones that a man had raked from the ashes. 'Tell her to be quiet,' I snarled.

'They're dogs' bones, lord.' The man with the rake bowed to me.

The hall dogs, the ones Sigunn loved. They were small terriers, adept at killing rats. The man pulled a melted silver dish from the ash. 'They didn't come to kill me,' I said, staring at the small ribcages.

'Who else?' Sihtric asked. Sihtric had been my servant once and was now a house-warrior and a good one.

14

'They came for Sigunn,' I said, because I could think of no other explanation.

'But why, lord? She's not your wife.'

'He knows I'm fond of her,' I said, 'and that means he wants something.'

'Cnut Longsword,' Sihtric said ominously.

Sihtric was no coward. His father had been Kjartan the Cruel, and Sihtric had inherited his father's skill with weapons. Sihtric had stood in the shield wall with me and I knew his bravery, but he had sounded nervous when he spoke Cnut's name. No wonder. Cnut Ranulfson was a legend in the lands where the Danes ruled. He was a slight man, very pale skinned with hair that was bone-white though he was no old man. I guessed he was now close to forty, which was old enough, but Cnut's hair had been white from the day he was born. And he had been born clever and ruthless. His sword, Ice-Spite, was feared from the northern isles to the southern coast of Wessex, and his renown had attracted oath-men who came from across the sea to serve him. He and his friend, Sigurd Thorrson, were the greatest Danish lords of Northumbria, and their ambition was to be the greatest lords of Britain, but they had an enemy who had stopped them repeatedly.

And now Cnut Ranulfson, Cnut Longsword, the most feared swordsman in Britain, had taken that enemy's woman. 'He wants something,' I said again.

'You?' Osferth asked.

'We'll find out,' I said, and so we did.

We discovered what Cnut Ranulfson wanted that evening when Father Cuthbert came home. The priest was brought by a merchant who traded in pelts, and he had Father Cuthbert on his wagon. It was Mehrasa who alerted us. She screamed.

I was in the big barn that the Danes had not had time to burn, and which we could use for a hall until I built another, and I was watching my men make a hearth from stones when I heard the scream and ran out to see the wagon lurching up the lane. Mehrasa was tugging at her husband while Cuthbert was flailing with his long skinny arms. Mehrasa was still screaming. 'Quiet!' I shouted.

15

My men were following me. The pelt-trader had stopped his wagon and fallen to his knees as I approached. He explained that he had found Father Cuthbert to the north. 'He was at Beorgford, lord,' he said, 'by the river. They were throwing stones at him.'

'Who was throwing stones?'

'Boys, lord. Just boys playing.'

So Cnut had ridden to the ford where, presumably, he had released the priest. Cuthbert's long robe was mud stained and torn, while his scalp was crusted with blood clots. 'What did you do to the boys?' I asked the trader.

'Just chased them away, lord.'

'Where was he?'

'In the rushes, lord, by the river. He was crying.'

'Father Cuthbert,' I said, walking to the wagon.

'Lord! Lord!' he reached a hand for me.

'He couldn't cry,' I told the trader. 'Osferth! Give the man money.' I gestured at the priest's rescuer. 'We'll feed you,' I told the man, 'and stable your horses overnight.'

'Lord!' Father Cuthbert wailed.

I reached into the cart and lifted him. He was tall, but surprisingly light. 'You can stand?' I asked him.

'Yes, lord.'

I put him on the ground, steadied him, then stepped away as Mehrasa embraced him.

'Lord,' he said over her shoulder, 'I have a message.'

He sounded as if he was crying, and perhaps he was, but a man with no eyes cannot cry. A man with two bloody eye-holes cannot cry. A blinded man must cry, and cannot.

Cnut Ranulfson had gouged out his eyes.

Tameworþig. That was where I was to meet Cnut Ranulfson. 'He said you would know why, lord,' Father Cuthbert told me.

'That's all he said?'

'You'd know why,' he repeated, 'and you will make it good,

16

and you're to meet him before the moon wanes or he'll kill your woman. Slowly.'

I went to the barn door and looked up into the night, but the moon was hidden by clouds. Not that I needed to see how slender its crescent glowed. I had one week before it waned. 'What else did he say?'

'Just that you're to go to Tameworþig before the moon dies, lord.'

'And make good?' I asked, puzzled.

'He said you'd know what that means, lord.'

'I don't know!'

'And he said . . .' Father Cuthbert said slowly.

'Said what?'

'He said he blinded me so I couldn't see her.'

'See her? See who?'

'He said I wasn't worthy to look on her, lord.'

'Look on who?'

'So he blinded me!' he wailed and Mehrasa started screeching and I could get no sense from either.

But at least I knew Tameworþig, though fate had never taken me to that town, which lay at the edge of Cnut Ranulfson's lands. It had once been a great town, the capital of the mighty King Offa, the Mercian ruler who had built a wall against the Welsh and dominated both Northumbria and Wessex. Offa had claimed to be the king of all the Saxons, but he was long dead and his powerful kingdom of Mercia was now a sad remnant split between Danes and Saxons. Tameworþig, which had once housed the greatest king of all Britain, the fortress city that had sheltered his feared troops, was now a decayed ruin where Saxons slaved for Danish jarls. It was also the most southerly of all Cnut's halls, an outpost of Danish power in a disputed borderland.

'It's a trap,' Osferth warned me.

I somehow doubted it. Instinct is everything. What Cnut Ranulfson had done was dangerous, a great risk. He had sent men, or brought men, deep into Mercia where his small raiding band could easily have been cut off and slaughtered to the last man. Yet

17

something had driven him to that risk. He wanted something, and he believed I possessed it, and he had summoned me, not to one of the great halls deep in his own land, but to Tameworþig that lay very close to Saxon territory.

'We ride,' I said.

I took every man who could mount a horse. We numbered sixty-eight warriors, mailed and helmeted, carrying shields, axes, swords, spears and war-hammers. We rode behind my banner of the wolf, and we rode northwards through chill summer winds and sudden spiteful showers of rain. 'The harvest will be poor,' I told Osferth as we rode.

'Like last year, lord.'

'We'd best look to see who's selling grain.'

'The price will be high.'

'Better that than dead children,' I told him.

'You're the hlaford,' he said.

I turned in my saddle. 'Æthelstan!'

'Lord Uhtred?' The boy quickened his stallion's pace.

'Why am I called a hlaford?'

'Because you guard the loaf, lord,' he said, 'and a hlaford's duty is to feed his people.'

I grunted approval of his answer. Hlaford is a lord, the man who guards the hlaf, the loaf. My duty was to keep my people alive through winter's harshness and if that took gold, then gold must be spent. I had gold, but never enough. I dreamed of Bebbanburg, of the fortress in the north that had been stolen from me by Ælfric, my uncle. It was the impregnable fort, the last refuge on Northumbria's coast, so grim and formidable that the Danes had never captured it. They had taken all of northern Britain, from the rich pastures of Mercia to the wild Scottish frontier, but they had never taken Bebbanburg, and if I was to take it back I needed more gold for men, more gold for spears, more gold for axes, more gold for swords, more gold so that we could beat down the kinsmen who had stolen my fortress. But to do that we would have to fight through all the Danish lands, and I had begun to fear I would die before I ever reached Bebbanburg again.

18

We reached Tameworþig on the second day of our journey. Somewhere we crossed the frontier between the Saxon and the Danish lands, a frontier that was no fixed line, but was a broad stretch of country where the steadings had been burned, the orchards cut down, and where few animals except the wild beasts grazed. Yet some of those old farms had been rebuilt; I saw a new barn, its timber bright, and there were cattle in some of the meadows. Peace was bringing men to the frontier lands. That peace had lasted since the battle in East Anglia that had followed Alfred's death, though it had ever been an uncomfortable peace. There had been cattle raids, and slave raids, and squabbles over land boundaries, but no armies had been raised. The Danes still wanted to conquer the south, and the Saxons dreamed of taking back the north, but for ten years we had lived in morose quiet. I had wanted to disturb the peace, to lead an army north towards Bebbanburg, but neither Mercia nor Wessex would give me men and so I too had kept the peace.

And now Cnut had disturbed it.

He knew we were coming. He would have posted scouts to watch all the tracks from the south and so we took no precautions. Usually, when we rode the wild border, we had our own scouts far ahead, but instead we rode boldly, keeping to a Roman road, knowing that Cnut was waiting. And so he was.

Tameworþig was built just north of the River Tame. Cnut met us south of the river, and he wanted to overawe us because he had more than two hundred men standing in a shield wall athwart the road. His banner, which showed a war axe shattering a Christian cross, flew at the line's centre, and Cnut himself, resplendent in mail, cloaked in dark brown with fur shrouding his shoulders, and with his arms bright with gold, waited on horseback a few paces ahead of his men.

I stopped my men and rode forward alone.

Cnut rode towards me.

We curbed our horses a spear's length from each other. We looked at one another.

His thin face was framed by a helmet. His pale skin looked

19

drawn, and his mouth, which usually smiled so easily, was a grim slash. He looked older than I remembered and it struck me at that moment, watching his grey eyes, that if Cnut Ranulfson were to achieve his life's dreams then he must do it soon.

We watched each other and the rain fell. A raven flew from some ash trees and I wondered what kind of omen that was. 'Jarl Cnut,' I broke the silence.

'Lord Uhtred,' he said. His horse, a grey stallion, skittered sideways and he slapped its neck with a gloved hand to still it. 'I summon you,' he said, 'and you come running like a scared child.'

'You want to trade insults?' I asked him. 'You, who were born of a woman who lay with any man who snapped his fingers?'

He was silent for a while. Off to my left, half hidden by trees, a river ran cold in that bleak summer's rain. Two swans beat up the river, their wings slow in the chill air. A raven and two swans? I touched the hammer about my neck, hoping those omens were good.

'Where is she?' Cnut spoke at last.

'If I knew who she was,' I said, 'I might answer you.'

He looked past me to where my men waited on horseback. 'You didn't bring her,' he said flatly.

'You're going to talk in riddles?' I asked him. 'Then answer me this one. Four dilly-dandies, four long standies, two crooked pandies and a wagger.'

'Be careful,' he said.

'The answer is a goat,' I said, 'four teats, four legs, two horns and a tail. An easy riddle, but yours is difficult.'

He stared at me. 'Two weeks ago,' he said, 'that banner was on my land.' He pointed to my flag.

'I did not send it, I did not bring it,' I said.

'Seventy men, I'm told,' he ignored my words, 'and they rode to Buchestanes.'

'I've been there, but not in many years.'

'They took my wife and they took my son and daughter.'

I gazed at him. He had spoken flatly, but the expression on his face was bitter and defiant. 'I had heard you have a son,' I said.

20

'He is called Cnut Cnutson and you captured him, with his mother and sister.'

'I did not,' I said firmly. Cnut's first wife had died years before, as had his children, but I had heard of his new marriage. It was a surprising marriage. Men would have expected Cnut to marry for advantage, for land, for a rich dowry, or for an alliance, but rumour said his new wife was some peasant girl. She was reputed to be a woman of extraordinary beauty, and she had given him twin children, a boy and a girl. He had other children, of course, bastards all, but the new wife had given him what he most wanted, an heir. 'How old is your son?' I asked.

'Six years and seven months.'

'And why was he at Buchestanes?' I asked. 'To hear his future?'

'My wife took him to see the sorceress,' Cnut answered.

'She lives?' I asked, astonished. The sorceress had been ancient when I saw her and I had assumed she was long dead.

'Pray that my wife and children live,' Cnut said harshly, 'and that they are unharmed.'

'I know nothing of your wife and children,' I said.

'Your men took them!' he snarled. 'It was your banner!' He touched a gloved hand to the hilt of his famed sword, Ice-Spite. 'Return them to me,' he said, 'or your woman will be given to my men, and when they have done with her I'll flay her alive, slowly, and send you her skin for a saddlecloth.'

I turned in the saddle. 'Uhtred! Come here!' My son spurred his horse. He stopped beside me, looked at Cnut, then back to me. 'Dismount,' I ordered him, 'and walk to Jarl Cnut's stirrup.' Uhtred hesitated a heartbeat, then swung out of the saddle. I leaned over to take his stallion's bridle. Cnut frowned, not understanding what was happening, then glanced down at Uhtred, who was standing obediently beside the big grey horse. 'That is my only son,' I said.

'I thought . . .' Cnut began.

'That is my only son,' I said angrily. 'If I lie to you now then you may take him and do as you wish with him. I swear on my only son's life that I did not take your wife and children away.

21

I sent no men into your land. I know nothing of any raid on Buchestanes.'

'They carried your banner.'

'Banners are easy to make,' I said.

The rain hardened, driven by gusts of wind that shivered the puddles in the ruts of the nearby fields. Cnut looked down at Uhtred. 'He looks like you,' he said, 'ugly as a toad.'

'I did not ride to Buchestanes,' I told him harshly, 'and I sent no men into your land.'

'Get on your horse,' Cnut told my son, then looked at me. 'You're an enemy, Lord Uhtred.'

'I am.'

'But I suppose you're thirsty?'

'That too,' I said.

'Then tell your men to keep their blades sheathed, tell them that this is my land and that it will be my pleasure to kill any man who irritates me. Then bring them to the hall. We have ale. It isn't good ale, but probably good enough for Saxon swine.'

He turned and spurred away. We followed.

The hall was built atop a small hill, and the hill was ringed with an ancient earth wall that I supposed had been made on the orders of King Offa. A palisade topped the wall, and inside that wooden rampart was a high-gabled hall, its timbers dark with age. Some of those timbers had been carved with intricate patterns, but lichen now hid the carvings. The great door was crowned with antlers and wolf skulls, while inside the ancient building the high roof was supported by massive oak beams from which more skulls hung. The hall was lit by a fierce fire spitting in the central hearth. If I had been surprised by Cnut's offer of hospitality I was even more surprised when I walked into that high hall, for there, waiting on the dais and grinning like a demented weasel, was Haesten.

Haesten. I had rescued him years before, given him his freedom and his life, and he had rewarded me with treachery. There had been a time when Haesten was powerful, when his armies had threatened Wessex itself, but fate had brought him low. I had forgotten how many times I had fought him, and I had beaten him every time, yet he survived like a snake wriggling free of a peasant's rake. For years now he had occupied the old Roman fort at Ceaster, and we had left him there with his handful of men, and now he was here, in Tameworþig. 'He swore me loyalty,' Cnut explained when he saw my surprise.

'He's sworn that to me too,' I said.

'My Lord Uhtred.' Haesten hurried to meet me, his hands outstretched in welcome and a smile wide as the Temes on his face. He looked older, he was older; we were all older. His fair hair had turned silver, his face was creased, yet the eyes were still shrewd, lively and amused. He had evidently prospered. He wore gold on his arms, had a gold chain with a gold hammer about his neck, and another gold hammer in his left ear lobe. 'It is always a pleasure to see you,' he told me.

'A one-sided pleasure,' I said.

'We must be friends!' he declared. 'The wars are over.'

'They are?'

'The Saxons hold the south, and we Danes live in the north. It is a neat solution. Better than killing each other, yes?'

'If you tell me the wars are over,' I said, 'then I know the shield walls will be made very soon.' They would too if I could provoke it. I had wanted to kick Haesten out of his refuge in Ceaster for a decade, but my cousin Æthelred, Lord of Mercia, had always refused to lend me the troops I would need. I had even begged Edward of Wessex, and he had said no, explaining that Ceaster lay inside Mercia, not Wessex, and that it was Æthelred's responsibility, but Æthelred hated me and would rather have the Danes in Ceaster than my reputation enhanced. Now, it seemed, Haesten had gained Cnut's protection, which made capturing Ceaster a much more formidable task.

'My Lord Uhtred doesn't trust me,' Haesten spoke to Cnut, 'but I am a changed man, is that not so, lord?'

'You're changed,' Cnut said, 'because if you betray me I'll extract the bones from your body and feed them to my dogs.'

'Your poor dogs must go hungry then, lord,' Haesten said.

Cnut brushed past him, leading me to the high table on the dais. 'He's useful to me,' he explained Haesten's presence.

'You trust him?' I asked.

'I trust no man, but I frighten him, so yes, I trust him to do my bidding.'

'Why not hold Ceaster yourself?'

'How many men does it take? A hundred and fifty? So let Haesten feed them and spare my treasury. He's my dog now. I scratch his belly and he obeys my commands.' He nevertheless gave Haesten a place at the high table, though far away from the two of us. The hall was large enough to hold all Cnut's warriors and my men, while at the farther end, a long way from the fire and close to the main door, two tables had been provided for cripples and beggars. 'They get what's left over,' Cnut explained.

The cripples and beggars ate well because Cnut gave us a feast that night. There were haunches of roasted horse, platters of beans and onions, fat trout and perch, newly baked bread, and big helpings of the blood puddings I liked so much, all served with ale that was surprisingly good. He served the first horn to me himself, then stared morosely to where my men mixed with his. 'I don't use this hall much,' he said, 'it's too close to you stinking Saxons.'

'Maybe I should burn it for you?' I suggested.

'Because I burned your hall?' That thought seemed to cheer him. 'Burning your hall was a revenge for *Sea Slaughterer*,' he said, grinning. *Sea Slaughterer* had been his prized ship, and I had turned her into a scorched wreck. 'You bastard,' he said, and touched his ale-horn to mine. 'So what happened to your other son? Did he die?'

'He became a Christian priest, so, as far as I'm concerned, yes he died.'

He laughed at that, then pointed to Uhtred, 'And that one?'

'Is a warrior,' I said.

'He looks like you. Let's hope he doesn't fight like you. Who's the other boy?'

'Æthelstan,' I said, 'King Edward's son.'

Cnut frowned at me. 'You bring him here? Why shouldn't I hold the little bastard as a hostage?'

'Because he is a bastard,' I said.

'Ah,' he said, understanding, 'so he won't be King of Wessex?'

'Edward has other sons.'

'I hope my son holds onto my lands,' Cnut said, 'and perhaps he will. He's a good boy. But the strongest should rule, Lord Uhtred, not the one who slides out from between a queen's legs.'

'The queen might think differently.'

'Who cares what wives think?' He spoke carelessly, but I suspected he lied. He did want his son to inherit his lands and fortune. We all do, and I felt a shiver of rage at the thought of Father Judas. But at least I had a second son, a good son, while Cnut had only one, and the boy was missing. Cnut cut into a haunch of horsemeat and held a generous portion towards me. 'Why don't your men eat horse?' he asked. He had noticed how many had left the meat untouched.

'Their god won't allow it,' I said.

He looked at me as if judging whether I made a joke. 'Truly?'

'Truly. They have a supreme wizard in Rome,' I explained, 'a man called the pope, and he said Christians aren't permitted to eat horse.'

'Why not?'

'Because we sacrifice horses to Odin and Thor and eat the meat. So they won't.'

'All the more for us,' Cnut said. 'A pity their god doesn't teach them to leave women alone.' He laughed. He had always been fond of jokes and surprised me by telling one now. 'You know why farts smell?'

'I don't.'

'So the deaf can enjoy them too.' He laughed again and I wondered why a man who was so bitter about his missing wife and children could be so light-hearted. And perhaps he read my thoughts because he suddenly looked serious. 'So who took my wife and children?'

'I don't know.'

25

He tapped the table with his fingertips. 'My enemies,' he said after a few heartbeats, 'are all the Saxons, the Norse in Ireland, and the Scots. So it's one of those.'

'Why not another Dane?'

'They wouldn't dare,' he said confidently. 'And I think they were Saxons.'

'Why?'

'Someone heard them speaking. She said they spoke your foul tongue.'

'There are Saxons serving the Norse,' I said.

'Not many. So who took them?'

'Someone who'll use them as hostages,' I said.

'Who?'

'Not me.'

'For some reason,' he said, 'I believe you. Maybe I'm getting old and gullible, but I'm sorry I burned your hall and blinded your priest.'

'Cnut Longsword apologises?' I asked in mock astonishment.

'I must be getting old,' he said.

'You stole my horses too.'

'I'll keep those.' He stabbed a knife into a hunk of cheese, cut off a lump, then gazed down the hall, which was lit by a great central hearth round which a dozen dogs slept. 'Why haven't you taken Bebbanburg?' he asked.

'Why haven't you?'

He acknowledged that with a curt nod. Like all the northern Danes he lusted after Bebbanburg, and I knew he must have wondered how it could be captured. He shrugged. 'I'd need four hundred men,' he said.

'You have four hundred. I don't.'

'And even then they'll die crossing that neck of land.'

'And if I'm to capture it,' I told him, 'I'd have to lead four hundred men through your land, through Sigurd Thorrson's land, and then face my uncle's men on that neck.'

'Your uncle is old. I hear he's sick.'

'Good.'

'His son will hold it. Better him than you.'

'Better?'

'He's not the warrior you are,' Cnut said. He gave the compliment grudgingly, not looking at me as he spoke. 'If I do you a favour,' he went on, still gazing at the great fire in the hearth, 'will you do one for me?'

'Probably,' I said cautiously.

He slapped the table, startling four hounds who had been sleeping beneath the board, then beckoned to one of his men. The man stood; Cnut pointed at the hall door and the man obediently went into the night. 'Find out who took my wife and children,' Cnut said.

'If it's a Saxon,' I said, 'I can probably do that.'

'Do it,' he said harshly, 'and perhaps help me get them back.' He paused, his pale eyes staring down the hall. 'I hear your daughter's pretty?'

'I think so.'

'Marry her to my son.'

'Stiorra must be ten years older than Cnut Cnutson.'

'So? He's not marrying her for love, you idiot, but for an alliance. You and I, Lord Uhtred, we could take this whole island.'

'What would I do with this whole island?'

He half smiled. 'You're on that bitch's leash, aren't you?'

'Bitch?'

'Æthelflaed,' he said curtly.

'And who holds Cnut Longsword's leash?' I asked.

He laughed at that, but did not answer. Instead he jerked his head towards the hall door. 'And there's your other bitch. She wasn't harmed.'

The man dispatched by Cnut had fetched Sigunn, who stopped just inside the door and looked around warily, then saw me on Cnut's dais. She ran up the hall, round the table's end and threw her arms around me. Cnut laughed at the display of affection. 'You can stay here, woman,' he told Sigunn, 'among your own people.' She said nothing, just clung to me. Cnut grinned at me over her shoulder. 'You're free to go, Saxon,' he said, 'but find out who hates me. Find out who took my woman and children.'

'If I can,' I said, but I should have thought harder. Who would dare capture Cnut Longsword's family? Who would dare? But I did not think clearly. I thought their capture was meant to harm Cnut, and I was wrong. And Haesten was there, sworn man to Cnut, but Haesten was like Loki, the trickster god, and that should have made me think, but instead I drank and talked and listened to Cnut's jokes and to a harpist singing of victories over the Saxons.

And next morning I took Sigunn and went back south.

Two

My son, Uhtred. It seemed strange calling him that, at least at first. He had been called Osbert for almost twenty years and I had to make an effort to use his new name. Perhaps my father had felt the same when he renamed me. Now, as we rode back from Tameworþig, I called Uhtred to my side. 'You haven't fought in a shield wall yet,' I told him.

'No, Father.'

'You're not a man till you do,' I said.

'I want to.'

'And I want to protect you,' I said. 'I've lost one son, I don't want to lose another.'

We rode in silence through a damp, grey land. There was little wind and the trees hung heavy with wet leaves. The crops were poor. It was dusk and the west was suffused with a grey light that glinted off the puddled fields. Two crows flew slowly towards the clouds that shrouded the dying sun. 'I can't protect you for ever,' I said. 'Sooner or later you'll have to fight in a shield wall. You have to prove yourself.'

'I know that, Father.'

Yet it was not my son's fault that he had never proved himself. The uneasy peace that had settled on Britain like a damp fog had meant that warriors stayed in their halls. There had been many skirmishes, but no battle since we had cut down the spear-Danes in East Anglia. The Christian priests liked to say that their god had granted the peace because that was his will, but it was the will of men that was lacking. King Edward of Wessex was content to defend what he had inherited from his father and showed little ambition to increase those lands, Æthelred of Mercia sulked in Gleawecestre, and Cnut? He was a great warrior, but also a cautious one, and perhaps the new pretty wife had been entertainment enough for him, except now someone had taken that wife and his twin children. 'I like Cnut,' I said.

'He was generous,' my son said.

I ignored that. Cnut had indeed been a generous host, but that was the duty of a lord, though once again I should have thought more carefully. The feast at Tameworþig had been lavish, and it had been prepared, which meant Cnut knew he would entertain me rather than kill me. 'One day we'll have to kill him,' I said, 'and his son, if he ever finds his son. They stand in our way. But for the moment we'll do what he asked. We'll find out who captured his wife and children.'

'Why?' he asked.

'Why what?'

'Why help him? He's a Dane. He's our enemy.'

'I didn't say we're helping him,' I growled. 'But whoever took Cnut's wife is planning something. I want to know what.'

'What is Cnut's wife called?' he asked.

'I didn't ask him,' I said, 'but I hear she's beautiful. Not like that plump little seamstress you plough every night. She's got a face like the backside of a piglet.'

'I don't look at her face,' he said, then frowned. 'Did Cnut say his wife was captured at Buchestanes?' he asked.

'That's what he said.'

'Isn't that a long way north?'

'Far enough.'

'So a Saxon band rides that deep into Cnut's land without being seen or challenged?'

'I did it once.'

'You're Lord Uhtred, miracle-worker,' he said, grinning.

'I went to see the sorceress there,' I told him, and remembered that strange night and the beautiful creature who had come to me in my vision. Erce, she had been called, yet in the morning there had only been the old hag, Ælfadell. 'She sees the future,' I said, but Ælfadell had said nothing to me of Bebbanburg, and that was what I had wanted to hear. I wanted to hear that I would retake that fortress, that I would become its rightful lord, and I thought of my uncle, old and sick, and that made me angry. I did not want him to die until I had hurt him. Bebbanburg. It haunted me. I had spent the last years trying to amass the gold needed to go north and assault those great ramparts, but bad harvests had bitten into my hoard. 'I'm getting old,' I said.

'Father?' Uhtred asked, surprised.

'If I don't capture Bebbanburg,' I told him, 'then you will. Take my body there, bury it there. Put Serpent-Breath in my grave.'

'You'll do it,' he said.

'I'm getting old,' I said again, and that was true. I had lived more than fifty years and most men were lucky to see forty. Yet all old age was bringing was the death of dreams. There had been a time when all we wanted was one country, free of Danes, a land of the English kin, but still the Northmen ruled in the north and the Saxon south was riddled with priests who preached turning the cheek. I wondered what would happen after my death, whether Cnut's son would lead the last great invasion, and the halls would burn and the churches would fall and the land Alfred had wanted to call England would be named Daneland.

Osferth, Alfred's bastard son, spurred to catch us up. 'That's odd,' he said.

'Odd?' I asked. I had been daydreaming, noticing nothing, but now, looking ahead, I saw that the southern sky was glowing red, a lurid red, the red of fire.

'The hall must still be smouldering,' Osferth said. It was dusk and the sky was dark except in the far west and above the fire to our south. The flames reflected from the clouds and a smear of smoke drifted eastwards. We were close to home and the smoke had to be coming from Fagranforda. 'But it can't have burned that long,' Osferth went on, puzzled. 'The fire was out when we left.'

'And it's rained ever since,' my son added.

For a moment I thought of stubble burning, but that was a nonsense. We were nowhere near harvest time and so I kicked my heels to hurry Lightning. The big hooves splashed in puddled ruts and I kicked him again to make him gallop. Æthelstan, on his lighter and smaller horse, raced past me. I called to the boy to come back, but he kept riding, pretending not to have heard me. 'He's headstrong,' Osferth said disapprovingly.

'He needs to be,' I said. A bastard son must fight his own way in the world. Osferth knew that. Æthelstan, like Osferth, might be the son of a king, but he was not the son of Edward's wife, and that made him dangerous to her family. He would need to be headstrong.

We were on my land now and I cut across a waterlogged pasture to the stream that watered my fields. 'No,' I said in disbelief because the mill was burning. It was a watermill I had built and now it was spewing flames, while close to it, dancing like demons, were men in dark robes. Æthelstan, far ahead of us, had curbed his horse to stare beyond the mill to where the rest of the buildings were aflame. Everything that Cnut Ranulfson's men had left unburned was now blazing: the barn, the stables, the cow shelters, everything; and all about them, capering black in the flamelight, were men.

There were men and some women. Scores of them. And children too, running excitedly around the roaring flames. A cheer went up as the ridge of the barn collapsed to spew sparks high into the darkening sky, and in the burst of flames I saw bright banners held by dark-robed men. 'Priests,' my son said. I could hear singing now and I kicked Lightning and beckoned my men so that we galloped across the waterlogged meadow towards the place that had been my home. And as we approached I saw the dark robes gather together and saw the glint of weapons. There were hundreds of folk there. They were jeering, shouting, and above their heads were spears and hoes, axes and scythes. I saw no shields. This was the fyrd, the gathering of ordinary men to defend their land, the men who would garrison the burhs if the Danes came, but now they had occupied my estate and they had seen me and were screaming insults.

A man in a white cloak and mounted on a white horse pushed through the rabble. He held up his hand for silence and when it did not come he turned his horse and shouted at the angry crowd. I heard his voice, but not his words. He calmed them, stared at them for a few heartbeats, and then wrenched his horse around and spurred towards me. I had stopped. My men made a line on either side of me. I was watching the crowd, looking for faces I knew and saw none. My neighbours, it seemed, had no stomach for this burning.

The horseman stopped a few paces from me. He was a priest. He wore a black robe beneath the white cloak and a silver crucifix was bright against the black weave. He had a long face carved with shadowed lines, a wide mouth, a hook of a nose, and deep-set dark eyes beneath thick black brows. 'I am Bishop Wulfheard,' he announced. He met my eyes and I could see nervousness beneath the defiance. 'Wulfheard of Hereford,' he added as if the name of his bishopric would give him added dignity.

'I've heard of Hereford,' I said. It was a town on the border between Mercia and Wales, a smaller town than Gleawecestre yet, for some reason that only the Christians could explain, the small town had a bishop and the larger did not. I had heard of Wulfheard too. He was one of those ambitious priests who whisper into kings' ears. He might be Bishop of Hereford, but he spent his time in Gleawecestre where he was Æthelred's puppy.

I looked away from him, staring instead at the line of men who barred my path. Perhaps three hundred? I could see a handful of swords now, but most of the weapons had come from farm steadings. Yet three hundred men armed with timber axes, with hoes and with sickles could do lethal damage to my sixty-eight men.

'Look at me!' Wulfheard demanded.

I kept my eyes on the crowd and touched my right hand to Serpent-Breath's hilt. 'You do not give me orders, Wulfheard,' I said, not looking at him.

'I bring you orders,' he said grandly, 'from Almighty God and from the Lord Æthelred.'

'I'm sworn to neither,' I said, 'so their orders mean nothing.'

33

'You mock God!' the bishop shouted loud enough for the crowd to hear.

That crowd murmured and a few even edged forward as if to attack my men.

Bishop Wulfheard also edged forward. He ignored me now and called to my men instead. 'The Lord Uhtred,' he shouted, 'has been declared outcast of God's church! He has killed a saintly abbot and wounded other men of God! It has been decreed that he is banished from this land, and further decreed that any man who follows him, who swears loyalty to him, is also outcast from God and from man!'

I sat still. Lightning thumped a heavy hoof on the soft turf and the bishop's horse shifted warily away. There was silence from my men. Some of their wives and children had seen us and they were streaming across the meadow, seeking the protection of our weapons. Their homes had been burned. I could see the smoke sifting up from the street on the small western hill.

'If you wish to see heaven,' the bishop called to my men, 'if you wish your wives and children to enjoy the saving grace of our Lord Jesus, then you must leave this evil man!' He pointed at me. 'He is cursed of God, he is cast into an outer darkness! He is condemned! He is reprobate! He is damned! He is an abomination before the Lord! An abomination!' He evidently liked that word, because he repeated it. 'An abomination! And if you remain with him, if you fight for him, then you too shall be cursed, both you and your wives and your children also! You and they will be condemned to the everlasting tortures of hell! You are therefore absolved of your loyalty to him! And know that to kill him is no sin! To kill this abomination is to earn the grace of God!'

He was inciting them to my death, but not one of my men moved to attack me, though the rabble found new courage and shuffled forward, growling. They were nerving themselves to swarm at me. I glanced back at my men and saw they were in no mood to fight this crowd of enraged Christians because my men's wives were not seeking protection, as I had thought, but trying to pull them away from me, and I remembered something Father Pyrlig

34

had once said to me, that women were ever the most avid worshippers, and I saw that these women, all Christians, were undermining my men's loyalties.

What is an oath? A promise to serve a lord, but to Christians there is always a higher allegiance. My gods demand no oaths, but the nailed god is more jealous than any lover. He tells his followers that they can have no other gods beside himself, and how ridiculous is that? Yet the Christians grovel to him and abandon the older gods. I saw my men waver. They glanced at me, then some spurred away, not towards the ranting mob, but westwards away from the crowd and away from me. 'It's your fault.' Bishop Wulfheard had forced his horse back towards me. 'You killed Abbot Wihtred, a holy man, and God's people have had enough of you.'

Not all my men wavered. Some, mostly Danes, spurred towards me, as did Osferth. 'You're a Christian,' I said to him, 'why don't you abandon me?'

'You forget,' he said, 'that I was abandoned by God. I'm a bastard, already cursed.'

My son and Æthelstan had also stayed, but I feared for the younger boy. Most of my men were Christians and they had ridden away from me, while the threatening crowd was numbered in the hundreds and they were being encouraged by priests and monks. 'The pagans must be destroyed!' I heard a black-bearded priest shout. 'He and his woman! They defile our land! We are cursed so long as they live!'

'Your priests threaten a woman?' I asked Wulfheard. Sigunn was by my side, mounted on a small grey mare. I kicked Lightning towards the bishop, who wrenched his horse away. 'I'll give her a sword,' I told him, 'and let her gut your gutless guts, you mouse-prick.'

Osferth caught up with me and took hold of Lightning's bridle. 'A retreat might be prudent, lord,' he said.

I drew Serpent-Breath. It was deep dusk now, the western sky was a glowing purple shading to grey and then to a wide blackness in which the first stars glittered through tiny rents in the clouds. The light of the fires reflected from Serpent-Breath's wide blade.

'Maybe I'll kill myself a bishop first,' I snarled, and turned Lightning back towards Wulfheard, who rammed his heels so that his horse leaped away, almost unsaddling his rider.

'Lord!' Osferth shouted in protest and kicked his own horse forward to intercept me. The crowd thought the two of us were pursuing the bishop and they surged forward. They were screaming and shouting, brandishing their crude weapons and lost in the fervour of their God-given duty, and I knew we would be over-whelmed, but I was angry too and I thought I would rather carve a path through that rabble than be seen to run away.

And so I forgot the fleeing bishop, but instead just turned my horse towards the crowd. And that was when the horn sounded.

It blared, and from my right, from where the sun glowed beneath the western horizon, a stream of horsemen galloped to place them-selves between me and the crowd. They were in mail, they carried swords or spears, and their faces were hidden by the cheek-pieces of their helmets. The flamelight glinted from those helmets, turning them into blood-touched spear-warriors whose stallions threw up gouts of damp earth as the horses slewed around so that the newcomers faced the crowd.

One man faced me. His sword was lowered as he trotted his stallion towards Lightning, then the blade flicked up in a salute. I could see he was grinning. 'What have you done, lord?' he asked.

'I killed an abbot.'

'You made a martyr and a saint then,' he said lightly, then twisted in the saddle to look past the horsemen at the crowd, which had checked its advance but still looked threatening. 'You'd think they'd be grateful for another saint, wouldn't you?' he said. 'But they're not happy at all.'

'It was an accident,' I said.

'Accidents have a way of finding you, lord,' he said, grinning at me. It was Finan, my friend, the Irishman who commanded my men if I was absent, and the man who had been protecting Æthelflaed.

And there she was, Æthelflaed herself, and the angry murmur of the rabble died away as she rode slowly to face them. She was

36

mounted on a white mare, wore a white cloak, and had a circlet of silver about her pale hair. She looked like a queen, and she was the daughter of a king, and she was loved in Mercia. Bishop Wulfheard, recognising her, spurred to her side where he spoke low and urgently, but she ignored him. She ignored me too, facing the crowd and straightening in her saddle. For a while she said nothing. The flames of the burning buildings flickered reflections from the silver she wore in her hair and about her neck and on her slim wrists. I could not see her face, but I knew that face so well, and knew it would be icy stern. 'You will leave,' she said almost casually. A growl sounded and she repeated the command in a louder voice. 'You will leave!' She waited until there was silence. 'The priests here, the monks here, will lead you away. Those of you who have come far will need shelter and food, and you will find both in Cirrenceastre. Now go!' She turned her horse and Bishop Wulfheard turned after her. I saw him plead with her, and then she raised a hand. 'Who commands here, bishop,' she demanded, 'you or I?' There was such a challenge in those words.

Æthelflaed did not rule in Mercia. Her husband was the Lord of Mercia and, if he had possessed a pair of balls, might have called himself king of this land, but he had become the thrall of Wessex. His survival depended on the help of West Saxon warriors, and those only helped him because he had taken Æthelflaed as his wife and she was the daughter of Alfred, who had been the greatest of the West Saxon kings, and she was also the sister of Edward, who now ruled in Wessex. Æthelred hated his wife, yet needed her, and he hated me because he knew I was her lover, and Bishop Wulfheard knew it too. He had stiffened at her challenge, then glanced towards me, and I knew he was half tempted to meet her challenge and try to reimpose his mastery over the vengeful crowd, but Æthelflaed had calmed them. She did rule here. She ruled because she was loved in Mercia, and the folk who had burned my steading did not want to offend her. The bishop did not care. 'The Lord Uhtred,' he began and was summarily interrupted.

'The Lord Uhtred,' Æthelflaed spoke loudly so that as many folk as possible could hear her, 'is a fool. He has offended God and

37

man. He is declared outcast! But there will be no bloodshed here! Enough blood has been spilled and there will be no more. Now go!' Those last two words were addressed to the bishop, but she glanced at the crowd and gestured that they should leave too.

And they went. The presence of Æthelflaed's warriors was persuasive, of course, but it had been her confidence and authority that overrode the rabid priests and monks who had encouraged the crowd to destroy my estate. They drifted away, leaving the flames to light the night. Only my men remained, and those men who were sworn to Æthelflaed, and she turned towards me at last and stared at me with anger. 'You fool,' she said.

I said nothing. I was sitting in the saddle, gazing at the fires, my mind as bleak as the northern moors. I suddenly thought of Bebbanburg, caught between the wild northern sea and the high bare hills.

'Abbot Wihtred was a good man,' Æthelflaed said, 'a man who looked after the poor, who fed the hungry and clothed the naked.'

'He attacked me,' I said.

'And you are a warrior! The great Uhtred! And he was a monk!' She made the sign of the cross. 'He came from Northumbria, from your country, where the Danes persecuted him, but he kept the faith! He stayed true despite all the scorn and hatred of the pagans, only to die at your hands!'

'I didn't mean to kill him,' I said.

'But you did! And why? Because your son becomes a priest?'

'He is not my son.'

'You big fool! He is your son and you should be proud of him.'

'He is not my son,' I said stubbornly.

'And now he's the son of nothing,' she spat. 'You've always had enemies in Mercia, and now they've won. Look at it!' She gestured angrily at the burning buildings. 'Æthelred will send men to capture you, and the Christians want you dead.'

'Your husband won't dare attack me,' I said.

'Oh he'll dare! He has a new woman. She wants me dead, and you dead too. She wants to be Queen of Mercia.'

I grunted, but stayed silent. Æthelflaed spoke the truth, of course.

Her husband, who hated her and hated me, had found a lover called Eadith, a thegn's daughter from southern Mercia, and rumour said she was as ambitious as she was beautiful. She had a brother named Eardwulf who had become the commander of Æthelred's household warriors, and Eardwulf was as capable as his sister was ambitious. A band of hungry Welshmen had ravaged the western frontier and Eardwulf had hunted them, trapped them, and destroyed them. A clever man, I had heard, thirty years younger than me, and brother to an ambitious woman who wanted to be a queen.

'The Christians have won,' Æthelflaed told me.

'You're a Christian.'

She ignored that. Instead she just gazed blankly at the fires, then shook her head wearily. 'We've had peace these last years.'

'That's not my fault,' I said angrily. 'I asked for men again and again. We should have captured Ceaster and killed Haesten and driven Cnut out of northern Mercia. It isn't peace! There won't be peace till the Danes are gone.'

'But we do have peace,' she insisted, 'and the Christians don't need you when there's peace. If there's war then all they want is Uhtred of Bebbanburg fighting for them, but now? Now we're at peace? They don't need you now, and they've always wanted to be rid of you. So what do you do? You slaughter one of the holiest men in Mercia!'

'Holy?' I sneered. 'He was a stupid man who picked a fight.'

'And the fight he picked was your fight!' she said forcibly. 'Abbot Wihtred was the man preaching about Saint Oswald! Wihtred had the vision! And you killed him!'

I said nothing to that. There was a holy madness adrift in Saxon Britain, a belief that if Saint Oswald's body could be discovered then the Saxons would be reunited, meaning that those Saxons under Danish rule would suddenly become free. Northumbria, East Anglia and northern Mercia would be purged of Danish pagans, and all because a dismembered saint who had died almost three hundred years in the past would have his various body parts stitched together. I knew all about Saint Oswald: he had once ruled in Bebbanburg, and my uncle, the treacherous Ælfric, possessed one of the dead man's arms. I had escorted the saint's head to safety years before, and the rest of him was supposed to be buried at a monastery somewhere in southern Northumbria.

'Wihtred wanted what you want,' Æthelflaed said angrily, 'he wanted a Saxon ruler in Northumbria!'

'I didn't mean to kill him,' I said, 'and I'm sorry.'

'You should be sorry! If you stay here there'll be two hundred spearmen coming to take you to judgement.'

'I'll fight them.'

She scorned that with a laugh. 'With what?'

'You and I have more than two hundred men,' I said.

'You're more than a fool if you think I'll tell my men to fight other Mercians.'

Of course she would not fight Mercians. She was loved by the Mercians, but that love would not raise an army sufficient to defeat her husband because he was the gold-giver, the hlaford, and he could raise a thousand men. He was forced to pretend that he and Æthelflaed were on cordial terms because he feared what would happen if he attacked her openly. Her brother, King of Wessex, would want revenge. He feared me too, but the church had just stripped me of much of my power. 'What will you do?' I asked her.

'Pray,' she said, 'and I'll take your men into service.' She nodded towards those of my men whose religion had taken away their loyalty. 'And I shall stay quiet,' she said, 'and give my husband no cause to destroy me.'

'Come with me,' I said.

'And tie myself to an outcast fool?' she asked bitterly.

I looked up to where smoke smeared the sky. 'Did your husband send men to capture Cnut Ranulfson's family?' I asked.

'Did he do what?' she sounded shocked.

'Someone pretending to be me captured his wife and children.'

She frowned. 'How do you know?'

'I just came from his hall,' I said.

'I would have heard if Æthelred had done that,' she said. She had her spies in his household, just as he had them in hers.

40

'Someone did it,' I said, 'and it wasn't me.'

'Other Danes,' she suggested.

I slid Serpent-Breath back into her scabbard. 'You think because Mercia has been peaceful these last years,' I said, 'that the wars are over. They're not. Cnut Ranulfson has a dream; he wants it to come true before he's too old. So keep a good watch on the frontier lands.'

'I already do,' she said, sounding much less certain now.

'Someone is stirring the pot,' I said. 'Are you sure it's not Æthelred?'

'He wants to attack East Anglia,' she said.

It was my turn to be surprised. 'He wants to do what?'

'Attack East Anglia. His new woman must like marshland.' She sounded bitter.

Yet attacking East Anglia made some sense. It was one of the lost kingdoms, lost to the Danes, and it lay next to Mercia. If Æthelred could capture that land then he could take its throne and its crown. He would be King Æthelred, and he would have the fyrd of East Anglia and the thegns of East Anglia and he would be as powerful as his brother-in-law, King Edward.

But there was one problem about attacking East Anglia. The Danes to the north of Mercia would come to its rescue. It would not be a war between Mercia and East Anglia, but between Mercia and every Dane in Britain, a war that would drag Wessex into the fight, a war that would ravage the whole island.

Unless the Danes to the north could be kept quiet, and how better than to hold hostage a wife and children whom Cnut held dear? 'It has to be Æthelred,' I said.

Æthelflaed shook her head. 'I'd know if it was. Besides, he's scared of Cnut. We're all scared of Cnut.' She gazed sadly at the burning buildings. 'Where will you go?'

'Away,' I said.

She reached out a pale hand and touched my arm. 'You are a fool, Uhtred.'

'I know.'

'If there is war . . .' she said uncertainly.

'I'll come back,' I said.

'You promise?'

I nodded curtly. 'If there's war,' I said, 'I will protect you. I swore that to you years ago and a dead abbot doesn't change that oath.'

She turned to look again at the burning buildings and the light of the fires made her eyes appear wet. 'I'll take care of Stiorra,' she said.

'Don't let her marry.'

'She's ready,' she said, then turned back to me. 'So how will I find you?' she asked.

'You won't,' I answered, 'I'll find you.'

She sighed, then turned in the saddle and beckoned to Æthelstan. 'You're coming with me,' she ordered. The boy looked at me and I nodded.

'And where will you go?' she asked me again.

'Away,' I said again.

But I already knew. I was going to Bebbanburg.

The assault of the Christians left me with thirty-three men. A handful, like Osferth, Finan and my son, were also Christians, but most were Danes or Frisians and followers of Odin, of Thor, and of the other gods of Asgard.

We dug out the hoard that I had buried beneath the hall, and afterwards, accompanied by the women and children of the men who had stayed loyal to me, we went eastwards. We slept in a copse not far from Fagranforda. Sigunn was with me, but she was nervous and said little. They were all nervous of my bleak, angry mood, and only Finan dared talk with me. 'So what happened?' he asked me in the grey dawn.

'I told you. I killed some damned abbot.'

'Wihtred. The fellow who's preaching Saint Oswald.'

'Madness,' I said angrily.

'It probably is,' Finan said.

'Of course it's madness! What's left of Oswald is buried in Danish territory and they'll have pounded his bones to dust long ago. They're not idiots.'

'Maybe they dug the man up,' Finan said, 'and maybe they didn't. But sometimes madness works.'

'What does that mean?'

He shrugged. 'I remember in Ireland there was a holy fellow preaching that if we could only play a drum with the thigh bone of Saint Athracht, poor woman, then the rain would stop. There were floods then, you see. Never seen rain like it. Even the ducks were tired of it.'

'What happened?'

'They dug the creature up, hammered a drum with her long bone, and the rain stopped.'

'It would have stopped anyway,' I snarled.

'Aye, probably, but it was either that or build an ark.'

'Well, I killed the bastard by mistake,' I said, 'and now the Christians want my skull as a drinking bowl.'

It was morning, a grey morning. The clouds had thinned during the night, but now they closed down again and spat showers. We rode on tracks that led through damp fields where the rye, barley and wheat had been beaten down by rain. We rode towards Lundene, and off to my right I caught glimpses of the Temes flowing slow and sullen towards the far-off sea. 'The Christians have been looking for a reason to be rid of you,' Finan said.

'You're a Christian,' I said, 'so why did you stay with me?'

He gave a lazy grin. 'What one priest decrees another priest denies. So if I stay with you I go to hell? I'm probably going anyway, but I'll easily find a priest who'll tell me different.'

'Why didn't Sihtric think that?'

'It's the womenfolk. They're more scared of the priests.'

'And your woman isn't?'

'I love the creature, but she doesn't rule me. Mind you, she'll wear her knees out with praying, though,' he said, grinning again. 'And Father Cuthbert wanted to come with us, poor man.'

'A blind priest?' I asked. 'What use is a blind priest? He's better off with Æthelflaed.'

43

'But he wanted to stay with you,' Finan said, 'so if a priest wanted that then how sinful is it for me to want the same thing?' He hesitated. 'So what are we doing?'

I did not want to tell Finan the truth, that I was going to Bebbanburg. Did I even believe that myself? To take Bebbanburg I needed gold and hundreds of men, and I was leading thirty-three. 'We're going viking,' I said instead.

'I thought as much. And we'll be back.'

'We will?'

'It's fate, isn't it? One moment we're in the sunlight, and the next every dark cloud in Christendom is pissing all over us. So Lord Æthelred wants to go to war?'

'So I hear.'

'His woman and her brother want it. And when he's driven Mercia into chaos they'll be screaming for us to come back and save their miserable lives.' Finan sounded so confident. 'And when we do come back they'll forgive us. The priests will be putting wet kisses all over our arses, so they will.'

I smiled at that. Finan and I had been friends for so many years. We had shared slavery together, and then stood shoulder to shoulder in the shield wall, and I glanced at him and saw the grey hair showing beneath his woollen cap. His grizzled beard was grey too. I supposed I was the same. 'We get old,' I said.

'We do, but no wiser, eh?' he laughed.

We rode through villages and two small towns and I was wary, wondering if the priests had sent word that we were to be attacked, but instead we were ignored. The wind turned east and cold, bringing more rain. I glanced behind often, wondering if Lord Æthelred had sent men in pursuit, but none appeared and I assumed he was content to have driven me from Mercia. He was my cousin, my lover's husband, and my enemy, and in that dank summer he had finally won the victory over me that he had sought so long.

It took us five days to reach Lundene. Our journey had been slow, not just because the roads were waterlogged, but because we did not have enough horses to carry wives, children, armour, shields and weapons.

44

I have always liked Lundene. It is a vile, smoky, stinking place, the streets thick with sewage. Even the river smells, yet the river is why Lundene exists. Go west and a man can row deep into Mercia and Wessex, go east and the rest of the world lies before his prow. Traders come to Lundene with shiploads of oil or pelts, wheat or hay, slaves or luxuries. It is supposed to be a Mercian city, but Alfred had made sure it was garrisoned by West Saxon troops, and Æthelred had never dared challenge that occupation. It was really two towns. We came to the new town first, built by the Saxons and spreading along the northern bank of the wide, sluggish Temes, and we threaded the long street, finding our way past carts and herds, through the slaughter district where the alleys were puddled in blood. The tanners' pools lay just to the north and gave off their stench of urine and shit, and then we dropped down to the river that lay between the new and old towns, and I was assailed by memories. I had fought here. In front of us was the Roman wall and the Roman gate where I had repelled a Danish attack. Then up the hill and the guards on the gate stood aside, recognising me. I had half expected to be challenged, but instead they bowed their heads and welcomed me back, and I ducked under the Roman arch and rode into the old city, the city on its hill, a city made by the Romans in stone and brick and tile.

We Saxons never liked living in the old city. It made us nervous. There were ghosts there, strange ghosts we did not understand because they had come from Rome. Not the Rome of the Christians; that was no mystery. I knew a dozen men who had made that pilgrimage and they had all come back to talk of a marvellous place of columns and domes and arches, all in ruins, and of wolves among the broken stones and of the Christian pope who spread his poison from some decayed palace beside a rancid river, and that was all understandable. Rome was just another Lundene, only bigger, but the ghosts of Lundene's old town had come from a different Rome, a city of enormous power, a city that had ruled all the world. Its warriors had marched from the deserts to the snow and they had crushed tribes and countries, and then, for no reason that I knew, their power had fled. The great legions had become weak, the beaten tribes revived, and the glory of that great city had become ruin. That was true in Lundene too. You could see it! There were magnificent buildings falling into decay, and I was assailed, as I always was, by the sense of waste. We Saxons built in wood and thatch, our houses rotted in the rain and were torn by the wind, and there was no man alive who could remake the Roman glory. We descend towards chaos. The world will end in chaos when the gods fight each other, and I was convinced, I still am, that the inexplicable rise of Christianity is the first sign of that encroaching ruin. We are children's toys swept along a river towards a killing pool.

I went to a tavern beside the river. It was properly named Wulfred's Tavern, though everyone called it the Dead Dane because the tide had dropped one day to reveal a Danish warrior impaled on one of the many rotting stakes that stab the mud where once there were wharves. Wulfred knew me, and if he was surprised that I wanted space in his cavernous buildings, he had the grace to hide it. I was usually a guest in the royal palace that was built on the hill's top, but here I was, offering him coins. 'I'm here to buy a ship,' I told him.

'Plenty of those.'

'And find men,' I said.

'No end of men will want to follow the great Lord Uhtred,' he said.

I doubted that. There had been a time when men begged to give me their oath, knowing that I was a generous lord, but the church would have spread the message that I was cursed now, and the fear of hell would keep men away.

'But that's good,' Finan said that night.

'Why?'

'Because the bastards who want to join us won't be frightened of hell.' He grinned, showing three yellow teeth in his empty gums. 'We need bastards who'll fight through hell.'

'We do too,' I said.

'Because I know what's in your mind,' he said.

'You do?'

He stretched on the bench, casting an eye across the great room

46

where men drank. 'How many years have we been together?' he asked, but did not wait for an answer. 'And what have you dreamed of all those years? And what better time than now?'

'Why now?'

'Because it'll be the last thing the bastards expect, of course.'

'I'll have fifty men, if I'm lucky,' I said.

'And how many does your uncle have?'

'Three hundred? Maybe more?'

He looked at me, smiling. 'But you've thought of a way in, haven't you?'

I touched the hammer hanging about my neck and hoped that the old gods still had power in this mad, declining world. 'I have.'

'Then Christ help the three hundred,' he said, 'because they're doomed.'

It was madness.

And, as Finan had said, sometimes madness works.

She was called *Middelniht*, a strange name for a war boat, but Kenric, the man selling her, said she had been built from trees cut down at midnight. 'It gives a boat good luck,' he explained.

Middelniht had benches for forty-four oarsmen, an unstepped mast made of spruce, a mud-coloured sail reinforced by hemp ropes, and a high prow with a dragon's head. A previous owner had painted the head red and black, but the paint had faded and peeled so the dragon looked as if it suffered from scurvy.

'She's a lucky boat,' Kenric told me. He was a short wide man, bearded and bald, who built ships in a yard just to the east of the Roman city's walls. He had forty or fifty workers, some of them slaves, who used adzes and saws to make merchant ships that were fat, heavy and slow, but *Middelniht* was of a different breed. She was long, and her midships were wide, flat and lay low in the water. She was a sleek beast.

'You built her?' I asked.

'She was wrecked,' Kenric said.

'When?'

'A year ago on Saint Marcon's day. Wind blew up from the north, drove her onto Sceapig Sands.'

I walked along the wharf, looking down into *Middelniht*. Her timbers had darkened, but that was likely to have been the recent rain. 'She doesn't look damaged,' I said.

'Couple of bow strakes were stove in,' Kenric said. 'Nothing that a man couldn't make good in a day or two.'

'Danish?'

'Frisian built,' Kenric said. 'Good tight oak, better than the Danish crap.'

'So why didn't the crew salvage her?'

'Silly bastards went ashore, made a camp and got caught by Centish men.'

'Then why didn't the Centish men keep her?'

'Because the silly bastards fought each other to a standstill. I went down and found six Frisians still alive, but two of them died, poor bastards.' He made the sign of the cross.

'And the other four?'

He jerked a thumb towards his slaves working on a new boat. 'They told me her name. If you don't like it you can always change it.'

'It's bad luck to change a boat's name,' I said.

'Not if you get a virgin to piss in the bilge,' Kenric said, then paused. 'Well, that might be difficult.'

'I'll keep her name,' I said, 'if I buy her.'

'She's well made,' Kenric said grudgingly, as if he doubted that any Frisian could build ships as well as he did.

But the Frisians were renowned shipbuilders. Saxon boats tended to be heavy, almost as if we were frightened of the sea, but the Frisians and the Northmen built lighter ships that did not plough through the waves, but seemed to skim across them. That was a nonsense, of course; even a sleek ship like *Middelniht* was laden with stone ballast and could no more skim than I could fly, but there was some magic in her construction that

48

made her appear light. 'I planned to sell her to King Edward,' Kenric said.

'He didn't want her?'

'Not big enough.' Kenric spat in disgust. 'West Saxons have always been the same. They want big boats, then they wonder why they can't catch the Danes. So where are you going?'

'Frisia,' I said, 'maybe. Or south.'

'Go north,' Kenric said.

'Why?'

'Not so many Christians up north, lord,' he said slyly.

So he knew. He might call me 'lord' and be respectful, but he knew my fortunes were at a low ebb. That would affect the price. 'I'm getting too old for sleet, snow and ice,' I said, then jumped down onto *Middelniht*'s foredeck. She shivered beneath my feet. She was a war boat, a predator, built of fine-grained Frisian oak. 'When was she last caulked?' I asked Kenric.

'When I repaired her strakes.'

I pulled out two of the deck boards and peered down at the ballast stones. There was water there, but that was hardly surprising in a boat that had been left unused. What mattered was whether it was rainwater or the saltwater brought upriver on the tide. The water lay too low to be reached and so I spat and watched as the blob of spittle floated on the dark water, suggesting it was fresh. Spittle spreads and vanishes in saltwater. So she was a tight boat. If the water in her bilge was fresh then it had come from the clouds above, not from the sea below.

'She's staunch,' Kenric said.

'Her hull needs cleaning.'

He shrugged. 'I can do it, but the yard's busy. I'll charge.'

I could find a beach and do the job myself between the tides. I looked across Kenric's slipways to where a small, dark merchant ship was moored. She was half the size of *Middelniht*, but every bit as wide. She was a tub, made for carrying heavy cargo up and down the coast. 'You want that instead?' Kenric asked, amused.

'One of yours?'

'I don't build shit like that. No, she belonged to an East Saxon. Bastard owed me money. I'll break it up and use the timber.'

'So how much for *Middelniht*?'

We haggled, but Kenric knew he had the whip and I paid too much. I needed oars and lines too, but we agreed a price and Kenric spat on his hand and held it out to me. I hesitated, then took his hand. 'She's yours,' he said, 'and may she bring you fortune, lord.'

I owned *Middelniht*, a ship built from timbers cut in darkness.

I was a shipmaster again. And I was going north.

PART TWO

Middelniht

Three

I love the whale's path, the long waves, the wind flecking the world with blown spray, the dip of a ship's prow into a swelling sea and the explosion of white and the spatter of saltwater on sail and timbers, and the green heart of a great sea rolling behind the ship, rearing up, threatening, the broken crest curling, and then the stern lifts to the surge and the hull lunges forward and the sea seethes along the strakes as the wave roars past. I love the birds skimming the grey water, the wind as friend and as enemy, the oars lifting and falling. I love the sea. I have lived long and I know the turbulence of life, the cares that weigh a man's soul and the sorrows that turn the hair white and the heart heavy, but all those are lifted along the whale's path. Only at sea is a man truly free.

It had taken six days to settle matters in Lundene, the chief of which was to find a place where my men's families could live in safety. I had friends in Lundene and, though the Christians had sworn to break and kill me, Lundene is a forgiving city. Its alleys are places where foreigners can find refuge, and though there are riots and though the priests condemn other gods, most of the time the folk know to leave each other alone. I had spent many years in the city, I had commanded its garrison and rebuilt the Roman walls of the old town, and I had friends there who promised to look after our families. Sigunn wanted to come with me, but we were going to where the blades would draw blood and that was no place for a woman. Besides, I could not let her come if I forbade my men to bring their women, and so she stayed with a purse of my gold and a promise that we would return. We bought salt fish and salt meat, we filled the casks with ale and stowed them aboard *Middelniht*, and only then could we row downriver. I had left two of the older men to guard our families, but the four enslaved Frisians who had been part of *Middelniht*'s wrecked crew all joined me, and so I led thirty-five men downriver. We used the tide to carry us round the wide bends I knew so well, past the mudbanks where the reeds stirred and the birds cried, past Beamfleot where I had won a great victory that had inspired the poets and left the ditches red with blood, and then out to the wild wind and the endless sea.

We stranded *Middelniht* in a creek somewhere on the East Anglian coast and spent three days scraping her hull clean of weeds and scum. We did the work during the low tides, first scraping one side and recaulking the seams, then using a high tide to float her, spill her over and so expose her other flank. Then it was back to sea, rowing out of the creek to raise the sail and head her dragon prow northwards. We shipped the oars, letting an east wind drive us, and I felt the happiness I always felt when I had a good ship and a fast wind.

I made my son take the steering oar, letting him get used to the feel of a ship. At first, of course, he pushed or pulled the oar too far, or else he corrected too late and *Middelniht* lurched or yawed, losing speed, but by the second day I saw Uhtred smiling to himself and I knew that he could feel that long hull trembling through the oar's loom. He had learned and knew the joy of it.

We spent the nights on land, nosing into a creek on some empty shore and pulling back to sea in the first light. We saw few ships other than fishing craft who, seeing our high prow, hauled their nets and rowed frantically towards the land. We slid past, ignoring them. On the third day I glimpsed a mast far to the east, and Finan, whose eyes were like a hawk's, saw it at the same time and he opened his mouth to tell me, but I cautioned him to silence, jerking my head towards Uhtred in explanation. Finan grinned. Most of my men had also seen the distant ship, but they saw what I intended and kept quiet. *Middelniht* forged on and my son, the wind blowing his long hair about his face, gazed enraptured at the oncoming waves.

The distant ship drew nearer. She had a sail grey as the low clouds. It was a big sail, wide and deep, crossed with hemp lines to reinforce the weave. No trader, probably, but almost certainly another lean, fast ship made for fighting. My crew was now watching the ship, waiting for the first glimpse of her hull above the ragged horizon, but Uhtred was frowning at our sail's trailing edge, which was fluttering. 'Should we tighten it?' he asked.

'Good idea,' I said. He half smiled, pleased at my approval, but then did nothing. 'Give the order, you damned fool,' I said in a tone that took the smile straight off his face. 'You're the steersman.'

He gave the order and two men tightened the sheet till the flutter vanished. *Middelniht* dipped into a trough, then reared her prow up a green wave and as we reached the top I looked eastwards and saw the prow of the approaching ship. It showed a beast's head, high and savage. Then the ship vanished behind a screen of wind-blown spray. 'What's the first duty of a steersman?' I asked my son.

'To keep the ship safe,' he answered promptly.

'And how does he do that?'

Uhtred frowned. He knew he had done something wrong, but did not know what, and then, at last, he saw the crew staring fixedly towards the east and turned that way. 'Oh God,' he said.

'You're a careless fool,' I snarled at him. 'Your job is to keep a lookout.' I could see he was angry at my public reproof, but he said nothing. 'She's a warship,' I went on, 'and she saw us a long time ago. She's curious and she's coming to smell us. So what do we do?'

He looked again at the ship. Her prow was constantly visible now, and it would not be long before we saw her hull. 'She's bigger than us,' Uhtred said.

'Probably, yes.'

'So we do nothing,' he said.

It was the right decision, one I had made just moments after seeing the far ship. She was curious about us and her course was converging on ours, but once she was close she would see we were dangerous. We were not a merchant ship loaded with pelts, pottery or anything else that could be stolen and sold, we were warriors, and even if her crew outnumbered us by two to one she would take casualties that no ship could afford. 'We hold our course,' I said.

Northwards. North to where the old gods still had power, north to where the world shaded into ice, north towards Bebbanburg. That fortress brooded over the wild sea like the home of a god. The Danes had taken all of Northumbria, their kings ruled in Eoferwic, yet they had never succeeded in capturing Bebbanburg. They wanted it. They lusted after it like a dog smelling a bitch in heat, but the bitch had teeth and claws. And I had one small ship, and dreamed of capturing what even whole armies of Danes could not conquer.

'She's East Anglian.' Finan had come to stand beside me. The stranger was closing on us now, aiming her prow well ahead of ours, but angling towards us, and because she was the larger ship she was faster than *Middelniht*.

'East Anglian?'

'That's not a dragon,' Finan jerked his chin towards the ship, 'it's that weird thing King Eohric put on all his ships. A lion.' Eohric was dead and a new king ruled in East Anglia, but perhaps he had kept the old symbol. 'She's got a full crew too,' Finan went on.

'Seventy men?' I guessed.

'Near enough.'

The other crew was dressed for battle in mail and helmets, but I shook my head when Finan asked if we should make similar preparations. They could see we were no merchantman. They might be trying to overawe us, but I still doubted they would try to trouble us, and there was small point in dressing for war unless we wanted battle.

The East Anglian ship was well sailed. She curved in close to us and then shook out her sail to slow the hull so that she kept pace with *Middelniht*. 'Who are you?' a tall man called across in Danish.

56

'Wulf Ranulfson!' I called back, inventing a name.

'From where?'

'Haithabu!' I shouted. Haithabu was a town in southern Daneland, a long way from East Anglia.

'What's your business here?'

'We escorted a pair of merchantmen to Lundene,' I called, 'and we're going home. Who are you?'

He seemed surprised I had asked. He hesitated. 'Aldger!' he finally called. 'We serve King Rædwald!'

'May the gods grant him long life!' I shouted dutifully.

'You're well to the west if you're going to Haithabu!' Aldger bellowed. He was right, of course. Had we been bound for southern Daneland we would have crossed the sea much further south and be feeling our way up the Frisian coast.

'Blame this wind!'

He was silent. He watched us for a time, then gave the order for his sail to be sheeted home, and the larger ship drew ahead of us. 'Who is Rædwald?' Finan asked.

'He rules in East Anglia,' I said, 'and from what I hear he's old, sick and about as much use as a gelding in a whorehouse.'

'And a weak king invites war,' Finan said. 'No wonder Æthelred is tempted.'

'King Æthelred of East Anglia,' I said scornfully, but doubtless my cousin wanted that title, though whether East Anglia would want him was another matter. It was a strange kingdom, both Danish and Christian, which was confusing, because most of the Danes worship my gods and the Saxons worship the nailed one, but the East Anglian Danes had adopted Christianity, which made them neither one thing nor the other. They were allies to both Wessex and to Northumbria, and Wessex and Northumbria were natural enemies, which meant that the East Anglians were trying to lick one arse while they kissed the other. And they were weak. The old King Eohric had tried to please the northern Danes by attacking Wessex, and he and many of his great thegns had died in a slaughter. That had been my slaughter. My battle, and the memory filled me with the rage of the betrayed. I had fought so

57

often for the Christians, I had killed their enemies and defended their lands, and now they had spat me out like a scrap of rancid gristle.

Aldger crossed our bow. He deliberately swung his bigger ship close to us, perhaps wanting us to baulk at the last moment, but I growled at Uhtred to hold his course, and our bow sliced within a sword's length of Aldger's steering oar. We were close enough to smell his boat, even though he was upwind. I waved to him, then watched as he swung his bows northwards again. He kept pace with us, but I reckoned he was merely bored. He stayed with us for an hour or more, then the long ship turned away, the sail filled full from aft, and she sped off towards the distant land.

We stayed at sea that night. We were out of sight of land, though I knew it lay not far to our west. We shortened the great sail and let *Middelniht* plunge northwards through short, steep waves that spattered the deck with cold spray. I had the oar for most of the night and Uhtred crouched beside me as I told him tales of Grimnir, the 'masked one'. 'He was really Odin,' I told him, 'but whenever the god wanted to walk among humans he would wear his mask and take a new name.'

'Jesus did that,' he said.

'He wore a mask?'

'He walked amongst men.'

'Gods can do whatever they want,' I said, 'but from here on we wear a mask too. You don't mention my name or your name. I'm Wulf Ranulfson and you're Ranulf Wulfson.'

'Where are we going?' he asked.

'You know where we're going,' I said.

'Bebbanburg.' He said the name flatly.

'Which belongs to us,' I said. 'You remember Beocca?'

'Of course.'

'He gave me the charters,' I said. Dear Father Beocca, so ugly, so crippled, and so earnest. He had been my childhood tutor, a friend to King Alfred, and a good man. He had died not long before and his twisted bones were buried in Wintanceaster's church, close to the tomb of his beloved Alfred, but before he died he had sent me the charters that proved my ownership of Bebbanburg, though no man living needed to see a charter to know that I was the rightful lord of the fortress. My father had died while I was a child, and my uncle had taken Bebbanburg, and no amount of ink on parchment would drive him out. He had the swords and the spears, and I had *Middelniht* and a handful of men.

'We're descended from Odin,' I told Uhtred.

'I know, Father,' he said patiently. I had told him of our ancestry so many times, but the Christian priests had made him suspicious of my claims.

'We have the blood of gods,' I said. 'When Odin was Grimnir he lay with a woman, and we came from her. And when we reach Bebbanburg we shall fight like gods.'

It was Grimesbi that had made me think of Grimnir. Grimesbi was a village that lay not far from the open sea on the southern bank of the Humbre. Legend said that Odin had built a hall there, though why any god would choose to make a hall on that wind-swept stretch of marsh was beyond my imagining, but the settlement provided a fine anchorage when storms ravaged the sea beyond the river's wide mouth.

Grimesbi was a Northumbrian town. There had been a time when the kings of Mercia ruled all the way to the Humbre, and Grimesbi would have been one of their most northerly possessions, but those days were long past. Now Grimesbi was under Danish rule, though like all sea ports it would welcome any traveller, whether he was Danish, Saxon, Frisian, or even Scottish. There was a risk putting into the small port because I did not doubt that my uncle would listen for any news of my coming northwards, and he would surely have men in Grimesbi who were paid to pass on news to Bebbanburg. Yet I also needed news, and that meant risking a landing in Grimesbi because the harbour was frequented by seamen, and some of them would surely know what happened behind Bebbanburg's great walls. I would try to lessen the risk by emulating Grimnir. I would wear a mask. I would be Wulf Ranulfson out of Haithabu.

I gave my son the steering oar. 'Should we go west?' he asked.

'Why?'

He shrugged. 'We can't see the land. How do we find Grimesbi?'

'It's easy,' I said.

'How?'

'When you see two or three ships, you'll know.'

Grimesbi was on the Humbre, and that river had been a path into central Britain for thousands of Danes. I was sure we would see ships, and so we did. Within an hour of Uhtred's question we found six sailing westwards and two rowing eastwards, and their presence told me I had come to the place I wanted to be, to the sea-road that led from Frisia and Daneland to the Humbre. 'Six!' Finan exclaimed.

His surprise was somehow no surprise. All six ships travelling towards Britain were war boats, and I suspected all six were well crewed. Men were coming from across the sea because rumour said there were spoils to be won, or because Cnut had summoned them. 'The peace is ending,' I said.

'They'll be crying for you to return,' Finan said.

'They can kiss my pagan arse first.'

Finan chuckled, then gave me a quizzical glance. 'Wulf Ranulfson,' he said. 'Why that name?'

'Why not?' I shrugged. 'I had to invent a name, why not that one?'

'Cnut Ranulfson?' he suggested. 'And Wulf? I just find it strange that you chose his name.'

'I wasn't thinking,' I said dismissively.

'Or you were thinking of him,' Finan said, 'and you think he's marching south?'

'He will be soon,' I said grimly.

'And they can kiss your pagan arse,' he said. 'What if the Lady Æthelflaed calls?'

I smiled, but said nothing. There was land in sight now, a grey line on a grey sea, and I took the steering oar from Uhtred. I had travelled the Humbre so often, yet I had never been into Grimesbi. We were still under sail, and *Middelniht* curved into the river mouth from the east, passing the long spit of sand that was called the

Raven's Beak. The seas broke white on that sand where the bones of ships were black and stark, but as we passed the tip of the beak the water settled and the waves were tamed and we were in the river. It was wide here, a vast expanse of grey water beneath a grey wind-scoured sky. Grimesbi lay on the southern shore. We took down the sail and my men grumbled as they pushed the oars into their tholes. They always grumbled. I have never known a crew not to grumble when asked to row, but they still pulled on the looms willingly, and *Middelniht* slid between the bare withies thrust as markers into the hidden mudbanks where fish traps were staked in long tangles of black nets, and then we were inside Grimesbi's anchorage where there was a score of small fishing boats and a half-dozen larger ships. Two of the larger craft were like *Middelniht*, ships made for fighting, while the others were trading boats, all of them tied against a long wharf made of dark timbers. 'The pier looks rotten,' Finan observed.

'It probably is,' I said.

Beyond the pier was a small village, the wooden houses as dark as the wharf. Smoke rose along the muddy shore where fish were being smoked or salt was being boiled. There was a gap between two of the larger ships, a gap just wide enough to let *Middelniht* tie up to the wharf at the pier's end. 'You'll never slide her into that hole,' Finan said.

'I won't?'

'Not without hitting one of the ships.'

'It'll be easy,' I said. Finan laughed, and I slowed the oar-beat so that *Middelniht* crept through the water.

'Two West Saxon shillings says you can't do it without hitting one of those boats,' Finan said.

'Done,' I held out a hand. He slapped it, and I ordered the oars shipped to let *Middelniht*'s small speed carry her into the gap. I could see no one ashore other than the small boys employed in scaring gulls away from the fish-drying racks, yet I knew we were being watched. It's strange how much we care that we show seamanship. Men were judging us, even though we could not see them. *Middelniht* glided closer, her oars held aloft so their blades

61

swayed against the grey sky, her prow heading for the stern of a long warship. 'You're going to hit her,' Finan said happily.

I heaved on the steering oar, thrusting it hard, and if I had judged it right then we should slew round and the last of our momentum should carry *Middelniht* into the gap, though if I had judged it wrong we would either be left floating out of reach of the wharf or else would slam into its timbers with a hull-jarring crash, but *Middelniht* coasted into that space as sweetly as any sailor could wish and she was barely moving as the first man leaped up onto the wharf planks and took the thrown stern line. Another man followed, carrying the bow line, and the *Middelniht*'s flank kissed one of the pilings so gently that the hull barely quivered. I let go of the steering oar, grinned and held out a hand. 'Two shillings, you Irish bastard.'

'Just luck,' Finan grumbled, taking the coins from his pouch.

The crew was grinning. 'My name,' I told them, 'is Wulf Ranulfson, out of Haithabu! If you've never been to Haithabu say that I recruited you in Lundene.' I pointed at my son. 'He's Ranulf Wulfson, and we're provisioning here before going home across the sea.'

Two men were coming towards us along the rickety walkway that jutted to the wharf across a stretch of mud. Both were cloaked and both wore swords. I scrambled onto the planks and went to meet them. They looked relaxed. 'Another rainy day!' one of them greeted me.

'It is?' I asked. There was no rain, though the clouds were dark.

'It will be!'

'He thinks he can tell the weather from his bones,' the other man said.

'Rain and more rain coming,' the first man said. 'I'm Rulf, reeve of the town, and if your boat's staying there you have to give me money!'

'How much?'

'All you've got would be nice, but we settle for a silver penny a day.'

So they were honest. I gave them two silver slivers cut from

62

an arm ring, which Rulf pushed into a pouch. 'Who's your lord?'
I asked.

'Jarl Sigurd.'

'Sigurd Thorrson?'

'That's him, and a fair man.'

'I've heard of him,' I said. I had not only heard of him, but I
had killed his son in the last great battle between Danes and Saxons.
Sigurd hated me, and he was Cnut's closest friend and ally.

'And you've heard nothing bad, I dare say,' Rulf said, then
moved to look down into *Middelniht*. 'And your name?' he asked.
He was counting the men, and noting the shields and swords
stacked in the hull's centre.

'Wulf Ranulfson,' I said, 'out of Lundene, going home to
Haithabu.'

'You're not looking for trouble?'

'We're always looking for trouble,' I said, 'but we'll settle for
ale and food.'

He grinned. 'You know the rules, Wulf Ranulfson. No weapons
in town.' He jerked his head towards a long low building with a
black-thatched reed roof. 'That's the tavern. There's two ships in
from Frisia, try not to fight them.'

'We're not here to fight,' I said.

'Otherwise the Jarl Sigurd will hunt you down, and you don't
want that.'

The tavern was large, the town small. Grimesbi had no wall,
only a stinking ditch that circled the huddled houses. It was a
fishing town and I guessed most of the men were out on the rich
ocean banks. Their houses were built close together as if they could
shelter each other against the gales that must roar off the nearby
sea. The largest buildings were warehouses full of goods for seamen;
there were hemp lines, smoked fish, salted meat, seasoned timbers,
shaped oars, gutting knives, hooks, thole pins, horsehair for
caulking: all things that a ship sheltering from the weather might
want to make repairs or replenish supplies. This was more than a
fishing port, it was a travellers' town, a place of refuge for ships
plying the coast, and that was why I had come.

I wanted news, and I expected to find it from another visiting ship, which meant a long day in the tavern. I left *Middelniht* under Osferth's command, telling him that he could let the crew go ashore in small groups. 'No fighting!' I warned them, then Finan and I followed Rulf and his companion along the pier.

Rulf, a friendly man, saw us following and waited for us. 'You need supplies?' he asked.

'Fresh ale, maybe some bread.'

'The tavern will supply both. And if you need me for anything you'll find me in the house beside the church.'

'The church?' I asked in surprise.

'Has a cross nailed to the gable, you can't miss it.'

'The Jarl Sigurd allows that nonsense here?' I asked.

'He doesn't mind. We get a lot of Christian ships, and their crews like to pray. And they spend money in town so why not make them welcome? And the priest pays the jarl a rent on the building.'

'Does he preach to you?'

Rulf laughed. 'He knows I'll pin his ears to his own cross if he does that.'

It began to rain, a slanting, stinging rain that swept from the sea. Finan and I walked about the town, following the line of the ditch. A causeway led south across the ditch, and a skeleton hung from a post on its far side. 'A thief, I suppose,' Finan said.

I gazed across the rain-swept marsh. I was putting the place in my mind because a man never knew where he might have to fight, though I hoped I would never have to fight here. It was a bleak, damp place, but it provided ships with shelter from the storms that could turn the sea into grey-white chaos.

Finan and I settled in the tavern where the ale was sour and the bread rock hard, but the fish soup was thick and fresh. The long, wide room was low-beamed, warmed by an enormous drift-wood fire that burned in a central hearth, and even though it was not yet midday the place was crowded. There were Danes, Frisians and Saxons. Men sang and whores worked the long tables, taking their men up a ladder to a loft built into one gable and provoking cheers whenever the loft's floorboards bounced up and down to sift dust onto our ale pots. I listened to conversations, but heard no one claim to have worked their way south along the Northumbrian coast. I needed a man who had been to Bebbanburg and I was willing to wait as long as I needed to find him.

But instead he found me. Sometime in the afternoon a priest, I assumed it was the priest who rented the small church in the town's centre, came through the tavern door and shook rain from his cloak. He had two burly companions who followed him as he went from table to table. He was an older man, skinny and white-haired, with a shabby black robe stained with what looked like vomit. His beard was matted, and his long hair greasy, but he had a quick smile and shrewd eyes. He looked our way and saw the cross hanging at Finan's neck and so threaded the benches to our table, which was beside the ladder used by the whores. 'My name is Father Byrnjolf,' he introduced himself to Finan, 'and you are?'

Finan did not give his name. He just smiled, stared fixedly at the priest and said nothing.

'Father Byrnjolf,' the priest said hurriedly, as if he had never meant to ask Finan for his name, 'and are you just visiting our small town, my son?'

'Passing through, father, passing through.'

'Then perhaps you'd be good enough to give a coin for God's work in this place?' the priest said and held out a begging bowl. His two companions, both formidable-looking men with leather jerkins, wide belts and long knives, stood at his side. Neither smiled.

'And if I choose not to?' Finan asked.

'Then God's blessing be upon you anyway,' Father Byrnjolf said. He was a Dane and I bridled at that. I still found it hard to believe that any Dane was a Christian, let alone that one could be a priest. His eyes flicked to my hammer and he took a pace back. 'I meant no offence,' he said humbly, 'I am just doing God's work.'

'So are they,' I said, glancing up to the loft floorboards that were moving and creaking.

He laughed at that, then looked back to Finan. 'If you can help the church, my son, God will bless you.'

Finan fished in his pouch for a coin and the priest made the

65

sign of the cross. It was plain he tried to approach none but Christian travellers and his two companions were there to keep him out of trouble if any pagan objected. 'How much rent do you pay to the Jarl Sigurd?' I asked him. I was curious, hoping that Sigurd was taking an outrageously large sum.

'I pay no rent, God be praised. The Lord Ælfric does that. I collect for the poor.'

'The Lord Ælfric?' I asked, hoping the surprise did not show in my voice.

The priest reached for Finan's coin. 'Ælfric of Bernicia,' he explained. 'He is our patron, and a generous one. I've just visited him.' He gestured at the stains on his black robe as if they had some relevance to his visit to Ælfric.

Ælfric of Bernicia! There had been a kingdom called Bernicia once, and my family had ruled it as kings, but that realm had long vanished, conquered by Northumbria, and all that was left was the great fortress of Bebbanburg and its adjacent lands. But my uncle liked to call himself Ælfric of Bernicia. I was surprised he had not taken the title of king.

'What did Ælfric do,' I asked, 'throw the kitchen slops at you?'

'I am always sick at sea,' the priest said, smiling. 'Dear sweet Lord but how I do hate ships. They move, you know? They go up and down! Up and down till your stomach can take no more and then you hurl good food to the fishes. But the Lord Ælfric likes me to visit him three times a year, so I must endure the sickness.' He put the coin into his bowl. 'Bless you, my son,' he said to Finan.

Finan smiled. 'There's a sure cure for the seasickness, father,' he said.

'Dear God, there is?' Father Byrnjolf looked earnestly at the Irishman. 'Tell me, my son.'

'Sit under a tree.'

'You mock me, my son, you mock me.' The priest sighed, then looked at me with an astonished expression, and no wonder. I had just rapped a gold coin on the table.

'Sit and have some ale,' I told him.

He hesitated. He was nervous of pagans, but the gold tempted him. 'God be praised,' he said, and sat on the bench opposite.

I looked at the two men. They were large men, their hands stained black with the tar that coats fishing nets. One looked particularly formidable; he had a flattened nose in a weather-darkened face and fists like war-hammers. 'I'm not going to kill your priest,' I told the two men, 'so you don't need to stand there like a pair of bullocks. Go find your own ale.'

One of them glanced at Father Byrnjolf who nodded assent, and the two men crossed the room. 'They're good souls,' Father Byrnjolf said, 'and like to keep my body in one piece.'

'Fishermen?'

'Fishermen,' he said, 'like our Lord's disciples.'

I wondered if one of the nailed god's disciples had a flattened nose, scarred cheeks and bleak eyes. Maybe. Fishermen are a tough breed. I watched the two men settle at a table, then spun the coin in front of the priest's eyes. The gold glittered, then made a thrumming noise as the spin lost speed. The coin clattered for an instant and then fell flat. I pushed it a little way towards the priest. Finan had called for another pot and poured ale from the jug. 'I have heard,' I said to Father Byrnjolf, 'that the Lord Ælfric pays for men.'

He was staring at the coin. 'What have you heard?'

'That Bebbanburg is a fortress and safe from attack, but that Ælfric has no ships of his own.'

'He has two,' Father Byrnjolf said cautiously.

'To patrol his coast?'

'To deter pirates. And yes, he does hire other ships at times. Two are not always sufficient.'

'I was thinking,' I said, and I tipped the coin upwards and spun it again, 'that we might go to Bebbanburg. Is he friendly to folk who are not Christian?'

'He's friendly, yes. Well,' he paused, then corrected himself, 'perhaps not friendly, but he is a fair man. He treats folk decently.'

'Tell me about him,' I said.

The coin caught the light, flickered and gleamed. 'He's unwell,' Father Byrnjolf said, 'but his son is a capable man.'

'And the son is called?' I asked. I knew the answer, of course. Ælfric was my uncle, the man who had stolen Bebbanburg, and his son was named Uhtred.

'He's called Uhtred,' Father Byrnjolf said, 'and he has a son of the same name, a fine boy! Just ten years old but stout and brave, a good lad!'

'Also called Uhtred?'

'It is an old family name.'

'Just the one son?' I asked.

'He had three, but the two youngest died.' Father Byrnjolf made the sign of the cross. 'The eldest thrives, God be praised.'

The bastard, I thought, meaning Ælfric. He had named his son Uhtred, and Uhtred had named his son the same, because the Uhtreds are the lords of Bebbanburg. But I am Uhtred and Bebbanburg is mine, and Ælfric, by naming his son Uhtred, was proclaiming to all the world that I had lost the fortress and that his family would now possess it to the end of time. 'So how do I get there?' I asked. 'He has a harbour?'

And Father Byrnjolf, transfixed by that gold coin, told me so much I already knew, and some that I did not know. He told how we would need to negotiate the narrow entrance north of the fortress and so take *Middelniht* into the shallow harbour that lay protected by the great rock on which Bebbanburg was built. We would be allowed to go ashore, he said, but to reach the Lord Ælfric's hall we would need to take the uphill path to the first gate, called the Low Gate. That gate was immense, he told us, and reinforced by stone walls. Once through the Low Gate there was a wide space where a smithy stood next to the fortress stables, and beyond that another steep path climbed to the High Gate, which protected Ælfric's hall, the living quarters, the armoury and the lookout tower. 'More stone?' I asked.

'The Lord Ælfric has made a stone wall there, yes. No one can pass.'

'And he has men?'

'Some forty or fifty live in the fortress. He has other warriors, of course, but they plough his land or live in halls of their own.'

And that I knew too. My uncle could summon a formidable war-band, but most of them lived on outlying farms. It would take at least a day or two for those hundreds of men to assemble, which meant I had to deal with the housecarls, the forty or fifty trained warriors whose job was to keep Ælfric's nightmare from coming true. I was the nightmare. 'You'll be going north soon then?' Father Byrnjolf asked.

I ignored the question. 'And the Lord Ælfric needs ships,' I asked, 'to protect his traders?'

'Wool, barley and pelts,' Father Byrnjolf said. 'They're sent south to Lundene or else across the sea to Frisia, so yes, they need protection.'

'And he pays well.'

'He's renowned for his generosity.'

'You've been helpful, father,' I said, and flicked the coin across the table.

'God be with you, my son,' the priest said, scrambling for the coin that had fallen among the floor rushes. 'And your name?' he asked when he had retrieved the gold.

'Wulf Ranulfson.'

'God bless your northward voyage, Wulf Ranulfson.'

'We may not go north,' I said as the priest stood. 'I hear there's trouble brewing in the south.'

'I pray not,' he sounded hesitant, 'trouble?'

'In Lundene they said that the Lord Æthelred thinks East Anglia is there for the taking.'

Father Byrnjolf made the sign of the cross. 'I pray not, I pray not,' he said.

'There's profit in trouble,' I said, 'so I pray for war.'

He said nothing, but hurried away. I had my back to him. 'What's he doing?' I asked Finan.

'Talking to his two fellows. Looking at us.'

I cut a piece of cheese. 'Why does Ælfric pay to keep a priest in Grimesbi?'

'Because he's a good Christian?' Finan suggested blandly.

'Ælfric's a treacherous piece of slug-shit,' I said.

69

Finan glanced towards the priest and looked back to me. 'Father Byrnjolf takes your uncle's silver.'

'And in return,' I said, 'he tells Ælfric who moves through Grimesbi. Who comes, who goes.'

'And who asks questions about Bebbanburg.'

'Which I just did.'

Finan nodded. 'You just did. And you paid the bastard too much, and you asked too many questions about the defences. You might just as well have told him your real name.'

I scowled, but Finan was right. I had been too eager to get information, and Father Byrnjolf must be more than suspicious. 'So how does he get news to Ælfric?' I asked.

'The fishermen?'

'And in this wind,' I suggested, looking towards a shutter that banged and rattled against its latches, 'it will be two days' sailing? Or a day and a half if they use something the size of *Middelniht*.'

'Three days if they put ashore at night.'

'And did the bastard tell me the truth?' I wondered aloud.

'About your uncle's garrison?' Finan asked, then used a forefinger to trace a pattern with spilled ale on the table top. 'It sounded likely enough.' He half smiled. 'Fifty men? If we can get inside we should be able to kill the bastards.'

'If we can get inside,' I said, then turned and pretended to look towards the big central hearth where flames leaped up to meet the rain spitting through the roof-hole. Father Byrnjolf was deep in conversation with his two big companions, but even as I watched they turned and hurried towards the tavern door.

'What's the tide?' I asked Finan, still watching the priest.

'Be high tonight, ebbing at dawn.'

'Then we leave at dawn,' I said.

Because the *Middelniht* was going hunting.

We left at dawn on the ebbing tide. The world was sword grey. Grey sea, grey sky and a grey mist, and the *Middelniht* slid through that greyness like a sleek and dangerous beast. We were only using twenty oars and they rose and fell almost silently, just a creak from the tholes and sometimes a splash as a blade dipped. The wake rippled behind us, black and silver, widening and fading as the *Middelniht* slipped between the withies marking the channel.

We let the tide take us to sea. The mist thickened, but the tide would carry us safely, and it was not till the bows bucked to bigger waves that I turned our course northwards. We rowed slowly. I could hear the distant sound of seas breaking on the Raven's Beak and steered away from it, waiting till it faded, and by then the grey mist had thickened but grown brighter. The rain had stopped. The sea was idle, lazy, slapping petulantly against the hull, the small waves remnants of the bad weather, but I sensed a wind would come again and hoisted the damp sail to be ready.

The wind came, still from the east, and the sail bellied and the oars were stowed and the *Middelniht* surged northwards. The mist lifted and I could see fishing boats inshore of us, but I ignored them, heading north, and the gods were with me for the wind swung a little southwards as the sun climbed through ragged clouds. Sea-birds shrieked at us.

We made good progress so that by late afternoon we were in sight of the chalk cliffs of Flaneburg. That was a famous landmark. How often I've sailed by that great promontory with its cave-riddled white cliffs. I could see the waves breaking white on those cliffs and, as we drew nearer, hear the boom of water crashing into the caves. 'Flaneburg,' I told my son, 'remember the place!'

He was gazing at the turmoil of water and stone. 'It's hard to forget.'

'It's best to sail well away from it,' I told him. 'The currents run hard around the cliffs, but it's easier offshore. And if you're running from a northerly gale don't look for shelter on its south side.'

'No?'

'The water's shallow,' I said, pointing to the dark bones of ships showing above the fretting waves. 'Flaneburg takes ships and men. Avoid it.'

The tidal current had turned and was against us now. *Middelniht* buffeted the waves and I ordered the sail dropped and the men to the oars. The sea was trying to drive us south, and I needed to shelter on Flaneburg's northern side where the water was deeper and where any boat coming from the south would not see us. I steered close to the cliffs. Gannets wheeled about our mast and puffins flew fast and low above the broken water. The waves shattered on the rocks and seethed across ledges, draining back into an angry confusion of swirling white. High up, where I could see wind-flattened grass on the cliff top, two men stared down at us. They were watching to see if we landed, but I had never tried grounding a boat in the tiny cove on Flaneburg's northern flank and I was not going to try now.

Instead we turned the bows into the sea's current and held her there with the oars. There had been five fishing craft close to the great chalk head when we arrived. Two had been east of the cliffs and three to the north, but all of them fled our coming. We were a wolf, and the sheep knew their place and so, as the shadows lengthened across the sea, we were left alone. The wind dropped, though that did nothing to lessen the churning sea. The current was running stronger so that my men had to pull hard on the oars to hold *Middelniht* in place. The shadows turned to gathering darkness, the sea from grey to near black, though the blackness was rifted with breaking white water. The sky was grey again, but luminous. 'Maybe they won't come tonight.' Finan joined me by the steering oar.

'They can't go by land,' I said, 'and they'll be in a hurry.'

'Why not by land?' my son asked.

'Don't ask stupid questions,' I said angrily.

He glared at me. 'They're Danes,' he said forcefully. 'Didn't you say the priest was Danish?' He did not wait for me to answer. 'The two fishermen might be Christians and Saxons,' he went on, 'but the Jarl Sigurd tolerates their religion. They could ride through Northumbria without being harassed.'

'He's right,' Finan said.

'He's wrong,' I insisted. 'Going by horse will take too long.'

I hoped I was right. I knew Father Byrnjolf would much rather have travelled to Bebbanburg on horseback, but the need to take his news quickly should force him into seasickness. My guess was that the fishermen would carry him close to the coast and, should some savage ship of hungry spear-Danes appear, they could run for a harbour or, if there was none, ground their boat on a beach. Travelling on a small boat close to shore was safer than riding the long northern roads.

I looked westwards. The first stars pricked between dark clouds. It was almost night, but a moon was rising. 'They know we left Grimesbi,' my son said, 'and they must worry we're waiting for them.'

'Why should they worry?' I asked.

'Because you asked about Bebbanburg,' Finan said drily.

'And they counted us,' I said, 'thirty-six of us. What hope do thirty-six men have against Bebbanburg?'

'They'll think none,' Finan said. 'And perhaps they believed your tale. Perhaps Father Byrnjolf isn't sending a warning?'

It was night now. The sea was moon-washed but the land was dark. Somewhere far to the north a fire glimmered on the shore, but all the rest was black; even the chalk cliffs were black. The sea was black, rilled with silver, grey and white. We pulled *Middelniht* a few boat lengths north to hold her off the night cliffs. Any ship out at sea would not see her against the land. The wolf was hidden.

Then, quite suddenly, the prey was there.

She appeared from the south, a small ship with a square sail, and it was the dark sail I saw first. She was perhaps half a mile from Flaneburg's eastern tip, and I instinctively pushed the steering oar away from me, and Finan gave the order for the oars to bite, and *Middelniht* slid out of her shadowed hiding place.

'Row hard,' I growled at Finan.

'Hard as we can,' he said. A wave broke at the bow and slung water down the deck. The men were hauling on the looms, the oars were bending, the ship was moving fast. 'Faster!' Finan called and stamped his foot to call the rhythm.

'How do you know it's them?' Uhtred asked me.

'I don't.'

They had seen us. Perhaps it was the white water at our bows or the sound of our heavy oars splashing, but I saw the short hull turn partly away from us and saw a man scrambling to haul on a line to tighten the sail, and then they must have realised there was no escape by fleeing from us and so they turned their boat towards us. Their sail flapped for a heartbeat, was tightened again, and the small ship was bows on to us. 'What he wants to do,' I told Uhtred, 'Is veer off course at the last moment and shatter one of our oar banks. The man's no fool.'

'Which oar bank though?'

'If I knew that . . .' I said, and left the rest unsaid.

There was more than one man in the approaching craft. Two maybe? Three? It was a fishing boat, wide-hulled, stable and slow, but heavy enough to splinter our oars.

'He'll go that side,' I said, pointing southwards. Uhtred looked at me, his face pale in the moonlight. 'Look at him,' I said, 'the steersman is standing beside the steering oar. He hasn't got room to pull the oar towards him, not enough room anyway, so he'll push it away.'

'Row, you bastards!' Finan shouted.

A hundred paces, fifty, and the fishing boat held its course, bows to bows, and now I could see there were three men aboard, and the ship came closer, closer, until I lost the hull under our bows and could only see the dark sail getting still closer, and then I hauled the steering oar towards me, hauled it hard and saw their boat turn at the same moment, but I had anticipated them and they turned the way I had expected and our beast-headed prow rode up over their low hull. I felt *Middelniht* shiver, heard a shout, heard the sound of wood shattering, saw the mast and sail vanish and then our oars bit again and something scraped down our hull and the water was full of broken timbers. 'Stop rowing!' I shouted.

We had dragged the swamped boat with us, though most of the broken hull, weighted down by ballast stones, had gone to the sea's bed where the monsters lurk. The sail was gone; there was only shattered wood, an empty wicker fish basket, and one

74

man splashing desperately, flailing in the heaving seas to reach *Middelniht*'s side.

'He's one of the men who was with Father Byrnjolf,' Finan said.

'You recognise him?'

'That flattened nose?'

The man reached up to grasp an oar, then pulled himself towards our flank, and Finan stooped to pick up an axe. He looked at me, I nodded, and the axe blade caught the moonlight as it slashed down. There was the butcher's sound and a spray of blood, black as the land, from the shattered skull, then the man drifted away.

'Hoist the sail,' I said, and, when the oars were stowed and the sail drawing, I turned *Middelniht*'s bows north again.

The *Middelniht* had killed our enemies in the middle of the night, and now we were going to Bebbanburg. Ælfric's nightmare was coming true.

Four

The weather calmed in the night and that was not what I wanted.

Nor did I want to remember the face of that fisherman with his flattened nose and the scars on his sun-darkened cheek, and how his eyes had looked up, desperate, pleading and vulnerable, and how we had killed him, and how his black blood had sprayed the black night and vanished in the swirl of black water beside *Middelniht*'s hull. We are cruel people.

Hild, whom I had loved and who had been an abbess in Wessex and a good Christian, had so often spoken wistfully of peace. She had called her god the 'prince of peace' and tried to persuade me that if only the worshippers of the real gods would acknowledge her nailed prince then there would be perpetual peace. 'Blessed are the peacemakers,' she liked to tell me, and she would have been pleased these last few years because Britain had known its uneasy peace. The Danes had done little more than raid for cattle, sometimes for slaves, and the Welsh and Scots had done the same, but there had been no war. That was why my son had not stood in the shield wall, because there had been no shield walls. He had practised time and again, day after day, but practice is not the real thing, practice is not the bowel-loosening terror of facing a mead-crazed maniac who is within arm's length and carrying a lead-weighted war axe.

And some men had preached that the peace of these last few years was the Christian god's will, and that we should be glad because our children could grow without fear and what we sowed

76

we could harvest, and that it was only during a time of peace that the Christian priests could preach their message to the Danes, and that when that work was done we would all live in a Christian world of love and friendship.

But it had not been peace.

Some of it was exhaustion. We had fought and fought, and the last battle, a welter of blood-letting in the winter marshland of East Anglia, where King Eohric had died and Æthelwold the Pretender had died and Sigurd Thorrson's son had died, that battle had been a slaughter so great it had slaked the appetite for more battle. Yet it had changed little. The north and east were still Danish, and the south and west still Saxon. All those graves had yielded little land for either side. And Alfred, who wanted peace, but had known there could be no peace while two tribes fought for the same pastures, had died. Edward, his son, was king in Wessex, and Edward was content to let the Danes live in peace. He wanted what his father had wanted, all the Saxons living under one crown, but he was young, he was nervous of failure, and he was wary of those older men who had advised his father, and so he listened to the priests who told him to hold hard to what he possessed and to let the Danes stay where they were. In the end, the priests said, the Danes would become Christians and we should all love one another. Not all the Christian priests preached that message. Some, like the abbot I had killed, urged the Saxons to war, claiming that the body of Saint Oswald would be a sign of victory.

Those belligerent priests were right. Not about Saint Oswald, at least I doubted that, but they were surely right to preach that there never could be a lasting peace while the Danes occupied lands that had once been Saxon. And those Danes still wanted it all; they wanted the rest of Mercia and all of Wessex. It did not matter what banner they fought under, whether it was the hammer or the cross, the Danes were still hungry. And they were powerful again. The losses of the wars had been made good, they were restless, and so was Æthelred, Lord of Mercia. He had lived all his life under the thrall of Wessex, but now he had a new woman and he was getting old and he wanted reputation. He wanted the poets to sing of his triumphs, he wanted the chronicles to write his name in history, and so he would start a war, and that war would be Christian Mercia against Christian East Anglia, and it would draw in the rest of Britain and there would be shield walls again.

Because there could not be peace, not while two tribes shared one land. One tribe must win. Even the nailed god cannot change that truth. And I was a warrior, and in a world at war the warrior must be cruel.

The fisherman had looked up and there had been pleading in his eyes, but the axe had fallen and he had gone to his sea grave. He would have betrayed me to Ælfric.

I told myself there would be an end to the cruelty. I had fought for Wessex all my life. I had given the nailed god his victories, and the nailed god had turned around and spat in my face, so now I would go to Bebbanburg and, once I had captured it, I would stay there and let the two tribes fight. That was my plan. I would go home and I would stay at home and I would persuade Æthelflaed to join me, and then not even the nailed god could prise me out of Bebbanburg because that fortress is invincible.

And in the morning I told Finan how we would capture it.

He laughed when he heard. 'It could work,' he said.

'Pray to your god to send the right weather,' I said. I sounded gloomy, and no wonder. I wanted hard weather, ship-threatening weather, and instead the sky was suddenly blue and the air warm. The wind had turned light and southerly so that our sail flapped at times, losing all power and causing *Middelniht* to slop lazily in a sun-glittering sea. Most of my men were sleeping, and I was content to let them rest rather than take to the oars. We had steered well offshore and were alone under that empty sky.

Finan looked up to see where the sun was. 'This isn't the way to Bebbanburg,' he said.

'We're going to Frisia.'

'Frisia!'

'I can't go to Bebbanburg yet,' I explained, 'and I can't stay on the Northumbrian coast because Ælfric will discover we're here, so we must hide for a few days. We'll hide in Frisia.'

And so we crossed the sea to that strange place of islands and water and mudbanks and reeds and sand and driftwood, and of channels that shift in the night, and land that is there one day and not the next. It is a home for herons, for seals and for outcasts. It took us three days and two nights to make the crossing, and in the third day's dusk, when the sun had turned all the west into a cauldron of glowing fire, we crept into the islands with a man in our bows testing the depth by probing with an oar.

I had spent time here. It was in these shoals that I had ambushed Skirnir and watched him die, and in his hall on the island of Zegge I had discovered his paltry treasure. I had left his hall intact and we searched for it now, but the island had gone, washed out by the relentless tides, though we did find the crescent-shaped sand-bank where we had tricked Skirnir into dividing his forces, and so we beached *Middelniht* there and made a camp on the dunes.

I needed two things: a second ship and bad weather. I did not dare search for the ship because we were in waters where another man held sway, and if I took the ship too early that man would have time to seek me out and demand to know why I poached in his waters. He found us anyway, arriving on our second day in a long, low vessel rowed by forty men. His ship came fast and confident through the unmarked channel that twisted towards our refuge, then the prow grated on the sand as the steersman bellowed at the oarsmen to back water. A man leaped ashore; a big man with a face as broad and flat as a spade's blade and with a beard reaching to his waist. 'And who,' he bellowed cheerfully, 'are you?'

'Wulf Ranulfson,' I answered. I was sitting on a bleached drift-wood log and I did not bother to stand.

He paced up the beach. It was a warm day, but he wore a thick cloak, high boots, and a chain-mail hood. His hair was matted and long, hanging to his shoulders. He had a long-sword strapped at his waist and a tarnished silver chain half hidden by his beard. 'And who is Wulf Ranulfson?' he demanded.

'A traveller out of Haithabu,' I answered mildly, 'and on his way back there.'

'So why are you on one of my islands?'

'We're resting,' I said, 'and making repairs.'

'I charge for rest and repairs,' he said.

'And I don't pay,' I responded, still speaking softly.

'I am Thancward,' he boasted, as if he expected me to recognise the name. 'I have sixteen crews, and ships for all of them. If I say you pay, you pay.'

'And what payment do you want?'

'Enough silver to make two more links for this chain,' he suggested.

I stood slowly, lazily. Thancward was a big man, but I was taller and I saw the slight surprise on his face. 'Thancward,' I said, as if trying to remember the name. 'I have not heard of Thancward, and if he had sixteen ships why would Thancward come to this miserable beach himself? Why would he not send his men to run his paltry errand? And his ship has benches for fifty rowers, yet only forty are at the oars. Maybe Thancward has mislaid his men? Or perhaps he believes we're a trading ship? Perhaps he thinks he didn't need to bring many warriors because we're weak?'

He was no fool. He was just a pirate, and I suspected he had two or three ships, of which perhaps only the one he was using was seaworthy, but he was trying to make himself lord of these shoals so that any passing ship would pay him passage money. But to do that he needed men, and if he fought me then he would lose men. He smiled suddenly. 'You're not a trading ship?'

'No.'

'You should have said!' He managed to make his surprise sound genuine. 'Then welcome! You need supplies?'

'What do you have?'

'Ale?' he suggested.

'Turnips?' I countered. 'Cabbages? Beans?'

'I shall send them,' he said.

'And I shall pay for them,' I promised, and each of us was satisfied. He would receive a scrap of silver, and I would be left alone.

The weather stayed obstinately warm and calm. After that bleak, cold, wet summer there were three days of burning sun and small wind. Three days of practising sword-craft on the beach and three days of fretting because I needed bad weather. I needed a north wind and high seas. I needed the view from Bebbanburg's ramparts to be of chaos and white water, and the longer that sun shone on a limpid sea the more I worried that Father Byrnjolf might have sent another warning to Bebbanburg. I was fairly sure the priest had died when *Middelniht* crushed the fishing boat, but that did not mean he had not sent a second message by some trader travelling north on the old roads. That was unlikely, but it was a possibility and it gnawed at me.

But then on the fourth morning the north-eastern sky slowly filled with dark cloud. It did not pile up with a ragged edge, but made a line straight as a spear-shaft across the sky; one side of the line was a deep summer blue and the rest of the sky was dark as a pit. It was an omen, but of what I could not tell. The darkness spread, a shield wall of the gods advancing across the heavens, and I took the omen to mean that my gods, the northern gods, were bringing a great storm south. I stood on top of a dune and the wind was strong enough to blow the sand off the dune's crest and the sea was stirring into whitecaps and the breakers were seething white on the long shoals and I knew it was time to sail into the storm.

It was time to go home.

Weapons sharp and shields stout. Swords, spears and axes had been ground with whetstones, shields bound with leather or iron. We knew we were sailing to battle, but the first fight was against the sea.

She is a bitch, the sea. She belongs to Ran, the goddess, and Ran keeps a mighty net in which to snare men, and her nine daughters are the waves that drive ships into the snare. She is married to a giant, Ægir, but he is an indolent beast, preferring to lie drunk in the halls of the gods while his bitch-wife and her vicious daughters gather ships and men to their cold unloving breasts.

81

So I prayed to Ran. She must be flattered, she must be told she is lovely, that no creature in the sky or on the earth or beneath the earth can compare to her beauty, that Freyja and Eostre and Sigyn and all the other goddesses of the heavens are jealous of her beauty, and if you tell her that over and over again she will reach for her polished silver shield to gaze at her own reflection, and when Ran looks upon herself the sea calms. And so I told the bitch of her loveliness, how the gods themselves shuddered with desire when she walked by, how she dimmed the stars, how she was the most beautiful of all the gods.

Yet Ran was bitter that night. She sent a storm out of the north-east, a storm that raced from the lands of ice and whipped the sea to anger. We had sailed westwards all day in a hard, lashing wind, and if that wind had lasted we would have been cold, wet and safe, but as night fell the wind increased, it howled and screamed, and we had to drop the sail and use the oars to hold *Middelniht*'s head towards the vicious seas that crashed about her prow, that reared in the darkness as unseen, white-topped monsters that heaved the hull up and then let it fall into a trough so that the timbers creaked, the hull strained and the water swirled about wet oarsmen. We bailed, hurling water over the side before the *Middelniht* was swallowed into Ran's net, and still the wind shrieked and the waters clawed at us. I had two men helping me on the steering oar, and there were times I thought it must break, and times I thought we were sinking, and I shouted my prayers to the bitch goddess and knew every man aboard was also praying.

The dawn showed chaos. Just grey light revealing white horrors on top of short, steep waves, and the light grew greyer to reveal a sea whipped to fury. Our faces stung from the spray, our bodies ached, we wanted nothing but sleep, but still we fought the sea. Twelve men rowed, three fought the loom of the steering oar, and the others used helmets and buckets to empty the boat of the water that crashed over the prow or poured over the side as the hull tipped or a wave suddenly rose like a beast from the deep. When we were at the peak of a wave I could see nothing but

82

turmoil, and then we would plunge into a swirling valley and the wind would vanish for a few heartbeats and the water would reach for us as the next sea roared from ahead and threatened to fall and break us.

I told that bitch Ran that she was beautiful, I told that sea-hag that she was the dream of men and the hope of gods, and perhaps she heard me and looked at her reflection in the silver shield because slowly, imperceptibly, the fury allayed. It did not die. The sea was still ragged ruin and the wind was like a madman, but the waves were lower and men could pause in their bailing, though the oarsmen still had to struggle to keep the bows headed into the anger. 'Where are we?' Finan asked. He sounded exhausted.

'Between the sea and the sky,' was all the answer I could give. I had a sunstone, which was a slab of glassy pale rock the size of a man's hand. Such stones come from the land of ice, and it had cost me precious gold, but by holding a sunstone to the sky and sweeping it from horizon to horizon, the stone will betray the sun's position behind the clouds, and when a man knows where the sun is, whether it is high or low, he can judge which way to travel. The sunstone glimmers when it looks toward the hidden sun, but that day the clouds were too dense and the rain too hard, and so the sunstone stayed sullen and mute. Yet I sensed the wind had shifted eastwards, and, around mid-morning, we half raised the sail and that snarling wind bellied the rope-strengthened cloth so that *Middelniht* raced ahead, crashing her prow into waves, but riding them now instead of fighting them. I blessed the Frisians who had built her, and I wondered how many men had gone to their wet graves that night, and then I turned *Middelniht*'s prow to what I thought was halfway between north and west. I needed to go north and west, always north and west, and I had no idea where we were, or which way to steer, except to follow the whisper of instinct that is a shipmaster's friend. It is a warrior's friend too, and as that day passed my mind wandered as a ship wanders in a ship-killing wind. I thought of battles long ago, of shield walls, of the fear, and of the prickling sense that an enemy is near, and I tried to find an omen in every cloud, every sea-bird, and every breaking wave. I thought of Bebbanburg, a fortress that had defied the Danes for all my lifetime, and the madness of planning to capture it with a small band of tired, wet, storm-beaten men, and I prayed to the Norns, those three goddesses who weave our fate at the foot of the world's tree, to send me a sign, an omen of success.

We sailed and I had no idea where we were, only that my weary men could sleep while I steered, and when I could stay awake no longer Finan took the oar and I slept like the dead. I woke at night and still that sea seethed and the wind screamed, and I struggled forward, past sleeping men and half-woken men, to stand beneath the dragon's head and peer into the darkness. I was listening rather than looking, listening for the sound of breakers crashing against the land, but all I could hear was the roar of water and wind. I shivered. My clothes were soaked, the wind was cold, I felt old.

The storm still blew in the early grey light, though nowhere near so fiercely as before, and I turned *Middelniht* west as if we fled the dawn. And the Norns loved us because we found land, though whether it was Northumbria or Scotland I had no idea. I was sure it was not East Anglia because I could see high rocky bluffs where breakers splintered into great gouts of spray. We turned northwards, and *Middelniht* battled the waves as we sought some place to rest from the sea's assault, and then at last we rounded a small headland and I saw a sheltered cove where the water shivered rather than broke and the cove was edged with a great long beach and the gods must have loved me because there was the ship I sought.

She was a trading ship, half *Middelniht*'s length, and she had been driven ashore by the storm, but the impact had not broken her. Instead she stood canted on the beach, and three men were trying to dig a channel through the sand to refloat her. They had already lightened their stranded ship because I could see the unloaded cargo heaped above the high-tide line, and nearby was a great driftwood fire where the crew must have warmed and dried themselves. That crew had seen us, and, as *Middelniht* drew closer, they backed away, retreating to some dunes that overlooked the beach. 'That's the ship we need,' I told Finan.

'Aye, she'll do well,' he said, 'and those poor bastards have done half the work of salvage already.'

The poor bastards had made a beginning, but it still took most of the day to wrestle the stranded ship off the sand and back into the water. I took twenty men ashore and we ended up emptying the ship of all her ballast, unstepping the mast, and then putting oars beneath the hull to lift her from the sand's sucking embrace. The impact of her stranding had sprung some of her planks, but we stuffed the seams with seaweed. She would leak like a sieve, but I did not need her to float for long. Just long enough to deceive Ælfric.

The crew of the ship found the courage to come back down to the beach while we were still digging the trenches that would let us slide the lifting oars beneath the hull. There were two men and a small boy, all Frisians. 'Who are you?' one of the men asked nervously. He was a big man, broad-shouldered, with the weather-worn face of a sailor. He carried an axe low in one hand, as if to demonstrate that he meant me no harm.

'I'm no one you know,' I said, 'and you are?'

'Blekulf,' he growled the name, then nodded at the ship, 'I built her.'

'You built her and I need her,' I said bluntly. I walked to where he had piled his cargo. There were four barrels in which glassware had been packed in straw, two barrels of copper nails, a small box of precious amber, and four heavy quern stones, shaped and finished. 'You can keep all this,' I said.

'For how long?' Blekulf asked sourly. 'What good is cargo without a ship?' He looked inland, though there was little to be seen except rain clouds hanging low over a bleak landscape. 'The bastards will strip me bare.'

'What bastards?' I asked.

'Scots,' he said. 'Savages.'

So that was where we were. 'Are we north or south of Foirthe?' I asked him.

'South,' he said, 'I think. We were trying to make the river when the storm came.' He shrugged.

'You were taking that cargo to Scotland?' I asked him.

'No, to Lundene. There were eight of us.'

'Eight crew?' I asked, surprised that so many had been aboard.

'Eight ships. As far as I know we're the only one left.'

'You did well to survive,' I said.

He had survived through good seamanship. He had realised the sudden storm was going to be brutal so he had taken the sail off the yard, split it so that it could be fitted around the mast, then used the nails from his cargo to fasten the sail to the ship's sides to fashion a makeshift deck. It had kept the small boat from being swamped, but made it almost impossible to row, and so he had been driven onto this long, lonely strand. 'There was a savage here this morning,' he said glumly.

'Just one?'

'He had a spear. He watched us, then went.'

'So he'll be coming back with his friends,' I said, then looked at the small boy who I reckoned was eight or nine years old. 'Your son?'

'My only son,' Blekulf said.

I called to Finan. 'Take the boy on board *Middelniht*,' I ordered him, then looked back to the Frisian. 'Your son is my hostage, and you're coming with me. If you do everything I say then I'll give you the ship back, with its cargo.'

'And what must I do?' he asked suspiciously.

'For a start,' I said, 'keep your ship safe through tonight.'

'Lord!' Finan called, and I turned to see him pointing northwards. A dozen men mounted on small ponies had appeared on the dunes. They carried spears. But we outnumbered them and they had the sense to keep their distance as we struggled to relaunch Blekulf's ship, which he said was named *Reinbôge*. It seemed an odd name to me.

'It rained all the time we built her,' he explained, 'and on the day we launched her there was a double rainbow.' He shrugged. 'My wife named her.'

We finally had the *Reinbôge* lifted and could move her. We chanted Ran's mirror song as we edged her down the beach and into the water. Finan went back aboard *Middelniht* and we fastened a line from the warship's stern to the *Reinbôge*'s bow, and towed the smaller ship clear of the breaking waves. Then we had to pile ballast and cargo back into her fat belly. We stepped the mast and tensioned it with braided leather lines. The pony-riders watched us, but did not try to interfere. They must have thought the stranded ship would be easy prey, but *Middelniht*'s arrival had spoiled their hopes, and, as dusk fell, they turned and rode away.

I left Finan to command *Middelniht*, while I sailed in *Reinbôge*. She was a good ship, taut and solid, though we needed to bail her constantly because of the sprung planks, but she rode the uneasy sea with competent ease. The wind dropped in the night. It still blew fiercely, but the anger was gone from the waves. The sea was now a confusion of scudding whitecaps that faded into the darkness as we rowed offshore. All night the wind blew, gusting sometimes, but never reaching the rage of the storm's height, and in the clouded dawn we set *Reinbôge*'s torn sail and surged ahead of *Middelniht*. We went southwards.

And at midday, under a torn sky and on a broken sea, we came to Bebbanburg.

That is where it all began, a lifetime ago.

I had been a child when I saw the three ships.

In my memory they slid from a bank of sea mist, and perhaps they did, but memory is a faulty thing and my other images of that day are of a clear, cloudless sky, so perhaps there was no mist, but it seemed to me that one moment the sea was empty and the next there were three ships coming from the south.

They had been beautiful vessels. They had appeared to rest weightless on the ocean, and when their oars dug into the waves they skimmed the water. Their prows and sterns curled high and were tipped with gilded beasts, with serpents and dragons, and on

87

that far-off summer's day I thought that the three boats danced on the water, propelled by the rise and fall of their silver winged oar banks. I had stared entranced. They had been Danish ships, the first of the thousands that came to ravage Britain.

'The devil's turds,' my father had growled.

'And may the devil swallow them,' my uncle had said. That was Ælfric, and that had been a lifetime ago. Now I sailed to meet my uncle again.

And what did Ælfric see on that morning when the storm was still grumbling and the wind whipping about the wooden ramparts of his stolen fortress? First he saw a small trading ship struggling southwards. The ship was under sail, but it was a sail torn to shreds and tatters that streamed off the yard. He saw two men trying to row the heavy hull, and every few moments they needed to stop rowing to bail water.

Or rather Ælfric's sentries saw the *Reinbôge* struggling. The current was against her and the ripped sail and twin oars were fighting against it. The men watching from Bebbanburg must have thought she was a tired, battered ship, low in the water and lucky to be afloat, and we made it look as if we were trying to round the shallows off Lindisfarena to bring her safe into the shelter of the shallow harbour behind the fortress. The sentries would have seen that attempt fail, and watched as the wind drove us southwards down the coast, past the high ramparts and through the treacherous gap between the shore and the bird-shrieking Farnea Islands, and all the time the foundering ship came closer to land where the sea exploded in high shattering foam until she vanished behind the southern headland. All that they would have seen, and those men watching from Bebbanburg would have guessed that the *Reinbôge* was being shipwrecked close to Bedehal.

That is what they saw. They saw two men struggling with long oars and a third man steering the ship, but they did not see the seven warriors hidden down with the cargo, all of whom were covered by cloaks. They would have seen plunder, not peril, and they were distracted because, not long after the *Reinbôge* passed their stronghold, they saw a second ship, the *Middelniht*, and she

88

was far more dangerous because the *Middelniht* was a warship, not a trading craft. She too was struggling. Men were bailing water, others were rowing, and the men on the high ramparts would see she had a depleted crew, that she only had ten oars, though those ten were enough to bring her safe around Lindisfarena and across the ragged water to the shallow entrance of the harbour behind Bebbanburg. So perhaps an hour after the *Reinbôge* disappeared, the *Middelniht* slid into Ælfric's harbour.

So Ælfric's men saw two ships. They saw two survivors of a terrible storm. They saw two ships seeking shelter. That was what Ælfric's men saw, and that was what I wanted them to see.

I was still on board *Reinbôge*, while Finan commanded *Middelniht*. He knew that once inside Bebbanburg's haven he would be questioned, but he had his answers ready. He would say they were Danes going south to East Anglia and were prepared to pay the Lord Ælfric for the privilege of shelter while they repaired their ship from the storm's ravages. The story would suffice. Ælfric would not question it, but doubtless he would demand a high payment, and Finan had gold coins ready. I did not think Ælfric would want anything more than money. He lived among Danes and, though they were his enemies, he gained nothing by provoking their anger. He would take the gold and lie quiet, and all Finan had to do was tell his tale, pay the coin, and wait. He would have anchored as close to the fortress entrance as he could, and his men would be sprawled in apparent weariness. None wore mail, none had a sword, though both mail and swords were close to hand.

So Finan waited.

And I let the *Reinbôge* drive up onto the beach south of Bedehal's headland and waited too.

It was now up to Ælfric, and he did just what I expected him to do. He sent his reeve to the *Middelniht* and the reeve took the gold coins and told Finan he could stay three days. He insisted that no more than four men could go ashore together, and none must carry weapons, and Finan agreed to it all. And while the reeve was dealing with *Middelniht*, my uncle would send men southwards to find the shipwrecked *Reinbôge*. Shipwrecks were profitable; there was timber, cargo, cordage and sailcloth to be had, and though any villagers nearby would be hungry for such a windfall they knew better than to interfere with the privileges of the man who ruled the great nearby fortress and who would claim the salvage rights.

So I waited in the stranded *Reinbôge*, touched the hammer about my neck and prayed to Thor, asking for success.

Some folk had appeared among the dunes to the north of the beach where the *Reinbôge* had driven ashore. There was a weather-beaten village at the sea's edge, inhabited mostly by fishermen whose small boats were sheltered from storms by a rill of rock that ran south from Bedehal's low headland, and some of those villagers watched, doubtless puzzled, as we unfastened the leather line that ran from the masthead to the *Reinbôge*'s stern. They could only see three of us. They watched as we lowered the mast, letting it fall across the boat with its ragged sail still attached. The tide was low, but rising, and the *Reinbôge* kept shifting and lurching up the beach as the waves pounded in.

Poor Blekulf was agonised over his boat, fearing that every impact on the sand would spring another leak or enlarge an existing one. 'I'll buy you another ship,' I said.

'I built her,' he answered gloomily, suggesting that no boat I bought him could ever be half as good as the one he had crafted himself.

'Then pray you built her well,' I said, and then told Osferth, who was hidden low in the *Reinbôge*'s hold, to take command. 'You know what to do.'

'I do, lord.'

'You stay here with Osferth,' I told Blekulf, then ordered Rolla, a vicious Dane, to choose his weapons and follow me. We jumped off the boat's stem and trudged up the beach and into the dunes. I carried Serpent-Breath. I knew the men coming from the fortress would arrive soon and that meant Serpent-Breath's moment was coming. The villagers must have seen us carry the swords up the beach, but they made no move towards us, nor towards the horsemen who came fast from the north.

I peered through wind-whipped dune grass and saw seven men on seven horses. They were all in mail, wore helmets and carried weapons. Their speed and the spiteful wind raised the seven riders' cloaks and blew the sand thrown up by the hooves. They were cantering, eager to get their errand done and so back to the fortress. It was beginning to rain, a stinging rain blown from the sea, and that was good. It would make the seven men even more eager to finish the business. It would make them careless.

The seven rode onto the beach. They saw a stranded ship with a fallen mast and a wind-ragged sail flapping uselessly. Rolla and I were moving now, crouching behind the dunes as we hurried northwards. No one could see us. We ran to the place where the horsemen had come through the dunes, the same path they would take back to the fortress, and we waited there, swords drawn, and I edged up a sandy slope and peered over the summit.

The seven horsemen reached *Reinbôge*, curbing their stallions just short of the seething waves that ran up the beach past the canted hull. Five of them dismounted. I could see them calling to Blekulf, who was the only man visible. He could have warned them, of course, but his son and crewman were both on board *Middelniht* and he feared for his boy's life and so he said nothing to betray us. Instead he told them he had been shipwrecked, nothing more, and the five men waded towards the ship. None had a drawn sword. The two horsemen waited on the beach, and then Osferth struck.

Seven of my men suddenly appeared, leaping over the *Reinbôge*'s bows with swords, axes and spears. The five men went down with appalling speed, hacked savagely with axe blows to the neck, while Osferth rammed a spear at the nearest horseman. That man turned away, escaping the thrust and spurred away from the sudden massacre that had left blood spreading in the swirling wave-froth. His companion dug in spurs and followed. 'Two of them,' I told Rolla, 'coming now.'

We crouched, one on either side of the path. I heard the hoof-beats coming nearer. Serpent-Breath was in my hand and anger in my soul. I had gazed at Bebbanburg as the *Reinbôge* had struggled

91

past and I had seen my inheritance, my fortress, my home, the place I had dreamed of since the day I left, the place stolen from me, and now I would take it back and slaughter the men who had usurped me.

And so I started my revenge. The leading horseman came into sight and I leaped at him, sword swinging, and his horse reared and twisted sideways so that my cut missed the rider entirely, but the horse was falling, its hooves throwing up gouts of sand, and the second horse crashed into the first and it too was going down and Rolla was gritting his teeth as his blade lunged up into the rider's chest. The horses, eyes white, struggled to their feet and I seized one set of reins, placed my foot on the fallen rider's chest and put Serpent-Breath at his throat.

'You fool,' the man said, 'don't you know who we are?'

'I know who you are,' I said.

Rolla had taken the second horse and now finished off its rider with a short, hard stab that sprayed the sand with blood. I looked back towards *Reinbôge* and saw that Osferth had captured the remaining five horses and that his men had hauled the corpses out of the shallow water and were stripping them of their mail, cloaks and helmets.

I bent down and unbuckled my captive's sword belt. I tossed it to Rolla, then told the man to stand. 'What's your name?' I asked.

'Cenwalh,' he muttered.

'Louder!'

'Cenwalh,' he said.

It began to rain harder, a malevolent heavy rain driving off the disturbed sea. And suddenly I laughed. It was insane. A small group of wet, desperate men against the grimmest fortress in Britain? I jabbed Serpent-Breath, driving Cenwalh back a pace. 'How many men in Bebbanburg?' I asked.

'Enough to kill you ten times over,' he snarled.

'That many? And how many is that?'

He did not want to answer, then thought he could deceive me. 'Thirty-eight,' he said.

I flicked my wrist so that the tip of Serpent-Breath's blade broke the skin of his neck. A bead of blood showed there, then trickled down beneath his mail. 'Now try the truth,' I said.

He put a hand to the trickle of blood. 'Fifty-eight,' he said sullenly.

'Including you and these men?'

'Including us.'

I judged he was telling the truth. My father had kept a garrison of between fifty and sixty men and Ælfric would be reluctant to have more because each housecarl had to be armed, given mail, fed and paid. If Ælfric had warning of real danger then he could summon more men from the land Bebbanburg ruled, but raising that force would take time. So we were outnumbered by about two to one, but I had expected nothing less.

Osferth and his men reached us, leading the five horses and carrying the clothes, mail, helmets and weapons of the men they had killed. 'Did you notice which man was riding which horse?' I asked him.

'Of course, lord,' Osferth replied, turning to look at his men and their captured horses, 'brown cloak on the brindled stallion, blue cloak on the black gelding, leather jerkin on the . . .' He hesitated.

'On the piebald mare,' my son carried on, 'the black cloak was on the smaller black stallion and . . .'

'Then change,' I interrupted them, and looked back to Cenwalh. 'You, undress.'

'Undress?' He gaped at me.

'You can take your clothes off,' I said, 'or we can strip your corpse. You choose.'

There had been seven horsemen, so the guards on Bebbanburg's gate must see seven horsemen return. Those guards would be totally familiar with the seven men, they would see them and their horses day after day, and so when we rode to the fortress those guards must see what they expected to see. If Cenwalh's brown and white striped cloak was draped over the rump of the wrong horse then the guards would sense something was wrong, but if they saw that cloak on a rider mounted on Cenwalh's tall chestnut stallion they would assume life was going on as it always did.

We changed clothes. Cenwalh, reduced to a woollen shirt that hung to his arse, shivered in the cold wind. He was staring at me, watching as I put a stranger's pale blue cloak over my mail coat. He saw me push Thor's hammer beneath the mail to hide it. He had heard Osferth call me 'lord', and he was slowly realising who I was. 'You're . . .' he began, then paused. 'You're . . .' he started again.

'I am Uhtred Uhtredson,' I snarled, 'the rightful Lord of Bebbanburg. You want to swear loyalty to me now?' I hung a dead man's heavy silver cross around my neck. The helmet would not fit me, it was far too small, so I kept my own, but the cloak had a hood that I pulled up over the silver wolf that crested my helmet. I strapped my own sword belt round my waist. It would be hidden by the cloak and I wanted Serpent-Breath as my companion.

'You are Uhtred the Treacherous,' Cenwalh said tonelessly.

'Is that what he calls me?'

'That and worse,' Cenwalh said.

I took Cenwalh's sword from Rolla and drew it from the scabbard. It was a good blade, well kept and sharp. 'My uncle lives?' I asked Cenwalh.

'He lives.'

'Lord,' Osferth chided Cenwalh, 'you call him "lord".'

'Ælfric must be old,' I said, 'and I hear he is sick?'

'He lives,' Cenwalh said, stubbornly refusing to call me lord.

'And he ails?'

'An old man's ailments,' Cenwalh said dismissively.

'And his sons?' I asked.

'The Lord Uhtred has the command,' Cenwalh said. He meant my cousin, Uhtred, son of Ælfric and father of yet another Uhtred.

'Tell me of Ælfric's son,' I said.

'He looks like you,' Cenwalh replied, making it sound an ill fortune.

'And what would he expect of you?' I asked him.

'Expect of me?'

'He sent seven of you. To do what?'

He frowned, not understanding the question, then flinched as

I brought the blade close to his face. He glanced towards the *Reinbôge*, which was still being pounded by surf as the rising tide drove her up the beach. 'We came to look at her,' he said sullenly.

'And you found us instead,' I said, 'but what would you have done if we hadn't been here?'

'Secured her,' he said, still looking at the stranded ship.

'And emptied her cargo? Who would have done that? You?'

'Plenty of men in the village,' he said.

So Cenwalh would have made certain the *Reinbôge* was properly stranded at high tide, then forced the villagers to empty her cargo. That meant he would have left men to make sure the work was done properly and that none of the valuables was stolen, and that in turn meant that the fortress would not expect to see seven men returning. I thought for a few moments. 'And if she was carrying nothing but ballast?' I asked.

He shrugged. 'Depends whether she's worth saving. She looks well built.'

'In which case you'd secure her, then leave her till the weather calms?'

He nodded. 'And if Lord Ælfric doesn't want her? We would break her up, or sell her.'

'Now tell me about the fortress,' I said.

He told me nothing I did not know. The Low Gate was approached by a road that snaked over the narrow neck of land and climbed steeply to the big wooden arch, and beyond that gate was the wide space where the stables and blacksmith's forge were built. That outer yard was protected by a high palisade, but the inner space, which occupied the high rocky summit, had another wall, even higher, and a second gate, the High Gate. It was there, on the peak of the rock, that Ælfric had his great hall and where smaller halls served as living quarters for the housecarls and their families. The key to Bebbanburg was not the Low Gate, formidable though it was, but the High Gate.

'The High Gate,' I asked, 'is it kept open?'

'It's closed,' Cenwalh said defiantly, 'it's always closed, and he's expecting you.'

I looked at him. 'Expecting me?'

'The Lord Ælfric knows your son became a priest, he knows you were outlawed. He thinks you'll come north. He thinks you're mad. He says you have nowhere to go so you'll come here.'

And Ælfric was right, I thought. A gust of wind brought a hard spatter of heavy rain. The surf seethed around *Reinbôge*. 'He knows nothing,' I said angrily, 'and won't know it till my sword is in his gullet.'

'He'll kill you,' Cenwalh sneered.

And Rolla killed him. I nodded to the Dane who was standing behind the shivering Cenwalh, who knew nothing of his death until it surprised him. The sword took him in the neck, a massive, killing, merciful blow. He crumpled to the sand.

'Mount,' I growled at my men.

Seven of us were mounted, three others would walk as though they were prisoners.

And so I went home.

Five

There will be an end to the killing.

That is what I told myself as I rode towards Bebbanburg, towards my home. There will be an end to the killing. I would slaughter my way into the fortress, then close its gates and let the world squabble its way to chaos and back, but I would be at peace inside those high wooden walls. I would let the Christians and pagans, Saxons and Danes fight each other till there was not one left standing, but inside Bebbanburg I would live like a king and persuade Æthelflaed to be my queen. Merchants travelling the coast road would pay us taxes, ships passing would pay for the privilege, and the coins would pile up and we would let life slip by.

When hell freezes over.

Father Pyrlig was fond of that saying. I missed Pyrlig. He was one of the good Christians, even though he was a Welshman, and after Alfred's death he had returned to Wales where, for all I knew, he still lived. He had been a warrior once, and I thought how he would have relished this impudent attack. Nine men against Bebbanburg. I did not count Blekulf, the owner of *Reinbôge*, though he walked with us. I had given him the choice of staying beside his beloved and beleaguered ship, but he feared the villagers and feared for his son and so he walked behind the horses.

Nine men. My son was one. Then there was Osferth, faithful Osferth who would have been a king had his mother been married to his father. I often thought Osferth disapproved of me, just as his father Alfred had, but he had stayed loyal when so many others had scurried away in fear. There was one other Saxon. Swithun was a West Saxon, named for one of their favourite saints, though this Swithun was anything but saintly. He was a tall, cheerful, quick-tempered young man with a mass of fair hair, innocent blue eyes, a ready laugh, and the swift fingers of a thief. He had been brought to me for justice by villagers tired of his crimes. They wanted me to brand him, maybe cut off a hand, but he had challenged me to fight instead and, amused, I gave him a sword. He was easy to beat, because he was untrained, but he had been strong and almost as fast as Finan, and I had pardoned his crimes on condition he swore loyalty and became my man. I liked him.

Rolla was a Dane. He was tall, sinewy and scarred. He had served another lord, one he never named, and he had fled that service, breaking his oath, because the lord had sworn to kill him. 'What did you do?' I asked him when he came and begged to give me his oath.

'His wife,' he said.

'Not a clever thing to do,' I had said.

'But enjoyable.'

He was weasel-fast in a fight, vicious and merciless, a man who had seen horrors and become accustomed to them. He worshipped the old gods, but had taken himself a plump little Christian wife who was with Sigunn in Lundene. Rolla frightened most of my men, but they admired him, and none more than Eldgrim, a young Dane whom I'd discovered drunk and naked in a Lundene alley. He had been robbed and beaten. He had a roundly innocent face and thick brown curls, and women adored him, but he was inseparable from Kettil, the third Dane who rode with me that day. Kettil, like Eldgrim, was perhaps eighteen or nineteen and thin as a harp string. He looked fragile, but that was deceptive because he was quick in a fight and strong behind a shield. A handful of my more foolish men had mocked Kettil and Eldgrim for their friendship, which went far beyond mere liking, but I had placed the hazel rods in Fagranforda's yard and incited the mockers to fight either of them, sword on sword, and the hazel rods had gone unused and the mockery had died.

Two Frisians rode from Bedehal to Bebbanburg. Folcbald was slow as an ox, but stubborn as a mule. Put Folcbald behind a shield and he was immovable. He was hugely strong and very slow of wit, but he was loyal and worth any two other men in a shield wall. Wibrund, his cousin, was excitable, easily bored and quarrelsome, but he was useful in a fight and unwearying behind an oar.

So we nine, accompanied by Blekulf, went to Bebbanburg. We followed the track that led north from Bedehal, and to our right were sand dunes while to our left was soggy farmland stretching to the dark inland hills. The rain was heavier, though the wind was dying. Osferth spurred his horse to ride beside me. He was wearing a heavy black cloak with a hood that concealed his face, but I saw the wry smile he offered me. 'You promised life would be interesting,' he said.

'I did?'

'All those years ago,' he said, 'when you rescued me from the priesthood.' His father had wanted his bastard son made into a priest, but Osferth had chosen the way of the warrior.

'You could finish your training,' I suggested, 'I'm sure they'd make you into one of their wizards.'

'They're not wizards,' he said patiently.

I grinned; it was always so easy to tease Osferth. 'You'd have been a good priest,' I told him, no longer teasing, 'and probably a bishop by now.'

He shook his head. 'No, perhaps an abbot, though?' He grimaced. 'An abbot of some remote monastery, trying to grow wheat in a swamp and saying prayers.'

'Of course you'd be a bishop,' I said savagely, 'your father was a king!'

He shook his head more forcibly. 'I am my father's sin. He would have wanted me far out of the way, hidden in that swamp where no one could see his sin.' He made the sign of the cross. 'I'm the child of sin, lord, and that means I'm doomed.'

'I've heard madmen make more sense than you,' I said. 'How can you worship a god who condemns you for your father's sin?'

'We can't choose gods,' he said gently, 'there is only one.'

That is such nonsense! How can one god look after the whole world? One god for every plover, kingfisher, otter, wren, fox, lapwing, deer, horse, mountain, spinney, perch, swallow, weasel, willow or sparrow? One god for every stream, every river, every beast or every man? I had said as much to Father Beocca once. Poor Father Beocca, dead now, but like Pyrlig, another good priest. 'You don't understand! You don't understand!' he had answered excitedly. 'God has a whole army of angels to take care of the world! There are seraphim, cherubim, principalities, powers and dominions all around us!' He had waved a crippled hand. 'There are unseen angels, Uhtred, all about us! God's winged servants watch over us. They even see the smallest sparrow fall!'

'And what do the angels do about the falling sparrow?' I had asked him, but Beocca had no answer to that.

I hoped the low dark clouds and beating rain would hide Bebbanburg from any watching angels. My uncle and cousin were Christians, so the angels might protect them, if such magical winged creatures even exist. Perhaps they do. I believe in the Christian god, but I do not believe he is the only god. He is a jealous, sullen, solitary creature who hates the other gods and conspires against them. Sometimes, when I think about him, I see him as being like Alfred, except Alfred had some decency and kindness, but Alfred never stopped working or thinking or worrying. The Christian god also never stops working and planning. My gods like to loll in the feasting-hall or take their goddesses to bed, they are drunk, dissolute and happy, and while they feast and fornicate, the Christian god is capturing the world.

A gull flew across our path and I tried to judge whether its flight was a good or a bad omen. Osferth would have denied any omen, but he was deep in gloom. He believed that because he was a bastard he was beyond his wretched god's salvation, and that the curse would last through ten generations. He believed it because

100

the Christian's holy book preached it. 'You're thinking about death,' I accused him.

'Every day,' he said, 'but today more than most.'

'You have omens?'

'Fears, lord,' he said, 'just fears.'

'Fears?'

He laughed grimly. 'Look at us! Nine men!'

'And Finan's men,' I said.

'If he gets ashore,' Osferth said pessimistically.

'He will,' I said.

'Perhaps it's just the weather,' Osferth said. 'It's hardly cheerful.'

But the weather was on our side. Men keeping watch from a fortress grow bored. Standing guard is to endure day after day after yet another day of little happening, of the same coming and goings, and a man's senses grow dull under the weight of such a routine. It is worse at night, or in foul weather. This rain would make Bebbanburg's sentinels miserable, and cold wet men make bad sentries.

The road dropped slightly. To my left were stacks of hay piled in a small pasture and I noted with approval the thick layer of bracken beneath each stack. My father used to get angry with the ceorls who did not use enough bracken beneath their haystacks. 'You want rats, you fart-brained idiots?' he would shout at them. 'You want the hay to rot? You want silage instead of hay? Do you know nothing, you piss-for-brains fools?' In truth he knew little about farming himself, but he did know that a foundation of bracken stopped the damp rising and deterred the rats, and he enjoyed displaying that small scrap of knowledge. I smiled at the memory. Perhaps, when I ruled again from Bebbanburg, I could afford to get angry about haycocks. A small black and white dog barked from a hovel, then ran at the horses who, evidently accustomed to the animal, ignored it. A man put his head through the hovel's low opening and snarled at the dog to be silent, then bowed his head in acknowledgement of our presence. The road climbed again, only a few feet, but as we reached the crest there, suddenly, was Bebbanburg.

Ida, my ancestor, had sailed from Frisia. Family lore said he brought three boats of hungry warriors, and he had landed somewhere on this wild coast and the natives retreated to a wooden-walled fort built atop the long rock that lay between the bay and the sea, and that was the rock that became Bebbanburg. Ida, who was called the Flamebearer, burned their wooden wall and slaughtered them all, soaking the rock in blood. He piled their skulls to face the land as a warning to others what would happen if they dared attack the new fortress he made on the bloody rock. He had captured it, he kept it, and he ruled all the land within a day's hard riding from its new high walls, and his kingdom was called Bernicia. His grandson, King Æthelfrith, scourged all of northern Britain, driving the natives to the wild hills, and he took a wife, Bebba, after whom his great fortress was named.

And now it was mine. We no longer had a kingdom, because Bernicia, like other small kingdoms, had been swallowed into Northumbria, but we still had Bebba's great fortress. Or rather Ælfric held the fortress, and on that cold, grey, dark, wet morning I rode to retake it.

It loomed, or perhaps that was my imagination because the image of the fortress had been in my heart since the day I left it. The rock on which Bebbanburg is built runs as a ridge north and south, so from the south it does not look vast. Closest to us was the outer wall made of great oak trunks, but where the wall was most vulnerable, in places where dips in the rock allowed men to get close, the lower portion had been remade in stone. That was new since my father's day. The Low Gate was an arch with a fighting platform above, and that gate was Bebbanburg's best defence because it could only be approached along a narrow path that followed the sandy spit from the mainland. The spit was wide enough, but then the dark rock erupted from the sand and the path became narrow as it climbed to that massive gateway, which was still decorated with men's skulls. I do not know if they are the same skulls that Ida the Flamebearer had flensed of flesh in a cauldron of boiling water, but they were certainly ancient and they bared their yellow teeth in a warning to would-be attackers. The

102

Low Gate was Bebbanburg's most vulnerable place, but it was still daunting. Hold that Low Gate and Bebbanburg was safe unless men landed from the sea to assault the higher walls, and that was a daunting prospect because the rock was steep and the walls high, and the defenders could rain spears, boulders and arrows down onto the attackers.

Yet even if an assault took the Low Gate they would still not have captured the fortress because that skull-hung arch led only to the lower courtyard. I could see the roofs above the wall. There were stables, storerooms and the smithy in that lower courtyard. Dark smoke came from the smithy, blowing inland with the rain-heavy wind. Beyond it the rock loomed again, and on its summit was the inner wall, higher than the outer, reinforced with great stone blocks and pierced by another formidable gateway. Beyond that High Gate was the fortress proper where the great hall was built and where more smoke showed above the hall roof over which the banner of my family flew. The wolf standard flapped sullen in that wet wind. That banner made me angry. It was my standard, my emblem, and my enemy was flying it, but I was the wolf that day and I had come back to my lair.

'Slouch!' I told my men.

We must ride like tired, bored men, and so we slumped in our saddles, letting the slow horses find their own way on a path they knew better than any of us. I knew it, though. I had spent my first ten years here and I knew the path and the rock and the beach and the harbour and the village. The fortress reared above us, and to its left was the wide and shallow sea-lake that was Bebbanburg's harbour. That harbour was entered by a channel north of the fortress, and, once inside, a boat had to take care not to be stranded. I could see *Middelniht* now. There were a half-dozen smaller boats, fishing craft, and two ships as large or larger than *Middelniht*, though none of those boats appeared to have any crew aboard. Finan would have seen us by now.

Beyond the harbour, where the hills rose, was the small village where fishermen and farmers lived. There was a tavern there, and another smithy, and a shingle beach where fires smoked beneath racks of drying fish. As a small child I had been given the job of chasing the gulls away from the fish-racks, and I could see children there now. I smiled, because this was home, and then stopped smiling because the fortress was close now. The path divided, one branch going west to circle the lower harbour to reach the village, the other climbing towards the Low Gate.

And that gate was open. They suspected nothing. I guessed the gate was always open in daylight, just like a town gate. The sentries would have plenty of time to see an approaching threat and close the massive gates, but all they saw on that wet morning was what they expected to see and so none of them moved from the high fighting platform.

Finan and three men jumped off the *Middelniht*'s bow and started wading to the shore. So far as I could see they had no weapons, though that did not matter as we all carried our own and the ones we had captured. I assumed, rightly, that Finan had been told how many men could come ashore at any time, and that such men must be unarmed. I wished for more than four, because now we were thirteen, not counting Blekulf, and thirteen is a bad omen. Everyone knows that, and even the Christians allow that thirteen is bad. The Christians claim that thirteen is unlucky because Judas was the thirteenth guest at the last supper, but the real reason is that Loki, the malevolent murdering trickster god, is the thirteenth deity in Asgard.

'Folcbald!' I called.

'Lord?'

'When we reach the gate you're to stay under the arch with Blekulf.'

'I'm to stay . . .' He did not understand. He expected to fight and I was telling him to stay behind. 'You want me to . . .'

'I want you to stay with Blekulf!' I interrupted him. 'Keep him under the arch until I tell you to join us.'

'Yes, lord,' he said. Now we were twelve.

Finan was ignoring me. He was some fifty paces away, trudging slowly towards the fortress. We were closer to the Low Gate, much closer, and our horses began to climb the shallow slope and the vast skull-hung arch was looming now. I kept my head down and let my stallion amble. Someone called something from the gate-house summit, but the wind and rain snatched the words away. It sounded like a greeting and I just waved a tired hand in answer. We left the sandy track and the hooves clattered on the path that had been cut through the dark rock. The hoofbeats sounded loud, like a great war-rhythm. Still the horses ambled and I slouched in the saddle and kept my head low and then the gloom of the day was suddenly darker still and the rain no longer beat on my hooded cloak and I glanced up to see that we were in the gate tunnel.

I was home.

I was carrying Cenwalh's sword concealed beneath the heavy cloak, but now I let it drop so that Finan would have a weapon. My men did the same, the weapons falling loud on the stone roadway. My horse shied from the sound, but I caught him and ducked my head beneath the heavy wooden beam that formed the inner arch.

The Low Gate had been left open, but that made sense because there would be constant coming and going in the daytime. A heap of baskets and woven bags lay just inside the gate, left there for the villagers who brought fish or bread to the fortress. The gate would be closed at dusk, and guarded day and night, but the High Gate, Cenwalh had told me, was kept closed. And that made sense too. An enemy could capture the Low Gate and all the courtyard beyond, but unless he could take the High Gate and its formidable stone-reinforced rampart he would still be no nearer to capturing Bebbanburg.

And as I rode out from beneath the inner arch I saw that the High Gate was open.

For a heartbeat I did not believe what I saw. I had expected a frantic and sudden fight to capture that gate, but it was open! There were guards on the platform above it, but none in the archway itself. I felt I was in a dream. I had ridden into Bebbanburg and not one man had challenged me, and the fools had left the inner gate wide open! I checked my horse and Finan caught up with me.

'Get the rest of the crew ashore,' I told him.

Off to my right there was a group of men practising shield drill. There were eight of them under the command of a squat, bearded man who was shouting at them to overlap their shields. They were youngsters, probably boys from the local farms who would be required to fight if Bebbanburg's land was attacked. They were using old swords and battered shields. The man teaching them glanced our way and saw nothing to alarm him. In front of me was the wide open High Gate, just a hundred or so paces away, while to my left was the smithy with its dark smoke. Two guards armed with spears slouched by the smithy door. A man called down from the gate above me. 'Cenwalh!' he called, and I ignored him. 'Cenwalh!' he called again, and I waved a hand, and that response seemed to satisfy him because he said nothing more. It was time to fight. My men were waiting for the signal, but for a moment I seemed suspended in disbelief. I was home! I was inside Bebbanburg, and then my son spurred his horse beside me.

'Father?' he asked, sounding worried.

It was time to unleash the fury. I touched my heels to the horse, which immediately went to the left, following its regular path to the stables that lay close to the smithy. I pulled the rein, heading it for the High Gate.

And the dogs saw me.

There were two of them, great shaggy wolfhounds who were sleeping under a crude wooden shelter where hay was stored beside the stables. One saw us and uncurled himself and loped towards us with his tail wagging. Then he stopped, suddenly wary and I saw his teeth bared. He snarled, then howled. The second dog woke fast. Both were howling now and racing towards me, and my horse shied away violently.

The squat man who was training the boys was efficient. He knew something was wrong and he did the right thing. He bellowed at the guards on the High Gate, 'Shut it! Shut it now!'

I kicked the horse towards the gate, but the two dogs were in its face. Perhaps they had been Cenwalh's hounds because they alone in all the fortress had realised something was wrong. They knew I was not Cenwalh. One leaped as if to bite my horse and I drew Serpent-Breath as the stallion snapped its teeth at the hound. 'Ride for the gate!' I shouted at my men.

'Close it!' the squat man bellowed.

A horn sounded. I kicked the horse past the hounds, but it was already too late. The huge gates were being pulled shut and I heard the crash of the locking bar falling into its brackets. I cursed uselessly. Men were appearing on the rampart above the High Gate, too many men. They would be twenty feet above me and it was hopeless to try and assault that vast wooden arch. My only hope had been to take the gate by surprise, but the hounds had prevented that.

The squat man ran towards me. The sensible thing to do now was to retreat, to realise that I had lost and, while there was still time, flee through the Low Gate and run to *Middelniht*, but I was reluctant to give up so easily. My men had paused in the centre of the courtyard, unsure what to do, and the squat man was shouting at me, demanding to know who I was, and the hounds were still howling and my horse was skittering sideways to escape them. More dogs were barking from the inner fortress. 'Take the gate!' I called to Osferth, pointing at the Low Gate. If I could not capture the inner rampart I would at least hold the outer one. The rain was slanting across the fortress, driven by the sea wind. The two guards by the smithy had their spears levelled, but neither had moved towards me, and Finan now led two of his men towards them.

I could not watch what happened to Finan because the squat man had seized my bridle. 'Who are you?' he demanded. The dogs calmed, perhaps because they recognised the man. 'Who are you?' he asked again. His eight youngsters watched wide-eyed, their shields and practice swords forgotten. 'Who are you?' he shouted at me a third time, then swore. 'Christ, no!'

He was looking towards the smithy. I glanced that way and saw Finan had begun the killing. The two guards were on the ground, though Finan and his men had vanished, and then I kicked my feet from the stirrups and slid from the saddle.

I was doing everything wrong. I was confused. Confusion is inevitable in battle, but indecision is unforgivable, and I had hesitated to make any decision and then made all the wrong ones. I should have withdrawn fast, instead I had been reluctant to abandon Bebbanburg so I had allowed Finan to slaughter the two guards. I had sent Osferth to capture the Low Gate and that meant I had men in and around that archway and more men in the smithy, while the crew of the *Middelniht* was presumably still wading ashore, but I was isolated in the courtyard where the squat man chopped at me with his sword. And still I did the wrong thing. Instead of calling Finan and trying to get all my men into one place, I parried the hard blow with Serpent-Breath and, almost without thinking, drove the man back with two hard strikes, took a pace back to let him attack and, as he took the bait and came forward, I lunged into his belly with the blade. I felt the blade burst the mail links, I felt it puncture leather and slide into softness. He shuddered as I twisted Serpent-Breath in his guts, then he staggered down to his knees. He fell forward when I jerked the blade out of his belly. Two of his youngsters started towards me, but I turned on them, my sword red. 'You want to die?' I snarled, and they stopped. I had pushed the hood away from my crested helmet and closed the cheek-pieces. They were boys and I was a warlord.

And I was a fool because I had done everything wrong. And then the High Gate opened.

Men poured through. Men in mail, men with swords, men with spears and shields. I lost count at twenty, and still they came.

'Lord!' Osferth called from the Low Gate. He had captured it and I could see my son up on the high fighting platform. 'Lord!' Osferth called again. He wanted me to back away, to join him, but instead I looked to the smithy where the two guards lay in the rain. There was no sign of Finan.

And then the spears and blades crashed on shields and I saw my uncle's forces had made a shield wall in front of the High Gate. There were at least forty men there and they were beating their blades rhythmically on the willow boards. They were confident, and led by a tall man with fair hair who wore mail, but no helmet. He carried no shield, just a drawn sword. The shield wall was crammed on the roadway between the rocks, just twelve men wide. My own crew was arriving now, coming through the Low Gate and making a wall of their own, but I knew I had lost. I could attack, and we might even fight our way uphill into those tight ranks, but we would have to hack and lunge for every inch, and above us, on the High Gate's fighting platform, there were men ready to hurl spears and rocks onto our heads. And even if we did force the passage, the gates were now closed again. I had lost.

The tall man at the front of the enemy snapped his fingers and a servant brought him a helmet and cloak. He donned both, took the sword back and walked slowly towards me. His men stayed behind. The two hounds who had caused all the trouble ran to him, and he snapped his fingers again to make them lie down. He stopped some twenty paces from me, holding his sword low. It was an expensive blade, its hilt heavy with gold and the blade shimmering with the same swirling patterns that glistened on Serpent-Breath's rain-cleansed steel. He looked at the horses we had been riding. 'Where is Cenwalh?' he asked. And, when I said nothing, added, 'Dead, I suppose?' I nodded. He shrugged. 'My father said you'd come.'

So this was Uhtred, my cousin, the Lord Ælfric's son. He was some years younger than me, but I could have been looking at myself. He had not inherited his father's dark looks and narrow build, but was burly, fair and arrogant. He had a short beard, fair in colour and trimmed close, and his eyes were very blue. His helmet was crested with a wolf, like mine, but his cheek-pieces were chased with gold inlay. His cloak was black and edged with wolf-fur. 'Cenwalh was a good man,' he said. 'Did you kill him?' I still said nothing. 'Lost your tongue, Uhtred?' he sneered.

'Why waste words on a goat's turd?' I asked.

'My father always says that a dog returns to its vomit, which is how he knew you would come here. Maybe I should welcome you? I do! Welcome, Uhtred!' He offered me a mocking bow. 'We have ale, we have meat, we have bread: will you eat with us in the high hall?'

'Why don't you and I fight here,' I said, 'just you and I?'

'Because I outnumber you,' he said easily, 'and if we are to fight then I'd rather slaughter you all, not just give your guts to my dogs.'

'Then fight,' I said aggressively. I turned and pointed to my crew whose shield wall guarded the Low Gate. 'They're holding your entrance. You can't get out until you defeat us, so fight.'

'And how will you hold the entrance when you find a hundred men behind you?' Ælfric's son asked. 'By tomorrow morning, Uhtred, you will find the causeway blocked. You have enough food, perhaps? There's no well out here, but you brought water or ale?'

'Then fight me now,' I said, 'show me you have some bravery.'

'Why fight you when you're already beaten?' he asked, then raised his voice so my men could hear him. 'I offer you life! You may leave here! You can go to your ship and leave! We shall do nothing to hinder you! All I demand is that Uhtred stays here!' He smiled at me. 'You see how eager we are for your company? You are family, after all, you must let us welcome you properly. Is your son with you?'

I hesitated, not because I doubted my answer, but because he had said son and not sons. So he knew what had happened, knew I had disowned my eldest.

'Of course he is,' Ælfric's son said, and raised his voice again. 'Uhtred will stay here, as will his whelp! The rest of you are free to leave! But if you choose to stay then you will never leave!'

He was trying to turn my men against me and I doubted it would work. They were sworn to me and, even if they wished to take his offer, they would not break their oaths so easily. If I died, then some would bend the knee, but right now none wanted to show disloyalty in front of their companions. Ælfric's son also knew that, but his offer was really intended to take away my crew's confidence. They knew I was beaten and were waiting to see what I decided to do before they made any choice.

110

My cousin looked at me. 'Drop your sword,' he commanded.

'I shall bury her in your belly,' I said.

It was a pointless defiance. He had won, I had lost, but there was still a chance we could reach *Middelniht* and escape the harbour, but I dared not lead my men back to the shore until Finan and his two men had reappeared. Where was he? I could not abandon him, not ever. We were closer than brothers, Finan and I, and he had vanished into the smithy and I feared he and his two men had been overwhelmed and were lying dead or, worse, were already taken captive.

'You will find,' my cousin said, 'that our men are lethal. We train, as you do, we practise, as you do. It is why we still hold Bebbanburg, because not even the Danes want to feel our blades. If you fight then I shall regret the men I will lose, but I promise that you will pay for their deaths. Your own death won't be quick, Uhtred, and you won't have a sword in your hand. I shall kill you slowly, in exquisite pain, but not till I have done the same to your son. You will watch him die first. You will hear him call for his dead mother. You will hear him beg for mercy and there will be none. Is that what you want?' He paused, waiting for an answer that I did not give him. 'Or you can drop the sword now,' he went on, 'and I promise you both a swift and painless death.'

I was still hesitating, still indecisive. Of course I knew what to do, I knew I should take my men back to *Middelniht*, but I dared not do that while Finan was still missing. I wanted to look at the smithy, but did not want to draw my cousin's attention to it, so I just stared at him and, as my mind raced, and as I tried to find some other way out of this defeat, I suddenly sensed that he was nervous too. It did not show. He looked magnificent in his black cloak, and with his wolf-crowned helmet incised with Christian crosses, and holding his blade that was as formidable as Serpent-Breath, but beneath that confidence there was a fear. I had not seen it at first, but it was there. He was tense.

'Where's your father?' I asked. 'I'd like him to see you die.'

'He will watch you die,' cousin Uhtred said. Had he bridled at my question? My sense of his discomfort was slight, but it was there. 'Drop your sword,' he ordered me again and in a much firmer voice.

'We shall fight,' I said just as firmly.

'So be it.' He accepted the decision calmly. So it was no fear of fighting that made him nervous, and perhaps I had misjudged him? Perhaps there was no uncertainty in him. He turned to his men. 'Keep Uhtred alive! You will slaughter the rest, but keep Uhtred and his son alive!' He walked away, not bothering to look back at me.

And I walked back to the Low Gate where my crew was waiting with their shields overlapping and weapons ready. 'Osferth!'

'Lord?'

'Where's Finan?'

'He went to the smithy, lord.'

'I know that!' I hoped that Finan might have left the smithy and that I had not seen him leave, but Osferth confirmed he had not come out. So three of my men were inside that dark building, and I feared they were dead, that other guards had been inside and had overwhelmed them, but if that was the case why had those guards not appeared at the smithy door? I wanted to send men to discover Finan's fate, but that would weaken my already weak shield wall.

And my cousin's men had begun beating their shields again. They were beating a rhythm with steel on wood, and they were advancing.

'In a moment,' I spoke to my men, 'we'll make the swine's horn. Then we'll break them.'

It was my only hope. The swine's horn was a wedge of men that would charge the enemy's shield wall like a wild boar. We would go fast and the hope was that we could pierce their wall, break it and so begin to slaughter them. That was the hope, but the fear was that the swine's horn would crumple. 'Uhtred!' I called.

'Father?'

'You should take a horse and ride now. Ride south. Keep riding till you reach friends. Keep our family alive and come back one day and take this fortress.'

112

'If I die here,' my son said, 'then I'll hold this fortress till Judgement Day.'

I had expected that answer, or something like it, and so I did not argue. Even if he rode south I doubted he would reach safety. My uncle would send men in pursuit, and between Bebbanburg and Saxon-ruled Britain there was nothing but enemies. Still, I had offered him the chance. Perhaps, I thought, my eldest son, the priestly son who was no longer my son, would marry and have children, and one of those sons would hear of this fight and want revenge.

The three Fates were laughing at me. I had dared and I had lost. I was trapped, and my cousin's men reached the end of the rock-bound path and spread now. Their shield wall was wider than mine. They would overlap us, they would curl around our flanks and chew us with axes, spears and swords.

'Step back,' I told my men.

I still planned the swine's horn, but for now I would let my cousin believe that I was going to make a wall inside the arch of the Low Gate. That would stop him from flanking me. It would make him cautious, and then I could charge him and hope to break him. Osferth stood beside me, my son behind me. We were under the arch now and I sent Rolla, Kettil and Eldgrim to the fighting platform so they could hurl stones at the advancing men. Osferth had told me the stones were piled there, ready, and I dared to hope we could survive this fight. I doubted I could take the High Gate, but just to survive and reach *Middelniht* would be victory enough.

My cousin took his shield. It was round, iron-bound willow with a big bronze boss. The boards had been painted red, and the wolf's head badge was grey and black against that blood-coloured field. The enemy tightened their ranks, their shields overlapping. The rain was slicing from the sea, heavy again, dripping from helmet rims and shield rims and from spear-blades. It was cold, wet and grey.

'Shields,' I said, and our brief front rank, just six men constrained by the oak walls of the arch's tunnel, touched shields. Let them come,

113

I thought. Let them die on our shield wall rather than go to them. If I used the swine's horn I would have to leave the shelter of the gate. I was still being indecisive, but the enemy had stopped advancing. That was normal. Men have to steel themselves to fight. My cousin was talking to them, but I could not hear his words. I did hear them cheer as they started forward again. They came sooner than I had expected. I had thought they would take time to ready themselves, time in which they would hurl insults, but they were well trained and confident. They came slowly, deliberately, their shields locked. They came as warriors advancing to a fight they expected to win. A big black-bearded man holding a long-hafted war axe was at their line's centre, next to my cousin. He was the man who would attack me. He would try to tear down my shield with the axe, leaving me open to my cousin's sword thrust. I hefted Serpent-Breath, then remembered that my hammer of Thor was still hidden beneath the mail. That was a bad omen, and a man should never have to fight under the thrall of a bad omen. I wanted to tear the silver cross from about my neck, but my left hand was threaded into the shield's grips and my right was holding Serpent-Breath.

And the bad omen told me I would die there. I gripped Serpent-Breath more tightly, for she was my passage to Valhalla. I would fight, I thought, and I would lose, but the Valkyries would take me to that better world that lies beyond this one. And what better place to die than Bebbanburg?

And then a horn blew again.

It was a loud squawk, nothing like the brave, bold note of the first horn that had sounded the alarm from the High Gate. This horn sounded as if it was being blown by an enthusiastic child, and its raucous tone made my cousin look towards the smithy, and I looked too, and there at the door was Finan. He blew the horn a second time and, disgusted by the crude noise it made, threw it down.

He was not alone.

A few paces in front of him was a woman. She looked young and was wearing a white dress belted with a golden chain. Her

114

hair was pale gold, so pale it was almost white. She had no cloak or cape and the rain was plastering the dress to her slim body. She stood motionless, and even at this distance I could see the anguish on her face.

And my cousin started towards her, then stopped because Finan had drawn his sword. The Irishman did not threaten the woman, but just stood, grinning, with his long blade naked. My cousin glanced at me, uncertainty on his face, then looked back to the smithy just as Finan's two companions appeared, and each had a captive.

One captive was my uncle, Lord Ælfric, the other was a boy. 'You want them dead?' Finan called to my cousin. 'You want me to slit their bellies open?' He tossed his sword high into the air so that it turned end over end. It was an arrogant display and every man in the courtyard watched as he deftly caught the falling weapon by its hilt. 'You want their guts fed to the dogs? Is that what you want? I'll oblige you, by the living Christ I'll oblige you! It would be a pleasure. Your dogs look hungry!' He turned and took the small boy into his grasp. I saw my cousin motion to his men, ordering them to stay still. Now I knew why he had seemed nervous: because he had known his only son was in the smithy.

And Finan now had the boy. He held him by one arm and brought him towards me. Ulfar, another of my Danes, followed with my uncle, while the woman, evidently the boy's mother, walked with them. No one held her, but she was clearly reluctant to leave her son.

Finan was still grinning as he reached me. 'This wee bastard says his name is Uhtred. Would you believe today is his birthday? He's eleven years old today and his grandfather bought him a horse, a fine one too! They were shoeing it, so they were. Just enjoying a sweet family outing which I interrupted.'

Relief was coursing through me like water pouring down a dry stream bed. A moment before I had been trapped and doomed, now I had my cousin's son as a hostage. And his wife, I assumed, and his father. I smiled at my black-cloaked enemy. 'It's time for you to drop your sword,' I told him.

'Father!' The boy struggled to escape Finan's grasp, lunging towards his father, and I hit him with my shield, a stinging blow from the heavy iron-rimmed boards that prompted a cry of pain and a protest from his mother.

'Stay still, you little bastard,' I said to him.

'He's not going any place,' Finan said, still holding the child's arm.

I looked at the woman 'And you are?' I demanded.

She stiffened defiantly, straightening her back and staring me in the eyes. 'Ingulfrid,' she said coldly.

Interesting, I thought. I knew my cousin had taken a Danish wife, but no one had told me what a fine-looking woman she was. 'This is your son?' I asked her.

'He is,' she said.

'Your only son?' I asked.

She hesitated, then nodded abruptly. I had heard that she had given birth to three boys, but only the one had lived.

'Uhtred!' my cousin called.

'Father?' the boy answered. He had a smear of blood where my shield had broken the skin over his right cheekbone.

'Not you, boy. I'm talking to him.' My cousin pointed his sword at me.

I dropped my shield and walked towards my cousin. 'So,' I said, 'it seems we have each other at a disadvantage. Shall we fight? You and I? The law of the hazel rods?'

'Fight him!' my uncle called.

'Let my wife and son go,' my cousin said, 'and you can leave in peace.'

I pretended to consider that, then shook my head. 'It will take more than that. And you don't want your father back?'

'Him too, of course.'

'You give me one thing,' I said, 'which is to go unharmed, and I have to give you three? That doesn't make sense, cousin.'

'What do you want?'

'Bebbanburg,' I said, 'because it's mine.'

'It is not yours!' my uncle snarled. I turned to look at him. He was old now, old and bent, his dark face deep-lined, but he still had clever eyes. His dark hair had turned white and hung lank to his thin shoulders. He was dressed richly in embroidered robes with a heavy fur-trimmed cloak. When my father rode off to war, only to die at Eoferwic, Ælfric had sworn on the comb of Saint Cuthbert that he would give the fortress to me when I came of age, but instead he had tried to kill me. He had tried to buy me from Ragnar, the man who had raised me, and later he had paid to have me sold into slavery, and I hated him more than I have ever hated any creature on this earth. He had even been betrothed to my beloved Gisela, though I had taken her long before she could reach his bed. That had been a small victory, but this was a greater one. He was my captive, though nothing in his demeanour suggested he thought the same thing. He stared at me disdainfully. 'Bebbanburg is not yours,' he said.

'It is my birthright,' I said.

'Your birthright,' he spat. 'Bebbanburg belongs to the man strong enough to hold it, not to some fool who waves parchment deeds. Your father would have wanted that! He told me often enough you were an irresponsible lackwit. He meant Bebbanburg to go to your elder brother, not to you! But it's mine now, and one day it will belong to my son.'

I wanted to kill the lying bastard, but he was old and frail. Old, frail and as poisonous as a viper. 'My Lady Ingulfrid,' I said to Osferth, 'is wet and cold. Give her my uncle's cloak.'

If Ingulfrid was grateful she did not show it. She took the cloak willingly enough and pulled the heavy fur collar around her neck. She was shivering, but stared at me with loathing. I looked back to my cousin, her husband. 'Maybe you should buy your family,' I said, 'and the price will be gold.'

'They're not slaves to be bought and sold,' he snarled.

I gazed at him and pretended to be struck by a sudden thought. 'There's an idea! Slaves! Finan!'

'Lord?'

'How much does a fine Saxon boy fetch in Frankia these days?'

'Enough to buy a coat of Frankish mail, lord.'

117

'That much?'

Finan pretended to appraise the boy. 'He's a fine-looking lad. Got meat on his bones. There are men who'll pay well for a plump little Saxon rump, lord.'

'And the woman?'

Finan looked her up and down, then shook his head. 'She's fair enough looking, I suppose, but she's used goods, lord. Maybe she still has a few years left in her? So she might fetch enough to buy a packhorse. More if she can cook.'

'Can you cook?' I asked Ingulfrid and received nothing more than a hate-filled stare for answer. I looked back to my cousin. 'A packhorse and a coat of mail,' I told him, then pretended to think about it. 'It's not enough,' I said, shaking my head. 'I want more than that. Much more.'

'You can leave unharmed,' he offered, 'and I shall pay you gold.'

'How much gold?'

He glanced at his father. It was plain that Ælfric had yielded the day-to-day command of the fortress to his son, but when it came to matters of money then my uncle was still in charge. 'His helmet,' Ælfric said sullenly.

'I will fill your helmet with gold coins,' my cousin offered.

'That will buy your wife,' I said, 'but how much for your heir?'

'The same,' he said bitterly.

'Not nearly enough,' I protested, 'but I'll exchange all three for Bebbanburg.'

'No!' my uncle cried loudly. 'No!'

I ignored Ælfric. 'Give me back what is mine,' I told my cousin, 'and I will give you what is yours.'

'You can make other sons!' Ælfric snarled at his son, 'and Bebbanburg is not yours to give. It is mine!'

'It's his?' I asked my cousin.

'Of course it's his,' he answered stubbornly.

'And you are his heir?'

'I am.'

I stepped back to the prisoners and seized my uncle by the nape of his scrawny neck. I shook him like a terrier shaking a rat, then

118

turned him so I could smile down into his face. 'You knew I would come back,' I said.

'I hoped you would,' he retorted.

'Bebbanburg is mine,' I said, 'and you know it.'

'Bebbanburg belongs to the man who can hold it,' he said defiantly, 'and you failed.'

'I was ten when you stole it,' I protested, 'younger even than him!' I pointed at his grandson.

'Your father didn't hold it,' my uncle said, 'and like a fool he rode to his death, and you're the same. You're a fool. You're impetuous, feckless, irresponsible. Suppose for a moment you retook Bebbanburg? How long would you hold it? You, who has never held onto any estate? Whatever land you had, you lost; whatever fortune you made, you threw away!' He looked at his son. 'You will hold Bebbanburg,' he ordered, 'whatever the price!'

'The price is your son's life,' I told my cousin.

'No!' Ingulfrid screamed.

'We will not pay your price,' my uncle said. He looked up at me with his dark eyes. 'So kill the boy,' he said. He waited, then sneered. 'Kill him! You named the price, and I won't pay it! So kill him!'

'Father . . .' my cousin said nervously.

Ælfric turned snake-fast towards his son. I was still holding him, tightly gripping the nape of his neck, but he made no effort to escape me. 'You can breed more sons!' he spat towards my cousin. 'Sons are easily made! Haven't enough of your whores whelped boys? The village is crawling with your bastards, so marry another wife and give her sons, but don't ever yield the fortress! Bebbanburg is not worth a son's life! There will never be another Bebbanburg, but there will always be more sons!'

I looked at my cousin. 'Give me Bebbanburg,' I said, 'and I will give you back your son.'

'I have refused that price!' my uncle snarled.

So I killed him.

It took him by surprise; indeed, it took everyone by surprise. I had been holding the old man by his neck and all I had to do was lift Serpent-Breath and draw her blade across his throat. And so I did. It was fast, much faster than he deserved. The sword felt the resistance of his skinny gullet and he twisted like an eel, but I quickened the blade and dragged it fast and she broke through the muscles and tendons, through the windpipe and the blood vessels, and he gasped, a curious almost feminine noise, and then the only sound he could make was gurgling, bubbling, and the blood was pouring onto the ground as he collapsed to his knees in front of me. I put a boot on his spine and thrust him forward so that he fell flat. He jerked for some seconds, still fighting for breath, and his hands curled as if to hold the soil of his fortress. Then he twitched a last time and was still, and I felt a vague disappointment. I had dreamed of killing this man for years. I had planned his death in my dreams, I had devised ever more painful deaths for him, and now I had just cut his throat with a merciful swiftness. All that dreaming for nothing! I prodded the dead man with my foot then looked up to his son. 'Now you're the one who has to make the decision,' I said.

No one spoke. The rain fell and the wind blew, and my cousin's men stared at the corpse and I knew their world had suddenly changed. All of them, for all of their lives, had been under the command of Ælfric and suddenly there was no Ælfric. His death had shocked them. 'Well?' I demanded of my cousin. 'Will you buy your son's life?'

He stared at me, said nothing.

'Answer me, you weasel vomit,' I said. 'Will you exchange Bebbanburg for your son?'

'I will pay you for Bebbanburg,' he said uncertainly. He looked down at his father's corpse. I guessed that they had suffered an uneasy relationship, just as I had with my father, but he was still horrified. He looked up at me again, frowning. 'He was old!' he protested. 'You had to kill an old man?'

'He was a thief,' I said, 'and I have dreamed of killing him for a lifetime.'

'He was old!' he protested again.

'He was lucky,' I snarled, 'lucky that he died so fast. I dreamed of killing him slowly. But fast or slow, he's gone to the

Corpse-Ripper in the underworld, and if you don't give me Bebbanburg then I shall send your son to the Corpse-Ripper too.'

'I will pay you gold,' he said, 'much gold.'

'You know my price,' I said, pointing Serpent-Breath's bloodied blade at his son. The rainwater was dripping pink from the sword's tip. I moved the sword closer to the boy and Ingulfrid screamed.

I had been indecisive and hesitant, now it was my cousin's turn. I could see the indecision on his face. Was Bebbanburg really worth his son's life? Ingulfrid was begging him. She had an arm around her son, tears were streaming down her face. My cousin seemed to grimace when she shrieked at him, but then he surprised me by turning and ordering his men back to the High Gate. 'I shall give you time to consider,' he said, 'but know this. I will not yield Bebbanburg. So, for this day's work you can end with a dead boy or with a fortune in gold. Tell me which you want before nightfall.' He walked away.

'Lord!' Ingulfrid appealed to her husband.

He turned back, but spoke to me instead of her. 'You'll release my wife,' he demanded.

'She's not a captive,' I said, 'she's free to go wherever she likes, but I keep the boy.'

Ingulfrid kept hold of her son's shoulders. 'I stay with my son,' she said fiercely.

'You'll come with me, woman,' my cousin snarled.

'You don't command here,' I said. 'Your wife pleases herself.'

He looked at me as though I was utterly mad. 'Pleases herself?' He did not say the words, but rather mouthed them in astonishment, then shook his head in disbelief and turned again. He took his men away, leaving us in control of the outer courtyard.

Finan took the boy from his mother and gave him to Osferth. 'Don't let go of the little bastard,' he said, then crossed to me and watched as my cousin led his men through the High Gate. He waited till the last man had disappeared and the gate slammed shut again. 'He'll pay a lot of gold for his boy,' Finan said in a low voice.

'Gold is good,' I said with deliberate carelessness. I heard the High Gate's locking bar drop into its brackets.

121

'And a dead boy is worth nothing,' Finan said more forcibly.

'I know.'

'And you're not going to kill him anyway,' Finan said. He still spoke quietly so that only I could hear him.

'I'm not?'

'You're not a child-killer.'

'Maybe now's the time to start.'

'You won't kill him,' Finan said, 'so take the gold.' He waited for me to say something, but I kept quiet. 'The men need reward,' Finan said.

And that was true. I was their hlaford, their gold-giver, but in the last weeks I had led them only to this failure. Finan was hinting that some of my men would leave. They had taken oaths, but the truth is that we only sanctify oaths with such high promise because they are so easily broken. If a man thought he could find wealth and honour with another lord then he would leave me, and I had few enough men anyway. I smiled at him. 'You trust me?'

'You know I do.'

'Then tell the men that I shall make them rich. Tell them I shall write their names in the chronicles. Tell them they will be celebrated. Tell them they will have reputation.'

Finan gave me a crooked grin. 'And how will you do that?'

'I don't know,' I said, 'but I will.' I walked back to where Ingulfrid stood watching her son. 'And what,' I asked, 'will your husband pay for you?'

She did not answer, and I suspected the answer would have been demeaning. My cousin had treated his wife with careless scorn and I suspected her value as a hostage was almost nothing. But the boy was worth a fortune.

And instinct told me to forgo the fortune, at least for this day. I looked at him. He was defiant, close to tears, brave. I weighed the choice again, to take the gold or trust my instinct? I had no idea what the future held, none, and keeping the boy would be a nuisance, but instinct told me to take the less appealing choice. The gods were telling me that. What else is instinct?

'Finan.' I turned sharply and pointed to the shelter where the two hounds had been sleeping. 'Get all that hay,' I told him, 'and spread it around the palisade. Some in the gatehouse, too.'

'You're going to burn the place?'

'The hay will get wet,' I said, 'but pile it thickly enough and some will stay dry. And the gatehouse, smithy and stables will burn. Burn it all!'

My cousin was not going to yield Bebbanburg because without the fortress he was nothing. He would be a Saxon lost in Danish territory. He would need to go viking, or else kneel in homage to Edward of Wessex. But in Bebbanburg he was king of all the land he could reach in a day's ride and he was rich. So Bebbanburg was worth a son's life. It was worth two sons' lives and, as Ælfric had said, he could always make more. My cousin would keep his fortress, but I would burn what I could.

So we took the horses out of the stables and drove them out of the fortress to run wild, then we burned the courtyard. My cousin made no attempt to stop us, he just watched from the high inner rampart, and, as the smoke mingled with the rain, we went back to *Middelniht*. We waded out to her, taking Ingulfrid and her son with us, and we scrambled over the low midships. My cousin would pursue us in his long warships and I wanted to burn them, but their timbers were rain-soaked, so Finan took three men and they slashed the cords holding the masts aloft, then hacked great gashes on the water-lines with their axes. Both ships were settling onto the harbour's muddy bottom as I ordered my men to *Middelniht*'s oars. It was still raining, but the flames of the burning buildings were bright and high, and the smoke poured up to the low smoke-coloured clouds.

The wind had dropped, though the seas were still high and the waves broke white in the shallow harbour entrance. We rowed into that white chaos and the water shattered on *Middelniht*'s high prow and my cousin and his men watched from the heights as we pulled the ship out to sea. We went far out to sea, out beyond the islands, out among the wild waves, and there we hoisted the *Middelniht*'s sail and turned her south.

And so were gone from Bebbanburg.

PART THREE

Rumours of War

Six

I had sailed south to convince my cousin that I was returning to southern Britain, but as soon as the smoke of burning Bebbanburg was nothing but a grey smear against the grey clouds I turned eastwards.

I did not know where to go.

To the north was Scotland, inhabited by savages only too glad for a chance to slaughter a Saxon. Beyond them were the Norse settlements, which were full of grim folk in stinking sealskin furs who clung to their rocky islands and, like the Scots, were far more likely to kill than offer a welcome. The Saxon lands lay to the south, but the Christians had made sure I was not wanted in either Wessex or Mercia, and I saw no future in East Anglia and so I turned back towards the lonely Frisian islands.

I did not know where else to go.

I had been tempted to take my cousin's offer of gold. Gold is always useful. It can buy men, ships, horses and weapons, but I had kept the boy because of instinct. I called the boy to me as we coursed eastwards, driven by a brisk north wind that blew steady and sure. 'What is your name?' I asked him.

He looked puzzled and glanced back at his mother, who was watching anxiously. 'My name is Uhtred,' he said.

'No it isn't,' I said. 'Your name is Osbert.'

'I am Uhtred,' he insisted bravely.

I hit him hard with my open hand. The blow stung my palm and must have made his ears ring because he staggered and might have gone overboard if Finan had not grabbed and pulled him back. His mother cried out in protest, but I ignored her. 'Your name is Osbert,' I said again, and this time he said nothing, just stared at me with tears and obstinacy in his eyes. 'What is your name?' I asked him, and still he just looked at me and I could see the temptation in his stubborn face so I drew my hand back again.

'Osbert,' he muttered.

'I can't hear you!'

'Osbert,' he said louder.

'You hear that!' I shouted to my crew. 'This boy's name is Osbert!'

His mother looked at me, opened her mouth to protest and closed it again.

'My name is Uhtred,' I told the boy, 'and my son's name is Uhtred, which means there are too many Uhtreds on this boat already so you're now Osbert. Go back to your mother.'

Finan was crouched in his usual position beside me on the steering platform. The waves were still large and the wind brisk, but not every wave was crested with breaking white and the wind was tamer. The rain had stopped and there were even breaks in the clouds through which shafts of sunlight poured to glitter on patches of the sea. Finan stared out at the water. 'We could have been counting gold coins, lord,' he said, 'and instead we have a woman and a child to guard.'

'Hardly a child,' I said, 'almost a man.'

'He's a thing worth gold, whatever he is.'

'You think I should have ransomed him?'

'You tell me, lord.'

I thought about it. I had kept the boy on instinct and was still not sure why I had done that. 'As far as the world is concerned,' I said, 'he's the heir to Bebbanburg, and that makes him valuable.'

'It does.'

'Not just to his father,' I said, 'but to his father's enemies.'

'And they are?'

'The Danes, I suppose,' I said vaguely, because I was still not sure why I had kept the boy.

128

'Strange, isn't it?' Finan went on, 'Cnut Ranulfson's wife and children are hostages somewhere, and now we have those two. It's the season for capturing wives and children, I suppose?' He sounded amused.

And who, I wondered, had taken Cnut Ranulfson's family? I told myself it was none of my business, that I had been thrown out of Saxon Britain, but the question still gnawed at me. The obvious answer was that the Saxons had made the capture to keep Cnut quiet while they attacked either the Danish lords of northern Mercia or the enfeebled kingdom of East Anglia, but Æthelflaed had heard nothing. She had spies in both her husband's household and in her brother's court, and she would surely have known if either Æthelred or Edward had taken Cnut's wife, yet those spies had told her nothing. And I did not believe Edward of Wessex would send men to capture Cnut's family. He was too nervous of Danish unrest and too much under the influence of timorous priests. Æthelred? It was possible that his new woman and her belligerent brother had taken the risk, but Æthelflaed would surely have learned of it if they had. So who had taken them?

Finan was still staring at me, wanting an answer. I offered him a question instead. 'So who is our most dangerous enemy?'

'Your cousin.'

'If I'd taken the gold,' I said and I was explaining to myself as much as to Finan, 'he'd still send men to kill us. He'd want the gold back. But he'll be cautious so long as we hold his wife and child.'

'That's true,' he allowed.

'And the price won't go down just because we wait for payment,' I said. 'My cousin will pay next month or next year.'

'Unless he takes a new wife,' Finan said sceptically, 'because he won't pay much for her.' He nodded towards Ingulfrid who was huddled just forward of the steering platform. She still wore Ælfric's cloak and was clutching her son protectively.

'He didn't sound fond of her,' I said, amused.

'He has another woman to keep his bed warm,' Finan suggested, 'and this one is just his wife.'

'Just?' I asked.

'He didn't marry her for love,' Finan said, 'or if he did the edge went off that blade long ago. He probably married her for her land, or for her father's alliance.'

And she was Danish. That interested me. Bebbanburg was a small patch of Saxon land in a Danish kingdom and the Danes would dearly love to take it. Yet a Danish wife suggested that my cousin had a Danish ally. 'My lady,' I called to her. She looked up at me, but said nothing. 'Come here,' I ordered her, 'and you can bring Osbert.'

She bridled, whether at my giving her a command or calling her son by another name, and for a brief instant I thought she would disobey, then she climbed to her feet and, holding her son by the hand, came aft. She staggered as the ship heaved on a wave and I held out an arm which she grasped, then looked disgusted as if she had gripped a piece of slimy filth. She let go and put her free hand against the stern post. 'Who's your father?' I asked her.

She hesitated, weighing the danger of such a question and, evidently finding none, shrugged. 'Hoskuld Leifson,' she said.

I had never heard of him. 'Who does he serve?' I asked.

'Sigtrygg.'

'Sweet Jesus,' Finan exclaimed, 'the fellow who was in Dyflin?'

'He was,' she said with some bitterness.

Sigtrygg was a Norseman, a warrior, and he had carved a kingdom for himself in Ireland, but Ireland is never an easy place for outsiders and the last I had heard was that the self-styled King of Ireland had been kicked back across the sea to Britain. 'So you're Norse?' I asked her.

'I'm Danish,' she said.

'So where's Sigtrygg now?' I asked.

'The last I heard he was in Cumbraland.'

'He's in Cumbraland,' Osferth confirmed. He had followed Ingulfrid up to the steering platform, which struck me as strange. Osferth liked his own company and rarely joined me at the ship's stern.

'So what does your father do for Sigtrygg?' I asked Ingulfrid.

'He commands the house-warriors.'

'So tell me,' I asked, 'why did Ælfric marry his son to a Dane who served Sigtrygg?'

'Why not?' she retorted, still with bitterness in her voice.

'Did he marry you so he'd have a refuge in Ireland if he lost Bebbanburg?' I suggested.

'Bebbanburg will never be lost,' she said. 'It can't be captured.'

'I almost captured it.'

'Almost isn't enough, is it?'

'No,' I conceded, 'it is not. So why the marriage, my lady?'

'Why do you think?' she spat back at me.

Because Bebbanburg ruled a small patch of land surrounded by enemies, and the marriage had brought an alliance with a man who shared those enemies. Sigtrygg was ambitious, he wanted a kingdom, and if it could not be in Ireland then he would hack it out of British land. He was not strong enough to attack Wessex, Wales would be as troublesome to him as Ireland, and Scotland was even worse, so he was looking at Northumbria. That meant his enemies were Cnut Ranulfson and Sigurd Thorrson, so had it been Sigtrygg who captured Cnut's wife? It was a possibility, but Sigtrygg must have been very confident of his ability to withstand an attack by Cnut if he had dared to do that. For the moment he was safe enough in Cumbraland. That was a wild place of mountains, rain and lakes, and Cnut was evidently content to let Sigtrygg rule over those barren wastes. And Sigtrygg? He doubtless wanted land that Cnut ruled, but the Norseman was no fool and was unlikely to provoke a war he must inevitably lose.

I leaned on the steering oar. The *Middelniht* was sailing fast and the loom of the steering oar was quivering in my hands, always a sign that a ship is happy. The clouds were being blown ragged as they were scoured away southwards and the *Middelniht* suddenly sailed into a patch of sunlight. I smiled. There are few things so exhilarating as a good ship in a good wind.

'What's the stench?' Ingulfrid asked indignantly.

'Probably Finan,' I said.

'It's Lord Uhtred,' Finan said at the same moment.

131

'It's the sail,' Osferth explained to her. 'It's smeared with cod oil and mutton fat.'

She looked appalled. 'Cod oil and mutton fat?'

'It does stink,' I allowed.

'And it attracts the flies,' Finan added.

'So why do it then?'

'Because it catches the wind better,' I said. She grimaced. 'Are you not used to ships, my lady?'

'No. And I think I hate them.'

'Why?'

She looked at me, said nothing for a few heartbeats, then scowled. 'Why do you think? I'm the only woman on board.'

I was about to reassure her that she was safe, then understood what she was saying. It was easy for men, we just pissed overboard, taking care never to face upwind, but Ingulfrid could hardly do the same. 'Eldgrim!' I called. 'Put a bucket under the steering platform and rig a curtain!' I looked back to her. 'It's a little cramped under there, but you'll be hidden.'

'I'll do it,' Osferth interrupted hastily. He waved Eldgrim away and busied himself with two cloaks that would hang like curtains over the dank, dark space beneath our feet. Finan looked at me, twitched his head towards Osferth and grinned. I pretended not to notice. 'There, my lady,' Osferth said in his most solemn tone, 'and I'll stand guard to make sure no one disturbs you.'

'Thank you,' she said, and Osferth bowed to her. Finan made a choking noise.

Osbert tried to stay with his mother when she climbed down from the platform. 'Stay here, boy,' I said. 'I'll teach you to steer a ship.'

Ingulfrid ducked out of sight. *Middelniht* soared on, happy in this wind and in these seas. I gave the boy the steering oar and showed him how to anticipate the ship's motion, and let him feel the power of the sea in that long oar-loom. 'Don't over correct,' I told him, 'it slows the boat. Treat her like a good horse. Be gentle and she'll know what to do.'

'Why teach him if you're going to kill him?' his mother asked when she reappeared. I watched her climb back to the steering platform. The wind caught loose strands of her hair and whipped them across her face. 'Well?' she demanded sharply. 'Why teach him?' Her anger gave her a stern, sharp beauty.

'Because it's a skill every man should have,' I said.

'So he'll live to be a man?' she asked defiantly.

'I don't kill children, my lady,' I said gently, 'but I didn't really want your husband to know that.'

'So what will you do with him?'

'He won't hurt him, my lady,' Osferth put in.

'Then what will he do with him?' she demanded.

'I'll sell him,' I said.

'As a slave?'

'I suspect your husband will pay more than any slaver. Or perhaps your husband's enemies will pay?'

'There are plenty of those,' she said, 'but you're chief among them.'

'And the least dangerous,' I said, amused. I nodded towards my crew. 'These are all the men I have.'

'And yet you still attacked Bebbanburg,' she said, and I could not tell from her tone whether she thought me a complete fool or had a reluctant admiration for my having dared to make the assault.

'And almost succeeded,' I said wistfully, 'though I confess I'd probably be dead by now if you hadn't taken your son to see his new horse being shod.' I offered her a bow. 'I owe my life to you, my lady, I thank you.'

'You owe it to my son,' she said, the bitterness back in her voice, 'I'm worth nothing, but Uhtred?'

'Osbert, you mean?'

'I mean Uhtred,' she said defiantly, 'and he's the heir to Bebbanburg.'

'Not while my son lives,' I said.

'But your son must first take Bebbanburg,' she retorted, 'and he won't. So my Uhtred is the heir.'

'You heard my uncle,' I said harshly. 'Your husband can make another heir.'

133

'Oh, he can,' she said savagely, 'he spawns bastards like a dog makes puppies. He prefers to make bastards, but he's proud of Uhtred.'

The sudden savagery in her voice had surprised me, as had her admission about her husband. She stared at me belligerently, and I thought what a fine face she had, hard-boned and strong-jawed, but a face softened by generous lips and pale blue eyes that, like the sea, were flecked by silver. Osferth evidently thought the same because he had hardly taken his eyes from her since he had joined us. 'Then your husband is a fool,' I said.

'A fool,' Osferth echoed.

'He likes his women fat and dark,' she said.

Her son had been listening and now frowned unhappily at his mother's bitter words. I grinned at the boy. 'Fat, dark, fair or thin,' I told him, 'they're all women, and all to be cherished.'

'Cherished?' he repeated the word.

'Five things make a man happy,' I told him, 'a good ship, a good sword, a good hound, a good horse, and a woman.'

'Not a good woman?' Finan asked, amused.

'They're all good,' I said, 'except when they're not, and then they're better than good.'

'Dear God,' Osferth said in a pained voice.

'Praise God,' Finan said.

'So your husband,' I looked back to Ingulfrid, 'will want his son back?'

'Of course he will.'

'And so pursue us?'

'He'll pay someone to find you.'

'Because he's a coward and won't come himself?'

'Because the Lord Ælfric's law was that the Lord of Bebbanburg doesn't leave the fortress unless the heir stays behind. One of them must always be within the walls.'

'Because it's easy to kill one of them outside the walls,' I said, 'but almost impossible to kill a man when he's safe inside?'

She nodded. 'So unless he's changed his father's law then he'll send other men to kill you.'

'Many have tried, lady,' I said gently.

'He has gold,' she said, 'he can afford to send many men.'

'He'll need to,' Finan said drily.

Next day we came to the islands. The sea was calm now, the sun bright and the wind so gentle that we were forced to row. We went very cautiously with a man standing in the bows probing the water's depth with an oar.

'Where are we?' Ingulfrid asked.

'The Frisian Islands,' I told her.

'You think you can hide here?'

I shook my head. 'There's nowhere to hide, lady. Your husband will know what choices I have, and he'll know this is one of them.'

'Dunholm,' she said.

I looked at her sharply. 'Dunholm?'

'He knows Ragnar was your friend.'

I did not respond. Ragnar had been more than a friend, he had been a brother. His father had raised me and if fate had decreed differently then I would have stayed with Ragnar and fought beside him to the end of time, but the three Norns make our destiny, and Ragnar had stayed as a lord in the north and I had gone south to join the Saxons. He had been sick, and news of his death had come the previous winter. That had not surprised me even though it saddened me. He had become fat and short of breath, lazy and lame, yet he had died with a sword in his hand, placed there by Brida, his woman, as he lay dying. So he would go to Valhalla, where, for all time, or at least until the final chaos overwhelms us, he would be the old Ragnar, strong and lively, full of laughter, generous and brave. 'Lord Ælfric knew you were an outcast,' Ingulfrid went on, 'and that you had too few men to attack Bebbanburg, so he thought you'd go to Dunholm.'

'Without Ragnar?' I asked, then shook my head. 'Without Ragnar there's nothing for me at Dunholm.'

'Ragnar's woman,' she suggested, 'and his sons?'

I smiled. 'Brida hates me.'

'You fear her?'

I laughed at that, though in truth I did fear Brida. She had been my lover once, and now she was my enemy, and a grudge, for

Brida, was like an itch that never went away. She would scratch the itch until it became a sore, and gouge the sore to suppurating blood and pus. She hated me because I had not fought for the Danes against the Saxons and it did not matter that she was a Saxon herself. Brida was all passion.

'Lord Ælfric hoped you'd go to Dunholm before coming to Bebbanburg,' Ingulfrid said.

'Hoped it?'

She hesitated, as though fearing she was about to reveal too much, then shrugged. 'He has an agreement with Brida.'

Why was I surprised? Our enemy's enemy is our friend, or at least our ally. 'He hoped she'd kill me?'

'She promised to poison you,' Ingulfrid said, 'and he promised her gold.'

And I was not surprised by that. Brida would never forgive me. She would carry that hatred to her death and, if she could, prolong it by sorcery long past her death. 'Why tell me that?' I asked Ingulfrid. 'Why not encourage me to go to Dunholm?'

'Because if you went to Dunholm,' she answered, 'Brida will keep my son and demand more gold than you ever will. She's bitter.'

'And cruel,' I said, then forgot Brida because the man in the prow was calling out warnings of shallow water. We were feeling our way through a channel that twisted towards a deserted sandbank where dune grass grew. The channel turned west, then north, then east again and the *Middelniht* touched bottom four times before we reached a stretch of deeper water that curved around the island's eastern flank. 'This will do,' I told Finan, and we rowed a few strokes to run the bows up onto the sand. 'Home for the moment,' I told my crew.

This was my new kingdom, my realm, my patch of sea-washed, wind-blown sand on the edge of Frisia, and I would hold it only so long as no stronger enemy decided to swat me like a fly. And that would happen unless I could find more men, but for the moment I just needed to keep my present crew busy and so I sent my son and a dozen men away in *Middelniht* to scour the nearby sandbanks for driftwood so we could make huts. There was some driftwood already on the island and I watched as Osferth made a shelter for Ingulfrid. My son brought back more wood, enough to make a fire as well as to build shelters, and that night we sang around a great blaze that spewed sparks into the starry sky. 'You want folk to know we're here?' Finan asked me.

'They know already,' I said. A couple of boats had slid past us during the day and the news of our presence would be spreading through the islands and along the marshy mainland shore. Thancward, the man who had challenged our presence before, would probably come again, though I doubted he wanted to fight. We would be at peace for a few days, I reckoned.

I could see Finan was worried about me. I had not spoken much all evening, nor joined in the singing. The Irishman had kept glancing at me. I suspected he knew what worried me. It was not my cousin, nor any forces my cousin could muster against me. My concern was broader and deeper than that: it was an inability to see a way ahead. I had no idea what to do, yet I had to do something. I led a crew, I had a ship, we carried swords, and we could not just rot on a beach, yet I did not know where to lead them. I was lost.

'Are you setting sentries?' Finan asked deep in the night.

'I'll stand guard,' I said. 'And make sure the men know that the Lady Ingulfrid is not here for their amusement.'

'They already know that. Besides, the preacher will kill any man who looks at her.'

I laughed. 'The preacher' was Osferth's nickname. 'He does seem fascinated,' I said mildly.

'Poor bastard's in love,' Finan said.

'About time he was,' I said, then gently slapped Finan's shoulder. 'Sleep, my friend, sleep well.'

I walked the beach in the dark. On this side of the island the waves made feeble slapping sounds, though I could hear the beat and suck of the bigger waves on the western side of the dune. The fire died slowly until it was just smouldering embers, and still I walked. The tide was low and *Middelniht* was a dark shadow canted on the sand.

137

I am a hlaford, a lord. A lord must provide for his men. He is their gold-giver, their ring-giver, their silver-lord. He must feed his men, shelter them and enrich them, and in return they serve him and make him a great lord, one whose name is spoken with respect. And my men had a homeless lord, a lord of sand and ashes, a one-ship lord. And I did not know what to do.

The Saxons hated me because I had killed an abbot. The Danes would never trust me, and besides I had killed Sigurd Thorrson's son and Sigurd, who was friend to Cnut Ranulfson, was sworn to avenge that death. Ragnar, who would have welcomed me as a brother and given me half his wealth, was dead. Æthelflaed loved me, but Æthelflaed loved her church too and did not possess the strength to defend me against the Mercians who followed her estranged husband. She was protected by her brother, Edward of Wessex, and he would probably welcome me, though he would demand a wergild for the death of the priest and force me to make a grovelling apology to his priests. He would not give me land. He might protect me and use me as a warrior, but I would not be a lord.

And I was getting old. I knew that, I could feel it in my bones. I was at an age when men lead armies. When they stood in the rear ranks of the shield wall and left the fighting to the young men at the front. I had grey hairs and a beard streaked white. So I was old, I was hated, I was outcast, and I was lost, yet I had been worse. My uncle had once sold me into slavery and that had been a bad time, except I had met Finan and together we had survived, and Finan had had the pleasure of killing the bastard who had branded us, and I had just been given the joy of killing the bastard who had betrayed me. The Christians talk of the wheel of fortune, a vast wheel that turns constantly and sometimes it lifts us up into the sunlight and at others it drags us down to the shit and mud. And there I was now, in the shit and muck. So perhaps stay here, I thought. A man could do worse than rule a few Frisian islands. I did not doubt I could defeat Thancward, take his surviving men into my service and then forge a small kingdom of sand dunes and seal-shit. I smiled at the thought.

'Osferth says you really won't kill my son.' She spoke from behind me. I turned to see Ingulfrid. She was a shadow against the dune. I said nothing. 'He says you're really a kind man.'

I laughed at that. 'I have made more widows and orphans than most men,' I said. 'Is that kind?'

'He says you're decent, honourable, and . . .' she hesitated, 'headstrong.'

'Headstrong is right,' I said.

'And now you're lost,' she said. She spoke mildly, all the defiance and anger gone from her voice.

'Lost?' I asked.

'You don't know where to go,' she said, 'and you don't know what to do.'

I smiled because she was right, then watched as she stepped cautiously down the beach. 'I don't know where to go,' I admitted.

She went to the remnants of the fire, crouched there and held her hands towards the dully glowing embers. 'I've felt that way for fifteen years,' she said bitterly.

'Then your husband is a fool,' I said.

She shook her head. 'So you keep telling me,' she said, 'but in truth he's a clever man, and you did him a favour.'

'By taking you?'

'By killing Lord Ælfric.' She stared into the smouldering timbers, watching the small remnant flames twist, fade and glow again. 'Now my husband is free to do whatever he wants.'

'And what's that?'

'To be safe in Bebbanburg,' she said. 'Not to go to sleep every night wondering where you are. And right now? I suspect he wants his son back. For all his faults he is fond of Uhtred.'

So that, I thought, was why she was talking to me without scorn or bitterness. She wanted to plead for her son. I sat on the far side of the fire and nudged the charred logs with a foot to make the small flames leap up. 'He won't be safe in Bebbanburg,' I said, 'while Cnut Ranulfson and Sigurd Thorrson live. They want Bebbanburg too, and one day they'll try to capture it.'

'But my husband's priests say that Northumbria is fated to be

Christian,' she said, 'so the Danes will be defeated. It's the Christian god's will.'

'Are you a Christian?' I asked.

'They say I am,' she said, 'but I'm not sure. My husband insisted I was baptised and a priest put me in a barrel of water and pushed my head under. My husband laughed when they did that. Then they made me kiss Saint Oswald's arm. It was dry and yellow.'

Saint Oswald. I had forgotten that new excitement that had been stirred by the abbot I had killed. Saint Oswald. He had been King of Northumbria in the old times. He had lived at Bebbanburg and ruled over all the north until he went to war with Mercia and was defeated in battle by a pagan king. The nailed god did not help him much that day, and his body was chopped to pieces, but because he was a saint as well as a king, people collected the butchered remains and preserved them. I knew that the saint's left arm had been given to Lord Ælfric, and long before that I had helped escort Oswald's severed head across the hills of the north.

'The priests say that if Oswald's body can be put together,' Ingulfrid said, 'then all the Saxon lands will be ruled by one lord. One king.'

'Priests never stop talking nonsense.'

'And Æthelred of Mercia begged Lord Ælfric for the arm,' she went on, ignoring my comment.

That caught my interest. I looked up at her flame-lit face. 'And what did Ælfric say?'

'He said he would exchange the arm for your body.'

'Truly?'

'Truly.'

I laughed at that, then went silent as I thought. Æthelred wanted to reassemble the dead Oswald? Was that his ambition? To be king of all the Saxons? And did he believe the priestly nonsense that whoever possessed the corpse of Saint Oswald could not be defeated in battle? Legend claimed that most of Oswald's body had been taken to a monastery in Mercia where the monks had refused to accept the relics because, they claimed, Oswald had been an enemy of their kingdom, but that night, while the corpse lay outside the

140

monastery gates, a great light had pierced the heavens to shine on the body, and the column of light had persuaded the monks to accept the saint's remains. The monastery had then been conquered by the Danes who had swallowed its lands into Northumbria, and Æthelred wanted to find that dry corpse? If I had ruled that part of Northumbria I would long ago have dug up the corpse, burned it and scattered its ashes to the winds. But presumably Æthelred believed the body still lay in its grave, but to claim the body he needed to fight against the Northumbrian lords. Did he plan a war against Cnut? East Anglia first, then Northumbria? That was madness. 'You think Æthelred wants to invade Northumbria?' I asked her.

'He wants to be King of Mercia,' Ingulfrid said.

He had always wanted that, but he had never dared defy Alfred, but Alfred had been dead these many years and Edward was king. Æthelred had fretted under Alfred and I could only imagine how he resented being in thrall to the younger Edward. And Æthelred was growing old like me, and he was thinking of his reputation. He did not want to be remembered as the vassal of Wessex, but as the King of Mercia, and the king moreover who had added East Anglia to Mercia's lands. And why stop there? Why not invade Northumbria and become king of all the northern Saxons? And once he had added East Anglia's thegns to his army, he would be strong enough to defy Cnut, and the possession of Saint Oswald's body would convince the northern Christians that their nailed god was on Æthelred's side and those Christians might well rise against their Danish lords. Æthelred would be remembered as the king who had made Mercia strong again, maybe even as the man who united all the Saxon kingdoms. He would set Britain ablaze to write his name in the chronicles of history.

And the biggest obstacle to that ambition was Cnut Ranulfson, Cnut Longsword, the man who wielded Ice-Spite. And Cnut's wife and children were missing, presumably held hostage. I asked Ingulfrid if she had heard of their capture.

'Of course I heard about it,' she said, 'all Britain knows of it.' She paused. 'Lord Ælfric thought you had taken them.'

'Whoever took them,' I said, 'wanted folk to think that. They rode under my banner, but it wasn't me.'

She gazed into the tiny flames. 'Your cousin Æthelred stands to gain most from their capture,' she said.

She was a clever woman, I realised, clever and subtle. My cousin, I thought, was a fool to despise her. 'Æthelred didn't do it,' I said. 'He isn't that brave. He's scared of Cnut. He wouldn't risk Cnut's anger, not yet, not till he's far stronger.'

'Someone did,' she said.

Someone who benefited from Cnut's inaction. Someone stupid enough to risk Cnut's savage revenge. Someone clever enough to keep it secret. Someone who would do it on Æthelred's behalf, presumably for a great reward in gold or land, and someone who would blame me.

And suddenly it was as though dry tinder had been thrown onto the dying embers. The realisation was like a blaze of light, bright as the shaft that had descended from the sky to shine on Oswald's dismembered corpse. 'Haesten,' I said.

'Haesten,' Ingulfrid repeated the name as though she had known all along. I stared at her and she gazed back. 'Who else?' she asked simply.

'But Haesten . . .' I began, then fell silent.

Yes, Haesten was brave enough to defy Cnut, and treacherous enough to ally himself with Æthelred, but would he really risk Cnut's revenge? Haesten was no fool. He had survived defeat after defeat, yet he always wriggled free. He had land and men, though not much and not many of either, yet he had them. And if he really had kidnapped Cnut's wife he risked losing everything, his life chiefly, and that life would not end easily. It would be days of torture.

'Haesten is everyone's friend,' Ingulfrid said softly.

'Not mine,' I put in.

'And everyone's enemy,' she went on, ignoring my comment. 'He survives by swearing loyalty to everyone stronger than himself. He keeps quiet, he lies like a dog on the hearth and he wags his tail when anyone comes close. He swears loyalty to Cnut and to

Æthelred, but you know what the Christians say. No man can serve two masters.'

I frowned. 'He serves Æthelred?' I shook my head. 'No, he's an enemy. He serves Cnut. I know, I met him in Cnut's hall.'

Ingulfrid smiled secretly, she paused, then asked. 'Do you trust Haesten?'

'Of course not.'

'My father first came to Britain in Haesten's service,' she said, 'and he left him to join Sigtrygg. He says Haesten is as trustworthy as a serpent. If he takes your hand, my father says, you should count your fingers.'

None of that was astonishing. 'All true,' I said, 'but he's weak, he needs Cnut's protection.'

'He does,' she agrees, 'but suppose he sent an envoy to Æthelred? A secret envoy?'

'It wouldn't surprise me.'

'And Haesten offers to serve Æthelred,' she continued, 'by sending him news and by doing what services he can without arousing Cnut's suspicion. And in return Æthelred promises not to attack Haesten.'

I thought about it, then nodded. 'I've spent eight years wanting to attack Haesten,' I said, 'and Æthelred refuses to give me the men.' Haesten occupied Ceaster, and that great Roman fortress would have protected Mercia's northern lands from attacks by the Irish Norse or from the Danes and Norse in Cumbraland, yet Æthelred had refused to countenance an assault. I had thought his refusal was simply to deny me the chance of adding to my reputation, and so I had been forced to let my men just watch Ceaster to make sure Haesten caused no trouble.

Ingulfrid half frowned. She was still looking into the small flames as she spoke. 'I don't know if any of what I'm saying is true,' she said, 'but I remember hearing about Cnut's wife and I instantly thought of Haesten. He's treacherous and clever. He could persuade Æthelred that he is loyal, but Haesten will always serve the stronger man, not the weaker. He will be smiling at Æthelred, but licking Cnut's backside, and Æthelred thinks Cnut dare not attack because

143

his wife is a hostage, but . . .' She paused and raised her head to look straight at me. '. . . just suppose that's what Cnut and Haesten want Æthelred to think?'

I stared at her as I tried to comprehend what she was suggesting. It made sense. Cnut's wife and children had never been captured at all, it was just a ruse to make Æthelred feel safe. I thought back to my meeting with Cnut. That would all have been part of the deception. He had seemed angry, but then he had turned friendly, and Haesten had been there, smiling his smirking smile all the time. And why had Cnut never swatted Haesten aside? Ceaster was a fort worth having for it controlled much of the traffic between Britain and Ireland, it lay between Mercia and Northumbria and between the Welsh and the Saxons, yet Cnut had allowed Haesten to keep it. Why? Because Haesten was useful? So was Ingulfrid right, and was Haesten hiding Cnut's wife and children? And telling Æthelred that he had captured them and was holding them hostage? 'So Cnut is deceiving Æthelred,' I said slowly.

'And if Æthelred feels safe to attack East Anglia?' she asked me.

'Then he'll march,' I said, 'and the moment his troops have left Mercia the Danes will attack there.'

'The Danes will attack Mercia,' she agreed. 'It's probably happening now. Æthelred thinks he's safe, and he's been fooled. The Mercian army is in East Anglia, and Cnut and Sigurd are in Mercia, destroying, burning, stealing, raping, killing.'

I watched the fire die. There was grey light over the mainland now, a grey light touching the inner sea with its ghostly shimmer. Dawn, the coming of light, and it was flooding into my thoughts at the same time. 'It makes sense,' I said uncertainly.

'Lord Ælfric had his spies everywhere,' she said, 'though he failed to find one in your household. But they were everywhere else and they sent their news to Bebbanburg. The men talked in the high hall and I listened. They never listened to me, but they let me hear. And sometimes my husband tells me things, if he's not beating me.'

'He beats you?'

144

She looked at me as though I was a fool. 'I'm his wife,' she said. 'If I displease him of course he beats me.'

'I've never beaten a woman.'

She smiled at that. 'Lord Ælfric always said you were a fool.'

'Maybe I am,' I said, 'but he was frightened of me.'

'He was terrified,' she agreed, 'and with every breath he drew he cursed you and prayed for your death.'

And it was Ælfric, not I, who had gone to the Corpse-Ripper. I watched the grey light brighten. 'Saint Oswald's arm,' I said, 'Bebbanburg still has it?'

She nodded. 'It's kept in the chapel, in a silver box, but my husband wants to give it to Æthelred.'

'To encourage him?'

'Because Cnut wants him to give it.'

'Ah,' I said, understanding. Cnut was encouraging Æthelred to invade East Anglia, and Æthelred would do that if he thought he could gain the magical assistance of Saint Oswald's body.

'Bebbanburg is weak,' Ingulfrid said. 'The fortress itself isn't weak. The fortress is hugely strong, and they can raise enough men to defend it against most enemies, but they daren't provoke a really dangerous enemy. So they stay safe by being agreeable to their neighbours.'

'Agreeable to the Danes.'

'To the Danes,' she said.

'So your husband is like Haesten,' I said, 'he survives by lying low and wagging his tail.'

She hesitated a heartbeat, then nodded. 'Yes.'

And Bebbanburg did not matter to the Danes. It mattered to me, but it was just an itch to the Danes. They wanted Bebbanburg, of course they did, but they wanted so much more. They wanted the rich fields, the slow rivers and thick woods of Mercia and Wessex. They wanted a country called Daneland. They wanted everything, and, while I was stranded on a Frisian beach, they were probably taking it.

And I thought of Æthelflaed. She was caught in the madness.

I did not know if that was true. At that moment, as the sun

145

blazed the east red, I knew nothing of what happened in Britain. It was all surmise. For all I knew the long peace had continued and I was just imagining chaos, but instinct told me otherwise. And if instinct is not the voice of the gods, what is it?

But why should I care? The Christians had spurned me and burned my estate. They had driven me from Mercia and outlawed me to this barren sand dune. I owed them nothing. If I had any sense, I thought, I should go to Cnut and offer him my sword, and then carry it through all Mercia and all Wessex, carry it clear to the southern coast and crush the pious fools who had spat in my face. I would have the bishops and abbots and priests kneeling to me and begging for my mercy.

And I thought of Æthelflaed.

And knew what I must do.

'So what do we do?' Finan greeted me next morning.

'Food,' I said, 'enough for three or four days at sea.'

He stared at me, surprised by the decisiveness in my voice, then nodded. 'There's plenty of fish and seal-meat,' he said.

'Smoke it,' I ordered. 'What about ale?'

'We've enough for a week. We took two barrels out of *Reinbôge*.'

Poor Blekulf. I had left him, his son and his crewman at Bebbanburg. He wanted to salvage the *Reinbôge*, but I told him to abandon it. 'Come with us,' I had said.

'Come with you where?'

'Frisia,' I had answered, and immediately regretted saying it. I had not been certain that Frisia would be my destination, though I could think of nowhere else to seek refuge. 'Sooner or later,' I had tried to cover my stupidity, 'we'll go to Frisia. I'm more likely to go to East Anglia first, but you can always get passage on a ship to Frisia from there.'

'I'll salvage *Reinbôge*,' Blekulf had insisted stubbornly, 'she's not stranded too high.' So he had stayed and I doubted he would have had time to refloat *Reinbôge* before my cousin's men found him, nor did I doubt that Blekulf would reveal that I was heading towards Frisia.

We could have sailed that day, or at least the next day if we stocked *Middelniht* with enough food, but we needed two or three days to recover from the storm. Weapons and mail had got wet and needed to be scoured with sand to grind away the last specks of rust, and so I told Finan we would leave after three nights.

'And where are we going?' he asked.

'To war,' I said grandly. 'We'll give the poets something to sing about. We'll wear their tongues out with singing! We're going to war, my friend,' I slapped Finan's shoulder, 'but right now I'm going to sleep. Keep the men busy, tell them they're going to be heroes!'

The heroes had to work first. There were seals to kill, fish to catch, and wood to collect so that the meat of both, cut into thin strips, could be smoked. Green wood is best for smoking and we had none, so we mixed the parched driftwood with seaweed and lit the fires and let the smoke smear the sky.

Middelniht had to be pampered. I had little enough material to make any repairs, but she needed little, and so we checked all her lines, sewed a rent in her sail, and cleaned her hull at low tide. It was during the same low tides that I took a dozen men and planted withies in the sandbanks. That was hard work. We had to dig holes in sand that was covered by shallow water, and as soon as we dug a pit the water and sand flowed back in. We kept digging, scrabbling with bare hands and broken boards, then thrust a pole as deep as we could before filling the hole with rocks to hold the withy upright. There were no rocks among the dunes and islets, so we used ballast stones from *Middelniht*, so many that we replaced the stones with sand. She would float a little high, but I reckoned she would be safe. It took two days, but then the withies showed above water even at high tide and, though a handful canted in the current and a couple floated away altogether, the rest showed a path through the treacherous shallows to our island refuge. A path for an enemy to follow.

And an enemy did come. It was not Thancward. He knew we

were back, and I saw his ship pass a couple of times, but he wanted no trouble and so ignored us. It was on our last day, a fine summer morning, that the ship arrived. She came just as we were leaving. We had burned the shelters, heaped our dried meat on board *Middelniht*, and now we hauled the anchor stone, put oars in tholes, and there she was, a ship come to fight.

She came from the west. We had been watching her approach and had seen the high, bright beast-head at her prow. The wind was westerly so she came under sail and as she drew nearer I saw the eagle pattern sewn into the thick sailcloth. A proud ship, a fine ship, and crammed with men whose helmets reflected back the sunlight.

To this day I do not know what ship that was or who commanded her. A Dane, I assume, and perhaps he was a Dane who wanted the reward my cousin promised to any man who killed me. Or perhaps he was just a passing predator who saw an easy capture, but whoever he was he saw our smaller ship and saw that *Middelniht* was trying to leave the islands, and he saw us row into the landward end of the channel I had marked with the rock-bolstered withies.

And he had me trapped. He was coming fast, driven by the wind in that rope-reinforced eagle-flaunting sail. All he needed to do was sail into the channel and slash his big hull down one of our flanks, snapping our oars, or else crash into us, hull against hull, and release his warriors into *Middelniht*'s belly where they would overwhelm us. And so they would, for his ship was twice the size of ours and his crew had more than twice our numbers.

I watched him come towards us as we rowed, and he was a fine sight. His dragon head was touched with gold, his eagle sail was woven with scarlet thread, and his banner on the masthead was a furl of sun-touched blue and gold. The water broke white at his prow. His men were mailed, armed, carrying shields and blades. He came for the kill, and he entered the marked channel and he could see we had no escape and I heard the roar of his men as they steeled themselves to our slaughter.

And then she struck.

The withies had led him onto a sandbank, which was why I had placed them so carefully.

She came, she struck, and the mast cracked and broke, so that the sail collapsed onto the bows and with it fell the heavy yard and splintered mast. Men were thrown forward by the impact as the heavy hull ground into the sand. One moment she had been a proud ship hunting prey, and now she was a wreck, her prow lifted by the sand and her hull filled with men struggling to their feet.

And I turned *Middelniht*'s steering oar so that we left the marked channel for the real channel, circling south around the sandbank where the proud ship was stranded. We rowed slowly, taunting that thwarted enemy, and as we passed her, just out of spear range, I waved a morning greeting to them.

Then we were at sea.

Ingulfrid and her son were close by me, Finan was beside me, my son and my men were at the oars. The sun shone on us, the water sparkled, the oar-blades dipped and we were gone.

Gone to make history.

Seven

The wheel of fortune was turning. I did not know it because most of the time we do not feel the wheel's motion, but it was turning fast as we sailed away from Frisia on that sun-bright summer's day.

I was going back to Britain. Going back to where the Christians hated me and the Danes mistrusted me. Going back because instinct told me the long peace was over. I believe instinct is the voice of the gods, but I was not so certain that those gods were telling me the truth. Gods lie and cheat too, they play tricks on us. I worried that we could have been sailing back to find a land at peace and that nothing had changed, so I was cautious.

If I had been certain of the gods' message I would have sailed north. I had thought about doing that. I had thought of sailing around the northern edge of the Scottish land, then south through the harsh islands and so down to the northern coast of Wales and east to where the rivers Dee and Mærse empty into the sea. It is only a short journey up the Dee to Ceaster, but though I suspected Haesten was concealing Cnut's family, I had no proof. Besides, with my small crew, what hope would I have against Haesten's garrison that was behind the Ceaster's harsh Roman walls?

So I was cautious. I sailed west, going to what I hoped would be a safe place where I might discover news. We had to row *Middelniht*, for the wind was against us, and all day we kept a slow oar-beat, using just twenty rowers so that men could take turns. I took my turn too.

That night was clear and we were alone beneath uncountable

stars. The milk of the gods was smeared behind the stars, an arch of light reflected from the waves. The world was made in fire and when it was finished the gods took the remnant sparks and embers and splashed them across the skies and I have never ceased to wonder at the glory of that great bright arch of milky starlight. 'If you're right,' Finan had joined me at the steering oar and broke my reverie, 'it could all be over.'

'The war?'

'If you're right.'

'If I'm right,' I said, 'then it hasn't started yet.'

Finan snorted at that. 'Cnut will chop Æthelred into scraps! It won't take him more than a day to fillet that gutless bastard.'

'I think Cnut will wait,' I said, 'and even then he won't attack Æthelred. He'll let him get tangled in East Anglia, he'll let him rot in the marshes, and then he'll march south into Mercia. And he'll wait for the harvest to be gathered before he marches.'

'There won't be much to harvest,' Finan said gloomily, 'not after this wet summer.'

'But he'll still want whatever he can steal,' I said, 'and if we're right about Haesten, then Æthelred thinks he's safe. He thinks he can fight in East Anglia without Cnut moving against him, so Cnut will wait just to convince Æthelred that he really is safe.'

'So Cnut attacks Mercia when?' Finan asked.

'A few days yet. It must be harvest time. Another week? Two?'

'And Æthelred will have his hands full in East Anglia.'

'And Cnut will take southern Mercia,' I said, 'then turn on Æthelred and keep a watch on Edward.'

'Will Edward march?'

'He has to,' I said with a vehemence that I hoped reflected the truth. 'Edward can't afford to let the Danes take all Mercia,' I went on, 'but those piss-brained priests might advise him to stay in his burhs. Let Cnut come to him.'

'So Cnut takes Mercia,' Finan said, 'then East Anglia, and marches on Wessex last.'

'That's what he wants to do. At least that's what I'd do if I was him.'

'So what are we doing?'

'Pulling the bastards out of the shit,' I said, 'of course.'

'All thirty-six of us?'

'You and me could do it alone,' I said scornfully.

He laughed at that. The wind was rising, heeling the ship. It was veering northwards too and if it continued to turn we would be able to raise the sail and pull the oars inboard. 'And what about Saint Oswald?' Finan asked.

'What about him?'

'Is Æthelred really trying to put the poor man back together?'

I was not sure about that. Æthelred was superstitious enough to believe the Christian claim that the saint's corpse had magical powers, but to get the corpse Æthelred would need to march into Danish-held Northumbria. So far as I knew he was willing to start a war with the East Anglian Danes, but would he risk another against the Northumbrian lords? Or did he believe that Cnut would never dare fight while his wife was held hostage? If he believed that then he might well risk a foray into Northumbria. 'We'll find out soon enough,' I said.

I gave the steering oar to Finan and left him to guide the ship while I picked my careful way through sleeping bodies, and past the twenty men who rowed slowly in the star-lightened darkness. I went to the prow, put a hand on the dragon post and gazed ahead.

I like standing at the prow of ships, and that night the sea was a spread of reflected starlight, a glittering path across the watery dark, but leading to what? I watched the sea wrinkle and sparkle, and listened to the water break and seethe on *Middelniht*'s hull as she rose and dipped to the small waves. The wind had veered enough to push us southwards, but as I had no clear idea where I wanted to go I did not call Finan and ask him to change course. I just let the ship follow that path of glittering light across the starlit sea.

'And what happens to me?'

It was Ingulfrid. I had not heard her come down the long deck, but I turned and saw her pale face framed by the hood of Ælfric's cloak. 'What happens to you?' I asked. 'You'll go home with your son when your husband pays the ransom, of course.'

'And what happens to me at home?'

I was about to answer that it was none of my concern what happened to her at Bebbanburg, then understood why she had asked the question, and why she had asked it in such bitter tones. 'Nothing,' I answered, knowing it was a lie.

'My husband will beat me,' she said, 'and probably worse.'

'Worse?'

'I'm a disgraced woman.'

'You're not.'

'And he'll believe that?'

I said nothing for a while, then shook my head. 'He won't believe it,' I said.

'So he'll beat me, and then in all likelihood he'll kill me.'

'He will?'

'He's a proud man.'

'And a fool,' I said.

'But fools kill too,' she said.

It crossed my mind to say that she should have thought of all those consequences before insisting on accompanying her son, then saw she was crying and so kept my words unsaid. She made no noise. She was just sobbing silently, then Osferth came from the rowers' benches and put an arm around her shoulders. She turned to him and leaned her head on his chest and just cried.

'She's a married woman,' I said to Osferth.

'And I am a sinner,' he said, 'cursed by God because of my birth. God can do no more harm to me, because my father's sin has already doomed me.' He looked at me defiantly and, when I said nothing, gently led Ingulfrid aft. I watched them go.

What fools we are.

We made landfall two mornings later, coming to the coast in a silvery mist. We were rowing, and for a time I followed the shore

153

that was a dull line to my right. The water was shallow, there was no wind, only thousands of sea-birds who flew from our approach to ruffle the flat sea with their wing-beats.

'Where are we?' Osferth asked me.

'I don't know.'

Finan was at the prow. He had the best eyes of any man I ever knew and he was watching that flat, dull shore for any sign of life. He saw none. He was also watching for sandbanks and we were rowing slowly for fear of going aground. The tide was carrying us, and our oars did little else than keep the ship steady.

Then Finan called that he had seen markers. Withies again, and a moment later he saw some hovels among the sand dunes and we turned towards the shore. I followed the channel marked by the withies, and it was a real channel that took us into the shelter of a low sandy headland and so to a small harbour where four fishing boats were grounded. I could smell the fires that smoked the fish and I ran *Middelniht* up onto the sand, knowing that the incoming tide would float her off, and so we came back to Britain.

I was dressed for war. I wore mail, a cloak, a helmet, and had Serpent-Breath at my side, though I could not imagine meeting any enemies in this bleak, mist-wrapped loneliness. Yet still I put on my battle-glory and, leaving Finan in command of *Middelniht*, took a half-dozen men ashore with me. Whoever lived in this tiny village on this desolate shore had seen us coming, and they had probably run away to hide, but I knew they would be watching us through the mist, and I did not want to overwhelm them by landing more than a handful of men. The houses were made of driftwood and thatched with reeds. One house, larger than the rest, was framed by the ribs of a wrecked ship. I ducked under its low lintel and saw a fire smoking in a central hearth, two rush beds, some pottery, and a big iron cauldron. In this place, I thought, such objects counted as wealth. A dog growled from the shadows and I growled back. There was no one inside.

We walked a short way inland. An earthen wall had been made at some time, a bank that stretched either side into the mist. The years had smoothed the earth wall and I wondered who had made it and why. It did not seem to protect anything, unless the villagers feared the frogs of the marsh that stretched bleakly north into the lightening mist. Wherever I looked I saw only bog land and reeds and damp and grass. 'Heaven on earth,' Osferth said. It was his idea of a jest.

My instinct told me we were in that strange bay that pierces the eastern flank of Britain between the lands of East Anglia and Northumbria. It is called the Gewæsc and is a vast bay, shallow and treacherous, edged by nothing but flat land, yet it sees many ships. Like the Humbre, the Gewæsc is a route into Britain and it had tempted scores of Danish boats, which had rowed up the bay to the four rivers that drained into the shallow waters, and if I was right then we had landed on the Gewæsc's northern shore and so were in Northumbria. My land. Danish land. Enemy land.

We waited a few paces beyond the old earth wall. A track led north, though it was little more than a path of trampled reeds. If we did nothing hostile then eventually someone would show themselves, and so they did. Two men, their nakedness half covered by sealskin, appeared on the track and walked cautiously towards us. They were both bearded and both had dark, greasy and matted hair. They could have been any age from twenty to fifty, their faces and bodies so grimed with dirt that they looked as though they had crept from some underground lair. I spread my hands to show I meant no harm. 'Where are we?' I asked them when they came into earshot.

'Botulfstan,' one of them answered.

Which meant we were at Botulf's stone, though there was no sign of anyone called Botulf, or his rock. I asked who Botulf was and they seemed to suggest he was their lord, though their accent was so mangled that it was hard to understand them. 'Botulf farms here?' I asked, this time in Danish, but they just shrugged.

'Botulf was a great saint,' Osferth explained to me, 'and a prayer to Saint Botulf will protect travellers.'

'Why travellers?'

'He was a great traveller himself, I suppose.'

'I'm not surprised,' I said, 'the poor bastard probably wanted to get away from this shit village.' I looked back to the two men. 'You have a lord? Where does he live?'

One of them pointed northwards and so we followed the track in that direction. Logs had been placed across the boggiest stretches, though they had long rotted and the damp timber crunched beneath our feet. The mist was obstinate. I could see the sun as a glowing patch of light, but even though the patch climbed higher in the sky the mist did not burn off. We seemed to walk for ever, just us and the marsh birds and the reeds and the long slimy pools. I began to think there would be no end to the desolation, but at last I saw a crude thorn fence and a small pasture where five sodden sheep with dung-clotted tails grazed among thistles. Beyond the sheep were buildings, at first just dark shapes in the mist, then I saw a hall, a barn and a palisade. A dog began to bark, and the sound brought a man to the open palisade gate. He was elderly, dressed in torn mail, and carrying a spear with a rusted blade. 'Is this Botulfstan?' I asked him in Danish.

'Botulf died long ago,' he said in the same language.

'Then who lives here?'

'Me,' he said helpfully.

'Gorm!' a woman's voice called from inside the palisade. 'Let them in!'

'And her,' Gorm said sullenly, 'she lives here too.' He stood aside.

The hall was made of timbers blackened by damp and age. The rush-thatched roof was thick with moss. A mangy dog was tied to a doorpost with a rope of plaited leather that strained as he leaped towards us, but the woman snapped at him and the dog lay down. She was an older woman, grey-haired, dressed in a long brown cloak gathered at her neck by a heavy silver brooch that was shaped like a hammer. No Christian then. 'My husband isn't here,' she greeted us brusquely. She spoke Danish. The villagers had been Saxons.

'And who is your husband?' I asked.

'Who are you?' she retorted.

'Wulf Ranulfson,' I said, using the name I had invented at Grimesbi, 'out of Haithabu.'

156

'You're a long way from home.'

'So is your husband it seems.'

'He is Hoskuld Irenson,' she said in a tone that suggested we should have heard of him.

'And he serves?' I asked.

She hesitated, as if reluctant to answer, then relented. 'Sigurd Thorrson.'

Sigurd Thorrson was Cnut Ranulfson's friend and ally, the second great Northumbrian lord, and a man who hated me because I had killed his son. True, the death had been in battle and the boy had died with a sword in his hand, but Sigurd would still hate me till his own death came.

'I have heard of Sigurd Thorrson,' I said.

'Who has not?'

'I have hopes of serving him,' I said.

'How did you come here?' she demanded, sounding indignant, as if no one should ever discover this rotting hall in its wide marsh.

'We crossed the sea, lady,' I said.

'The wrong sea,' she said, sounding amused, 'and you're a long way from Sigurd Thorrson.'

'And you, my lady, are?' I asked gently.

'I am Frieda.'

'If you have ale,' I said, 'we can pay for it.'

'Not steal it?'

'Pay for it,' I said, 'and while we drink it you can tell me why I have crossed the wrong sea.'

We paid a scrap of silver for ale that tasted of ditch-water, and Frieda explained that her husband had been summoned to serve his lord, that he had taken the six men from the estate who were skilled with weapons, and that they had ridden westwards. 'Jarl Sigurd said they should take their boat, but we don't have a ship.'

'Take it where?'

'To the western sea,' she said, 'the sea that lies between us and Ireland,' and she sounded vague as though Ireland was just a name to her, 'but we have no ship, so my husband went by horse.'

'The Jarl Sigurd is summoning his men?'

'He is,' she said, 'and so is the Jarl Cnut. And I pray they all return safely.'

From the western sea? I thought about that. It meant, surely, that Cnut and Sigurd were gathering ships and the only place on the western coast where they could assemble a fleet was close to Haesten's fortress at Ceaster. The coast to the south of Ceaster was Welsh, and those savages would not give shelter to a Danish fleet, while the shore to the north was Cumbraland, which is as wild and lawless as Wales, so the Danes must be gathering at Ceaster. So where would the fleet go? To Wessex? Frieda did not know. 'There will be war,' she said, 'and there already is war.'

'Already?'

She gestured northwards. 'I hear the Saxons are in Lindcolne!'

'Saxons!' I pretended surprise.

'The news came yesterday. Hundreds of Saxons!'

'And Lindcolne is where?' I asked.

'There,' she said, pointing north again.

I had heard of Lindcolne, though I had never visited the place. It had been an important town once, built by the Romans and made larger by the Saxons who captured the land when the Romans had left, though rumour said the town had been burned by the Danes who now occupied the fort on Lindcolne's high ground. 'How far is Lindcolne?' I asked her.

She did not know. 'But my husband can be there and back in two days,' she suggested, 'so it's not far.'

'And what are the Saxons doing there?' I asked.

'Dunging the ground with their filth,' she said, 'I don't know. I just hope they don't come here.'

Lindcolne lay north, well inside Northumbria. If Frieda was right then a Saxon army had dared invade Sigurd Thorrson's land, and they would only do that if they were sure of provoking no reprisals, and the only way to prevent such reprisals was if Cnut Longsword's wife and children were hostages in Saxon hands. 'Do you have horses, lady?' I asked.

'You're hungry?' she scoffed.

'I would borrow horses, lady, to find out more about these Saxons.'

She drove a hard bargain, making me rent the two miserable nags left in the stable. Both were mares, both were old, and neither looked as if she had stamina, but they were horses and we needed them. I told Osferth he would accompany me to Lindcolne and sent the other men back to *Middelniht*. 'Tell Finan we'll be back in three days,' I told them, hoping that was true.

Osferth was reluctant to leave *Middelniht* and Ingulfrid. 'She'll be safe,' I snarled at him.

'Yes, lord,' he said distantly.

'She'll be safe! Finan will make sure of that.'

He threw a saddle over the smaller mare. 'I know, lord.'

I was taking Osferth because he was useful. All I knew of the Saxons at Lindcolne was that they had come from Æthelred's army, which meant they were probably sworn to my destruction, but Osferth, even though he was bastard born, was Alfred's son and men treated him with the respect and deference due to the son of a king. He had a natural authority, and his Christianity was beyond argument, and I needed all the support his presence might give me.

Osferth and I mounted. The stirrup leathers were too short and the girths too big, and I wondered if we would ever make it to Lindcolne, but the two mares ambled northwards willingly enough, though neither seemed capable of going any faster than an exhausted walk. 'If we meet Danes,' Osferth said, 'we're in trouble.'

'They'd more likely die from laughing if they see these horses.'

He grimaced at that. The mist was slowly melting away to reveal a wide, empty land of marsh and reed. That was a bleak, treeless place. Some folk lived in the marshes because we saw their hovels in the distance and passed eel traps in dark ditches, but we saw no one. Osferth seemed to grow more gloomy with every mile we travelled. 'What will you do with the boy?' he asked after a while.

'Sell him back to his father, of course,' I said, 'unless someone else offers more money.'

'And his mother will go with him.'

'Will she?' I asked. 'You know better than I what she'll do.'

He was staring across the wetland. 'She'll die,' he said.

'So she says.'

'You believe her?' he challenged me.

I nodded. 'There's plainly no affection there. Everyone will assume we raped her, and her husband won't believe her denials, so yes, he'll probably kill her.'

'Then she can't go back!' Osferth said fiercely.

'That's her decision,' I said.

We rode in silence for a while. 'The Lady Ingulfrid,' he broke the silence, 'was not allowed to leave Bebbanburg for fifteen years. She might as well have been a prisoner.'

'Is that why she came with us? To smell the air outside?'

'A mother wants to be with her son,' he said.

'Or away from her husband,' I replied tartly.

'If we keep the boy . . .' he began, then faltered.

'He's no use to me,' I said, 'except for what his father will pay. I should have sold him when we were at Bebbanburg, but I wasn't sure we'd get out of the harbour alive unless we held him hostage. Since then he's just been a nuisance.'

'He's a good boy,' Osferth said defensively.

'And as long as he lives,' I said, 'the good boy believes he has a claim to Bebbanburg. I should cut his lousy throat.'

'No!'

'I don't kill children,' I said, 'but in another few years? In another few years I'll have to kill him.'

'I'll buy him from you,' Osferth blurted out.

'You? Where will you get the gold?'

'I'll buy him!' he said obstinately. 'Just give me time.'

I sighed. 'We'll sell the boy back to his father and persuade his mother to stay with us. That's what you want, isn't it?' He nodded, but said nothing. 'You're in love,' I said, and saw I had embarrassed him, but pressed on anyway, 'and being in love changes everything. A man will fight through the fires of Ragnarok because he's in love; he'll forget all the world and do insane things just for the woman he loves.'

'I know,' he said.

'You do? You've never had the madness before.'

'I've watched you,' he said, 'and you're not doing this for Wessex or for Mercia, you're doing this for my sister.'

'Who is a married woman,' I said harshly.

'We are all sinners,' he said and made the sign of the cross. 'God forgive us.'

We fell silent. The road was climbing now, though only to slightly higher ground where, at last, trees grew. They were alders and willow, all bent westwards from the cold wind of the sea. The higher ground was good pasture land, still flat, but hedged and ditched, and with cows and sheep at grass. There were villages and fine halls. It was afternoon by now and we stopped at one hall and asked for ale, bread and cheese. The servants in the hall were Danish and told us their lord had ridden westwards to join Sigurd Thorrson. 'When did he go?' I asked.

'Six days ago, lord.'

So Cnut and Sigurd had not launched their invasion yet, or else they were sailing even as we spoke. 'I heard the Saxons are in Lindcolne,' I said to the steward.

'Not in Lindcolne, lord. In Bearddan Igge.'

'Bearda's Island?' I repeated the name. 'Where's that?'

'Not far from Lindcolne, lord. A short ride to the east.'

'How many?'

He shrugged. 'Two hundred? Three?' He plainly did not know, but his answer confirmed my suspicion that Æthelred had not brought his whole army into Northumbria, but instead had sent a strong war-band.

'They're there to attack Lindcolne?' I asked.

He laughed. 'They daren't! They'd die!'

'Then why are they there?'

'Because they're fools, lord?'

'So what's at Bearddan Igge?' I asked.

'Nothing, lord,' the steward said, and I saw Osferth open his mouth to speak, then think better of it.

'There's a monastery at Bearddan Igge,' Osferth told me as we rode on, 'or there used to be before the pagans burned it.'

'Good to know they did something useful,' I said, and was rewarded with a glower.

'It is where Saint Oswald's body is buried,' Osferth said.

I stared at him. 'Why didn't you tell me that before?'

'I'd forgotten the name, lord, till the man said it. Bearddan Igge: it's a strange name, but a holy place.'

'And full of Æthelred's men,' I said, 'digging up a saint.'

The sun was low in the west as we approached Bearddan Igge. The land was still flat and the ground damp. We forded lazy streams and crossed drainage ditches that ran straight as arrows between soggy pastures. We had joined a larger road and that too ran straight as an arrow. We passed a Roman milestone, fallen over and half hidden by grass, and the carving on the stone said 'Lindum VIII' which meant, I assumed, that it was eight miles to the town we call Lindcolne. 'Did the Romans use miles?' I asked Osferth.

'They did, lord.'

It was not far beyond the fallen milestone that the war-band saw us. They were to our west where the sun was low and dazzling in the sky, and they saw us long before we saw them. There were eight of them, mounted on big stallions, the riders armed with spears or swords, and they galloped across the wetland, their hooves hurling up great clods of damp earth. We curbed our miserable nags and waited.

The eight men surrounded us. Their horses stamped the track as the riders inspected us. I saw their leader's eyes look at my hammer, then at the cross hanging at Osferth's neck. 'You call those things horses?' he sneered. Then, when neither of us answered, 'And who in God's name are you?'

'He's the priest-killer,' one of his men supplied the answer. He was the only man with a shield and that shield was painted with Æthelred's prancing white horse. 'I recognise him,' the man went on.

The questioner looked into my eyes. I could see surprise on his face. 'You're Uhtred?'

'He's Lord Uhtred,' Osferth said reprovingly.

'You'll come with us,' the man said curtly, and turned his horse.

162

I nodded at Osferth to indicate we would obey. 'We should take their swords,' another of the men suggested.

'Try,' I said pleasantly.

They decided not to try, leading us instead across waterlogged pastures, over ditches, and finally to a damp road that led north and east. I could see a mass of horses in the distance. 'How many men are you?' I asked. No one answered. 'And who leads you?'

'Someone who'll decide whether a priest-killer should live or die,' the man who was evidently the leader answered.

But the wheel of fortune was still hoisting me upwards because the decision-maker turned out to be Merewalh, and I saw the relief on his face when he recognised me. I had known him for years. He was one of Æthelred's men, and a good one. He and I had been together outside Ceaster, and Merewalh had always taken my advice and, so far as Æthelred allowed him, cooperated with me. He had never been close to Æthelred. Merewalh was a man who was chosen for the uncomfortable tasks, like riding the frontier between Saxon and Danish lands while other men basked in the comfort of Æthelred's approval. Now Merewalh had been given the job of leading three hundred men deep into Northumbria. 'We're looking for Saint Oswald,' he explained.

'What's left of him.'

'He's supposed to be buried here,' he said, and gestured at a field where his men had been digging so that the whole expanse of grass was pocked by opened graves, mounds of earth, and rows of bones. A few rotted posts showed where there had once been a monastery. 'The Danes burned it years ago,' Merewalh said.

'And they dug up Saint Oswald too,' I said, 'and they probably pounded his bones to dust and scattered them to the winds.'

Merewalh was a good friend, but there were also enemies waiting for me in that drab field called Bearddan Igge. There were three priests led by Ceolberht whom I recognised by his toothless gums, and my arrival spurred him to a new rant. I was to be killed. I was the pagan who had killed the saintly Abbot Wihtred. I had been cursed by God and by man. Men crowded around to hear him, listening as he spat his hatred. 'I command you,' Ceolberht spoke to Merewalh, but pointed to me, 'in the name of the Father and of the Son and of the Holy Ghost to put that evil man to death.'

But though these Mercians were Christians they were also nervous. They had been sent on an idiotic errand deep inside enemy land and they knew they were being watched by Danes patrolling from the high fort at Lindcolne. The longer they stayed at Bearddan Igge the more nervous they became, expecting any moment to be attacked by a larger and more powerful enemy. They wanted to be back with Æthelred's army, but the priests were insisting that Saint Oswald could be found and must be found. Ceolberht and his priests were insisting that I was an outlaw, fated to be killed, but these men also knew I was a warlord, that I had won battle after battle against the Danes, and at that moment they feared the Danes more then they feared the wrath of their nailed god. Ceolberht ranted, but no one moved to kill me.

'Have you finished?' I asked Ceolberht when he paused to catch his breath.

'You have been declared an . . .' he began again

'How many teeth do you have left?' I interrupted him. He said nothing, just gawped at me. 'So keep your mouth closed,' I said, 'if you don't want me to kick the rest of your rotten teeth out of your jaw.' I turned back to Merewalh. 'The Danes are just letting you dig?'

He nodded. 'They know we're here.'

'How long have you been here?'

'Three days. The Danes send men from Lindcolne to watch us, but they don't interfere.'

'They don't interfere,' I said, 'because they want you here.'

He frowned at that. 'Why would they want us here?'

I raised my voice. Most of Merewalh's men were close by and I wanted them to hear what I had to say. 'The Danes want you here because they want Æthelred to be bogged down in East Anglia while they attack Mercia.'

'You're wrong!' Father Ceolberht yapped triumphantly.

164

'I am?' I asked him mildly.

'God has delivered the Danes to us!' Ceolberht said.

'They won't attack Mercia,' Merewalh explained the priest's confidence, 'because we have Cnut's son as a hostage.'

'You do?' I asked.

'Well, not me, no.'

'So who does?'

Ceolberht was plainly unwilling to reveal anything to me, but Merewalh trusted me. Besides, what he told me was already known to his men. 'The Lord Æthelred,' he explained, 'made a truce with Haesten. You remember Haesten?'

'Of course I remember Haesten,' I said. Merewalh and I had met outside Haesten's fortress; we had become friends there.

'Haesten has become a Christian!' Father Ceolberht put in.

'And all Haesten wants,' Merewalh told me, 'is to be left in peace in Ceaster, so the Lord Æthelred promised to leave him there if he converted, and if he did us a service.'

'The Lord God disposes!' Ceolberht crowed.

'And the service,' I asked, 'was capturing Cnut's wife and two children?'

'Yes,' Merewalh said simply and proudly. 'So you see? Cnut won't move. He thinks the Lord Æthelred has his family.'

'The Lord God Almighty has delivered our enemies into our grasp,' Ceolberht shouted, 'and we lie under his divine protection. God be praised!'

'You're idiots,' I said, 'all of you! I was in Cnut's hall just after his wife was captured and who was there with him? Haesten! And what was he wearing around his neck? One of these!' I held up my own hammer of Thor. 'Haesten is no more a Christian than I am, and Haesten is sworn to Cnut Ranulfson's service, and Cnut Ranulfson has sent orders that his thegns, his followers, his warriors are to assemble at Ceaster. With ships!'

'He lies,' Ceolberht shouted.

'If I lie to you,' I said to the priest, but loudly enough for all Merewalh's men to hear, 'then my life is yours. If I lie to you then I shall bend my neck in front of you and you can hack off my

165

head.' That silenced the priest. He just stared at me. Merewalh believed me, and so did his men. I plucked Osferth's sleeve, bringing him to stand beside me. 'This man is a Christian. He is the son of King Alfred. He will tell you I speak the truth.'

'He does,' Osferth said.

'He lies!' Ceolberht said, but he had lost the argument. Men believed me, not the priest, and their world had changed. They were no longer safe, but poised on the edge of chaos.

I drew Merewalh aside to the shadows under a willow. 'The last time Cnut attacked,' I said, 'he took ships to the south coast of Wessex. He's gathering ships again.'

'To attack Wessex?'

'I don't know, but it doesn't matter.'

'No?'

'What matters,' I said, 'is that we have to make him dance to our drum. He thinks we're capering to his.'

'Æthelred won't believe you,' Merewalh said nervously.

I suspected that was true. Æthelred had launched his war and he would be unwilling to believe that he had started that war because he had been deceived. He would insist that he was right and his hatred of me would make him even more stubborn. I decided that did not matter. Æthelred would be forced to believe me soon enough. What mattered was to unbalance Cnut. 'You should send most of your men back to Æthelred,' I told Merewalh.

'Without the saint?'

I was about to snarl at him, but checked myself. Æthelred had promised his army the assistance of Saint Oswald, and though Æthelred's men were in the wrong place, and though Æthelred would be unwilling to abandon his war on East Anglia, it still made sense to give his army the confidence of magical assistance.

'Tomorrow,' I said, 'we'll make one last attempt to find Oswald. Then send him back to Æthelred.'

'Send him?'

'I have a ship less than a day's ride from here,' I told him. 'Forty of your men will go there with Osferth. They'll send my men back here on their horses. Until they arrive you can look for your saint.

If you find him you can send two hundred men back to Æthelred with the bones, but the rest will come with me.'

'But . . .' He fell silent. He was thinking that he could not detach men to follow me without incurring Æthelred's wrath.

'If you don't do what I say,' I told him, 'Æthelred will be dead within the month and Mercia will be Danish. If you trust me then both will be alive.'

'I trust you,' he said.

'Then get some sleep,' I told him, 'because tomorrow we're busy.'

I waited till the heart of the night, till the darkest hour when only the shadow-walkers tread the earth, when men sleep and owls fly, when the fox hunts and the world trembles at every small noise. The night is death's kingdom. Merewalh's sentries were awake, but they were at the edge of his encampment, and none was close to the sodden timber wreckage of the old monastery. Two fires smouldered there and by their small light I walked past the skeletons that had been prised from the earth and lain reverently in a long row. Father Ceolberht had declared that they must all be reburied with prayers, for these were the monks of Bearddan Igge, the monks who had lived here before the Danes came to burn, to steal and to kill.

The bones were wrapped in new woollen shrouds. I counted twenty-seven. At the far end of the row a shroud had been placed flat on the ground and heaped with more bones and skulls, orphan remains that had been unattached to any skeleton, and beyond that pile was a cart with a pair of high wheels. The cart was just big enough to contain a man. The flanks had been painted with crosses that I could just see in the faint glow of the dying fires. A folded cloth lay on the cart's bed and, when I touched it, I felt the smooth, expensive material that is called silk and is imported from some distant country to the east. The silk was obviously meant to be a new shroud for Saint Oswald, the only difficulty being that Saint Oswald no longer existed.

So it was time for another resurrection.

I wondered if anyone had counted the skeletons, or, if they had, whether they would count them again before they were reburied. Yet I had little time and I doubted I could discover yet another body, not without making enough noise to rouse the nearest sleepers who were only yards away, and so I picked a corpse at random and unwrapped the woollen winding sheet. I felt the bones. They were clean, suggesting that these skeletons had been washed before being shrouded, and when I lifted one dry arm the bones stayed connected, suggesting this monk had died not long before the monastery had been destroyed.

I crouched beside the dead man and felt in my pouch for the silver cross I had worn when we deceived the sentries on Bebbanburg's Low Gate. It was a heavy cross with garnets embedded into the arms. I had planned to sell it, but now it must serve another purpose, though first I had to dismember the skeleton. I used a knife to hack off one arm and the skull, then carried the severed parts to the heap of orphaned bones.

After that it was simple. I laid the silver cross inside the ribcage, tangling the chain around one rib, then used the woollen shroud to pick the man up and carry him west towards a sluggish stream. I laid him in the shallow water, pulled the shroud free and tugged an eel trap across the bones. I left the dead man to ripple the slow current as I wrung as much water from the shroud as I could, then dropped the damp wool onto a dying fire where it hissed and steamed. Most of it would be charred and unrecognisable by morning. I went back to the dead monks and moved the skeletons to disguise the gap I had made, then touched the hammer about my neck and prayed to Thor that no one made a new count of the bodies.

Then, because when dawn came I must be busy, I slept.

I called Osferth and Merewalh to me in the dawn, but a dozen other men came too. They were thegns, important men, landowners in Mercia who had brought their warriors to serve in Æthelred's army. They were subdued, perhaps because a thick mist draped the flat land, or because their confidence in Æthelred had been destroyed by my news of Haesten's true allegiance. We gathered round the cart, where servants brought us pots of weak ale and slabs of hard bread.

Merewalh was the Mercian leader, but Merewalh deferred to me, just as he had at Ceaster so many years before. 'You,' I pointed to Osferth, 'will ride back to *Middelniht* today.' I looked at Merewalh. 'You'll give him a good horse and forty men.'

'Forty?'

'A crew,' I explained, and looked back to Osferth. 'You send Finan and his men to me on the horses you take to *Middelniht*. Tell him to come quickly and to bring the rest of my war gear. After that you sail to Lundene and warn the garrison what's happening, then find your half-brother and tell him.' Osferth's half-brother was King of Wessex, and we would need the strong West Saxon army if Cnut was to be defeated. 'Tell him the Danes are coming either to Mercia or Wessex, that they're coming in force and he's to look for me in the west.'

'In the west,' Osferth repeated solemnly.

'I don't know where,' I said, 'but if Cnut attacks Mercia then King Edward should take his forces to Gleawecestre. If Cnut attacks Wessex then I'll join him, but I think it'll be Mercia, so send your brother to Gleawecestre.'

'Why Gleawecestre?' one of the thegns asked. 'We don't know what Cnut will do!'

'We know he'll attack,' I said, 'and as long as he's loose then he can march where he likes and do what damage he pleases, so we have to snare him. We have to make him fight where we want to fight, not where he chooses.'

'But . . .'

'I've chosen the west,' I snarled, 'and I'll make him fight where I choose.'

No one spoke. They probably did not believe me, but I was telling them the truth.

'I need a hundred of your men,' I told Merewalh, 'the best of them on the lightest horses. You can lead them.'

169

He nodded slowly. 'To go where?'

'With me,' I said. 'The rest of your men will rejoin Æthelred. Tell him you're sorry, but Saint Oswald was scattered to the winds long ago.'

'He won't like it,' a heavy-set man called Oswin said.

'He won't like any of the news,' I said, 'and he'll refuse to believe it. He'll stay in East Anglia till he's proved wrong, and then he'll be terrified of going home. But he has to go towards Gleawecestre.' I looked at Osferth. 'Have your brother send him orders.'

'I will,' Osferth said.

'And have Edward tell Æthelred that if he wants to stay Lord of Mercia he'd best move his arse quickly.'

'And what are you going to do?' Oswin asked indignantly.

'I'm going to kick Cnut's balls,' I said, 'and kick them so hard that he'll be forced to turn and deal with me, and then I'll hold him in place till the rest of you can come and kill the bastard once and for all.'

'We can't even be sure Cnut will attack,' another of the thegns said nervously.

'Wake up!' I shouted at him, startling all of the men gathered about the cart. 'The war has started! We just don't know where or how. But Cnut began it and we're going to finish it.'

No one said anything more because just at that moment there was another shout, a triumphant shout, and I saw men running towards the shallow stream that curled about the western end of the encampment. Father Ceolberht was there, waving his arms, and the two other priests were with him, both on their knees. 'God be praised!' one of them shouted.

Merewalh and his men stared towards the priests. Osferth looked at me.

'We've found him!' Ceolberht called. 'We've found the saint!'

'God be praised,' the priest called again.

We all walked toward the stream. 'You were so wrong!' Ceolberht greeted me, his voice made sibilant by his missing teeth. 'Our God is greater than you know. He has delivered the saint to us! Uhtred was wrong and we were right!'

170

Men were lifting the skeleton from the water, disentangling weeds and strands of willow that had broken from the fish trap. They carried the bones reverently towards the cart.

'You were wrong,' Merewalh said to me.

'I was wrong,' I said, 'indeed I was.'

'Victory will be ours!' Ceolberht said. 'Look! A cross!' He lifted the silver cross out of the ribcage. 'The cross of the blessed Saint Oswald.' He kissed the silver and gave me a look of pure hatred. 'You mocked us, but you were wrong. Our God is greater than you will ever know! It is a miracle! A miracle! Our God preserved the saint through trial and tribulation, and now he will grant us victory over the pagans.'

'God be praised,' Merewalh said, and he and his men stepped back reverently as the yellowed bones were laid on the cart's bed.

I let the Christians have their moment of happiness as I drew Osferth to one side. 'Take *Middelniht* to Lundene,' I told him, 'and take Ingulfrid and the boy with you.'

He nodded, began to say something and then decided to stay silent.

'I don't know what I'll do with the boy yet,' I said, 'and I have to deal with Cnut first, but keep him safe. He's worth a lot of gold.'

'I'll buy him from you,' Osferth said.

'Let his father do the buying,' I said, 'and you deal with the mother. But keep them both safe!'

'I shall keep them safe,' Osferth said. The priests had begun to sing, and Osferth watched them with his usual serious expression. There were times when he looked so like his father that I was almost tempted to call him 'lord'. 'I remember,' he still looked at the three chanting priests as he spoke, 'that you once told me your uncle was given an arm of Saint Oswald.'

'He was, yes. Ingulfrid has seen it. You can ask her.'

'The left arm, you said?'

'Did I?'

'I have a memory for these things,' he said solemnly, 'and you said it was the left arm.'

'I don't remember,' I said, 'and how would I have known which arm it was?'

171

'You said it was the left arm,' he insisted. 'One of your spies must have told you.'

'So it was the left arm,' I said.

'Then this truly is a miracle,' Osferth said, still gazing towards the men crowded about the cart, 'because that body is missing its right arm.'

'It is?'

'Yes, lord, it is.' He looked at me and surprised me by smiling. 'I shall tell Finan to hurry, lord.'

'Tell him I want him here tomorrow.'

'He'll be here, lord, and God speed you.'

'I hope he speeds you to Lundene,' I said. 'We need your brother's army.'

He hesitated. 'And what are you going to do, lord?'

'You'll tell no one?' I asked.

'I promise, lord,' he said, and when Osferth gave a promise I knew it would be kept.

'I'm going to do what I was accused of doing all those weeks ago,' I told him. 'I'm going to capture Cnut's wife and children.'

He nodded as if such a task was to be expected, then frowned. 'And will you make sure my sister is safe?'

'That above all,' I said.

Because I had made a promise to Æthelflaed, and that was one oath I had never broken.

Which meant I would be riding westwards. To meet Cnut Longsword.

Eight

We left Bearddan Igge in a thick fog just two mornings after Saint Oswald had been so miraculously discovered entangled in the fish trap.

One hundred and thirty-three men rode. We took fifty pack-horses to carry armour and weapons, and we carried two banners: the wolf's head of Bebbanburg and the white horse of Mercia, though for most of our journey those banners would have to stay hidden. We also took one priest, Father Wissian. Merewalh insisted that a priest accompany us. He said his men fought better when they had a priest to shepherd their souls, and I growled that they were warriors, not sheep, but Merewalh insisted in his polite way and so I grudgingly permitted Wissian to ride with us. He was a Mercian, a tall, thin young man with a perpetually nervous look and an unkempt shock of hair that had gone prematurely white. 'We'll be riding through Danish land,' I told him, 'and I don't want them knowing we're Saxons, which means you can't wear that dress,' I pointed to his long black priestly robe, 'so take it off.'

'I can't . . .' he began, then just stammered.

'Take it off,' I ordered him again, 'and borrow a mail coat or a leather jerkin.'

'I . . .' he began again and discovered he still could not talk, but he obeyed me and changed into a servant's drab clothes, which he then covered with a long black cloak that he belted at the waist with a length of twine so that he still looked like a priest, though at least his heavy wooden cross was covered.

We rode to save Christianity in Britain. Was that true? Father Ceolberht claimed it was true in a fiery sermon he had preached on the day we waited for Finan's arrival. The priest had harangued Merewalh's men, telling them that the Christian's holy book had foretold how the king of the north would attack the king of the south, and that this prophecy was being fulfilled, which meant it was now God's war. Perhaps it was, but Cnut was no king even though he did come from the north. I have often wondered whether, if the Danes had won and if I now lived in a country called Daneland, would we be Christians? I would like to think not, but the truth was that Christianity was already infecting the Danes. That long war was never about religion. Alfred believed it was, the priests proclaimed it a holy struggle, and men died under the banner of the cross in the belief that once we were all Christians, both Saxons and Danes, we would live in perpetual peace, but that was plain wrong. The Danes of East Anglia were Christians, but that did not stop the Saxons attacking them. The simple truth was that the Danes and the Saxons wanted the same land. The priests said that the lion would lie down with the lamb, but I never saw that happen. Not that I ever knew what a lion was. I once asked Mehrasa, Father Cuthbert's dark-skinned wife, if she had ever seen a lion and she said yes, she had, and that when she was a child the lions would come from the desert to kill cattle in her village, and that they were animals larger than any horse and had six legs, two forked tails, three horns made of molten iron and teeth like seaxes. Eohric, who had been King of East Anglia before we killed him, had a lion on his banner and his animal had only four legs and one horn, but I doubted Eohric had ever seen a lion so I suppose Mehrasa was right.

We rode anyway, and if we did not ride to save Christianity we did ride to save the Saxons.

Perhaps the most dangerous part of all that journey was the first, though it did not seem so at the time. We had to cross the river at Lindcolne and, to save time, and because we were shrouded by the thick fog, I chose to use the bridge. We knew there was a bridge because a frightened cowherd at Bearddan Igge stammered

174

that he had seen it. He knelt to me, awed by my mail, my helmet, my fur-edged cloak and my silver-spurred boots. 'You've seen the bridge?' I asked him.

'Once, lord.'

'Is it close to the fort?'

'No, lord, not close,' he frowned, thinking, 'the fort is on the hill,' he added as though that made everything clear.

'Is it guarded? The bridge?'

'Guarded, lord?' He seemed puzzled by that question.

'If you cross the bridge,' I asked patiently, 'do armed men stop you?'

'Oh no, lord,' he answered confidently, 'you never take your cows over a bridge in case the water spirits get jealous and then they get the dropsy.'

'So are there fords?'

He shook his head, though I doubted he knew the answer to that either. The man lived a short walk from Lindcolne, yet as far as I could discover he had only been there once. If the Danish garrison in Lindcolne had any sense then they would keep guards on the bridge, but I reckoned we would outnumber them, and by the time reinforcements arrived from the hill we would be long gone into the fog.

It was easy enough to find Lindcolne because the Romans had made a road and the road had their sign-stones counting down the miles, but the fog was so dense that I never saw the fort on its high hill and only realised we had reached the town when I rode beneath a crumbling and unguarded gate arch. The gates were long gone, as were the walls on either side.

And I rode through a place of ghosts.

We Saxons have always been unwilling to live in Roman buildings unless we disguise them with thatch and mud. The folk of Lundene had been forced to occupy the old city when the Danes attacked because that was the only part that was defended by a wall, but still they preferred their timber and thatch houses in the new city to the west. I had lived with Gisela in a big Roman house beside the river in Lundene and I never saw a ghost, but I had noticed how

175

Christians coming to the house made the sign of the cross and looked anxiously into its dark corners. Now our horses walked down a deserted street flanked by ruined houses. The roofs had fallen in, the pillars had collapsed, and the stonework was cracked and thick with moss. They would have made fine houses, but the Saxons who still lived in the town preferred to make a hovel of mud and wattle. Here and there a house was occupied, but only because the people had built a hut inside the shell of an old stone building.

The bridge was also made of stone. Its parapets were broken and a great hole gaped in its central span, but it was unguarded, and so we passed over the river and on into the wide fog-shrouded country beyond.

None of us knew the country, or which way we should go, so I simply followed the Roman road until it joined another that ran north and south. 'We keep going west,' I told Finan.

'Just west?'

'We'll find somewhere we know.'

'Or ride to the world's end,' he said happily.

The fog was lifting and the land rose slowly until we reached a rolling upland where there were fat farms and big halls half hidden by groves of good trees, and though I was sure folk saw us, no one came to enquire what brought us to their land. We were armed men, best left alone. I sent scouts ahead as I always did in hostile country, and this land was certainly hostile. We were either in Cnut's land or Sigurd's territory and all the halls would be Danish. The scouts rode either side of the road, using woods or hedgerows for cover and always looking for any sign of an enemy, but we met none. Once, on the second day, five horsemen came towards us from the north, but they saw our numbers and veered away.

We were among higher hills by then. The villages were smaller and more scattered, the halls less wealthy. I sent my Danes to purchase ale and food from the halls and the Saxons to buy provisions from the villages, but there was scarce any spare food because so many armed bands had been this way before us. I went to one hall where an old man greeted me. 'I am Orlyg Orlygson,' he said proudly.

'Wulf Ranulfson,' I responded.

'I have not heard of you,' he said, 'but you're welcome.' He limped because of an old wound in his left leg. 'And where does Wulf Ranulfson ride?'

'To join Jarl Cnut.'

'You're late,' he said, 'the summons was for the moon's death. She's growing again.'

'We'll find him.'

'I wish I could go,' Orlyg patted his injured leg, 'but what use is an old man?' He looked at my companions. 'Just seven of you?'

I gestured vaguely northwards. 'I've got three crews on the road.'

'Three! I can't feed that many. But I'll have my steward find you something. Come inside, come inside!' He wanted to talk. Like all of us, he welcomed travellers if they brought news, and so I sat in his hall and petted his hounds and invented tales about Frisia. I said the harvest there would be poor.

'Here too!' Orlyg said gloomily.

'But there is good news,' I went on, 'I heard that Uhtred Uhtredson attacked Bebbanburg and failed.'

'Not just failed,' Orlyg said, 'he was killed there!' I just stared at him and he grinned at the surprise on my face. 'You hadn't heard?' he asked.

'Uhtred Uhtredson was killed?' I could not keep the astonishment from my voice. 'I heard that he failed,' I went on, 'but he survived.'

'Oh no,' Orlyg said confidently, 'he died. The man who told me was a witness to the fight.' He pushed his fingers into his tangled white beard to touch the hammer at his neck. 'He was cut down by the Lord Ælfric. Or maybe it was Ælfric's son. The man wasn't sure, but it was one of them.'

'I heard Ælfric died,' I said.

'Then it must have been the son who dealt the blow,' Orlyg said, 'but it's true! Uhtred Uhtredson is dead.'

'That will make Jarl Cnut's life easier,' I said.

177

'They all feared Uhtred,' Orlyg said, 'and no wonder. He was a warrior!' He looked wistful for a moment. 'I saw him once.'

'You did?'

'A big man, tall. He carried an iron shield.'

'I heard that,' I said. I had never carried an iron shield in my life.

'He was fearsome, right enough,' Orlyg said, 'but a warrior.'

'He belongs to the Corpse-Ripper now.'

'Someone should go to the Lord Ælfric,' Orlyg suggested, 'and buy the fiend's corpse.'

'Why?'

'To make the skull into a drinking cup, of course! It would make a fine gift for Jarl Cnut.'

'The jarl will have drinking cups enough,' I said, 'when he's beaten Æthelred and Edward.'

'And he will,' Orlyg said enthusiastically. He smiled. 'At Yule, my friend, we shall all drink from Edward's skull and dine in Edward's hall and use Edward's wife for pleasure!'

'I heard Jarl Cnut's wife was captured by Uhtred,' I said.

'A rumour, my friend, a rumour. You can't believe everything you hear. I've learned that much over the years. Men come here and give me news and we celebrate it and then discover it isn't true at all!' He chuckled.

'So perhaps Uhtred lives,' I suggested mischievously.

'Oh no! That is true, my friend. He was chopped down in battle, and he still lived, so they tied him to a post and loosed the dogs on him. They tore him to bits!' He shook his head. 'I'm glad he's dead, but that's no way for a warrior to die.'

I watched as servants carried ale, bread and smoked meat to my men waiting in the orchard. 'To find the jarl,' I asked Orlyg, 'we keep going west?'

'Cross the hills,' he said, 'and just follow the road. The jarl won't be in any of his halls, he'll have sailed south by now.'

'To Wessex?'

'To wherever he wants!' Orlyg said. 'But if you follow the road west you'll come to Cesterfelda and you can ask there.' He frowned.

'I think you go from there to Buchestanes and the jarl has a hall there, a fine hall! One of his favourite halls, and there'll be men in the hall who'll tell you where to find him.'

'Buchestanes,' I repeated the name as if I had never heard it before, but my interest was roused. Cnut had told me his wife and two children had been captured while travelling to Buchestanes, and maybe Orlyg's mention of the town was just a coincidence, but fate does not like coincidences. I felt the hairs on the back of my neck prickle.

'A good town,' Orlyg said, 'it has hot springs. I went there two summers ago and sat in the water. It took away the pain.'

I paid him gold for his generosity. He had told me that his son had led twenty-three men to Cnut's service and I said I hoped they came back victorious, and so I left him.

'I'm dead,' I told Finan.

'You are?'

I told him Orlyg's tale and he laughed. We slept that night in Cesterfelda, a village I had never heard of and reckoned I might never see again, though it was a pleasant enough place with good farmland spread around the small village, which itself surrounded some fine Roman buildings, though of course they had decayed over the long years. A magnificent pillared hall, which I supposed had been a temple to the Roman gods, was now a cattle shelter. There was a fallen statue of a hook-nosed man draped in a sheet and with a wreath of leaves about his short-cut hair, and the statue was evidently used as a sharpening stone because it had been deeply grooved by blades. 'Pity it's not marble,' Finan said, kicking the statue.

'Wouldn't be here if it was,' I said. Sometimes a farmer finds a Roman statue made from marble and such a thing is valuable because it can be put in a furnace to make lime, but a stone statue is not worth anything. I looked down at the statue's hooked nose. 'Is that their god?' I asked Finan.

'The Romans were Christians,' my son answered instead.

'Some of them were Christians,' Finan said, 'but I think the others worshipped eagles.'

179

'Eagles!'

'I think so.' He gazed up at the cattle shed's gable that was cleverly carved with half-naked girls running through a forest pursued by a man with goat's legs. 'Maybe they worshipped goats?'

'Or tits,' my son said, staring up at the lissom girls.

'That would be a religion worth having,' I said.

Merewalh had joined us and he also stared up at the gable. The carving was distinct because the sun was low and the shadows long and sharp. 'When we take this land back,' he said, 'we'll pull all this down.'

'Why?' I asked.

'Because the priests won't like that.' He nodded at the long-legged girls. 'They'll order it destroyed. It's pagan, isn't it?'

'I think I'd like to have been a Roman,' I said, gazing upwards.

They laughed, but I was melancholy. The remnants of Rome always make me sad, simply because they are proof that we slide inexorably towards the darkness. Once there was light falling on marbled magnificence, and now we trudge through mud. Wyrd bið ful āræd.

We bought butter, oatcakes, cheese and beans, we slept under the naked girls in the empty cattle shelter and next morning rode on westwards. And the wind blew strong and the rain began again, and by mid-morning we were riding into a gale. The land was rising and the track we followed turned into a stream. Lightning flickered to the north and thunder rolled across the sky and I raised my face to the wind and rain and knew Thor was there. I prayed to him. I told him I had sacrificed my best animals to him, that I had been loyal, that he should give me aid, but I knew Cnut would be making the same prayer, and so would Cnut's friend, Sigurd Thorrson, and the gods, I feared, would favour the Danes because more of them were his worshippers.

The rain hardened, the wind shrieked and some of the horses shied from the hammer of Thor's wrath and so we sheltered beneath the gale-thrashed branches of an oak wood. It was hardly shelter, for the rain pierced the leaves and dripped incessantly.

180

Men walked their horses while Finan and I crouched by a thorn bush at the western edge of the trees. 'Never known a summer like it,' he said.

'It'll be a hard winter.'

'God help us,' he said grimly and made the sign of the cross. 'So what are we doing?'

'Travelling to Buchestanes.'

'To see the sorceress?'

I shook my head and wished I had not because the motion let rainwater trickle down inside my jerkin. 'To see her granddaughter perhaps,' I said, smiling. 'Cnut says the sorceress still lives, but she must be older than time.' The sorceress's name was Ælfadell and she was reputed to have greater powers than any other aglæcwif in Britain. I had visited her and drunk her potion and dreamed the dreams and been told my future. Seven kings would die, she had said, seven kings in one great battle.

'To see her granddaughter?' Finan asked. 'Is she the one who's deaf and dumb?'

'And the most beautiful creature I've ever seen,' I said wistfully.

Finan smiled. 'So if we're not going to see this creature,' he said after a pause, 'why are we going there?'

'Because it's on the way to Ceaster.'

'Just that?'

I shook my head. 'Cnut said his wife and son were captured while they were travelling to Buchestanes. And that old fellow yesterday said Cnut has a hall there, a fine hall.'

'So?'

'So he didn't have a hall there ten years ago. It's new.'

'If I remember,' Finan said, 'there's no wall at Buchestanes.'

I knew what he was saying. I was suggesting that the new hall was important to Cnut, and Finan was suggesting it was undefended and therefore not as important as I thought. 'There wasn't a wall ten years ago,' I said, 'but there could be now.'

'And you think his wife is there?'

'I don't know. Maybe.'

He frowned, then flinched as a gust of wind drove rain into our faces. 'Maybe?'

'We know Cnut went to Ceaster,' I said, 'and she probably went with him, but she wouldn't have sailed with him. Her children are too young. You don't take small children to war, so either she's still at Ceaster, or Cnut sent her somewhere further from Mercia.'

'Could be anywhere.'

'I'm groping in the dark,' I admitted.

'But you are always lucky.'

'Sometimes I'm lucky,' I said, and thought of the wheel of fate. Thor was in the sky and the wind bitter in my face. The omens were bad. 'Sometimes,' I said again.

We waited till the rain eased, then rode on.

Groping in the dark.

We reached Buchestanes the next day. I dared not enter the town for fear of being recognised and so I sent Rolla, Eldgrim and Kettil, three Danes, down into the hollow where the small town was cradled by hills. I could see that Cnut had made a palisade around the place, though it was hardly formidable, merely a wall the height of a man and better suited to keep cattle out than to deter enemies.

It was still raining. The clouds were low, the ground soaked, the rain persistent, but the wind had eased. I led my horsemen to the wood close to the cave where the sorceress wove her spells, then took my son, Finan and Merewalh up to the great limestone crag that was streaming with water. The rock was slashed with a crevice where ferns and moss grew thick, and the crevice led into the cave. I hesitated at the entrance, remembering my fear.

Caves are the entrances to the netherworld, to the dark places where the Corpse-Ripper lurks and where Hel, the grim goddess, rules. These are the lands of the dead where even most gods walk warily, where silence is a howl, where all the memories of all the living are endlessly echoed in misery, and where the three Norns weave our fates and play their jests. This is the netherworld.

It was dark beyond the low, narrow entrance, but the sound of my boots suddenly echoed loud and I knew I had come into the larger chamber. Water dripped. I waited. Finan blundered into me, I heard my son breathing. Slowly, so slowly, my eyes became accustomed to the dark, helped by what small grey light leaked from the crevice, and I saw the flat rock where the sorceress had worked her magic. 'Is anyone here?' I shouted and the echo of my voice was the only answer.

'What happened here?' my son asked in an awed tone.

'This was where Ælfadell the sorceress told the future,' I said, 'and maybe still does.'

'And you came here?' Merewalh asked.

'Just once,' I said, as if it were no great thing. Something moved in the back of the cave, a scrabbling noise, and the three Christians touched their crosses as I fingered Thor's hammer. 'Is anyone there?' I called, and again there was no answer.

'A rat,' Finan suggested.

'And what future did you discover, lord?' Merewalh asked.

I hesitated. 'It was nonsense,' I said harshly. Seven kings will die, she had said, seven kings and the women you love. And Alfred's son will not rule and Wessex will die and the Saxon will kill what he loves and the Danes will gain everything, and all will change and all will be the same. 'It was nonsense,' I said again, and I lied when I said it, though I did not know it. I know now, because everything she said came true except one thing, and perhaps that one thing still lies in the future.

And Alfred's son did rule, so was that wrong? In time I saw her meaning, but back then, standing on a floor made slippery with bat-shit and listening to the water run underground, I did not know the significance of what I had been told. Instead I was thinking of Erce.

Erce was the aglæcwif's granddaughter. I did not know her real name, only that she was called Erce after the goddess, and in my trance I had seen what I thought was the goddess come to me. She had been naked and beautiful, pale as ivory, lithe as a willow-wand, a dark-haired girl who had smiled as she rode me, her light hands touching my face as my fingers caressed her small breasts. Had she been real? Or a dream? Men said she was real, that she was deaf and dumb, but ever after that night I doubted their tales. Perhaps there was a granddaughter who could neither hear nor speak, but it was surely not the lovely creature I remembered from this dank cave. She had been a goddess, come to our middle earth to touch our souls with sorcery, and it was the memory of her that had drawn me to this cave. Did I expect to see her again? Or did I just want to remember that strange night?

Uhtred, my son, walked to the pale flat stone and ran his hand over its table-like surface. 'I'd like to hear the future,' he said wistfully.

'There's a sorceress in Wessex,' Finan said, 'and men say she speaks true.'

'The woman in Ceodre?' I asked.

'That's the one.'

'But she's a pagan,' my son said disapprovingly.

'Don't be an idiot,' I snarled. 'You think the gods speak only to Christians?'

'But a sorceress . . .' he began.

'Some folk are better than others at knowing what the gods are doing. Ælfadell was one of them. She talked to them in here; they used her. And yes, she was, is, a pagan, but that doesn't mean she can't see farther than the rest of us.'

'So what did she see?' my son asked. 'What did she tell of your future?'

'That I whelped idiots who would ask stupid questions.'

'So she really did see the future!' Uhtred said, and laughed. Finan and Merewalh laughed too.

'She said there would be a great battle and seven kings would die.' I spoke bleakly. 'It was like I said, just nonsense.'

'There aren't seven kings in Britain,' my son said.

'There are,' Merewalh said. 'The Scots have three at least, and God alone knows how many men call themselves king in Wales. Then there are the Irish kings.'

'A battle which everyone joins in?' Finan said lightly. 'We can't miss that.'

Rolla and his companions returned late in the afternoon, bringing bread and lentils. The rain had eased and they found us in the wood where we had lit a fire and were trying to dry our clothes. 'The woman's not there,' Rolla told me, meaning Cnut's wife.

'So who is there?'

'Thirty, forty men,' he said dismissively, 'most of them too old to go to war, and Cnut's steward. I told him what you told me to say.'

'He believed you?'

'He was impressed!' I knew that the folk inside Buchestanes's palisade would be curious, even suspicious, because we had not ridden into the town, but had stayed outside, so I had told Rolla to say I had sworn an oath to pass through no town walls until I assaulted a Saxon stronghold. 'I told him you were Wulf Ranulfson, out of Haithabu,' Rolla went on, 'and he said Cnut would welcome us.'

'But where?'

'He said to go to Ceaster, then just ride south if there are no ships.'

'Just south?'

'That's all he said, yes.'

And south could be either Mercia or Wessex, but instinct, that voice of the gods which we so often mistrust, told me it was Mercia. Cnut and Sigurd had attacked Wessex ten years before and had achieved nothing. They had landed their forces on the banks of the Uisc and marched two miles to Exanceaster where the walls of that burh had defeated them, and Wessex was full of such burhs, the fortified towns that Alfred had made and in which folk could shelter as the Danes roamed impotently outside. Mercia had burhs too, but fewer, and the Mercian army, which should have been prepared to attack the Danes as they besieged a burh, was a long way away in East Anglia.

'Then we'll do what he suggested,' I said. 'We'll go to Ceaster.'

'Why not head directly south?' Merewalh asked.

I knew what was in his mind. By going south we would reach

Mercia far more quickly than by travelling to Britain's west coast and, once at Ceaster, we would be on the very edge of Mercia, in a region already dominated by the Danes. Merewalh wanted to get back to his country fast, to find out what had happened, and perhaps to reunite his men with Æthelred's forces. Æthelred would be annoyed that Merewalh had accompanied me, and that worry was nagging at the Mercian.

'You'll gain nothing by going south now,' I explained.

'We save time.'

'I don't want to save time. I need time. I need time for Edward of Wessex and for Æthelred to join forces.'

'Then go back to East Anglia,' Merewalh said, but without much conviction.

'Cnut wants Æthelred in East Anglia,' I said, 'so why should we do what Cnut wants? He wants Æthelred to come to him and he'll wait for him on a hill or beside a river, and Æthelred will have to fight uphill or through deep water, and at the end of the day Æthelred will be dead and Cnut will be boiling his skull to make a drinking cup. Is that what you want?'

'Lord,' Merewalh protested.

'We have to make Cnut do what we want,' I said, 'so we go to Ceaster.'

So we rode to Ceaster. The countryside was strangely empty. There were harvesters in the fields and cowherds in the pastures, there were shepherds and woodsmen, but the warriors were gone. There were no men hawking, no men practising the shield wall or exercising horses, because the warriors were all gone southwards, leaving the halls protected only by old and injured men. We should have been challenged a hundred times on that journey, but the road had seen countless bands pass and folk assumed we were just another group seeking Jarl Cnut's generosity.

We followed a Roman road out of the hills. The fields either side were churned by hoofprints, all going west. The stones counted the miles down to Deva, because that was what the Romans had called Ceaster. I knew the place, as did Finan and Merewalh, indeed most of our men had spent time to the south of the town, riding the woods and fields on the southern bank of the River Dee and watching the Danes on Ceaster's ramparts. Those walls, and the river, protected the town, and if we had ever wanted to attack from the south we would have had to cross the Roman bridge that led to the town's southern gate, but now we came from the east and the road took us north of the river. We rode through heathland where a few scattered trees bent to the west wind. I could smell the sea. The rain had stopped and the sky was thronged with fast-moving clouds that threw vast scudding shadows across the lower country ahead of us. The river's coils glinted in that landscape, which, beyond the heath, was marsh and, way beyond that and nothing but a hazed glimmer on the skyline, was the sea.

I rode ahead with Finan, Merewalh, and my son. We slanted left, going to a stand of trees on a small hillock, and from there we could see Ceaster itself. Smoke rose from thatched roofs inside the walls. A few roofs were tile, and some buildings rose higher than others, and the stone of those high walls looked pale gold in the patchy sunlight. The town's defences were formidable. It was fronted with a ditch flooded by the river, and behind the ditch was an earthen bank topped by stone ramparts. Some of the stone had fallen, but timber palisades filled those gaps. There were stone towers studding the long walls, and timber towers stood above the four gateways, one gate in the centre of each long wall, but we had watched Ceaster long enough to learn that two of those gates were never used. The north gate and south gate had usually been busy, but none of us had ever seen men or horses use the east and west entrances, and I suspected they had been blocked up. Just outside the walls was a stone arena where the Romans had staged fights and slaughters, but cattle now grazed beneath the decaying arches. There were four ships downstream of the bridge, only four, but there must have been two or three hundred before Cnut left. Those ships would have rowed out through the river curves, past the wild sea-birds of the Dee's estuary to the open sea, and then where?

'That's a burh,' Finan said admiringly. 'Be a right bastard of a place to capture.'

'Æthelred should have captured it ten years ago,' I said.

187

'Æthelred couldn't capture a flea if it was biting his cock,' Finan said scornfully.

Merewalh cleared his throat as a mild protest against this insult to his sworn lord.

A banner flew above the gate-tower in the southern wall. We were too far away to see what was embroidered or daubed on the cloth, but I knew anyway. It would show Cnut's emblem of the axe and the shattered cross, and that flag was on the southern ramparts, facing Saxon country, the direction from which the garrison could expect an attack. 'How many men can you see?' I asked Finan, knowing his eyes were better than mine.

'Not many,' he said.

'Cnut told me the garrison was a hundred and fifty men.' I was remembering our conversation in Tameworþig. 'He could have been lying, of course.'

'A hundred and fifty men would be enough most of the time,' Finan said.

A hundred and fifty men would not have been enough to stop a determined attack on two or more of the four walls, but they would have been more than sufficient to defeat an assault coming across the long bridge against the southern gate. If the town was threatened by war then more men could be brought in to stiffen the garrison. King Alfred, who had always been precise in his calculations, demanded that four men should be stationed for every pole of a burh's wall. A pole was six paces, more or less, and I tried to reckon the length of Ceaster's ramparts and decided they would need a thousand men to defend against a determined attack, but how likely was such an attack? Æthelred had been supine, and now he was far away, and Cnut was on the rampage somewhere, and Cnut would want every available man for the battles he knew he must fight. Ceaster, I suspected, was very lightly defended.

'We just ride in,' I said.

'We do?' Merewalh sounded surprised.

'They're not expecting an attack,' I said, 'and I doubt there's as many as a hundred and fifty men there. Maybe eighty?'

Eighty men could stop us if we tried to assault the wall,

188

though without ladders such an assault was unthinkable. But would they try to stop us if we rode peaceably up the road? If we looked like all the other bands of men who had obeyed Cnut's summons?

'Why eighty?' my son asked.

'I've no idea,' I said, 'I made the figure up. There could be five hundred men in there.'

'And we just ride in?' Finan asked.

'You have a better plan?'

He shook his head, grinning. 'Just like Bebbanburg,' he said, 'we just ride in.'

'And pray for a better ending,' I added grimly.

And so we did.

We just rode in.

The road leading to the fortress's northern gate was paved with wide slabs, most of which were now cracked or canted. Grass grew thick on either verge, dunged by the hundreds of horses that had passed before us. There were rich farms on either side where slaves were using sickles to cut tall rye and rain-beaten barley. The farmhouses were made of stone, though all were patched with wattle and mud, and usually re-roofed with thatch. They, like the town, were Roman. 'I'd like to go to Rome,' I said.

'King Alfred went,' Merewalh said.

'Twice, he told me,' I replied, 'and all he saw were ruins. Great ruins.'

'They say the city was made of gold.' Merewalh sounded wistful.

'A city of gold on a river of silver,' I said, 'and once we've defeated Cnut we should go there and dig it all up.'

We were riding slowly, like tired men on weary horses. We wore no mail and carried no shields. The packhorses with the long battle-axes and heavy round shields were at the back of our column, while I had put my Danes at the front. 'Keep your Saxon mouth shut when we get to the gate,' I told Merewalh.

189

'A river of silver?' he asked. 'Is that true?'

'It's probably more like our rivers,' I said, 'full of piss, shit and mud.'

A beggar with half his face eaten by ulcers crouched in the ditch. He mewed as we passed and held out a crooked hand. Wissian, our Christian priest, made the sign of the cross to ward off any evil that the beggar might harbour and I snarled at him. 'The Danes will see you do that, you fool. Save it till we're out of their sight.' My son dropped a piece of bread close to the beggar who scrabbled after it on all fours.

We passed the great bend in the river east of the fortress and the road now turned south to run straight as a spear-shaft towards the town. There was a Roman shrine at the road's bend, just a stone shelter where, I supposed, the statue of a god had once stood, but now the small building housed an old one-legged man who was weaving baskets from willow wands. 'Has Jarl Cnut gone?' I asked him.

'Gone and gone,' he said. 'Half the world's gone.'

'Who's left?' I asked.

'None that matters, none that can row, ride, fly or crawl.' He cackled. 'Half the world went by and half the world has gone. Only the elf now!'

'The elf?'

'The elf is here,' he said very seriously, 'but all else is gone.' He was mad, I think, but his old hands wove the willow deftly. He tossed a finished basket onto a pile and took up more withies. 'All else is gone,' he said again, 'and only the elf be left.'

I spurred on. A pair of posts flanked the road, and on both posts a skeleton was lashed with hemp twine. They were warnings, of course, a warning that thieves would be killed. Most men would be content with a pair of skulls, but it was typical of Haesten to want more. The sight of the bones reminded me of Saint Oswald, and then I forgot that saint because our road ran straight towards Ceaster's northern gate and, even as I watched, that gate was pulled shut. 'That's a welcome,' Finan said.

'If you saw horsemen approaching, what would you do?'

'I thought the bastards would leave it open and make it easy for us,' he said.

The gate was formidable. A pair of stone towers flanked the gate's arch, though one of the towers had partially collapsed into the ditch that was crossed by a timber bridge. The fallen tower had been rebuilt in wood. The top of the arch was a platform where one man stood watching our approach, but as we drew nearer another three men joined him.

The gates, there were a pair, stood about twice the height of a man. They looked solid as rocks. Above them was an open space because the gates did not reach all the way up to the high fighting platform, which was protected by a timber wall and a stout-looking roof. One of the men in the shadow of the roof cupped his hands. 'Who are you?' he called.

I pretended not to hear. We ambled on.

'Who are you?' the man shouted again.

'Rolla of Haithabu!' Rolla called out the answer. I was deliberately staying behind my leading men and keeping my head down because it was possible some of these men had been at Tameworþig and would recognise me.

'You're late!' the man called. Rolla made no answer. 'You came to join the Jarl Cnut?' the man asked.

'From Haithabu,' Rolla shouted.

'You can't come in!' the man said. We were very close now and he had no need to shout.

'What are we supposed to do?' Rolla asked. 'Stay here and starve? We need food!'

Our horses had stopped just short of the bridge, which was as wide as the road and about ten paces long. 'Ride around the walls,' the man ordered, 'to the southern gate. Cross the bridge there and you can buy food in the village.'

'Where's Jarl Cnut?' Rolla demanded.

'You'll have to ride south,' the man said. 'But cross the river first. Leiknir will tell you what to do.'

'Who's Leiknir?'

'He commands here.'

'But why can't we come in?' Rolla asked.

'Because I say so. Because no one comes in. Because the jarl gave orders.'

Rolla hesitated. He did not know what to do and glanced back at me as if seeking guidance, but at that moment my son spurred his horse past me and onto the bridge. He looked up at the four men. 'Is Brunna still here?' he asked. He spoke in Danish, the language he had learned from his mother and from me.

'Brunna?' The man was puzzled, as well he might be because Brunna was the name of Haesten's wife, though I doubted my son knew that.

'Brunna!' my son said as if everyone would recognise the name. 'Brunna!' he said again. 'You must know Brunna the Bunny! The sweet little whore with bouncy tits and an arse to dream about?' He made a pumping motion with a fist.

The man laughed. 'That's not the Brunna I know.'

'You should meet her!' my son said enthusiastically. 'But only when I've finished with her.'

'I'll send her across the river,' the man said, amused.

'Whoa!' Uhtred shouted, not in excitement, but because his horse was skittering sideways. It looked accidental, but I had seen him rowel a spur, and the horse reacted by jerking away from the pain and the motion took Uhtred beneath the fighting platform so that he could not be seen by the four men above. Then, to my amazement, he kicked his feet from the stirrups and stood on the saddle. He did it smoothly, but it was a dangerous move because the horse was not his own, it had been borrowed from Merewalh's men and Uhtred could not have known how it would react to his strange behaviour. I held my breath, but the horse just tossed his head and stayed still, letting my son reach with both hands to the gate's top. He pulled himself up, straddled the gate and then dropped over. It took almost no time.

'What . . .' The man on the gate-tower leaned over, trying to see what was happening.

'Will you send all the town's whores across the river?' I called, to keep his attention.

Uhtred had vanished. He was inside the town. I waited to hear a shout, or a clash of swords, but instead heard the scrape of the locking bar being lifted from its brackets, a thump as it was dropped, and then one of the gates was being pushed open. The heavy iron hinges squealed. 'Hey!' the man called from above.

'Go!' I called. 'Go!'

I spurred my horse, driving Uhtred's riderless stallion ahead of me. We had planned what we would do if we got inside the town and those plans needed to be changed. The Romans built their towns to a pattern, with the four gates in the four walls and two streets running between the pairs of gates to make a crossroads at the town centre. My idea had been to go fast to that centre and make a shield wall there, inviting men to come and be killed. I would have then sent twenty men to the southern gate, to make sure it was closed and barred, but now I suspected most of the defending garrison would be concentrated at that southern gate, so that was where we would go to make our shield wall. 'Merewalh!'

'Lord?'

'Twenty men to guard this gate. Shut it, bar it, hold it! Finan! South gate!'

My son ran alongside his horse, reached for the pommel and leaped up into the saddle. He drew his sword.

And I drew mine.

Our hooves sounded loud on the paved street. Dogs barked and a woman screamed.

Because the Saxons had come to Ceaster.

Nine

A street was ahead of me. A long, straight street, while behind me horsemen were bursting through the gates. They began whooping as they spurred into the town.

Ceaster suddenly seemed vast. I remember thinking that this was stupidity, that I needed three times the number of men to take this place, but we were committed now. 'You're a fool!' I shouted at my son. He turned in his saddle and grinned. 'And well done!' I called to him.

The long street was edged with stone buildings. Ducks fled the leading horsemen and one bird was trampled by a heavy hoof. There was a squawk and white feathers flying. I kicked my heels to quicken my stallion as two armed men came from an alley. They stopped, astonished, and one had the sense to dart back into the shadows while the other was ridden down by Rolla, his sword slicing once, hard, and the pale stone of the nearest house was suddenly splattered with red. Blood and feathers. A woman screamed. Over a hundred of us were charging down the street. It had been paved once, but in places the stone slabs had gone and the hooves thumped in mud, then clattered on stone again. I had expected to see the southern gate at the street's far end, but a big pillared building blocked the view, and as I drew closer I saw there were four spearmen behind the pillars, running. One turned to face us. Eldgrim and Kettil, riding stirrup to stirrup, pushed their horses up the two stone steps leading onto the arcade that surrounded the huge building. I swerved left, heard a wail as

194

one man was cut down, then wrenched my horse to the right and saw more men, maybe half a dozen, standing at a vast door that led into the pillared building. 'Rolla! Twelve men. Keep those bastards here!'

I slewed right again, then left, and we crossed a wide square and galloped into another long street that ran spear-straight towards the southern gate. Five men were running ahead of us and lacked the sense to turn into an alleyway. I spurred behind one, saw his frightened face as he turned in panic, then Serpent-Breath slashed into the nape of his neck and I kicked my heels again and saw my son chop another of the men down. Three cows were at the street's edge. A red-faced woman was milking one and she stared at us with indignation, but kept on tugging at the udders as we crashed past. I could see spears and blades on the rampart above the southern gate. Cnut's banner of the axe and broken cross was flying there. The gate's arch was flanked by a pair of stone towers, but the rampart above was wooden. There were at least a score of men on the platform, and more were joining them. I could see no way up to the rampart and guessed the stairway was inside one of the towers. The big gates inside the arch were closed and the locking bar was in place. I was close to the gate now, still galloping, and saw an arrow whip from the gate's high platform to skid along the road's paving. I saw a second archer taking aim, and wrenched the reins and kicked my feet from the stirrups. 'Cenwalh!' I shouted at one of my younger Saxons. 'Look after the horses!'

I dismounted. A stone was hurled from the fighting platform to crash and break a paving slab. There was a doorway in the right-hand tower and I ran to it as a second stone narrowly missed me. A horse screamed as an arrow struck. There were stone stairs curving upwards into shadow, but they stopped after a few steps because much of the tower's inward face had collapsed. The masonry had been replaced by heavy oak timbers and the tower steps by a stout timber ladder. I climbed a few of the old Roman stairs, then peered upwards and had to jump back as a heavy stone crashed down. The stone hit the ladder's lowest rung, bounced off

195

without breaking it, and rolled down beside me. An arrow followed, only a hunter's arrow, but as I was not wearing mail it could easily have pierced my chest.

'Finan!' I bellowed as I went back to the tower's doorway. 'We need shields!'

'They're coming!' he shouted back. He had led my dismounted men into an alleyway because more arrows were flicking down from the high rampart. We were not carrying shields because I had not wanted to arouse the suspicions of the guards on the northern gate, which meant our best protection against the arrows was still heaped on the packhorses.

'Where are the packhorses?' I called.

'They're coming!' Finan shouted again.

I hesitated a few heartbeats then ran from the tower, dodging left and right as I hurried across the open space. I had limped slightly ever since the fight at Ethandun and could not run like a young man. An arrow slapped on the roadway to my right, I swerved that way and another slashed past my left shoulder, and then I was safe in the alleyway. 'There are two bastard archers,' Finan said.

'Where are the shields?'

'I told you, they're coming. Einar has an arrow in his leg.'

Einar was a Dane, a good man. He was sitting in the alley with the arrow sticking from his thigh. He drew a knife to cut the head out. 'Wait for Father Wissian,' I told him. Merewalh had told me the priest had a talent for healing.

'What can he do that I can't?' Einar asked. He gritted his teeth and plunged the knife into his leg.

'Jesus!' Finan said.

I peered out of the alley and immediately ducked back as an arrow flew. If I had been wearing mail and carrying a shield I would have been safe enough, but even a hunter's arrow can kill a man unprotected by mail. 'I want firewood,' I told Finan, 'a lot of firewood. Kindling as well.'

I looked for Merewalh and found him with the packhorses. The town's streets made a grid and the men leading the horses had possessed the sense to bring them by a parallel street and so out of sight of the two bowmen on the gate platform. 'We killed the men at the north gate,' Merewalh told me. He was pulling on a mail coat and his voice was muffled. 'And I left twelve men to hold it.'

'I want two more groups,' I told him, 'and they're to find their way onto the walls either side of this gate.' I meant the eastern and western walls. 'Twelve men in each group,' I told him. He grunted acceptance of the orders. 'And tell them to check the two other gates,' I ordered. 'I think they're blocked, but make certain of it!'

I was not sure how many men were on the southern gate's fighting platform, but there were at least twenty, and by sending Merewalh's men up onto the ramparts I should be able to trap those defenders. 'Warn them about the archers,' I told Merewalh, then unbuckled my sword belt and shrugged off the cloak. I pulled my mail coat over my head. The leather lining stank like a polecat's fart. I donned the helmet, then strapped my sword belt around my waist again. Other men were finding their mail. Finan handed me my shield. 'Get the firewood!' I told him.

'They're fetching it,' he said patiently.

Men had broken into a house and were smashing benches and a table. There was a pigsty in the back yard and we hauled down its thatch and ripped the beams apart. A fire, nothing but smoking embers contained in a ring of stones, smouldered in the yard. An old cauldron stood to one side of the fire and a dozen clay pots were on a small shelf propped against the wall. I picked up one of the pots, emptied it of dry beans and looked for a shovel. I found a ladle instead and used it to fill the pot with glowing embers, then put the pot inside the cauldron.

It was all taking time. I still had no idea how many of the enemy were inside the town, and I was dividing my own force into ever smaller groups, which meant that we could be overwhelmed one group at a time. We had taken the garrison by surprise, but they would be recovering fast and, if they outnumbered us, they could squash us like bedbugs. We needed to defeat them fast. I knew

197

that the men on the northern gate were already dead, and I assumed Rolla had bottled up the Danes in the big pillared building, but there could have been three or four hundred more angry Northmen in the parts of the town we had not seen. The enemies on this southern gate were certainly confident, which suggested they thought they would be rescued by reinforcements. They were shouting insults at us, inviting us to step out of the alley and be killed. 'Or you can wait there!' a man shouted. 'You're going to die anyway! Welcome to Ceaster!'

I needed to capture the walls. I suspected there were men outside the town, and we had to stop them from entering. I watched as men brought armfuls of thatch and broken timbers into the alley. 'I need four men,' I said. Any more than four would be too many for the ground floor of the tower. 'And six men in mail and with shields!'

I sent the six men first. They ran towards the tower and, sure enough, the archers released their arrows that thumped harmlessly into shields, and as soon as the bows were loosed I led the four men towards the tower. Stones rained down. I had my shield over my head and it shook as rocks hit the willow boards. I was carrying the cauldron in my sword hand.

I ducked into the tower. If the defenders had been thinking properly they would have sent men down the ladder to keep us away from the old Roman stairway, but they felt safer on the high platform and so they stayed there. But they knew we were inside the tower, and hurled stones down. I used my shield to cover my head as I climbed the few stone steps. The willow boards shook as the stones hit, but the shield protected me as I crouched at the ladder's foot and as men thrust handfuls of thatch and shattered timber up to me. I used my free hand to pile the firewood roughly around the ladder, then I took the scalding hot clay pot from the cauldron and spilt the embers into the straw and kindling. 'More timber!' I called. 'More!'

Yet I hardly needed more timber because the fire caught immediately, driving me fast down the few stone steps. The kindling flared, the wood caught fire and the tower seemed to suck the flames and smoke upwards, choking the men immediately above us so that the rain of stones stopped. The ladder would catch fire fast and that fire should spread to the oak timbers on the tower's face, and then to the platform itself and so drive the men down onto the flanking walls where Merewalh's men should be waiting. I ran back into the open air to see smoke churning from the tower's broken top and men abandoning the platform like rats fleeing a flooding bilge. They hesitated when they reached the wall's top, but must have seen Merewalh's men approaching because they simply abandoned the ramparts, jumping down into the ditch and so into the country beyond.

'Uhtred!' I called my son and pointed at the gates. 'The fire could spread to the gates, so find something to block the arch when they've burned out. Choose a dozen men. You're to hold the gateway.'

'You think they . . .'

'I don't know what they'll do,' I interrupted him, 'and I don't know how many there are. What I do know is that you're to stop any of them getting back into the town.'

'We can't hold for long,' he said.

'Of course we can't. There aren't enough of us. But they don't know that.' The fire caught Cnut's standard, which burst into sudden bright flame. One moment it was flying, the next it was a flare of fire and ash in the wind. 'Merewalh!' I looked for the Mercian. 'Put half your men on the ramparts!' I wanted any Danes outside the town to see spears and swords and axes on the walls. I wanted them to think we outnumbered them. 'Use the other half to clear the town.'

I sent most of my men up to the walls and took Finan and seven others back to the town's centre, to the big pillared building where I had left Rolla. He was still there. 'There's only the one entrance,' he told me, 'and there's a few of them inside. Shields and spears.'

'How many?'

'I've seen eight, could be more.' He jerked his head upwards. 'There are windows up there, but they're high and barred.'

'Barred?'

'Iron bars. Reckon the only way in and out is through these doors.'

The men inside had closed the doors, which were made of heavy timber studded with iron bolts. There was a latch on one door, but when I tugged it was evident that both doors were barred or bolted inside. I beckoned to Folcbald who was carrying a lead-weighted war axe. 'Break it down,' I told him.

Folcbald was the Frisian with the strength of an ox. He was slow, but give him a simple job and he could be remorseless. He nodded, took a breath, and swung the weapon.

The steel blade bit deep. Splinters flew. He jerked the axe free and struck again and both big doors shivered under the enormous blow. He gouged the blade loose and drew the weapon back for a third blow when I heard the locking bar grate in its brackets. 'Enough,' I told him, 'step back.'

The seven men I had brought were all in mail and all had shields, so we made a wall between the two pillars closest to the door. Rolla and his men were behind us. The locking bar scraped again, then I heard it thump as it fell on the floor inside. There was a pause, then the right-hand door was pushed open very slowly. It stopped when the opening was a mere hand's breadth wide and a sword was held out through the gap. The sword dropped onto the pavement. 'We'll give you a fight if that's what you want,' a man called from inside, 'but we'd rather live.'

'Who are you?' I asked.

'Leiknir Olafson,' the man said.

'And you serve?'

'The Jarl Cnut. Who are you?'

'The man who'll slaughter you if you don't surrender. Open both doors now.'

I closed my helmet's cheek-pieces and waited. I could hear low urgent voices inside the building, but the argument was brief and then both doors were pushed wide open. Maybe a dozen men stood in a shadowed corridor that led deep into the great building's darkness. The men were in mail, they had helmets and carried shields, but as soon as the doors were open they dropped their spears and swords onto the flagstones. A tall, grey-bearded man stepped towards us. 'I am Leiknir,' he announced.

'Tell your men to drop their shields,' I said, 'shields and helmets. You too.'

'You will let us live?'

'I haven't decided,' I said. 'Give me a reason why I should.'

'My wife is here,' Leiknir said, 'and my daughter and her babes. My family.'

'Your wife could find another husband,' I said.

Leiknir bridled at that. 'You have family?' he asked.

I did not answer that. 'Maybe I'll let you live,' I told him, 'and just sell your family. The Norse in Ireland pay well for slaves.'

'Who are you?' he asked.

'Uhtred of Bebbanburg,' I snarled at him, and the reaction was strange. It was also gratifying because a look of pure fear came to Leiknir's face. He stepped a pace backwards and put a hand to Thor's hammer about his neck.

'Uhtred is dead,' he said, and that was the second time I heard that rumour. Leiknir had plainly believed it because he was staring at me in horror.

'Shall I tell you what happened?' I asked. 'I died, and died without a sword in my hand, so I was sent to Hel and heard her dark cockerels crowing! They announced my coming, Leiknir, and the Corpse-Ripper came for me.' I took a pace towards him and he stepped back. 'The Corpse-Ripper, Leiknir, all rotted flesh peeling from his yellow bones and his eyes like fire and his teeth like horns and his claws like gelding knives. And there was a bone on the floor, a thigh bone, and I picked it up and I ripped it to a point with my own teeth and then I slew him.' I hefted Serpent-Breath. 'I am the dead, Leiknir, come to collect the living. Now kick your swords, spears, shields and helmets towards the door.'

'I beg for the life of my family,' Leiknir said.

'Have you heard of me?' I demanded, knowing well what the answer was.

'Of course.'

'And have you ever heard that I kill women and children?'

He shook his head. 'No, lord.'

'Then kick your weapons towards me and kneel down.'

They obeyed, kneeling against the corridor's wall. 'Guard them,' I told Rolla, then walked past the kneeling men. 'Leiknir,' I called, 'you come with me.' The passage walls were made from rough wood planks, so they were not Roman work. Doors opened on each side, leading into small chambers where straw mattresses lay. Another room held barrels. All the rooms were empty. At the corridor's end was a larger door that led into the western half of the great building. I went to that end door and pushed it open. A woman screamed.

And I stared. Six women were in the room. Four were apparently servants for they knelt in terror behind the other two, and those two I knew. One was Brunna, Haesten's wife. She was grey-haired, plump, round-faced and had a heavy cross hanging at her neck. She was clinging to the cross and mouthing a prayer. She had been baptised on King Alfred's orders and I had always thought that her acceptance of Christianity had been a cynical ploy arranged by her husband, but it seemed I was wrong. 'That's your wife?' I asked Leiknir who had followed me into the room.

'Yes, lord,' he said.

'I kill liars, Leiknir,' I said.

'She's my wife,' he said again, though defensively, as if the lie must be maintained even though it had failed.

'And is that your daughter?' I asked, nodding at the younger woman who was sitting beside Brunna.

This time Leiknir said nothing. Brunna was screaming at me now, demanding that I release her, but I ignored her. Two small children, twins, were clinging to the younger woman's skirts and she also said nothing, but just stared at me with large, dark eyes that I remembered so well. She was so beautiful, so fragile, so frightened, and she just stared at me and said nothing. She had grown older, but not as the rest of us had aged. I suppose she must have been fifteen or sixteen when I first met her, and now she was ten years older, but those years had merely added dignity to beauty.

202

'Is she your daughter?' I asked Leiknir again, savagely, and he said nothing.

'What is her name?' I demanded.

'Frigg.' Leiknir almost whispered the answer.

Frigg, wife of Odin, chief of all the goddesses in Asgard, the only one allowed to sit on Odin's high throne, and a creature of surpassing beauty who also had the great gift of prophecy, though she chose never to reveal what she knew.

And perhaps this Frigg also knew everything that would ever come to pass, but she would never tell because the girl I knew as Erce, granddaughter of Ælfadell the sorceress, was both deaf and dumb.

And she was also, I presumed, the wife of Jarl Cnut.

And I had found her.

Two hundred Danes had been left to guard Ceaster, though many of those were old or slowed by wounds. 'Why so few?' I asked Leiknir.

'No one expected Ceaster to be attacked,' he said bitterly.

I was walking through the captured town, exploring and admiring. Not even Lundene's old city, the part built on the hill, had so many Roman buildings in such good repair. If I ignored the thatch I could almost imagine myself back in the times when men could make such marvels, when half the world had been ruled from one shining city. How had they done that, I wondered, and how could such a people, so strong and so clever, have ever been defeated?

Finan and my son were with me. Merewalh and his men were on the ramparts, giving the impression that we numbered far more than a hundred and thirty-three men. Most of the defeated garrison was now outside the walls, gathered in the vast arena where the Romans had amused themselves with death, but we had captured their horses, almost all their supplies, and many of their women.

'So you were left to guard Frigg?' I asked Leiknir.

'Yes.'

'The Jarl Cnut won't be happy with you,' I said, amused. 'If I were you, Leiknir, I'd find somewhere a very long way away and hide there.' He said nothing to that. 'Haesten sailed with Jarl Cnut?' I asked.

'He did.'

'To where?'

'I don't know.'

We were standing in a pottery. The furnace, made of thin Roman bricks, was still burning. There were shelves of finished bowls and jugs, and a wheel on which a lump of clay had sagged. 'You don't know?' I asked.

'He didn't say, lord,' Leiknir said humbly.

I prodded the clay on the potter's wheel. The lump had hardened. 'Finan?'

'Lord?'

'There's firewood for that furnace?'

'There is.'

'Why don't you make it really hot and we'll put Leiknir's hands and feet inside. We'll start with his left foot.' I turned on the captured Dane. 'Take your boots off. You won't be needing them again.'

'I don't know!' he said frantically. Finan had tossed firewood into the furnace mouth.

'You were left to guard Jarl Cnut's most precious possession,' I said, 'and the Jarl Cnut wouldn't have just vanished. He would have told you how to send him news.' I watched as the fire roared. The sudden heat made me take a pace backwards. 'You'll be left with no hands and no feet,' I said, 'but I suppose you can shuffle around on your knees and wrist-stumps.'

'They went to the Sæfern,' he said desperately.

And I believed him. He had just revealed what Cnut was doing and it made sense. Cnut could have taken his fleet south around Cornwalum and attacked Wessex's southern coast, but that had been tried before and it had failed. So instead he was using the River Sæfern to take his army deep into Mercia, and the first great obstacle he would encounter was Gleawecestre. Gleawecestre was Æthelred's home, the most important town of Mercia, and it was a well-defended burh with high Roman walls, but how many men were left to defend those ramparts? Had Æthelred stripped his country of men for his invasion of East Anglia? And I felt a sudden fear, because Æthelflaed would surely have taken refuge in Gleawecestre. The moment folk heard that the Danes were in the river, that thousands of men and horses were being landed on the Sæfern's bank, they would flee to the nearest, strongest burh, but if that burh was inadequately defended it would become a trap for them.

'So what would you do if you needed to send a message to Cnut?' I asked Leiknir, who was watching the furnace fearfully.

'He said to send horsemen south, lord. He said they'd find him.'

And that was probably true. Cnut's army would be spreading through Saxon Mercia, burning halls, churches and villages, and the smoke of those fires would be beacons for any messenger. 'How many men does Cnut have?' I asked.

'Nearly four thousand.'

'How many ships sailed from here?'

'A hundred and sixty-eight, lord.'

That many ships could easily have carried five thousand men, but they had also taken horses and servants and baggage, so four thousand was probably accurate. That was a large army, and Cnut had been clever. He had lured Æthelred away to East Anglia and now he was deep inside Æthelred's land. What was Wessex doing? Edward would surely be gathering his army, but he would also be putting warriors into his burhs, fearing that the Danes might strike south across the Temes. My guess was that Edward would think of defending Wessex, which left Cnut free to ravage Mercia and to defeat Æthelred when that fool finally decided to march home. In another month all Mercia would be Danish.

Except I possessed Frigg. That was not her real name, but who knew what that was? She could not tell and, because she was deaf, she might not even know. Ælfadell had called her granddaughter Erce, but that goddess's name was just to impress the gullible. 'Jarl Cnut is fond of Frigg,' I suggested to Leiknir.

'He's like a man with a new sword,' he said, 'he can't bear to be out of her sight.'

'You can't blame him,' I said, 'she's a rare beauty. So why didn't she go south with him?'

'He wanted her kept safe.'

'And left just two hundred men to guard her?'

'He thought that was enough,' Leiknir said, then paused. 'He said there was only one man who was shrewd enough to attack Ceaster and that man was dead.'

'And here I am,' I said, 'back from Hel's kingdom.' I kicked the furnace's iron door shut. 'You can keep your hands and feet,' I said.

It was dusk. We left the pottery and walked towards the town's centre, and I was surprised to see a small building decorated with a cross. 'Haesten's wife,' Leiknir explained.

'He doesn't mind she's a Christian?'

'He says he might as well have the Christian god on his side as well.'

'That sounds like Haesten,' I said, 'dancing with two different women to two different tunes.'

'I doubt he likes dancing with Brunna,' Leiknir said.

I laughed. She was a vixen, that one, a stout, vicious-tempered, barrel-shaped vixen with a chin like a ship's prow and a tongue sharp as any blade. 'You can't keep us prisoner!' she told me when we were back inside the great pillared hall. I ignored her.

The building had been a hall once, and a magnificent hall. Perhaps it had been a temple, or even the palace of a Roman governor, but someone, I assumed Haesten, had divided the great chamber into separate rooms. The walls, made of wood, only reached halfway up and, in the daytime, light would stream in through the high windows, which were barred with iron. At night there were lamps and, in the big room where the women and children lived, an open fire that had stained the painted stonework of the high ceiling with soot and smoke. The floor was made of thousands upon thousands of small tiles arranged to make a pattern that showed some strange sea creature with a curling tail being hunted by three naked men with tridents. Two naked women rode giant scallop shells on a cresting wave to watch the hunt.

Brunna went on haranguing me and I went on ignoring her. The four women servants crouched with Frigg's twins at the edge of the room and watched me nervously. Frigg was wearing a cloak of feathers and was seated in a wooden chair at the room's centre. She also watched me, not with fear now, but with a child-like curiosity, her big eyes following me about the room as I examined the weird picture on the floor. 'They must have giant scallops in Rome,' I said, and no one answered. I walked to Frigg's chair and looked down at her and she gazed calmly back. Her cloak was made of thousands of feathers sewn into a linen cape. The feathers had been plucked from jays and ravens so that it seemed to shimmer blue and black. Beneath the strange feathered cloak she was hung with gold. Her slender wrists were ringed with gold, her fingers were bright with stones set in gold, her neck was hung with gold chains and her hair, black as one of Odin's ravens, was piled on her head and held in place by a net of gold.

'Touch her,' Brunna hissed, 'and you're a dead man!'

I had taken Brunna prisoner before, but Alfred, convinced she had become a true Christian, had insisted on releasing her. He had even stood as godfather to her two sons, Haesten the Younger and Horic, and I remembered the day she had been dunked in the holy water in the Lundene church where she had been given a new Christian name, Æthelbrun. Now, though still calling herself Brunna, she wore a big silver cross at her breasts. 'My husband will kill you,' she spat at me.

'Your husband has tried many times,' I said, 'and I still live.'

'We could kill her instead,' Rolla said. He looked tired of guarding the women, or at least of guarding Brunna. No man could tire of looking at Frigg.

I crouched in front of Frigg's chair and stared into her eyes. She smiled at me. 'Do you remember me?' I asked.

'She can't hear,' Leiknir said.

'I know,' I said, 'but does she understand?'

207

He shrugged. 'As well as a dog? Sometimes you think she knows everything, and at others?' He shrugged again.

'And the children?' I asked, glancing at the twins who watched me silent and wide-eyed from the edge of the chamber. They looked to be about six or seven years old, a boy and a girl, and both with their mother's dark hair.

'They can talk,' Leiknir said, 'and hear.'

'What are their names?' I asked.

'The girl is Sigril, the boy is Cnut Cnutson.'

'And they talk well enough?'

'They never stop usually,' Leiknir said.

And the twins could indeed talk because something strange happened at that moment, something I did not immediately understand. Merewalh came into the chamber, and with him was Father Wissian with his prematurely white hair and his long black cloak belted so it looked like a priest's robe and the small boy's face lit up. 'Uncle Wihtred!' Cnut Cnutson said. 'Uncle Wihtred!'

'Uncle Wihtred!' the girl echoed happily.

Wissian walked out of shadow into the firelight. 'My name's Wissian,' he said, and the twins' faces fell.

At the time I did not think about it because I was staring at Frigg, and the sight of that loveliness was enough to drive all sense from a man's head. I was still crouching, and I took one of her pale hands and it felt so light in mine, so light and fragile, like a bird held in a fist. 'Do you remember me?' I asked again. 'I met you and Ælfadell.'

She just smiled. She had been frightened when we first came, but now she seemed happy enough. 'You remember Ælfadell?' I asked, and of course she said nothing. I squeezed her hand very gently. 'You are coming with me,' I told her, 'you and your children, but I promise no harm will come to you. None.'

'Jarl Cnut will kill you!' Brunna screeched.

'One more word from you,' I said, 'and I'll cut your tongue out.'

'You dare . . .' she began, then screamed because I had stood and drawn a knife from my belt. And, to my surprise, Frigg laughed.

There was no sound to the laughter, other than a guttural choking noise, but her face was lit with sudden amusement.

I crossed to Brunna, who shrank away. 'You can ride a horse, woman?' I asked her. She just nodded. 'Then in the morning,' I said, 'you will ride south. You will go to that miserable wormcast you call a husband and tell him Uhtred of Bebbanburg has Jarl Cnut's wife and children. And you will tell him that Uhtred of Bebbanburg is in a mood to kill.'

I sheathed the knife and looked at Rolla. 'Have they eaten?'

'Not while I've been here.'

'Make sure they're fed. And safe.'

'Safe,' he said the word bleakly.

'Touch her,' I warned him, 'and you fight me.'

'They're safe, lord,' he promised.

Æthelred had started this war and Cnut had fooled him and now Cnut was loose in Mercia and convinced that his enemies were in disarray. The old dream of the Danes was coming true, the conquest of Saxon Britain.

Except I was still alive.

That night we hardly slept. There was work to do.

Finan found the best of the captured horses, for they would come with us. My son led search parties through the town, looking for hidden coins or anything of value that we could carry, while half of Merewalh's men guarded the walls and the rest tore apart buildings to make kindling and firewood.

The southern gates had burned and my son had blocked the entrance with two heavy carts. The Danes outside the town outnumbered us, though they did not know that, and I feared an attack in the night, but none came. I could see fires flickering in the old arena, and more by the bridge that lay a short ride to the south. There would be more fires soon.

Merewalh's men were laying the kindling and firewood beside every stretch of wooden palisade. Wherever the wall had been repaired we would set a fire. We would burn the gates of the town, we would burn the walls, and we would leave it stripped of any defence that was not made of stone.

I could not hold Ceaster. I would need ten times as many men and so I would abandon it, and doubtless the Danes would move back inside the Roman walls, but at least I could make it easier for a Saxon force to attack those walls. It would take six months to repair the damage I planned to do, six months of chopping down trees and trimming the trunks and burying them in the rubble of the broken ramparts. I hoped the Danes would not be given six months. And so, as the night wore on, we lit the fires, starting on the northern side of the town. Blaze after blaze brightened the late summer night, their flames beating up towards the stars, their smoke smearing the wide heaven. Ceaster was ringed with fire, loud with it, and the sparks from the fires blew onto thatch inside the town and that started burning too, but by the time the last fire was lit and much of the town was blazing, we were mounted and ready to leave. By then the last star was in the sky. Earendel, that star is called, the star of the morning, and Earendel still shone as we dragged the two carts aside and rode out through the southern gate.

We drove every horse out with us so that the watching Danes would see a horde erupting from the burning town. We took Haesten's wife, Cnut's wife and both her children, all of them close-guarded by my men, and we took the Danes who had surrendered to us. We were in war gear, dressed in mail and carrying shields, our naked blades reflecting the flames, and we galloped down the long straight road and I could see men waiting at the bridge, but those men were chilled, nervous and hugely outnumbered. They did not even try to stop us, instead they fled along the river's banks, and my horse's hooves suddenly thundered loud on the bridge's timber roadway. We stopped on the Dee's southern bank. 'Axes,' I said.

Beyond the river the fortress town of Ceaster burned. Thatch and timber flared and was consumed, turned into smoke, sparks and embers. The town itself, I thought, would live. It would be scorched, and the paved streets would be silted with ash, but what the Romans had made would still be there long after we were gone. 'We don't build,' I said to my son, 'we just destroy.'

He looked at me as if I was mad, but I just nodded towards our axemen who were destroying the bridge's roadway. I was making sure that the remaining Danes in Ceaster did not pursue us, and the quickest way to do that was to deny them the bridge. 'It's time you were married,' I told Uhtred.

He looked at me in surprise, then he grinned. 'Frigg will be a widow soon.'

'You don't need a deaf, dumb widow. But I'll find you someone.'

The last plank connecting two of the stone arches fell into the river. It was dawn and the rising sun was gilding the east, rifting low clouds with scarlet and gold. Men watched us from across the river.

The prisoners had ridden with us, each man with a noose about his neck, but now I ordered the nooses taken off. 'You're free to go,' I told them, 'but if I see you again, I'll kill you all. You take her with you.' I nodded towards Brunna who sat like a sack of oats on a stout mare.

'Lord,' Leiknir edged his horse towards me, 'I would come with you.'

I looked at him, so grey-haired and so beaten down, 'You're sworn to Jarl Cnut's service,' I said harshly.

'Please, lord,' he begged.

One of the other prisoners, a young man, kicked his horse next to Leiknir. 'Lord,' he said, 'may we have one sword?'

'You may borrow one sword,' I said.

'Please, lord!' Leiknir said. He knew what was about to happen.

'Two swords,' I said.

Leiknir had failed. He had been given a task and he had failed. If he returned to Cnut he would be punished for that failure and I did not doubt the punishment would be long, agonising and deadly. Yet I did not want him. He was a failure. 'What's your name?' I asked the young man.

'Jorund, lord.'

'Make it quick, Jorund. I take no joy in pain.'

He nodded and dismounted. My men moved their horses aside, making a crude ring about a patch of grass as Leiknir slid from his saddle. He looked defeated already.

We tossed two swords onto the grass. Leiknir let Jorund choose his weapon first, then picked up the other, but he made small effort to defend himself. He raised the blade, but without any enthusiasm. He just stared at Jorund and I saw how Leiknir was gripping the hilt with all his strength, intent on holding onto the weapon as he died.

'Fight!' Jorund goaded him, but Leiknir was resigned to death. He made a feeble lunge at the younger man and Jorund swept it aside, knocking Leiknir's blade wide, and Leiknir left it there, his arms spread, and Jorund drove his borrowed sword deep into the exposed belly. Leiknir bent over, mewing, his fist white as it gripped the sword. Jorund tugged his blade loose, releasing a spurt of thick blood, and stabbed again, this time into Leiknir's throat. He held the sword there as Leiknir dropped to his knees, then fell forward. The older man jerked on the grass for a few heartbeats, then was still. And the sword, I noted, was still in his grip.

'The swords,' I said.

'I need his head, lord,' Jorund pleaded.

'Then take it.'

He needed the head because Cnut would want proof that Leiknir was dead, that the older man had been punished for his failure to protect Frigg. If Jorund went to Cnut without such proof then he too could face punishment. The head of the dead man was Jorund's surety, a token that he had administered punishment and so might escape it himself.

There was a quarry close to the road. No one had worked it for years because the floor was thick with weeds and dotted with straggling saplings. I guessed it was the place where the Romans had cut the limestone to build Ceaster, and now we threw Leiknir's headless body down among the stones. Jorund had returned the two swords and had wrapped the bloody head in a cloak. 'We shall meet again, lord,' he said.

'Give the Jarl Cnut my greetings,' I said, 'and tell him his wife and children won't be harmed if he goes back home.'

'And if he does, lord, you'll return them?'

'He must buy them from me, tell him that. Now go.'

The Danes rode eastwards. Brunna was complaining as she went with them. She had demanded that two of the maidservants accompany her, but I kept them all to look after Frigg and her children. Cnut's wife was mounted on a grey mare and was wearing her feathered cloak, and she was a vision in that summer morning. She had watched Leiknir die and the slight smile on her face had not flickered as he choked and bubbled blood and twitched and went still.

And so we rode south.

Ten

'Will Cnut go home?' my son asked as we rode south through beech woods and beside a small, fast-flowing stream.

'Not till he's finished in Mercia,' I said, 'and maybe not then. He'd like to capture Wessex too.'

My son twisted in his saddle to look at Frigg. 'But you'll return her to him if he does go home? So he might?'

'Don't be a fool,' I said. 'We know he's fond of her, but he wouldn't walk ten paces to save her life.'

My son laughed in disbelief. 'I'd walk halfway round the world for her,' he said.

'That's because you're an idiot. Cnut isn't. He wants Mercia, he wants East Anglia, he wants Wessex, and those places are full of women, some of them almost as pretty as Frigg.'

'But . . .'

'I've touched his pride,' I interrupted him. 'She's not really a hostage because Cnut won't give a rat's turd to save her. He might lift a finger to rescue his son, but his woman? That's not why he'll hunt me. He'll hunt me because his pride is hurt. I've made him look like a fool and he won't abide that. He'll come.'

'With four thousand men?'

'With four thousand men,' I said flatly.

'Or he might ignore you,' my son suggested. 'You said yourself that Mercia is a bigger prize.'

'He'll come,' I said again.

'How can you be so certain?'

'Because,' I said, 'Cnut is like me. He's just like me. He's proud.'

My son rode in silence for a few paces, then gave me a stern look. 'Pride is a sin, Father,' he said in an unctuous voice, imitating a priest.

I had to laugh. 'You earsling!' I said.

'They do tell us that,' he said, serious now.

'The priests?' I asked. 'Do you remember Offa?'

'The dog man?'

'That one.'

'I liked his dogs,' Uhtred said. Offa had been a failed priest who travelled throughout Britain with a pack of trained dogs that performed tricks, though the dogs were merely his way of gaining acceptance in any lord's hall, and once in the hall he listened carefully. He was a clever man and he learned things. Offa had always known what was being plotted, who hated whom and who pretended otherwise, and he sold that information. He had betrayed me in the end, but I missed his knowledge.

'The priests are like Offa,' I said. 'They want us to be their dogs, well schooled, grateful and obedient, and why? So they can get rich. They tell you pride is a sin? You're a man! It's like telling you breathing is a sin, and once they've made you feel guilty for daring to breathe they'll give you absolution in return for a handful of silver.' I ducked my head under a low branch. We were following a wooded track that led south beside the fast-running stream. It was raining again, but not hard. 'The priests never minded my pride when the Danes were burning their churches,' I went on, 'but the moment they thought there was peace, that no more churches would be destroyed, then they turned against me. You watch. A week from now the priests will be licking my backside and begging me to save them.'

'And you will,' Uhtred said.

'Fool that I am,' I said gloomily, 'I will.'

We were in familiar ground because for years we had sent large bands of men to watch the Danes in Ceaster. All of northern Mercia was under Danish rule, but here, in the western part where we rode, the land was constantly threatened by the wild

215

Welsh tribesmen and it was hard to say who truly controlled the land. Jarl Cnut claimed the lordship, but he was too sensible to make enemies of the Welsh, who fought like fiends and could always retreat into their mountains if they were outnumbered. Æthelred claimed the land too, and he had offered silver to any Mercian willing to build a homestead in this contested place, but he had done nothing to protect those settlers. He had never built a burh this far north, and he had been reluctant to capture Ceaster because both the Danes and the Welsh would see such a capture as a threat. The last thing Æthelred had wanted was to provoke a war against Mercia's two most fearsome enemies, and so he had been content just to watch Ceaster. Now he had his war against the Danes, and I just prayed the Welsh would stay out of it. They claimed this land too, but in the long years that my men had ridden to keep a guard on Ceaster they had never interfered, but they had to be tempted now. Except the Welsh were Christians and most of their priests reluctantly sided with the Saxons because they all worshipped the same nailed god. But if the Danes and Saxons were killing each other then even the Welsh priests might see a god-given opportunity to plunder a swathe of rich land along Mercia's western boundary. Perhaps. Perhaps not. But I had scouts riding ahead just in case a war-band of Welsh warriors came from the hills.

And I thought we had found such a band when one of the scouts rode back to say there was smoke in the sky. I did not expect smoke this far north. Cnut's men would be ravaging southern Mercia, not the north, and a thick pillar of smoke suggested a hall was burning. The smoke was to our left, the east, and far enough away to be ignored, but I needed to know whether the Welsh had joined the chaos and so we crossed the stream and rode through thick oak woods towards the distant smear.

It was a farmstead that burned. There was no hall and no palisade, just a group of timber buildings in a clearing of the forest. Someone had settled here, had built a house and a barn, had cleared trees and raised cattle and grown barley, and now their small home was ablaze. We watched from the oaks. I could see eight or nine armed men, a couple of boys and two corpses. Some women and children were crouched under guard.

'They're not Welsh,' Finan said.

'You can tell?'

'Not enough of them. They're Danes.'

The men who carried spears and swords had long hair. That did not make them Danish, but most Danes wore their hair long and most Saxons preferred to keep it short and so I suspected Finan was right. 'Take twenty men to the eastern side,' I told him, 'then show yourselves.'

'Just show?'

'Just show.'

I waited till the men at the burning farm saw Finan. The two boys immediately ran to fetch horses, and the prisoners, the women and children, were goaded to their feet. The Danes, if they were Danes, began rounding up seven cows, and they were still herding the animals as I led my men out of the trees and down the long slope of stubble. The nine men saw us, seemed to panic as they realised they were trapped between two forces, but then calmed as they saw no threat. We did not charge, we just rode slowly and they would see that many of us had long hair. They held onto their weapons and stayed close together, but decided against flight. That was a mistake.

I checked most of my men in the stubble and took just three across a small stream and so into the heat of the burning buildings. I beckoned for Finan's men to join us, then stared into the flames of the burning granary. 'A good day for a fire,' I said in Danish.

'It's been a long time coming,' one of the men answered in the same language.

'Why's that?' I asked. I slid from the saddle, amazed at how stiff and sore I felt.

'They don't belong here,' the man said, indicating the two corpses, both men, both gutted like deer, and both lying in pools of blood that the small rain slowly diluted.

'You call me "lord",' I said mildly.

'Yes, lord,' the man said. He had only one eye, the other socket was scarred and weeping a trickle of pus.

'And who are you?' I asked.

They were indeed Danes, all of them older men and, reassured by the hammer hanging over my mail coat, they willingly explained that they came from settlements to the east and had resented the incursion of Saxons into their country. 'They're all Saxons,' the man told me, indicating the women and children who crouched beside the stream. Those women and children had been crying, but now watched me in terrified silence.

'They're slaves now?' I asked.

'Yes, lord.'

'Two more bodies over here,' Finan called. 'Old women.'

'What use are old women?' the man asked. One of his companions said something that I did not hear and the others all laughed.

'What's your name?' I asked the one-eyed man.

'Geitnir Kolfinnson.'

'And you serve the Jarl Cnut?'

'We do, lord.'

'I'm on my way to join him,' I explained, which was true, in a way. 'Did he tell you to attack these folk?'

'He wants the Saxon scum scoured away, lord.'

I looked at Geitnir Kolfinnson's men, seeing grey beards and lined faces and missing teeth. 'Your young men sailed with the jarl?'

'They did, lord.'

'And you're to clean the Saxon scum out of the district?'

'That's what the jarl wants,' Geitnir said.

'You've done a thorough job,' I said admiringly.

'It's a pleasure,' Geitnir said. 'I've been wanting to burn this place down for six years now.'

'So why didn't you do it before?'

He shrugged. 'Jarl Cnut said we should let Æthelred of Mercia go to sleep.'

'He didn't want to provoke a war?'

'Not then,' Geitnir said, 'but now?'

'Now you can treat the Saxon scum as they should be treated.'

218

'Not before time, lord, either.'

'I'm Saxon scum,' I said. There was silence. They were not sure they had heard me correctly. After all, they saw a man with long hair, wearing Thor's hammer, his arms rich with the rings that Danes wear as battle trophies. I smiled at them. 'I'm Saxon scum,' I said again.

'Lord?' Geitnir asked, puzzled.

I turned to the two boys. 'Who are you?' I asked them. They were Geitnir's grandsons, brought along to learn how to deal with Saxons. 'I'm not going to kill either of you,' I told the boys, 'so now you'll ride home and tell your mother that Uhtred of Bebbanburg is here. Say that name to me.' They dutifully repeated my name. 'And tell your mother I'm riding to Snotengaham to burn down Jarl Cnut's hall. Where am I going?'

'Snotengaham,' one of them muttered. I doubted they had heard of the place, and I had no intention of going anywhere near the town, but I wanted to spread rumours to keep Cnut off balance.

'Good boys,' I said. 'Now go.' They hesitated, uncertain about the fate of their grandfather and his men. 'Go!' I shouted. 'Before I decide to kill you too.'

They went, and then we killed the nine men. We took all their horses, except the two the boys had ridden in their panicked flight. I wanted rumours to start spreading in Danish Mercia, rumours that Uhtred had returned and was in a killing mood. Cnut believed that he had a free hand to do as he wished in Saxon Mercia, but within a day or two, once Brunna reached him and the rumours became louder, he would begin looking over his shoulder. He might even send men to Snotengaham where he kept one of his richer halls.

We left the Saxon women and children to fend for themselves and rode on south. We saw no more Danish bands and no Welsh warriors, and two days later we were in Saxon Mercia and the sky to the east and to the south was smirched with smoke, which meant that the Jarl Cnut was burning and plundering and killing.

And we rode on to Gleawecestre.

* * *

Gleawecestre was Æthelred's stronghold. It was a burh and it lay in the western part of Mercia on the River Sæfern where it defended Æthelred's territory from the marauding Welsh. That had been the burh's original purpose, but it was large enough to provide a refuge for folk in the surrounding country whatever enemy came. Like Ceaster and like so many other places in Mercia and Wessex, its defences had been made by the Romans. And the Romans had built well.

The city lay on flat land, which is not the easiest to defend, but like Ceaster the wall at Gleawecestre was surrounded by a ditch fed by the nearby river, only this ditch was much deeper and wider. Inside the ditch was an earthen bank studded with pointed stakes on top of which was the Roman wall, built with stone, and twice the height of a man. That wall was strengthened by over thirty fighting towers. Æthelred had kept those defences in good repair, spending money on masons to rebuild the walls wherever time had crumbled them. Gleawecestre was his capital and home, and when he left to invade East Anglia, he had made sure that his possessions were well guarded.

It was the fyrd who had the task of defending Gleawecestre. The fyrd was the citizen army, men who normally worked the land or beat iron in smithies or sawed timber. They were not the professional warriors, but place the fyrd behind a flooded ditch and on top of a stout stone wall and they became a formidable foe. I had been fearful when I first heard that Cnut had sailed to the Sæfern, but as I rode south I decided that Gleawecestre and its inhabitants were probably safe. Æthelred had too much treasure in the city to leave it lightly defended, and he might have left as many as two thousand men inside the city's walls. True, most of those men were the fyrd, but if they stayed behind the ramparts they would be hard to conquer.

Cnut must have been tempted to assault the city, but the Danes have never loved sieges. Men die on stone walls and drown in city ditches, and Cnut would want to keep his army strong for the battle he anticipated against Æthelred's forces as they returned from East Anglia. Win that battle and only then might he set his men to attack a Roman city-fort. Yet by leaving Gleawecestre alone he ran the risk that the garrison might sally from the city to attack his rear, but Cnut knew the Saxon fyrd. They could defend, but were fragile in attack. I suspected he would have left two or three hundred men to watch the walls and keep the garrison quiet. Three hundred would be more than enough because one trained warrior was worth six or seven men of the fyrd, and besides, to preserve their supplies the men inside the city would have few horses and, if they were to attack Cnut, they would need horses. They were not there to attack Cnut, but to defend Æthelred's lavish palace and treasury. Cnut's bigger fear, I was sure, was that Edward of Wessex would march to relieve the city, but by now I suspected Cnut's men were watching the Temes and ready to confront any West Saxon army that did appear. And that would not happen quickly. It would take days for Edward to summon his own fyrd to defend the West Saxon burhs and then assemble his army and decide what to do about the chaos to his north.

Or so I reckoned.

We rode through a waste land.

This was a rich land of good soil and fat sheep and heavy orchards, a land of plenty. Just days before there had been plump villages and noble halls and capacious granaries, but now there was smoke, ash and death. Cattle lay dead in the fields, their rotting flesh ripped by wolves, wild dogs and ravens. There were no people, except for the dead. The Danes who had caused this misery had ridden on to find more steadings to plunder, and the survivors, if there were any, would have fled to a burh. We rode in silence.

We followed a Roman road that ran straight across the desolation, the surviving marker stones counting down the miles to Gleawecestre. It was near a stone cut with the letters VII that the first Danes saw us. There were thirty of forty of them and they must have assumed we were also Danes because they rode towards us without fear. 'Who are you?' one of them called as they came nearer.

'Your enemy,' I said.

They curbed their horses. They were too close to turn and run safely, and perhaps they were puzzled by my answer. I checked my men and went forward alone. 'Who are you?' the man asked again. He was in mail, had a close-fitting helmet that framed a lean, dark face, and his arms were heavy with silver.

'I have more men than you,' I said, 'so you give me your name first.'

He thought about that for a few heartbeats. My men were spreading out, making a line of heavily armed horsemen who were plainly ready to attack. The man shrugged. 'I am Torfi Ottarson.'

'You serve Cnut?'

'Who doesn't?'

'I don't.'

He glanced at the hammer at my neck. 'Who are you?' he demanded a third time.

'I am called Uhtred of Bebbanburg,' I said, and was rewarded with a look of sudden alarm. 'You thought I was dead, Torfi Ottarson?' I asked. 'Perhaps I am. Who says the dead can't return to take revenge on the living?'

He touched his own hammer, opened his mouth to speak, then said nothing. His men watched me.

'So tell me, Torfi Ottarson,' I said, 'have you and your men come from Gleawecestre?'

'Where there are many more men,' he said defiantly.

'You're here to keep a watch on the city?' I asked.

'We do what we are told to do.'

'Then I shall tell you what to do, Torfi Ottarson. Who commands your forces at Gleawecestre?'

He hesitated, then decided there was no harm in answering. 'The Jarl Bjorgulf.'

It was not a name I knew, but presumably he was one of Cnut's trusted men. 'Then you will ride to the Jarl Bjorgulf now,' I said, 'and tell him that Uhtred of Bebbanburg is riding to Gleawecestre and that I will be allowed passage. He will let me pass.'

Torfi smiled grimly. 'You have reputation, lord, but even you can't defeat the men we have at Gleawecestre.'

222

'We're not going to fight,' I said.

'The Jarl Bjorgulf might wish otherwise?'

'He probably will wish otherwise,' I said, 'but you will tell him more.' I raised my hand and beckoned, and watched Torfi's face as he saw Finan and three of my men bring Frigg and the twins into sight. 'Do you know who they are?' I asked Torfi. He just nodded. 'So tell Jarl Bjorgulf that if he opposes me I shall kill the little girl first, then her mother, and the boy last.' I smiled. 'Jarl Cnut won't be happy, will he? His wife and children slaughtered and all because the Jarl Bjorgulf wanted a fight?'

Torfi was staring at Frigg and the twins. I think he was finding it difficult to believe his eyes, but at last he found his tongue. 'I shall tell the Jarl Bjorgulf,' he said in a voice suffused with amazement, 'and bring you his answer.'

'Don't trouble yourself,' I said, 'I know his answer. You ride and tell him that Uhtred of Bebbanburg is travelling to Gleawecestre and that he will not try to stop us. And think yourself lucky, Torfi.'

'Lucky?'

'You met me and lived. Now go.'

They turned and went. Their horses were much fresher than ours and they were soon so far ahead that we lost sight of them. I grinned at Finan. 'We should enjoy this,' I said.

'Unless they want to be heroes and rescue them?'

'They won't,' I said. I put the girl Sigril on Rolla's horse and he rode with a drawn sword, while the boy, Cnut Cnutson, was on Swithun's saddle, and Swithun, like Rolla, carried a naked blade. Frigg rode between Eldgrim and Kettil and seemed oblivious of what happened. She just smiled. In front of Frigg and her children, and leading our column, were two standard-bearers because, for the first time since leaving Bearddan Igge, we flew our flags, the prancing horse of Mercia and the wolf's head of Bebbanburg.

And the Danes just watched us pass.

We came in sight of Gleawecestre and I saw how the buildings outside the high walls had been burned and cleared away so the defenders could see any enemy approach. The walls bristled with spear-points that caught the late afternoon sun. To my left were

223

shelters put up by the Bjorgulf's Danes, the men who guarded the city to make sure the fyrd did not attempt to sally out. There were maybe four hundred Danes, it was hard to count them because once we were in sight they rode either side of us, but always keeping a respectful distance. They did not even shout insults, but just watched us.

A mile or so from the city's northern gate a heavy-set man with a red moustache turning grey spurred his horse towards us. He was accompanied by two younger men, and none carried a shield, just scabbarded swords. 'You must be Jarl Bjorgulf,' I greeted him.

'I am.'

'It's good to see the sun, isn't it?' I said. 'I can't remember such a wet summer. I was beginning to think it would never stop raining.'

'You would be wise,' he said, 'to give me the Jarl Cnut's family.'

'And whole fields of rye rotted by rain,' I said. 'I've never seen so many ruined crops.'

'The Jarl Cnut will be merciful,' Bjorgulf said.

'You should be worried about my mercy, not his.'

'If they're hurt . . .' he began.

'Don't be a fool,' I said harshly, 'of course they'll be hurt. Unless you do exactly what I tell you to do.'

'I . . .' he began again.

'Tomorrow morning, Bjorgulf,' I said as if he had not tried to speak, 'you will take your men away from here. You'll ride east, up into the hills, and by midday you'll all be gone.'

'We . . .'

'All of you, and your horses, up into the hills. And you'll stay there, out of sight of the city, and if I see one single Dane anywhere close to Gleawecestre after midday I'll rip the guts out of Cnut's daughter and send them to you as a present.' I smiled at him. 'It was a pleasure talking to you, Bjorgulf. When you send a messenger to the jarl give him my greetings and tell him I have done the favour he asked of me.'

Bjorgulf frowned. 'The jarl asked a favour of you?'

'He did. He asked me to discover who hates him, and to find out who took his woman and children. The answer to both

224

questions, Bjorgulf, is Uhtred of Bebbanburg. You can tell him that. Now go: you smell like a goat's turd soaked in cat's piss.'

And so we came to Gleawecestre, and the great northern gates were dragged open and the barricades inside were pulled away, and men cheered from the ramparts as my twin flags dipped to pass beneath the Roman arch. Horses' hooves clattered loud on ancient stone and in the street beyond, waiting for us, was Osferth, who looked happier than I had ever seen him, and, next to him, was Bishop Wulfheard who had burned my home, and, towering above both men on a horse caparisoned in silver, was my woman of gold. Æthelflaed of Mercia.

'I said I'd find you,' I told her happily.

And so I had.

Whenever I had visited my cousin Æthelred, which I did rarely and reluctantly, it had been at his hall outside Gleawecestre, a hall I presumed was now turned to ash. I had rarely been inside the city, which was even more impressive than Ceaster. The palace was a towering building made of thin Roman bricks that had once been clad in marble sheets, though almost all of those had been burned for lime, leaving only a few rusted iron brackets that had once held the marble in place. The bricks were now hung with leather panels depicting various saints, among them Saint Oswald being hacked down by a vicious-looking brute who snarled with bloodstained teeth while Oswald displayed a vacuous smile as if he welcomed death. What was ironic about the picture was that the vicious-looking brute was Penda, a Mercian, and the stupid-looking victim was a Northumbrian who had been an enemy of Mercia, but there is no point in looking for sense among Christians. Oswald was now venerated by his enemies and a Mercian army had crossed Britain to find his bones.

The floor of the hall was one of the intricate Roman tiled floors, this one depicting warriors hailing a chieftain who stood in a chariot being pulled by two swans and a fish. Maybe life was different in

225

those days. Great pillars held up an arched roof on which the remnants of plaster still showed, those remnants covered with paintings that could just be discerned among the water-stains, while the far end of the hall had a timber dais on which my cousin had placed a throne draped in scarlet cloth. A second lower throne was presumably for his new woman who so desperately wanted to be a queen. I kicked that seat off the dais and sat in the scarlet chair and looked down on the city's leaders. Those men, both church and laymen, stood on the picture of the chariot and looked sheepish. 'You're fools,' I snarled. 'You are all arse-licking, piss-dribbling, nose-picking fools.'

I was determined to enjoy myself.

There must have been two score of Mercians in the hall, all ealdormen, priests or thegns, the men left to guard Gleawecestre while Æthelred sought glory in East Anglia. Æthelflaed was there too, but my men surrounded her, separating her from the other Mercians. She was not the only woman in the hall. My daughter Stiorra, who lived in Æthelflaed's household, was standing by one of the pillars, and the sight of her long, serious and beautiful face brought a sudden sharp memory of her mother. Next to her was another girl, as tall as Stiorra, but fair where my daughter was dark, and she seemed familiar, but I could not place her. I gave her a long hard look, more on account of her undeniable prettiness than to try to provoke my memory, but I still could not identify her, and so turned to the body of the hall. 'And which of you,' I demanded, 'has command of the city's garrison?'

There was a pause. Finally Bishop Wulfheard took a pace forward and cleared his throat. 'I do,' he said.

'You!' I said, sounding shocked.

'The Lord Æthelred entrusted the city's safety to me,' he said defensively.

I stared at him. Let the silence stretch. 'Is there a church here?' I asked at last.

'Of course.'

'Then tomorrow I'll celebrate mass,' I said, 'and I'll preach a sermon. I can hand out stale bread and bad advice as well as anyone, can't I?' There was silence, except for a girlish giggle. Æthelflaed turned sharply to silence the sound, which came from the tall, fair, pretty girl standing next to my daughter. I recognised her then because she had ever been a light-headed, flippant creature. She was Æthelflaed's daughter, Ælfwynn, whom I still thought of as a child, but she was a child no longer. I winked at her, which only made her giggle again.

'Why would Æthelred put a bishop in charge of a garrison?' I asked, turning my attention back to Bishop Wulfheard. 'Have you ever fought in a battle? I know you burned down my barns, but that isn't a battle, you stinking piece of rat-gristle. A battle is the shield wall. It's smelling your enemy's breath while he tries to disembowel you with an axe, it's blood and shit and screams and pain and terror. It's trampling in your friends' guts as enemies butcher them. It's men clenching their teeth so hard they shatter them. Have you ever been in a battle?' He said nothing, just looked indignant. 'I asked you a question!' I shouted at him.

'No,' he admitted.

'Then you're not fit to be in charge of the garrison,' I said.

'The Lord Æthelred . . .' he began.

'Is pissing his breeches in East Anglia,' I said, 'and wondering how he'll ever get home again. And he only put you in charge because you're a grovelling lickspittle arsehole whom he trusted, just as he trusted Haesten. It was Haesten who assured you he'd captured Cnut's family, yes?'

A few men muttered assent. The bishop said nothing.

'Haesten,' I said, 'is a treacherous piece of slime, and he deceived you. He always served Cnut, but you all believed him because your shit-brained priests assured you that God was on your side. Well, he is now. He sent me, and I brought you Cnut's wife and children, and I am also angry.'

I stood on those last four words, stepped off the dais and stalked towards Wulfheard. 'I am angry,' I said again, 'because you burned my buildings. You tried to get that mob to kill me. You said any man who killed me would earn the grace of God. Do you remember that, you rancid piece of rat-dropping?'

227

Wulfheard said nothing.

'You called me an abomination,' I said. 'Do you remember?' I pulled Serpent-Breath from her sheath. She made a rasping noise, surprisingly loud, as her long blade scraped through the scabbard's throat. Wulfheard made a small scared noise and stepped back towards the protection of four priests who were evidently his followers, but I did not threaten him, I just reversed the sword and thrust the hilt towards him. 'There, you toad fart,' I said, 'earn the grace of God by killing a pagan abomination.' He stared at me puzzled. 'Kill me, you bile-brained slug,' I said.

'I . . .' he began, then faltered and took another backwards step.

I followed him, and one of the priests, a young man, moved to stop me. 'Touch me,' I warned him, 'and I'll spill your guts across the floor. I'm the priest-killer, remember? I'm an outcast of God. I'm an abomination. I'm the man you hate. I kill priests the way other men swat wasps. I am Uhtred.' I looked back to Wulfheard and held the sword to him again. 'So, you spavined weasel,' I challenged him, 'do you have the belly to kill me?' He shook his head and still said nothing. 'I'm the man who killed the Abbot Wihtred,' I said to him, 'and you cursed me for that. So why don't you kill me?' I waited, watching the fear on the bishop's face, and that was the moment I remembered the twins' strange reaction when Father Wissian had come into the great chamber at Ceaster. I turned towards Æthelflaed. 'You told me the Abbot Wihtred came from Northumbria?'

'He did.'

'And he suddenly appeared preaching about Saint Oswald?' I asked.

'The blessed Saint Oswald was a Northumbrian,' the bishop put in as if that might placate me.

'I know who he was!' I snarled. 'And did it occur to any of you that Cnut persuaded Abbot Wihtred to come south? Cnut rules in Northumbria, he wanted the Mercian army lured to East Anglia, and so he drew them there with promises of a dead saint's miraculous corpse. Wihtred was his man! His children called him uncle.' I did not know if all that was true, of course, but it seemed very likely. Cnut had been clever. 'You're fools, all of you!' I thrust the sword at Wulfheard again. 'Kill me, you slug-turd,' I said, but he just shook his head. 'Then you will pay me,' I said, 'for the damage you did at Fagranforda. You will pay me in gold and silver and I shall rebuild my halls and my barns and my cowsheds at your expense. You are going to repay me, aren't you?'

He nodded. He had little choice.

'Good!' I said cheerfully. I slammed Serpent-Breath back into her scabbard, and strode back to the dais. 'My Lady Æthelflaed,' I said very formally.

'My Lord Uhtred,' she answered just as formally.

'Who should command here?'

She hesitated, looking at the Mercians. 'Merewalh is as good as anyone,' she said.

'What about you?' I asked her. 'Why don't you command?'

'Because I go where you go,' she said firmly. The men in the room stirred uncomfortably, but none spoke. I thought about contradicting her, then decided it was best not to waste my breath.

'Merewalh,' I said instead, 'you're in charge of the garrison. I doubt Cnut will attack you because I intend to lure him northwards, but I could be wrong. How many trained warriors are in the city?'

'A hundred and forty-six,' Æthelflaed answered, 'most of them mine. Some used to be yours.'

'They'll all be riding with me,' I said. 'Merewalh, you can keep ten of your men, the rest go with me. And I might send for you when I know the city is safe because I'd hate for you to miss the battle. It's going to be a vicious one. Bishop! Would you like to fight the pagans?'

Wulfheard just stared at me. He was doubtless praying that his nailed god would send a lightning strike to shrivel me, but the nailed god did not oblige.

'So let me tell you what is happening,' I said, pacing the dais as I spoke. 'The Jarl Cnut has brought over four thousand men to Mercia. He's destroying Mercia, burning and killing, and Æthelred,' I deliberately did not call him Lord Æthelred, 'has to come back to stop the destruction. How many men does Æthelred have?'

229

'Fifteen hundred,' someone muttered.

'And if he doesn't come back,' I went on, 'Cnut will hunt him down in East Anglia. That's probably what Cnut is doing now. He's hunting Æthelred and hopes to destroy him before the West Saxons come north. So our job is to pull Cnut away from Æthelred and keep him busy while the West Saxons muster their army and march to join Æthelred. How many men can Edward bring?' I asked Osterth.

'Between three and four thousand,' he said.

'Good!' I smiled. 'We'll outnumber Cnut and we'll rip his guts out and feed them to the dogs.'

Ealdorman Deogol, a slow-witted man who held land just north of Gleawecestre, frowned at me. 'You'll lead men north?'

'I will.'

'And take almost all the trained warriors with you,' he said accusingly.

'I will,' I said.

'But there are Danes ringing the city,' he said plaintively.

'I got into the city,' I said, 'and I can get out.'

'And if they see the trained warriors leave,' his voice was rising, 'what's to stop them attacking?'

'Oh, they're leaving tomorrow,' I said, 'didn't I tell you that? They're leaving, and we're going to burn their ships.'

'They're leaving?' Deogol asked incredulously.

'Yes,' I said, 'they're leaving.'

And I hoped I was right.

'You were hard on Bishop Wulfheard,' Æthelflaed said to me that night. We were in bed. I assumed it was her husband's bed and I did not care. 'You were very hard on him,' she said.

'Not hard enough.'

'He's a good man.'

'He's an earsling,' I said. She sighed. 'Ælfwynn's grown into a pretty girl,' I went on.

'She has a head filled with feathers,' her mother said harshly.

'But very pretty feathers.'

'And she knows that,' Æthelflaed said, 'and she behaves like a fool. I should have given birth to sons.'

'I've always liked Ælfwynn.'

'You like all pretty girls,' she said disapprovingly.

'I do, yes, but you're the one I love.'

'And Sigunn, and a half-dozen others.'

'Only half a dozen?'

She pinched me for that. 'Frigg is pretty.'

'Frigg,' I said, 'is beautiful beyond words.'

She thought about that, then gave a grudging nod. 'Yes, she is. And Cnut will come for her?'

'He'll come for me.'

'You're such a humble man.'

'I've wounded his pride. He'll come.'

'Men and their pride.'

'You want me to be humble?'

'I might as well hope to see the moon turn somersaults,' she said. She tilted her head and kissed my cheek. 'Osferth is in love,' she said, 'it's rather touching.'

'With Ingulfrid?'

'I'd like to meet her,' Æthelflaed said.

'She's clever,' I said, 'very clever.'

'So is Osferth, and he deserves someone clever.'

'I'm sending him back to your brother,' I told her. Osferth had come north after taking his message to Edward, and Edward had sent him on to Gleawecestre to order Æthelflaed back to Wessex, a command she had predictably ignored. Osferth had arrived in Gleawecestre just hours before the Danes landed south of the city, and now he needed to go back to spur the West Saxons to haste. 'Is your brother mustering his army?'

'So Osferth says.'

'But will he bring it north?' I wondered aloud.

'He has to,' Æthelflaed said bleakly.

'I'll tell Osferth to kick Edward's arse,' I said.

231

'Osferth will do no such thing,' she said, 'and he'll be glad to go back to Wessex. He left his lady in Wintanceaster.'

'And I left mine in Gleawecestre,' I said.

'I knew you'd come back.' She stirred beside me, a small hand stroking my chest.

'I thought about joining Cnut,' I told her.

'No, you didn't.'

'He wanted me to be an ally,' I said, 'but instead I have to kill him.' I thought of Ice-Spite, Cnut's sword, and of his famed skill, and felt a shiver in the night.

'You will.'

'I will.' I wondered whether age had slowed Cnut. Had it slowed me?

'What will you do with the boy?'

'Ingulfrid's son? Sell him back to his father when I've settled Cnut.'

'Osferth said you very nearly captured Bebbanburg.'

'Nearly isn't enough.'

'No, I suppose not. What would you have done if you'd succeeded? Stayed there?'

'And never left,' I said.

'And me?'

'I'd have sent for you.'

'I belong here. I'm a Mercian now.'

'There won't be a Mercia,' I said truthfully, 'until we've killed Cnut.'

She lay in silence for a long time. 'What if he wins?' she asked after that long silence.

'Then a thousand ships will come from the north to join him, and men will come from Frisia, and every Northman who wants land will bring a sword, and they'll cross the Temes.'

'And there'll be no Wessex,' she said.

'No Wessex,' I said, 'and no Englaland.'

How odd that name sounds. It was her father's dream. To make a country called Englaland. Englaland. I fell asleep.

PART FOUR

Ice-Spite

Eleven

The Danes decided not to leave Gleawecestre.

It was not Bjorgulf's decision, at least I thought not, but he must have sent a messenger eastwards in search of orders or advice because, next morning, a delegation of Danes rode towards Gleawecestre's walls. They came on horseback, their stallions picking their way through the ruins of the houses that had been dismantled beyond the ramparts. There were six men, led by a standard-bearer who carried a leafy branch as a signal that they came to talk and not to fight. Bjorgulf was one of the six, but he hung back and left the talking to a tall, heavy-browed man with a long red beard that was plaited, knotted and hung with small silver rings. He was dressed in mail, had a sword at his side, but wore no helmet and carried no shield. His arms were bright with the rings of war, and a chain of heavy gold links hung at his neck. He motioned for his companions to stop some twenty paces from the ditch, then rode forward alone until he reached the ditch's edge where he curbed his horse and stared up at the ramparts. 'Are you Lord Uhtred?' he called to me.

'I am Uhtred.'

'I am Geirmund Eldgrimson,' he said.

'I have heard of you,' I said, and that was true. He was one of Cnut's battle-leaders, a man with a reputation for fearlessness and savagery. His estates, I knew, were in northern Northumbria, and he had earned his fame by fighting against the Scots, who were forever coming south to rob, rape and ravish.

'The Jarl Cnut sends you greetings,' Geirmund said.

'You will return my greetings to him,' I said, just as courteously.

'He heard you were dead.' Geirmund stroked his horse's mane with a gloved hand.

'I heard the same.'

'And he regretted that news.'

'He did?' I asked in surprise.

Geirmund offered me a grimace that I supposed was meant to be a smile. 'He had wanted the pleasure of killing you himself,' he explained. He spoke mildly, not wanting to provoke an exchange of insults. Not yet, anyway.

'Then he will be as pleased as I am that I live,' I said just as mildly.

Geirmund nodded. 'Yet the jarl sees no need to fight against you,' he said, 'and sends you a proposal.'

'Which I shall hear with great interest.'

Geirmund paused, looking left and right. He was examining the walls, seeing the ditch and the stakes, and estimating the number of spears that bristled above the high Roman parapet. I let him stare because I wanted him to see just how formidable these defences were. He looked back to me. 'The Jarl Cnut offers you this,' he said, 'if you return his woman and children unharmed then he will return to his own lands.'

'A generous offer,' I said.

'The jarl is a generous man,' Geirmund replied.

'I do not command here,' I said, 'but I shall talk with the city leaders and bring you their answer in one hour.'

'I advise you to accept the offer,' Geirmund said. 'The jarl is generous, but he is not patient.'

'One hour,' I repeated, and stepped back out of his sight.

And that was interesting, I thought. Had Cnut really made such an offer? If so then he had no intention of keeping to its terms. If I handed over Frigg and her children then we had lost what small hold we had on Cnut and as a result his savagery would double. So the offer was a lie, of that I was sure, but did it even come from Cnut? My suspicion was that Cnut and his main army

236

were on the other side of Mercia, waiting to pounce on Æthelred's smaller force as it left East Anglia, and if that suspicion was right then there was no possibility that a messenger could have reached him and returned to Gleawecestre in the one day since my arrival. I suspected Geirmund had invented the offer.

Bishop Wulfheard, of course, believed otherwise. 'If Cnut returns to his own land,' he said, 'then we have gained the victory we desire without the shedding of blood.'

'Victory?' I asked dubiously.

'The pagans will have left our land!' the bishop explained.

'And left it ravaged,' I said.

'There must be compensation, of course.' The bishop saw my point.

'You're a nose-picking idiot,' I said. We had gathered in the hall again where I had told the assembled thegns and churchmen of the Danish offer. I now told them it was a ruse. 'Cnut is miles away,' I explained. 'He's somewhere on the East Anglian frontier, and Geirmund didn't have time to send him a messenger and get a reply, so he invented the offer. He's trying to trick us into returning Cnut's family, and we have to persuade him to leave Gleawecestre.'

'Why?' a man asked. 'I mean if they're here we know where they are, and the city is strong.'

'Because Cnut has his fleet here,' I said. 'If things go badly for him, and I plan to make things go very badly for him, then he'll withdraw towards his boats. He doesn't want to lose a hundred and sixty-eight ships. But if we burn those ships then he'll withdraw northwards, and that's where I want him.'

'Why?' the man asked again. He was one of Æthelred's thegns, which meant he disliked me. All of Saxon Mercia was divided between those who followed Æthelred, and the supporters of his estranged wife, Æthelflaed.

'Because right now,' I said angrily, 'his army is in between Æthelred's forces and King Edward's army, and as long as he's there those two armies cannot join together, so I have to move him out of the way.'

237

'The Lord Uhtred knows what he is doing,' Æthelflaed chided the man mildly.

'You told them you would kill the children if they didn't leave.' The speaker was one of Wulfheard's priests.

'An empty threat,' I said.

'Empty?' The bishop sounded angry.

'I know this will astonish you,' I said, 'but I have a reputation for not killing women and children. Maybe that's because I'm a pagan, not a Christian.'

Æthelflaed sighed.

'But we still have to get the Danes away from Gleawecestre,' I went on, 'and unless I do slaughter one of the twins, Geirmund won't move.'

They understood that. They might not have liked me, but they could not dispute my reasoning. 'The girl, then,' Bishop Wulfheard said.

'The girl?' I asked.

'She's the least valuable,' he said and, when I did not respond, he tried to explain, 'she's a girl!'

'So we just kill her?' I asked.

'Isn't that what you suggested?'

'Will you do it?' I asked him.

He opened his mouth, discovered he had nothing to say, so closed it again.

'We do not kill small children,' I said. 'We wait till they're grown up and then we kill them. So. How do we persuade Geirmund to go away?' No one had an answer. Æthelflaed was watching me warily. 'Well?' I asked.

'Pay him?' Ealdorman Deogol suggested weakly. I said nothing and he looked around the hall seeking support. 'We guard the Lord Æthelred's treasure,' he said, 'so we can afford to pay him.'

'Pay a Dane to go away,' I said, 'and they come back next day to be paid again.'

'So what are we going to do?' Deogol asked plaintively.

'Kill the girl, of course,' I said. 'Bishop,' I looked at Wulfheard, 'be useful. Talk to the city's priests and discover if a small girl has

238

died in the last week. She needs to be six or seven years old. If she has, dig her up. Tell the parents she'll become a saint, or an angel, or whatever else will make them happy. Then bring the body to the ramparts, but don't let the Danes see it! Merewalh?'

'Lord?'

'Find me a piglet. Take it to the ramparts, but keep it below the parapet so the Danes don't know it's there. Finan? You'll bring Frigg and the twins to the walls.'

'Piglet,' Bishop Wulfheard said in a scornful tone.

I stared at him, then held up a hand to check Merewalh, who was about to leave the hall. 'Maybe we don't need a piglet,' I said slowly, as if an idea was just coming to me. 'Why waste a baby pig when there's a bishop available?'

Wulfheard fled.

And Merewalh fetched the piglet.

Geirmund was waiting, though now he had been joined by almost twenty other men. Their horses were picketed a hundred paces from the ditch, while the Danes were much closer, and all in a cheerful mood. Servants had brought ale, bread and meat, and there were half a dozen boys, presumably the sons of the warriors who had joined Geirmund to witness his confrontation with Uhtred of Bebbanburg whose reputation did not stretch to the slaughter of women and children. Geirmund was chewing on a goose-leg when I appeared, but he tossed it away and strolled towards the ramparts. 'You have come to a decision?' he called up to me.

'You forced me to a decision,' I said.

He smiled. He was not a man accustomed to smiling, so it looked more like a snarl, but at least he tried to smile. 'As I told you,' he said, 'the jarl is merciful.'

'And he will leave Saxon Mercia?'

'He has promised it!'

'And he will pay compensation for the damage he has done to Lord Æthelred's land?' I asked.

239

Geirmund hesitated, then nodded. 'There will be compensation, I'm sure. The jarl is not an unreasonable man.'

And you, I thought, are a lying bastard. 'So,' I asked, 'the jarl will pay us gold and return to his own land?'

'That is his wish, but only if you return his family unharmed.'

'They have neither been harmed nor molested,' I assured him, 'I swear it by Thor's spittle.' I spat to show the sincerity of that promise.

'I am glad to hear it,' Geirmund said, and spat to show that he accepted my promise, 'and the jarl will also be glad.' He tried to smile again because Frigg and her two children had just appeared on the high rampart. They were escorted by Finan and five men. Frigg looked scared and exquisitely beautiful. She was wearing a linen dress lent to her by Æthelflaed. The dress was dyed palest yellow, and the twins clung to the pretty garment's skirts. Geirmund bowed to her. 'My lady,' he said formally, then looked at me. 'Would it not be better, Lord Uhtred,' he suggested, 'if you were to allow the lady and her children to leave by the gate?'

'The gate?' I asked, pretending not to understand.

'You can't expect them to swim that filthy ditch?'

'No,' I said, 'I'll throw them to you.'

'You'll . . .' he began, then went silent because I had seized the girl, Sigril, and now held her in front of me. She screamed in terror and her mother lunged for her, but was restrained by Finan. I had my left arm around Sigril's throat, pinning her, and drew a knife from my belt with my right hand.

'I'll throw her to you in bits,' I called to Geirmund, and grasped Sigril's long black hair. 'Hold her,' I ordered Osferth and while he held her I cut the hair, sawing through the strands and tossing them over the wall to be caught by the wind. The girl was screaming wonderfully as I forced her down to the stones where the parapet hid her from Geirmund. I clapped a hand over her mouth and nodded to the man concealed behind the parapet, and he stabbed a knife into the piglet's neck. It gave a shriek and blood spattered and flew. The Danes, beyond the wall, would just see the blood and hear the terrified squealing, then they saw Rolla slam down an axe.

The dead child was yellow, waxen and stinking. Rolla had chopped off a leg, and the smell was like the stench of the Corpse-Ripper's lair. Rolla bent down, smeared the severed leg in the piglet's blood, then tossed it over the rampart. It splashed into the ditch, and he cut down again, this time taking an arm.

'Oh, sweet mother of God,' Osferth said faintly. Frigg was struggling, her mouth opening and closing in terror, her eyes wide. Her pretty dress was spattered with blood, and to the watching Danes it must have seemed she was seeing her daughter being butchered before her eyes, but in truth it was the horror of watching that half-decayed, liquid-oozing corpse being disjointed that was scaring her. Her son was screaming. I still had my hand over Sigril's mouth and the little bitch bit me hard enough to draw blood.

'Her head next,' I called to Geirmund, 'then we kill the boy, and after that we'll take the mother back for our amusement.'

'Stop!' he shouted.

'Why? I'm enjoying myself!' I used my free hand to throw the dead child's remaining foot over the wall. Rolla raised the axe that had been smeared with piglet blood. 'Chop her head off,' I ordered loudly.

'What do you want?' Geirmund called.

I held up a hand to check Rolla. 'I want you to stop telling me lies,' I said to Geirmund. I beckoned to Osferth and he knelt beside me and put his hand on Sigril's mouth. She managed a yelp as my bloodied hand left her lips and before Osferth's palm clamped down, but none of the Danes seemed to notice. They just saw Frigg's terrible distress and the boy's utter fear. I stood in the piglet's blood and stared down at Geirmund. 'You had no promise from Cnut,' I said, 'and he sent no message! He's too far away!' Geirmund said nothing, but his face betrayed that I had told the truth. 'But you will send him a message now!' I was shouting, so that all Geirmund's companions could hear me. 'Tell Jarl Cnut that his daughter is dead, and his son will be dead too if you're not gone from here in one hour. You leave! All of you! You go now! You go up to the hills and far away. You leave this place. If I see one Dane anywhere near Gleawecestre one hour from now then I shall

241

feed the boy to my wolfhounds and whore his mother for my men's pleasure.' I took hold of Frigg's arm and pulled her to the parapet so that the Danes could see that pretty dress with its pattern of blood spots. 'If you're not gone within one hour,' I told Geirmund, 'then Jarl Cnut's woman becomes our whore. You understand? You go east, up into the hills!' I pointed that way. 'Go to Jarl Cnut and tell him his wife and son will be returned unharmed if he goes back to Northumbria. Tell him that! Now go! Or else watch Cnut Cnutson's body being eaten by dogs!'

They believed me. They left.

And so, in that next hour as a pale cloud-shrouded sun climbed towards its noon height, we watched the Danes leave Gleawecestre. They rode east towards the Coddeswold hills, and the horsemen were followed by a crowd of women, children and servants on foot. The dead child's leg had drifted to the ditch's bank where two ravens came to feast. 'Bury the child again,' I told a priest, 'and send the parents to me.'

'To you?'

'So I can give them gold,' I explained. 'Go,' I told him, then looked at my son who was watching the retreating Danes. 'The art of war,' I told him, 'is to make the enemy do your bidding.'

'Yes, Father,' he said obediently. He had been distressed by Frigg's frantic and silent misery, though by now I supposed Æthelflaed would have calmed the poor woman. I had ruined little Sigril's hair, but it would grow again, and I had given her a dripping honeycomb as consolation.

So, for the price of one piglet and a small girl's hair, we had cleared the Danes away from Gleawecestre, and, as soon as they were gone, I took a hundred men to where their boats were tethered in the river. Some had been hauled onto land, but most were tied to the Sæfern's bank, and we burned them all except for one smaller craft. One by one the ships caught the fire and the flames leaped up the hemp ropes and the high masts crashed down in blasts of sparks and smoke, and the Danes saw it all. I might have told Geirmund to go all the way to the high ground, but I knew he would have men watching us and they saw their fleet turned to ash that turned the river grey as it floated seawards. Boat after boat burned, their dragon prows belching flame, their timbers cracking and their hulls hissing as the ships sank. I kept the one ship afloat and took Osferth aside. 'That ship's yours,' I said.

'Mine?'

'Take a dozen men,' I said, 'and row it downriver. Then up the Afen. Take Rædwulf.' Rædwulf was one of my older men, slow and steady, who had been born and raised in Wiltunscir and knew the rivers there. 'The Afen will take you deep into Wessex,' I went on, 'and I want you there fast!' That was why I had kept the one boat unburned; the journey would be far faster by water than by land.

'You want me to go to King Edward,' Osferth said.

'I want you to put on your heaviest boots and kick his arse hard! Tell him to get his army north of the Temes, but he's to look for Æthelred coming from the east. Ideally they should join up. Then they're to march towards Tameworþig. I can't tell you where we'll be, or where Cnut will be, but I'm trying to lure him north onto his own land.'

'Tameworþig?' Osferth asked.

'I'll start with Tameworþig and work my way north and east, and he'll come for me. He'll come fast, and he's going to outnumber me by twenty or thirty to one, so I need Edward and Æthelred.'

Osferth frowned. 'So why not stay in Gleawecestre, lord?' he asked.

'Because Cnut can put five hundred men here to keep us caged and do whatever he wants while we scratch our backsides. I can't let him trap me in a burh. He has to pursue me. I'm leading him in a dance, and you have to bring Edward and Æthelred to join it.'

'I understand, lord,' he said. He turned to look at the burning boats and at the great swathe of smoke darkening the sky above the river. Two swans went past, going southwards, and I took them for a good omen. 'Lord?' Osferth asked.

'Yes?'

'The boy,' Osferth sounded embarrassed.

243

'Cnut's son?'

'No, Ingulfrid's son. What will you do with him?'

'Do? I'd like to cut his miserable little throat, but I'll settle for selling him back to his father.'

'Promise me you won't hurt him, lord, or sell him to slavery.'

'Promise you?'

He looked defiant. 'It's important to me, lord. Have I ever asked you for a favour before?'

'Yes,' I said, 'you asked me to save you from being a priest, and I did.'

'Then I'm asking a second favour of you, lord. Please let me buy the boy from you.'

I laughed. 'You can't afford him.'

'I will pay you, lord, if it takes the rest of my life.' He stared at me so earnestly. 'I swear it, lord,' he said, 'on the blood of our Saviour.'

'You'll pay me,' I said, 'in gold?'

'If it takes my whole life, lord, I will pay you.'

I pretended to think about the offer, then shook my head. 'He's not for sale,' I said, 'except to his father. But I will give him to you.'

Osferth gazed at me. He was not sure he had heard correctly. 'Give him to me?' he asked faintly.

'You bring me Edward's army,' I said, 'and I'll give the boy to you.'

'Give?' he asked a second time.

'I swear on Thor's hammer that I will give you the boy if you bring me Edward's army.'

'Truly, lord?' He looked pleased.

'Get your skinny arse into that boat and go,' I said, 'and yes. But only if you bring me Edward and Æthelred. Or just Edward. And if you don't bring them,' I went on, 'the boy's yours anyway.'

'He is?'

'Because I'll be dead. Now go.'

The ships burned into the night. Geirmund would have seen the western sky aglow and he would know that everything had changed. His messengers would be riding eastwards to Cnut, telling him that his fleet was cinders and his daughter dead, and that Uhtred of Bebbanburg was loose in the west.

Which meant that the dance of death was about to begin.

And next morning, when the sky was still smeared with the smoke of the burning, we rode north.

Two hundred and sixty-nine warriors rode from Gleawecestre.

And one woman warrior. Æthelflaed insisted she would accompany us, and when Æthelflaed insisted then not all the gods of Asgard could change her mind. I tried. I might as well have attempted to turn back a tempest by farting into its face.

We took Frigg too, along with her son, her ragged-haired daughter and her servants. And we took a score of boys whose job was to look after the spare horses. One of those boys was Æthelstan, King Edward's eldest son though not his heir. I had insisted on leaving him behind under the care of Merewalh and Bishop Wulfheard, safe behind Gleawecestre's Roman walls, but fifteen miles up the road I saw him galloping a grey horse through a meadow where he was racing another boy. 'You!' I bellowed, and he slewed the stallion around and kicked it towards me.

'Lord?' he asked innocently.

'I ordered you to stay in Gleawecestre,' I snarled.

'And so I did, lord,' he said respectfully. 'I always obey you.'

'I should beat you till you bleed, you foul little liar.'

'But you didn't say how long I should stay, lord,' he said reprovingly, 'so I stayed a few minutes and then followed you. But I did obey you. I did stay.'

'And what will your father say when you die?' I demanded. 'Tell me that, you excrescence.'

He pretended to think about the question, then looked at me with his most innocent expression. 'He'll probably thank you, lord. Bastards are a nuisance.'

Æthelflaed laughed and I had to stop myself from laughing too.

245

'You're a hideous nuisance,' I told him. 'Now get out of my sight before I break your skull.'

'Yes, lord,' he said, grinning, 'and thank you, lord.' He turned his horse and rode back to his friends.

Æthelflaed smiled. 'He has spirit.'

'A spirit that will get him killed,' I said, 'but it probably doesn't matter. We're all doomed.'

'We are?'

'Two hundred and sixty-nine men,' I said, 'and one woman, while Cnut has between three and four thousand men. What do you think?'

'I think no one lives for ever,' she said.

And for some reason I thought of Iseult then, of Iseult the Shadow Queen, born into darkness and given the gift of prophecy, or so she had said, and she had also said Alfred would give me power and I would take back my northern home and my woman would be a woman of gold and I would lead armies that would crush the earth with their size and power. Two hundred and sixty-nine men. I laughed.

'You're laughing because I'm going to die?' Æthelflaed asked.

'Because almost none of the prophecies have come true,' I said.

'What prophecies?' she asked.

'I was promised that your father would give me power, that I would take back Bebbanburg, that I would lead armies to darken the land, and that seven kings would die. All false.'

'My father gave you power.'

'He gave it,' I agreed, 'and he took it away. He lent it to me. I was a dog and he held the leash.'

'And you will take back Bebbanburg,' she said.

'I tried, I failed.'

'And you will try again,' she said confidently.

'If I live.'

'If you live,' she said, 'and you will.'

'And the seven kings?'

'We'll know who they are,' she said, 'when they die.'

The men who had deserted me at Fagranforda were back now.

246

They had served Æthelflaed ever since my departure, but one by one they came to me and pledged their loyalty once again. They were embarrassed. Sihtric stammered his explanation, which I cut short. 'You were frightened,' I said.

'Frightened?'

'That you'd go to hell.'

'The bishop said we'd be cursed for ever, us and our children. And Ealhswith said . . .' His voice trailed away.

Ealhswith had been a whore, a good one too, and Sihtric had fallen in love with her and, against my advice, married her. It turned out he was right and I was wrong because the marriage was a happy one, but part of the price Sihtric had paid was to become a Christian, and, it seemed, a Christian who feared his wife as much as he feared the fires of hell.

'And now?' I asked.

'Now, lord?'

'Are you so sure you won't be cursed now? You're back under my command.'

He gave a quick smile. 'It's the bishop who's frightened now, lord.'

'So he should be,' I said. 'The Danes would feed him his own balls to eat, then turn him inside out, and not quickly either.'

'He gave us absolution, lord,' he stumbled over the long word, 'and said we wouldn't be doomed if we followed you.'

I laughed at that, then clapped his back. 'I'm glad you're here, Sihtric. I need you!'

'Lord,' was all he could say.

I needed him. I needed every man. Above all I needed Edward of Wessex to hurry. Cnut, once he decided to change his plans, and if he decided to change his plans, would move with lightning speed. His men, all mounted, would thunder across Mercia. It would be the wild hunt with thousands of hunters, and I would be the prey.

But first I had to draw him, and so we rode north, back into Danish territory. I knew we were being followed. Geirmund Eldgrimson would have men pursuing us, and I thought of turning

247

back to confront them, but reckoned they would simply ride away if they saw us threaten them. So let them follow. It would take two or three days for any news of our whereabouts to reach Cnut, and two or three more days for his forces to reach us, and I had no intention of staying in the same place for more than a day. Besides, I wanted Cnut to find me. What I did not want was for Cnut to catch me.

We crossed into Danish-held Mercia and we burned. We fired halls, barns and hovels. Wherever a Dane lived, we set fires. We filled the sky with smoke. We were making signals, telling the Danes where we were, but moving fast after each burning so that it must have seemed that we were everywhere. We were not opposed. The men from these steadings had been summoned to Cnut's army, leaving the old, the young and the women behind. I did not kill, not even livestock. We gave folk minutes to leave their homes, then used their hearths to fire the thatch. Other folk saw the smoke and fled before we arrived, and we would search the ground about such abandoned homes for signs of hasty digging. We found two hoards that way, one of them a deep hole filled with heavy silver bowls and jugs that we chopped to pieces. I remember one of those bowls, big enough to hold a pig's head, and decorated with bare-legged girls dancing. They held garlands and they were lithe, graceful and smiling, as if they danced in a forest glade for pure joy. 'It must be Roman,' I said to Æthelflaed. No one I knew could have made such a delicate thing.

'It is Roman,' she said, pointing to words incised about the rim.

I read the words aloud, stumbling over the unfamiliar syllables. *'Moribus et forma conciliandus amor,'* I read. 'And what does that mean?'

She shrugged. 'I don't know. *Amor* is love, I think. The priests would know.'

'We're blessedly short of priests,' I said. A couple had accompanied us because most of our men were Christians and wanted priests to be with them.

She ran a finger around the bowl's rim. 'It's beautiful. A pity to break it.'

We broke it anyway, hacking it to shreds with our axes. The ancient work of a craftsman, a thing of elegant beauty, was turned into hacksilver, and hacksilver was far more useful than a bowl of half-naked dancers. Hacksilver was easy to carry and it was money. The bowl yielded at least three hundred pieces, which we shared out, and then we rode on.

We slept in groves of trees, or else in abandoned halls that we would burn in the dawn. We never lacked food. The harvest had been gathered and there was grain, there were vegetables, and there was livestock. For a whole week we roamed Cnut's land and we ate his food and we burned his halls, and no hall-burning gave me as much pleasure as destroying his great feasting-hall at Tameworþig.

We had been riding in the countryside north of that town, deep inside Cnut's territory, but now we went south to where the rivers met and to where old King Offa had built his magnificent hall on Tameworþig's fortified hill. Spearmen manned the wooden palisade, but they were few in number, probably all old or injured men, and they made no attempt to resist us. As we came from the north they fled across the Roman bridge that spanned the Tame and vanished southwards.

We searched the high, old hall, seeking silver or better, but we found nothing. The feasting platters were clay, the drinking horns were undecorated, and the treasures, if there had been any, were gone. Saxons lived in the town that was built just north of the hill on which the great hall stood and they told us that men had carried four wagonloads of goods eastwards just two days before. Those men had stripped the hall, leaving only the antlers and skulls, and even the food stores were almost bare. We used hacksilver to buy bread, smoked meat and salt fish from the townspeople, and that night we slept in Cnut's hall, but I made certain there were sentries on the wall and more on the Roman bridge that led southwards.

And in the morning we put fire to Offa's hall. Was it King Offa's? I do not know; I only know it was age-blackened, and that Offa had built the fort there and must have had a hall inside its wall. Perhaps the hall had been rebuilt since his death, but whoever built it, it now burned. It blazed. It caught the fire with savage speed, the ancient timbers seeming to embrace their fate, and we drew back in awe as the high beams fell to erupt sparks, smoke and new bright flame. Men must have seen that burning from fifty miles away. I have never seen a hall burn so fierce or so fast. Rats fled it, birds panicked from the thatch, and the heat drove us down to the town where our horses were penned.

We had lit a signal to defy the Danes, and next morning, as the fires still burned and the smoke drifted in a cool, damp wind, I put two hundred men on the wall facing the river. Parts of the wall had burned, and much of the rest was scorched, but to anyone coming from south of the river it would look like a fiercely defended fortress. A fortress of smoke. I took the rest of my men to the bridge and there we waited.

'You think he'll come?' my son asked me.

'I think he'll come. Today or tomorrow.'

'And we fight him here?'

'What would you do?' I asked him.

He grimaced. 'We can defend the bridge,' he said uncertainly, 'but he can cross the river upstream or downstream. The water's not that deep.'

'So would you fight him here?'

'No.'

'Then we won't,' I said. 'I want him to think we will, but we won't.'

'Then where?' he asked.

'You tell me.'

He thought for a while. 'You don't want to go back north,' he said eventually, 'because that takes us away from King Edward.'

'If he's coming,' I said.

'And you can't go south,' he continued, ignoring my pessimism, 'and going east puts Cnut between us and Edward, so we have to go west.'

'You see?' I said. 'It's easy when you think.'

'And going west takes us towards the Welsh,' he said.

'So let's hope those bastards are sleeping.'

250

He stared at the long green weeds stirring languidly in the river. He was frowning. 'But why not go south?' he asked after a while. 'Why not try to join Edward's army?'

'If it's coming,' I said, 'and we don't know that.'

'We have no hope if it isn't,' he said grimly, 'so suppose that it is. Why don't we join it?'

'You Just said we couldn't.'

'But if we leave now? If we travel fast?'

I had thought of doing that. We could indeed hurry southwards, going towards the West Saxon army that I hoped was coming north, but I could not be sure that Cnut had not already blocked the way, or that he would not intercept us on the road, and then I would be forced to fight a battle in a place of his choosing, not mine. So we would go west and hope the Welsh were drunk and sleeping.

The Roman bridge was made of four stone arches and it was in surprisingly good repair. In the centre, built into one of the para- pets, was a wide limestone slab cut with words, *pontem perpetui mansurum in saecula*, and again I had no idea what it meant, though the word *perpetui* suggested the bridge was intended to last for ever. If so, it was untrue, because my men broke one of the two centre arches. We used massive hammers and it took most of the day, but eventually the old stones were all on the river's bed and we bridged the gap with baulks of timber taken from the town. We used more timber to make a barrier at the bridge's northern end, and behind that barrier we made our shield wall.

And waited.

And next day, as the sun sank scarlet in the west, Cnut came.

Cnut's scouts came first, riders on small, light horses that could travel fast. They reached the river and just stood there, watching us, all except a small group who rode along the Tame's bank, presumably to discover whether we had placed men to bar the next crossing place upstream.

251

The bulk of Cnut's forces arrived an hour or so after the scouts, and they covered the land, a horde of horsemen in mail and helmets, their round shields decorated with ravens, axes, hammers and hawks. It was impossible to count them because they numbered thousands. And nearly all had sacks or bags hanging from the cantles of their saddles: the plunder of Mercia. Those bags would have the valuable items, the silver, amber and gold, while the rest of the plunder would be on packhorses behind the vast army that threw long shadows as it advanced towards the bridge.

They stopped fifty paces short of the bridge to let Cnut ride forward. He was in a coat of mail polished silver-bright. He wore a white cloak, and rode a grey horse. With him was his close friend, Sigurd Thorrson, and where Cnut was all silver and white, Sigurd was dark. His horse was black, his cloak was black, and his helmet was crested with raven feathers. He hated me and I did not blame him for that hatred. I would hate any man who killed my son. He was a big man, heavily muscled, looming over his powerful horse, and beside him Cnut looked thin and pale. But of the two I feared Cnut more. He was snake-fast, weasel-cunning, and his sword, Ice-Spite, was famous as a drinker of blood.

Behind the two jarls were standard-bearers. Cnut's flag showed the axe and the broken cross, while Jarl Sigurd's displayed a flying raven. There were a hundred other standards among the army, but I looked for only one, and saw it. Haesten's bleached skull-symbol was held aloft on a pole in the army's centre. So he was here, but he had not been invited to accompany Cnut and Sigurd.

The banners of the broken cross and the flying raven halted at the bridge's southern end, while the two jarls rode on towards us. They checked their horses just short of the timber roadway. Æthelflaed, standing beside me, shivered. She hated the Danes and now she was within yards of the two most formidable jarls of Britain.

'This is what I shall do,' Jarl Cnut said without any greeting or even insult. He spoke in a reasonable voice, as if he merely arranged a feast or a horse race. 'I shall capture you alive, Uhtred of Bebbanburg, and I shall keep you alive. I shall tie you between two posts so that folk can mock you, and I shall have my men use your woman in front of your eyes until there is no use left in her.' He looked at Æthelflaed with his pale, cold eyes. 'I will bare you naked, woman, and give you to my men, even to the slaves, and you, Uhtred of Bebbanburg, will hear her sobbing, you will watch her shame and you will see her die. Then I shall begin on you. I have dreamed of it, Uhtred of Bebbanburg. I have dreamed of cutting you piece by piece until you have no hands, no feet, no nose, no ears, no tongue, no manhood. And then we shall peel your skin away, inch by inch, and rub salt on your flesh, and listen to your screams. And men will piss on you and women laugh at you, and all this you will see because I will have left you your eyes. But they will go. And then you will go, and so will end the tale of your miserable life.'

I said nothing when he had finished. The river seethed over the broken stones of the bridge.

'Lost your tongue already, you shit-slimed bastard?' Jarl Sigurd snarled.

I smiled at Cnut. 'Now why would you do that to me?' I asked. 'Did I not do your bidding? Didn't I discover who took your wife and children?'

'A child,' Cnut said passionately, 'a small girl! What had she done? And I will find your daughter, Uhtred of Bebbanburg, and when she has pleasured as many of my men who wish to use her I shall kill her as you killed my daughter! And if I find her before your death then you will witness that too.'

'So you'll do to her what I did to your daughter?' I asked.

'It is a promise,' Cnut said.

'Truly?' I asked.

'I swear it,' he said, touching the hammer hanging over his silver-shining mail.

I beckoned. The shield wall behind me parted, and my son brought Cnut's daughter to the barrier. He held her hand. 'Father!' Sigril shouted when she saw Cnut, and Cnut just stared at her in shock. 'Father!' Sigril called and tried to pull away from my son.

I took the girl from him. 'I am sorry about her hair,' I said to

Cnut, 'and it probably hurt her a little when I cut it because the knife wasn't nearly as sharp as I'd have liked. But hair does grow again and she'll be as beautiful as ever in a few months.' I picked the girl up, lifted her over the barricade and let her go. She ran to Cnut and I saw the joy and relief on his face. He leaned down and extended a hand to her, she gripped it and he raised her up so she could sit on his saddle. He hugged her, then stared at me with puzzlement

'Lost your tongue already, you shit-slimed bastard?' I asked pleasantly, then beckoned again, and this time Frigg was allowed through the shield wall. She ran to the barrier, looked at me, and I nodded. She climbed over it, making an incoherent sobbing noise, and ran to Cnut's side and he looked even more astonished as she gripped his leg and stirrup leather, clinging to them as if her life depended on it. 'She wasn't harmed,' I said, 'not even touched.'

'You . . .' he began.

'Geirmund was easy to fool,' I said. 'A piglet and a body were all we needed. And that was enough to clear him away so we could burn your ships. Yours too,' I added to Sigurd, 'but I expect you know that.'

'We know more, you pig-turd,' Sigurd said. He raised his voice so the men behind me could hear him. 'Edward of Wessex is not coming,' he shouted. 'He has decided to cower behind his town walls. Were you hoping he would come to rescue you?'

'Rescue?' I asked. 'Why would I want to share the glory of victory with Edward of Wessex?'

Cnut was still staring at me. He said nothing. Sigurd did all the talking. 'Æthelred is still in East Anglia,' he shouted, 'because he fears to come out from behind the rivers in case he meets a Dane.'

'That does sound like Æthelred,' I said.

'You're alone, you shit-slimed bastard.' Sigurd was almost shaking with his anger.

'I have my vast army,' I said, pointing to the small shield wall behind me.

'Your army?' Sigurd sneered, then went silent because Cnut had reached out and silenced him by touching his gold-ringed arm.

Cnut still held his daughter tightly. 'You can go,' he said to me.

'Go?' I asked. 'Go where?'

'I give you life,' he said, and touched Sigurd's arm again to still the protest.

'My life is not yours to give,' I told him.

'Go, Lord Uhtred,' Cnut said, almost pleading with me. 'Go south to Wessex, take all your men, just go.'

'You can count, Jarl Cnut?' I asked him.

He smiled. 'You have fewer than three hundred men,' he said, 'and as for me? I cannot count my men. They are as grains of sand on a wide beach.' He hugged his daughter with one arm and reached down to stroke Frigg's cheek with his other hand. 'I thank you for this, Lord Uhtred,' he said, 'but just go.'

Sigurd growled. He wanted my death, but he would agree to anything Cnut suggested.

'I asked if you could count,' I said to Cnut.

'I can count,' he said, puzzled.

'Then you might remember you had two children. A girl and a boy, remember? And I still have the boy.' He flinched at that. 'If you stay in Saxon Mercia or attack Wessex,' I said, 'perhaps you will only have a daughter?'

'I can make more sons,' he said, though without much conviction.

'Go back to your lands,' I told him, 'and your son will be returned to you.'

Sigurd began to speak, his tone angry, but Cnut checked him. 'We shall talk in the morning,' he told me, and turned his horse.

'We shall speak in the morning,' I agreed, and watched them ride away with Frigg running between them.

Except we would not speak in the morning, because once they had gone I had my men kick the timber roadway off the bridge, and then we left.

We went west.

And Cnut, I knew, would follow.

Twelve

Had Edward of Wessex decided to stay behind his burh walls? I could well believe that Æthelred was cowering in East Anglia because if he tried to return to Mercia he would be faced by a much larger enemy and he was probably terrified of facing Danes in open battle, but would Edward just abandon Mercia to Cnut's forces? It was possible. His advisers were cautious men, frightened of all the Northmen, but confident that the stout burh walls of Wessex could resist any attack. Yet they were not fools. They knew that if Cnut and Sigurd were to capture both Mercia and East Anglia then thousands of warriors would come from across the sea, all of them eager to feast off the carcass of Wessex. If Edward waited behind his walls then his enemies would grow in strength. He would not face four thousand Danes, but ten or twelve. He would be overwhelmed.

Yet it was possible he had decided to stay on the defensive.

On the other hand what else would Jarl Sigurd say to me? He would hardly tell me that the West Saxons were marching. He had wanted to unsettle me, and I knew that, yet I was still unsettled.

And what else could I tell my men except that Sigurd had lied? I could only sound confident. 'Sigurd has the greased tongue of a weasel,' I told them, 'and of course Edward is coming!'

And we were fleeing, riding westwards through the night. When I was young I liked the night. I taught myself not to fear the spirits that haunt the darkness, to walk like a shadow through the shadows, to hear the vixen's cry and the owl's call and not tremble.

The night is the domain of the dead, and the living fear it, but that night we rode through the dark as if we belonged to it.

We came to Liccelfeld first. I knew the town well. It was here that I had thrown the treacherous Offa's corpse into a stream. Offa, who had trained his dogs, sold news and posed as a friend, and then had tried to betray me. It was a Saxon town, yet mostly undisturbed by the Danes who lived all around it, and I assumed that most of the Saxons, like the dead Offa, purchased that peace by paying tribute to the Danes. Some of them were probably in Cnut's army and doubtless they had gone to the grave of Saint Chad in Liccelfeld's big church and prayed for Cnut's victory. The Danes permitted Christian churches, but if I had tried to make a shrine to Odin on Saxon land the Christian priests would be sharpening their gutting knives. They worship a jealous god.

Bats wheeled over the town's roofs. Dogs barked as we passed and were hushed by fearful folk who were wise to be frightened of hoofbeats in the night. Shutters stayed shut. We splashed through the stream where I had thrown Offa and I remembered his widow's shrill curses. The moon was almost full, silvering the road that now rose into low wooded hills. The trees cast hard black shadows. We rode in silence except for the thud of hooves and jangle of bridles. We were following the Roman road that led westwards from Liccelfeld, a road that ran spear-shaft straight across the low hills and wide valleys. We had ridden this road before, not often, but even by moonlight the land looked familiar.

Finan and I stopped at a bare hilltop from where we gazed southwards as the horsemen passed along the road behind us. A long slope of stubble fell away in front of us, and beyond it were dark woods and more hills, and somewhere far off a small glimmer of firelight. I turned to look eastwards, looking back the way we had come. Was there a glow in the sky? I wanted to see some proof that Cnut had stayed in Tameworþig, that his huge army was waiting for the dawn before marching, but I could see no fires lighting the horizon. 'The bastard's following us,' Finan grunted.

'Probably.'

But far off to the south there was a glow. At least I thought there was. It was hard to tell because it was so far away, and perhaps it was just a trick of the darkness. A hall burning? Or the camp fires of a distant army? An army I just hoped was there? Finan stared too and I knew what he was thinking, or what he was hoping, and he knew I was thinking and hoping the same, but he said nothing. I thought for a moment the glow lightened, but I could not be sure. Sometimes there are lights in the night sky, great shimmering sheets of brightness that ripple and tremble like water, and I wondered if this was one of those mysterious shinings that the gods cascade through the darkness, but the longer I stared the less I saw. Just night and the horizon and the black trees.

'We've come a long way since that slave ship,' Finan said wistfully.

I wondered what had made him remember those far-off days, then realised he was thinking that all his days would end soon, and a man facing death does well to look back on life. 'You make it sound like the end,' I chided him.

He smiled. 'What is it you like to say? Wyrd bið ful āræd?'

'Wyrd bið ful āræd,' I repeated.

Fate is inexorable. And right at that moment, as we gazed forlornly towards the darkness where we hoped to see the light, the three Norns were weaving my life's threads at the foot of the great tree. And one held a pair of shears. Finan still gazed south, hoping against hope that there was a glow in the sky that would announce the presence of another army, but that southern horizon was dark beneath the stars. 'The West Saxons have always been cautious,' Finan said ruefully, 'unless you were leading them.'

'And Cnut isn't cautious.'

'And he's coming for us,' Finan said. He looked back to the east. 'They'll be an hour behind us?'

'Their scouts will be, yes,' I said, 'but it will take Cnut the best part of the night to get his army across the river.'

'But once he's across . . .' Finan began and did not finish.

'We can't run for ever,' I said, 'but we'll slow them down.'

258

'We'll still have two or three hundred men biting our arses by dawn,' Finan said.

'We will,' I agreed, 'and whatever happens, it happens tomorrow.'

'So we have to find somewhere to fight.'

'That, and slow them down tonight.' I gave the south one last look, but decided the glow had been in my dreams.

'If I remember right,' Finan turned his horse towards the west, 'there's an old fort on this road.'

'There is,' I said, 'but it's too big for us.' The fort was Roman, four earth walls enclosing a great square space where two roads met. I could remember no settlement at the crossroads, just the remnants of the mighty fortress. Why had they built it? Had their roads been haunted by thieves?

'It's too big for us to defend,' Finan agreed, 'but we can slow the bastards there.'

We followed the column west. I twisted constantly in my saddle, looking for pursuers, but seeing none. Cnut must have known we would try to escape and he would have sent men on light horses across the river with orders to find us. Their job was to track us so that Cnut could follow and crush us. He was in a hurry, and he would also be angry, not with me, but with himself. He had abandoned his hunting of Æthelred and by now he must know that had been a bad decision. His army had been rampaging in Mercia for days, but it had yet to defeat any Saxon army, and those armies were getting stronger, perhaps even marching, and time was running out for him. But I had distracted him. I had taken his family, burned his ships and destroyed his halls, and he had turned on me in rage, only to discover he had been tricked and that his wife and children lived. If he had any sense he would abandon me because I was not the enemy he needed to defeat. He needed to massacre Æthelred's army and then go south to slaughter Edward's West Saxons, but I suspected he would still pursue me. I was too close, too tempting, and killing me would give Cnut even more reputation, and he knew our small war-band was easy prey. Kill us, rescue his son, then turn south to fight the real war. It would take him one day to crush us, then he could deal with the larger enemy.

And my only hope of living was if that larger enemy was not being cautious, but marching to help me.

The great fort was black with mooncast shadow. It was an immense place, an earthwork built on low land where the two roads crossed. I supposed it had once held wooden buildings where the Roman soldiers were quartered, but now the grass-grown walls enclosed nothing but a wide pasture inhabited by a herd of cows. I spurred through the shallow ditch and over the low rampart to be met by two howling dogs that were instantly silenced by the cowherd. He dropped to his knees when he saw my helmet and mail. He bowed his head, put his hands on the necks of his growling hounds and shivered with fear. 'What do you call this place?' I asked him.

'The old fort, master,' he said, not raising his head.

'There's a village?'

'Up yonder.' He jerked his head northwards.

'Its name?

'We calls it Pencric, master.'

I remembered the name when he said it. 'And there's a river here?' I asked, recalling the last time I had been on this road.

'Over yonder,' he said, jerking his bowed head westwards.

I tossed him a scrap of hacksilver. 'Keep your hounds quiet,' I said.

'Not a sound, master.' He gazed at the silver in the moonlit grass, then lifted his face to look at me. 'God bless you, master,' he said, then saw my hammer. 'The gods protect you, master.'

'Are you a Christian?' I asked him.

He frowned. 'I think so, master.'

'Then your god hates me,' I said, 'and you will too if your dogs make any noise.'

'Quiet as mouses they'll be, master, like little mouses. No noises, I swear.'

I sent most of my men on westwards, but with orders to turn south when they reached the nearby river, which, if I remembered rightly, was neither deep nor wide. 'Just follow the river south,' I told them, 'and we'll find you.'

260

I wanted Cnut to think we were fleeing westwards, aiming for the dubious sanctuary of the Welsh hills, but in truth the hoofmarks would betray our southerly turn. Still, if it gave him even a short pause that would help because I needed all the time I could gain, and so my horsemen vanished west towards the river while I stayed with fifty of my men behind the grassy ramparts of the ancient fort. We were lightly armed, carrying spears or swords, though Wibrund, the Frisian, carried an axe on my orders. 'Hard to fight on horseback with an axe, lord,' he had grumbled.

'You'll need it,' I said, 'so keep it.'

We did not wait long. Perhaps less than an hour passed before horsemen appeared on the eastern road. They were hurrying. 'Sixteen,' Finan said.

'Seventeen,' my son corrected.

'They should have sent more,' I told them, and watched the distant road in case more men appeared from the far woods. There would be more men coming, and soon, but these sixteen or seventeen had raced ahead, eager to find us and to report back to Cnut. We let them get close, then spurred the horses over the earthen rampart. Finan led twenty men hard to the east to cut off their retreat while I led the rest straight at the approaching men.

We killed most of them. It was not hard. They were fools, they rode rashly, they were not expecting trouble, they were outnumbered and they died. A few escaped southwards, then turned east in panic. I called to Finan to let them go. 'Now, Wibrund,' I said, 'cut off their heads. Do it quickly.'

The axe fell eleven times. We threw the headless corpses into the fort's old ditch, but arranged the heads across the Roman road with their dead eyes staring eastwards. Those dead eyes would greet Cnut's men and, I suspected, suggest that something dire and sorcerous had been done. They would smell magic and they would hesitate.

Just give me time, I prayed to Thor, just give me time.

And we rode on south.

*   *   *

We caught up with the rest of my men and rode through the dawn. Birds were singing everywhere, that joyful song of a new day, and I hated the sound because it greeted the day on which I thought I must die. Still we rode on south towards distant Wessex and hoped against hope that the West Saxons were riding towards us.

And then we just stopped.

We stopped because the horses were tired, we were tired. We had ridden through low hills and placid farmland and I had found nowhere I wanted to fight. What had I expected? A Roman fort small enough to be garrisoned by my two hundred and sixty-nine men? A fort on a convenient hill? An outcrop of steep rock where a man could die of old age while his enemies raged about the rock's base? There were just fields of stubble, pastures where sheep grazed, woods of ash and oak, shallow streams and gentle slopes. The sun rose higher. The day was warm and our horses wanted water.

And we had come to the river and so we just stopped.

It was not much of a river, more of a stream trying to be a river, and succeeding only in looking like a deep ditch, but it would cause problems for anyone trying to cross it. The ditch's banks were steep and muddy, though those banks became shallow and gentle where the road crossed the water. The ford was not deep. The river or stream spread there and at its centre the slow-moving water scarcely reached a man's thighs. The western bank was lined with pollarded willows, and still farther west was a low ridge where a few poor houses stood and I sent Finan to explore that higher ground while I roamed up and down the river's bank. I could find no fort, no steep hill, but there was this sluggish ditch that was just wide and deep enough to slow an attack.

And so we stopped there. We put the horses into a stone-walled paddock on the western bank and we waited.

We could have pressed on southwards, but Cnut would catch us sooner or later, and at least the river would slow him. Or so I told myself. In truth I had little hope, and even less when Finan came down from the low ridge. 'Horsemen,' he said bluntly, 'to the west.'

'To the west?' I asked, thinking he must have been mistaken.

'To the west,' he insisted. Cnut's men were north and east of us and I expected no enemies from the west. Or, rather, I hoped no enemies would come from the west.

'How many?'

'Scout parties. Not many.'

'Cnut's men?'

He shrugged. 'Can't say.'

'The bastard can't have crossed this ditch,' I said, though of course Cnut could have done just that.

'That's no ditch,' Finan said, 'it's the River Tame.'

I looked at the muddy water. 'That's the Tame?'

'So the villagers told me.'

I laughed sourly. We had ridden all the way from Tameworþig to find ourselves back on the headwaters of the same river? There was something futile about that, something that seemed fitting to this day on which I supposed I would die. 'So what do they call this place?' I asked Finan.

'Bastards don't seem to know,' he said, amused. 'One man called it Teotanheale and his wife said it was Wodnesfeld.'

So it was either Teotta's dell or Odin's field, but whatever it was called it was still the end of our road, the place where I would wait for a vengeful enemy. And he was coming. The scouts were visible across the ford now, which meant horsemen were north, east and west of us. At least fifty men were on the Tame's far bank, but still a long way from the river, and Finan had seen more horsemen to the west and I supposed Cnut had divided his army, sending some men down the west bank and some down the east.

'We could ride south still,' I said.

'He'll catch us,' Finan said bleakly, 'and we'll be fighting in open country. At least here we can retreat to that ridge.' He nodded to where the few hovels crowned the low hill.

'Burn them,' I said.

'Burn them?'

'Burn the houses. Tell the men it's a signal to Edward.'

The belief that Edward was close enough to see the smoke would give my few men hope, and men with hope fight better, and then I looked at the paddock where the horses were gathered. I was wondering whether we should ride west, beat our way through the few scouts who lurked in that direction and hope to reach still higher ground. It was probably a futile hope, and then I thought how strange it was that the paddock had a stone wall. This was a country of hedges, yet someone had gone to the immense trouble of piling heavy stones into a low wall. 'Uhtred!' I bellowed at my son

He ran to me. 'Father?'

'Take that wall apart. Get every man to help, and fetch me stones about the size of a man's head.'

He gaped at me. 'A man's head?'

'Just do it! Bring the stones here, and hurry! Rolla!'

The big Dane ambled over. 'Lord?'

'I'm going up to the ridge, and you're putting stones into the river.'

'I am?'

I told him what I wanted, watched him grin. 'And make sure those bastards,' I pointed to Cnut's scouts who were waiting well to the east, 'don't see what you're doing. If they come close just stop work. Sihtric!'

'Lord?'

'Banners, here.' I pointed to where the road led west from the ford. I would plant our standards there to show Cnut where we wanted to fight. To show Cnut where I would die. 'My lady!' I called to Æthelflaed.

'I'm not leaving,' she said stubbornly.

'Did I ask you to?'

'You will.'

We walked to the low ridge where Finan and a dozen men were shouting at the villagers to empty their cottages. 'Take everything you want!' Finan told them. 'Dogs, cats, children even. Your pots, your spits, everything. We're burning the houses!' Eldgrim was carrying an old woman from a house as her daughter screamed in protest.

'Must we burn the houses?' Æthelflaed asked.

264

'If Edward's marching,' I said bleakly, 'he has to know where we are.'

'I suppose so, yes,' she said simply. Then she turned to gaze eastwards. The scouts were still watching us from a safe distance, but there was no sign yet of Cnut's horde. 'What do we do with the boy?'

She meant Cnut's son. I shrugged. 'We threaten to kill him.'

'But you won't. And Cnut knows you won't.'

'I might.'

She laughed at that, a grim laugh. 'You won't kill him.'

'If I live,' I said, 'he'll be fatherless.'

She frowned in puzzlement, then saw what I meant. She laughed. 'You think you can beat Cnut?'

'We've stopped,' I said, 'we'll fight. Perhaps your brother will come? We're not dead yet.'

'So you'll raise him?'

'Cnut's son?' I shook my head. 'Sell him, probably. Once he's a slave there'll be no one to tell him who his father was. He won't know that he's a wolf, he'll think he's a puppy.' If I lived, I thought, and, truly, I did not expect to survive that day. 'And you,' I touched Æthelflaed's arm, 'should ride away.'

'I . . .'

'You're Mercia!' I snapped at her. 'Men love you, they follow you! If you die here then Mercia loses its heart.'

'And if I run away,' she said, 'then Mercia is cowardly.'

'You leave so that you can fight another day.'

'And how do I leave?' she asked. She was gazing westwards and I saw the horsemen there, just a handful, but they were also watching us. There were six or seven men, all of them at least two miles away, but they could see us. And there were probably others who were closer. If I was to send Æthelflaed away then those men would follow her, and if I sent her with an escort large enough to fight through whatever enemy she found then I just made my own death more certain. 'Take fifty men,' I told her, 'take fifty men and ride south.'

'I'm staying.'

'If you're captured . . .' I began.

'They'll rape and kill me,' she said calmly, then put a finger on my hand. 'It's called martyrdom, Uhtred.'

'It's called stupidity.'

She said nothing to that, just turned and looked north and east and there, at last, were Cnut's men. Hundreds upon hundreds of men darkening the land, coming south down the road from the Roman fort where we had left the severed heads. Their leading horsemen had almost reached the turn in the road that led west to the ford where my men laboured in the shallow water. Rolla must have seen the enemy because he called the men back to the river's western bank where we would make our shield wall.

'Did you ever hear of Æsc's Hill?' I asked Æthelflaed.

'Of course,' she said, 'my father loved to tell that tale.'

Æsc's Hill was a battle fought long ago, when I was a boy, and on that winter day I had been in the Danish army and we had been so confident of victory. Yet the frosted ground had been warmed by Danish blood and the cold air had been filled with Saxon cheers. Harald, Bagseg and Sidroc the Younger, Toki the Shipmaster, names from my past, they had all died, killed by the West Saxons who, under Alfred, had waited behind a ditch. The priests, of course, ascribed that unlikely victory to their nailed god, but in truth the ditch defeated the Danes. A shield wall is strong so long as it stays intact, shield against shield, men shoulder to shoulder, a wall of mail, wood, flesh and steel, but if the wall breaks then slaughter follows, and crossing the ditch at Æsc's Hill had broken the Danish wall and the Saxon foemen had made a great slaughter.

And my little shield wall was protected by a ditch. Except the ditch was broken by the ford, and it was there, in that shallow water, that we would fight.

The first cottage burst into flames. The thatch was dry under its moss and the flames were hungry. Rats scrambled from the roof as my men carried the fire to the other houses. I was sending a signal to whom? To Edward? Who might still be cowering behind his burh walls? I stared south, hoping against all hope to see

266

horsemen approaching, but there was just a falcon riding the high wind above the empty fields and woods. The bird was almost motionless, wings flickering, then it stooped, wings folded, streaking down to kill. A bad omen? I touched my hammer. 'You should go,' I told Æthelflaed, 'go south. Ride hard, ride fast! Don't stop at Gleawecestre, but keep going to Wessex. Go to Lundene! Those walls are strong, but if it falls you can take a ship to Frankia.'

'My banner is there,' she said, pointing to the ford, 'and where my banner is I am.' Her banner showed a white goose clutching a cross and a sword. It was an ugly flag, but the goose was the symbol of Saint Werburgh, a holy woman who had once frightened a flock of geese away from a cornfield, a feat that had earned her sainthood, and the goose-frightener was also Æthelflaed's protector. She would have to work hard this day, I thought.

'Who do you trust?' I asked her.

She frowned at that question. 'Trust? You, of course, your men, my men, why?'

'Find a man you trust,' I said. The fire of the nearest house was scorching me. 'Tell him to kill you before the Danes capture you. Tell him to stand behind you and make the stroke on the back of your neck.' I pushed a finger through her hair to touch her skin where the skull meets the spine. 'Just there,' I said, pressing my finger. 'It's fast, it's quick and it's painless. Don't be a martyr.'

She smiled. 'God is on our side, Uhtred. We shall win.' She spoke very flatly, as if what she said was beyond all contradiction, and I just looked at her. 'We shall win,' she said again, 'because God is with us.'

What fools these Christians are.

I went down to my death-place and watched the Danes approach.

There is a way of battle. In the end the shield walls must meet and the slaughter will begin and one side will prevail and the other will be beaten down in a welter of butchery, but before the blades clash and before the shields crash, men must summon the nerve to make the charge. The two sides stare at each other; they taunt and insult each other. The young fools of each army will prance ahead of the wall and challenge their enemy to single combat, they will boast of the widows they plan to make and of the orphans who will weep for their fathers' deaths. And the young fools fight and half of them will die, and the other half strut their bloody victory, but there is still no true victory because the shield walls have not met. And still the waiting goes on. Some men vomit with fear, others sing, some pray, but then at last one side will advance. It is usually a slow advance. Men crouch behind their shields, knowing that spears, axes and arrows will greet them before the shields slam together, and only when they are close, really close, does the attacker charge. Then there is a great bellow of noise, a roar of anger and fear, and the shields meet like thunder and the big blades fall and the swords stab and the shrieks fill the sky as the two shield walls fight to the death. That is the way of battle.

And Cnut broke it.

It began in the usual way. My shield wall stood at the very edge of the ford, which was no more than twenty paces across. We were on the western bank, Cnut's men were arriving from the east and, as they reached the crossroads, they dismounted. Boys took the horses and led them to a pasture while the warriors unslung their shields and looked for their battle-companions. They were arriving in groups. It was plain they had hurried and were strung out along the road, but their numbers grew swiftly. They gathered some five hundred paces from us where they formed a swine's horn. I had expected that.

'Confident bastards,' Finan muttered.

'Wouldn't you be?'

'Probably,' he said. Finan was to my left, my son to my right. I resisted the temptation to give Uhtred advice. He had practised the shield wall for years, he knew all I had to teach him, and to repeat it now would only betray my nervousness. He was silent. He just stared at the enemy and knew that in a few moments he would have to face his first battle of the shield walls. And, I thought, he would probably die.

I tried to count the arriving enemy and reckoned the swine's horn held about five hundred men. So, they outnumbered us two to one, and still more men were coming. Cnut and Sigurd were there, their banners bright above the shields. I could see Cnut because he was still mounted, his pale horse somewhere deep in the big wedge of men.

A swine's horn. I noticed that not one man had come forward to look at the ford, which told me they knew this stretch of country, or someone in their army knew it. They knew about the ditch-like river and they knew that the west-leading road had a shallow ford that would be easy to cross and so they did not need to make any exploration. They would just advance, and Cnut had formed them into the swine's horn to make that advance irresistible.

The shield wall is usually straight. Two straight lines that crash together and men struggle to break the opposing line, but a swine's horn is a wedge. It comes fast. The biggest and bravest men are placed at the point of the wedge and their job is to smash through the opposing shield wall like a spear shattering a door. And, once our line was broken, the wedge would widen as they hacked along our lines and so my men would die.

And to make sure of that Cnut had sent men to cross the river north of us. A boy rode down from the ridge where the houses burned to bring me that bad news. 'Lord?' he asked nervously.

'What's your name, boy?'

'Godric, lord.'

'You're Grindan's son?'

'Yes, lord.'

'Then your name is Godric Grindanson,' I said, 'and how old are you?'

'Eleven, lord, I think.'

He was a snub-nosed, blue-eyed boy wearing an old leather coat that had probably belonged to his father because it was so big. 'So what does Godric Grindanson want to tell me?' I asked.

He pointed a tremulous finger north. 'They're crossing the river, lord.'

'How many? And how far away?'

'Hrodgeir says there are three hundred men, lord, and they're still a long way north and more of them are crossing all the time, lord.' Hrodgeir was a Dane whom I had left on the ridge so he could keep watch on what the enemy did. 'And, lord . . .' Godric went on until his voice faltered.

'Tell me.'

'He says there are more men to the west, lord, hundreds!'

'Hundreds?'

'They're among trees, lord, and Hrodgeir says he can't count them.'

'He hasn't got enough fingers,' Finan put in.

I looked up at the frightened boy. 'Shall I tell you something about battles, Godric Grindanson?'

'Yes please, lord.'

'One man always survives,' I said. 'He's usually a poet and his job is to write a song that tells how bravely all his companions died. That might be your job today. Are you a poet?'

'No, lord.'

'Then you'll have to learn. So when you see us dying, Godric Grindanson, you ride south as fast as you can and you ride like the wind and you ride till you're safe and you write the poem in your head that tells the Saxons that we died like heroes. Will you do that for me?'

He nodded.

'Go back to Hrodgeir,' I told him, 'and tell me when you see the horsemen from the north or the ones from the west getting close.'

He went. Finan grinned. 'Bastards on three sides of us.'

'They must be scared.'

'Shitting themselves, probably.'

I was expecting Cnut to ride to the ford, bringing his war-leaders with him to enjoy his insults. I had thought to have his son at my side with a knife at his throat, but rejected the thought. Cnut Cnutson could stay with Æthelflaed. If he stayed with me I could only threaten him, and if Cnut dared me to cut the boy's throat, what would I do? Cut it? We would still have to fight. Let him

270

live? Then Cnut would despise me for being weak. The boy had served his purpose by luring Cnut away from the East Anglian borderlands to this corner of Mercia, and now he must wait till the battle was done to learn his fate. I gripped my shield and drew Serpent-Breath. In almost every clash of the shield walls I preferred Wasp-Sting, my short-sword that was so deadly when you were being forced into the embrace of your enemy, but today I would begin with the longer, heavier blade. I hefted her, kissed her hilt, and waited for Cnut's arrival.

Only he did not come to insult me, nor did any young men come forward to challenge us to single combat.

Instead Cnut sent the swine's horn.

Instead of insults and challenges there was a great roar of battle-shout from the mass of men assembled under the banners of Cnut and Sigurd, and then they advanced. They came down the road fast. The land was flat, there were no obstacles and they kept their tight formation. Their shields overlapped. We saw the painted symbols on the shields, the shattered crosses, ravens, hammers, axes, and eagles. Above those broad round shields were helmets with face-guards so that the enemy seemed to be black-eyed, steel-clad, and in front of the shields were the heavy spears, their blades catching the day's half-clouded light, and beneath the shields hundreds of feet trampled the ground in time to the heavy drums that had started to beat the war-rhythm behind the swine's horn.

No insults, no challenges. Cnut knew he outnumbered me by so many that he could afford to divide his army. I glanced to my left and saw still more horsemen crossing the ditch far to the north. Some five or six hundred men were pounding towards us in the swine's horn, and at least that many were now on our side of the river and ready to fall on our left flank. More men, those on slower horses, were still arriving, but Cnut must have known that his swine's horn would do the necessary work. It thundered towards us and as it came closer I could see faces behind the cheek-pieces, I could see eager eyes and grim mouths, I could see Danes coming to kill us.

'God is with us!' Sihtric shouted. The two priests had been

shriving men all morning, but now they retreated behind the shield wall and knelt in prayer, their clasped hands lifted to the sky.

'Wait for my order!' I called. My shield wall knew what they must do. We would advance into the ford as the swine's horn reached the far bank. I planned to meet the charge almost halfway across the river and there I planned a slaughter before I died. 'Wait!' I shouted.

And I thought Cnut should have waited. He should have let his swine's horn wait until the men to the north were ready to attack, but he was so confident. And why not? The swine's horn outnumbered us and it should have shattered our shield wall and scattered my men and led to a slaughter by the river, and so he had not waited. He had sent the swine's horn and it was almost at the far bank now.

'Forward!' I shouted. 'And slowly!'

We went forward steadily, our shields overlapping, our weapons held hard. We were in four ranks. I was in the front and at the centre, and the point of the swine's horn came straight at me like a boar's tusk ready to rip through flesh and muscle and sinew and mail to shatter bone and spill guts and wreath the slow river water with Saxon blood.

'Kill!' a man shouted from the Danish ranks and they saw how few we were and knew they would overwhelm us and now they quickened, eager to slay, cheering as they came, their voices raw with threat, their shields still touching, their mouths grimaces of battle-hate, and it was as if they raced to reach us in the certainty that their poets would sing of a great slaughter.

And then they reached the stones.

Rolla had made a ragged line of stones at the ford's deepest point. The stones were large, each about the size of a man's head, and they were invisible. Almost invisible. I knew they were there and could just see them, and I could see how the water rippled irritably about the sunken rocks, but the Danes could not see them because their shields were held high and those shields blocked their view downwards. They were staring at us over the shields' rims, planning our deaths, and instead they ran into the stones

272

and tripped. What had been a wedge of men charging irresistibly to our slaughter became a chaos of falling men, and even though those at the sides of the wedge tried to halt the men behind pushed them on and still more tripped on the hidden stones, and then we struck.

And we killed.

It is so easy to kill men who are in chaos, and every man we killed became an obstacle to the ones behind. The man at the point of the wedge had been a big, black-haired warrior. His hair sprang like a horse's wild mane from beneath his helmet, his beard half hid his mail coat, his shield bore the sign of Sigurd's raven and his arms were bright with the silver and gold he had earned as a warrior. He had taken the place of honour, the sharp point of the swine's horn, and he had carried an axe with which he had hoped to hack down my shield, break my skull open and cut his way through our wall.

Instead he sprawled in the river, face down, and Serpent-Breath stabbed down hard, piercing mail to cut his spine and he bent backwards as I twisted and ripped the blade and then I thrust my shield forward to crash against a man who was on his knees and trying desperately to stab me with his sword. I put my foot on the dying warrior's back, tore my blade free, and thrust it hard. Her point went into the second man's open mouth so that he seemed to swallow Serpent-Breath and I rammed her forward and watched his eyes widen as the blood gurgled from his open mouth, and all along the river my men were hacking and cutting and lunging at Danes who were fallen or off balance or dying.

And we screamed. We screamed our war cry, our shout of slaughter, our joy of being men in battle who are driven by terror. At that moment it did not matter that we were fated to die, that our enemy outnumbered us, that we could have killed all the swine's horn and still they would have enough numbers to over-whelm us. At that moment we were released to be death's servants. We were living and they were dying, and all the relief of being alive fed into our butchery. And we were butchers. The swine's horn had stopped dead, it was in utter disarray, the shield wall was broken and we were killing. Our shields were still touching, we were shoulder to shoulder, and we were advancing slowly, stepping on dead men, finding footholds between the stones, chopping and stabbing, spears lancing down into fallen men, axes splitting helmets, swords piercing flesh, and the Danes still did not understand what had happened. The men in the rear ranks were pressing forward and driving the front ranks onto the obstacles and onto our blades, except you could not talk of ranks any longer because Cnut's swine's horn had become a rabble. Chaos and panic spread through them as the river swirled with blood and the sky echoed with the screams of dying men whose guts were being washed by the Tame.

And someone on the Danish side realised that disaster was just begetting disaster, and that there was no need for more good men to be killed by Saxon blades. 'Back!' he shouted. 'Back!'

And we jeered them. We mocked them. We did not follow them because what small safety we had lay in staying west of the stones in the ford, and now those stones were humped with dead and dying men, a tangle of blood-laced bodies, and those bodies, weighed down by their mail, made a low wall across the river. We stood amidst that wall and called the Danes cowards, called them weaklings, and mocked their manhood. We lied, of course. They were warriors and brave men, but we were doomed men and we had our moment of triumph as we stood knee-deep in the river with our blades bloodied and with relief coursing through veins heated by fear and anger.

And the remnant of the swine's horn, a remnant that still outnumbered us, went back to the river's eastern bank and there they were formed into a new shield wall, a bigger shield wall because the latecomers were joining them. There were hundreds of men now, thousands perhaps, and we were prancing fools who had stung a boar that was about to eviscerate us.

'Lord!' It was Hrodgeir the Dane who had ridden down from the ridge where the fires still burned to send their futile message into the empty sky. 'Lord!' he called urgently.

'Hrodgeir?'

'Lord!' He turned in his saddle and pointed and I saw beyond the ridge, up the river's bank, a second shield wall. And that shield wall had hundreds too, and it was coming. Those men had crossed the ditch-like river, dismounted, and now they came towards us. 'I'm sorry, lord,' Hrodgeir said, as if he was responsible for not stopping that second attack.

'Uhtred!' a voice bellowed from across the river. Cnut stood there, legs apart, Ice-Spite in his hand. 'Uhtred Worm-shit!' he called. 'Come and fight!'

'Lord!' Hrodgeir called again and he was staring westwards and I turned to look that way and saw horsemen streaming from the woods to climb the ridge. Hundreds of men. So the enemy was in front of us, they were behind us, and they were to the north of us.

'Uhtred Worm-turd!' Cnut bellowed. 'You dare fight? Or have you lost your bravery? Come and die, you piece of shit, you turd, you piece of oozing shit! Come to Ice-Spite! She yearns for you! I'll let your men live if you die! You hear me?'

I stepped ahead of the shield wall and stared at my enemy. 'You'll let my men live?'

'Even that whore of yours can live. They can all go! They can live!'

'And what value is the promise of a man who dribbled from his mother's arse when he was born?' I called back.

'Does my son live?'

'Unharmed.'

'Your men can take him as surety. They will live!'

'Don't, lord,' Finan said urgently, 'he's too fast. Let me fight him!'

The three Norns were laughing. They sat at the foot of the tree and two of them held the threads, and one of them held the shears.

'Let me go, Father,' Uhtred said.

But wyrd bið ful āræd. I had always known it would come to this. Serpent-Breath against Ice-Spite. And so I clambered over the bodies of my enemies and went to fight Cnut.

Thirteen

Urðr, Verðandi and Skuld are the Norns, the three women who spin our threads at the foot of Yggdrasil, the massive ash tree that supports our world. In my mind I see them in a cave: not a cave like the one where Erce had straddled me, but something much larger and almost limitless, a terrifying emptiness through which the world tree thrusts its giant bole. And there, where the roots of Yggdrasil writhe and twist into the bedrock of creation, the three women weave the tapestry of all our lives.

And that day they held two threads away from the loom. I have always imagined my thread to be yellow like the sun. I do not know why, but so I imagine. Cnut's had to be white like his hair, like the ivory hilt of Ice-Spite, like the cloak he shrugged from his shoulders as he stepped towards me.

So Urðr, Verðandi and Skuld would decide our fate. They are not kindly women, indeed they are monstrous and malevolent hags, and Skuld's shears are sharp. When those blades cut they cause tears that feed the well of Urðr that lies beside the world tree, and the well gives the water that keeps Yggdrasil alive and if Yggdrasil dies then the world dies, and so the well must be kept filled and for that there must be tears. We cry so that the world can live.

The yellow and the white thread. And the shears hovering.

Cnut came slowly. We would meet close to the ford's eastern edge, where the water was shallow, scarce ankle-deep. He held Ice-Spite low in his right hand, but men said he could use either

276

hand with equal skill. He carried no shield because he needed none. He was quick, none faster, and he could parry with Ice-Spite.

I carried Serpent-Breath. She looked brutal compared to Ice-Spite. She was twice as heavy, a hand's breadth longer, and a man might be forgiven for thinking that her long blade would shatter Cnut's sword, but rumour said his blade had been forged in the ice caverns of the gods In a fire that burned colder than ice, and that it was the unbreakable sword, and swifter than a serpent's tongue. He held it low.

Ten paces divided us. He stopped and waited. He had a slight smile.

I took another pace. The water flowed around my boots. Get close to him, I thought, so he has no room to use that vicious blade. He would be expecting that. Maybe I should stand back, let him come to me.

'Lord!' a voice called behind me.

Cnut raised Ice-Spite, though he still held her lightly. She had a silvery gleam on the blade that shivered as she moved. He was watching my eyes. A man who uses a sword with lethal skill always watches his opponent's eyes.

'Lord!' It was Finan calling.

'Father!' Uhtred shouted urgently.

Cnut looked past me and his face suddenly changed. He had been looking amused, but now there was sudden alarm. I stepped back and turned.

And saw horsemen coming from the west, hundreds of horsemen climbing the ridge where the hovels burned to send their dark signal into the sky. How many? I could not tell, but maybe two, perhaps three hundred? I looked back to Cnut and his face betrayed that the newcomers were not his men. He had sent troops across the ditch to the north of us, but the newly arrived horsemen would block their advance on our flank. If they were Saxons.

I looked back again to see the newly arrived men dismounting and boys leading their horses back down the ridge, while on the low summit where the cottages burned a new shield wall was forming. 'Who are they?' I called to Finan.

'God knows,' he said.

And the nailed god did know, because a banner was suddenly unfurled on the skyline, a huge banner, and the new banner showed a Christian cross.

We were not alone.

I stepped back, almost tripping on a body. 'Coward!' Cnut shouted at me.

'You told me what would happen if I died,' I called to him, 'but what happens if you die?'

'If I die?' The question seemed to puzzle him as though such an outcome was an impossibility.

'Does your army surrender to me?' I asked.

'They'll kill you,' he snarled.

I jerked my head towards the ridge where the newcomers stood beneath the banner of the cross. 'You're going to find that a little more difficult now.'

'Just more Saxons to kill,' Cnut said. 'More filth to clean from the land.'

'So if you and I fight,' I said, 'and you win, then you go south to face Edward?'

'Maybe.'

'And if you lose,' I said, 'your army still goes south?'

'I won't lose,' he snarled.

'But you're not offering a fair fight,' I said. 'If you lose then your army must surrender to me.'

He laughed at that. 'You're a fool, Uhtred of Bebbanburg.'

'If my death makes no difference,' I said, 'why should I fight?'

'Because it's fate,' Cnut said, 'you and I.'

'If you die,' I insisted, 'then your army must take my orders. Tell them that.'

'I shall tell them to piss on your corpse,' he said.

But first he had to kill me and I was stronger now. The newcomers under the big banner of the cross were allies, not enemies. It must have been their scouts we had seen in the west, and now they were here and, though it was no army, there had to be two or three hundred men on the ridge's crest, enough to halt the Danes who had crossed the river to my north. 'If we fight,' I told Cnut, 'then we fight fair. If you win, my men live; if I win, your men take my orders.' He said nothing, and I turned from him and rejoined my men. I could see that the Danes to the north had stopped their advance, worried by the newcomers, while Cnut's larger force across the ford was still not arrayed in a shield wall. They had crowded along the ford's edge to watch us fight, and Cnut now bellowed at them to form ranks. He wanted to attack fast, but it would take a few moments for his men to make their ranks and lock their shields.

So while they made their new shield wall I pushed back through my ranks. Young Æthelstan was riding fast and careless down from the ridge. 'Lord! Lord!' he shouted. Æthelflaed was following him, but I ignored them both because two horsemen were also coming from the ridge. One was a big, bearded man in mail and helmet, while the other was a priest. The priest wore no armour, just a long black robe, and he smiled as he reached me. 'I thought you needed help,' he said.

'He always needs help,' the larger man said, 'Lord Uhtred stumbles into a pit of shit and we pull him out.' He grinned at me. 'Greetings, my friend.'

He was Father Pyrlig and he was my friend. He had been a great warrior before he became a priest. He was a Welshman, proud of his tribe. His beard had turned grey and the hair under his helmet was grey, but his face was lively as ever. 'Would you believe,' I asked him, 'that I'm glad to see you?'

'I believe you! Because this is as filthy a pit of shit as any I've seen,' Pyrlig said. 'I've got two hundred and thirty-eight men. How many bastards does he have?'

'Four thousand?'

'Oh, that's good,' Pyrlig said. 'It's lucky we're Welshmen. Four thousand Danes? No trouble for a few Welshmen.'

'You're all Welsh?' I asked.

'We asked for help,' the other priest said, 'to ensure that the light of the gospel isn't extinguished from Britain, so that the pagans are defeated utterly, and so the love of Christ will fill this land.'

'What he means,' Pyrlig explained, 'is that he knew you were in the shit so he came to me and asked for help, and I had nothing better to do.'

'We asked good Christian men to offer their services,' the younger priest explained earnestly, 'and these men came.'

'"And then I heard the voice of God",' Pyrlig said in a sonorous tone, and I realised he was quoting from the Christians' holy book, '"and He said, 'Whom shall I send? Who will go for me?' and I said, 'Here I am, Lord, send me.'"' He paused, then smiled at me. 'I always was an idiot, Uhtred.'

'And King Edward is coming,' the younger priest said. 'We just have to hold them here for a short while.'

'You know that?' I asked, still dazed.

'I know it . . .' he paused, 'Father.'

The younger priest was Father Judas, my son. The son I had insulted, beaten and rejected. I turned away from him so that he would not see the tears in my eyes.

'The armies met north of Lundene,' Father Judas went on, 'but that was over a week ago. Lord Æthelred joined his men to King Edward's and they're both coming north.'

'Æthelred left East Anglia?' I asked. I was finding it difficult to comprehend the news.

'As soon as you drew Cnut away from the frontier. He went south towards Lundene.'

'Lundene,' I said vaguely.

'He and Edward met somewhere just to the north of Lundene, I think.'

I sniffed. Still more Danes were arriving across the river where Cnut's shield wall was widening. Now it would overlap us at either end. That meant we must lose. I turned back to look at the man who had been my son. 'You blamed me for killing Abbot Wihtred,' I said.

'He was a holy man,' he said reprovingly.

'He was a traitor! Cnut sent him. He was doing their bidding.' I pointed Serpent-Breath at the Danes. 'It was all Cnut's idea!' Father Judas just stared at me. I could see he was trying to decide whether or not I was lying. 'Ask Finan,' I said, 'or Rolla. They were both there when Cnut's children talked about Uncle Wihtred. I did you damned Christians a service, but I get little thanks from you.'

'But why would Cnut send Æthelred chasing after the blessed Oswald's bones?' Pyrlig asked. 'He knew that finding them would encourage the Saxons, so why do it?'

'Because he'd already pounded the bones to dust or thrown them into the sea. He knew there were no bones.'

'But there were,' Father Judas said triumphantly. 'They found them, God be praised.'

'They found a skeleton I chopped up for them, you young fool. Ask Osferth if you live long enough to see him again. I even chopped off the wrong arm. And your precious Wihtred was sent by Cnut! So what do you have to say to that?'

He looked from me to the enemy. 'I'd say, Father, that you'd best retreat to the higher ground.'

'You insolent bastard,' I said. But he was right. The Danes were almost ready to advance, and their wall was far wider than mine, which meant we would be surrounded and we would die, and so our only hope now was to join the Welsh on the ridge's low crest and hope that together we could hold the enemy till help came. 'Finan,' I shouted, 'up the hill, fast! Now!'

I thought Cnut might attack when he saw us retreat, but he was too intent on gathering the men who still arrived and adding them to his shield wall, which was now over eight ranks deep. He could have hurried over the river and assaulted us while we went back to the ridge's top, but he must have thought we would reach that low summit long before he could catch us and he preferred to attack in his own time and with overwhelming force.

And so we went to the ridge, our last refuge. It was hardly a hill to frighten an enemy. The slope was gentle and easy to climb, but there were those burning houses and they made formidable obstacles. There were seven of them and all still burned. The roofs had collapsed so that each was now a smoking pit of fire, and our shield wall filled the gaps between the fierce blazes. The Welsh faced north towards the men who had crossed the river, and my men faced east and south towards Cnut's larger force, and there we touched our shields together and watched as Cnut's horde crossed the ford.

The Welsh were singing a psalm in praise of the nailed god. Their voices were strong, deep and confident. We had made a circle on the ridge's top, a circle of shields and weapons and fire. Æthelflaed was in the circle's centre where our banners flew, and where, I thought, the last survivors must eventually be crushed and cut down. Father Judas and two other priests were moving along the ranks giving men blessings. One by one the Christians knelt and the priests would touch the crest of their helmet. 'Believe in the resurrection of the dead,' Father Judas said to Sihtric in my earshot, 'and in the life everlasting, and may the peace of God shine upon you ever more.'

'Were you telling the truth about Wihtred?' Pyrlig asked me. He was standing behind me in our second rank. Today, it seemed, he would be a warrior again. He carried a heavy shield decorated with a dragon writhing about a cross, and in his other hand a short, stout spear.

'That he was doing Cnut's bidding? Yes.'

He chuckled. 'A clever bastard, our Cnut. How are you?'

'Angry.'

'Ah, nothing changes.' He smiled. 'Who are you angry with?'

'Everyone.'

'It's good to be angry before battle.'

I gazed southwards, looking for King Edward's army. It was strange how peaceful that land looked, just low hills and lush pastures, fields of stubble and stands of trees, and a swan flying westwards and the falcon high above just circling on its still, outstretched wings. It was all so beautiful, and so empty. No warriors.

'My lady!' I threaded our thin wall to face Æthelflaed. Cnut's son was beside her, guarded by a tall warrior who had a drawn seax.

'Lord Uhtred?' she said.

'Did you choose a man to do what I suggested?'

She hesitated, then nodded. 'But God will give us victory.'

I looked at the tall man with the drawn sword and he just lifted the short blade to show he was ready. 'Is it sharp?' I asked him.

'It will cut deep and swift, lord,' he said.

'I love you,' I said to Æthelflaed, not caring who heard me. I gazed at her for a moment, my woman of gold with her stern jaw and blue eyes, and then I turned back fast because a great shout deafened the sky.

Cnut was coming.

He came as I had expected. He came slowly. His massive shield wall was so big that most of his men would never have to fight, they just trailed behind the long front ranks that tramped towards the ridge. The pagan banners were held high. The Danes were beating blades against shields in a rhythm set by the big war drums behind their massive wall. They were chanting too, though I could not hear what words they said. The Welsh were still singing.

I pushed through to the front rank, taking my place between Finan and Uhtred, my son. Pyrlig was again behind me, his big shield raised to protect me from the spears and axes that would be hurled before the shield walls clashed.

Though the insults came first. The Danes were close enough now that we could see their helmet-framed faces, see the grimaces, the snarling. 'You're cowards,' they taunted us. 'Your women will be our whores!'

Cnut faced me. He was flanked by a pair of tall warriors in fine war gear, men heavy with arm rings, men whose reputations came from battle-slaughter. I sheathed Serpent-Breath and drew Wasp-Sting, the seax. She was much shorter than Serpent-Breath, but in the close embrace of a shield wall a long weapon is a hindrance, while a short blade can be lethal. I kissed the sword's hilt, then touched the hilt to the hammer about my neck. Cnut still carried Ice-Spite, though he had taken a shield for this assault. The shield was covered in cowhide on which his symbol of the axe-shattered cross was daubed in black paint. The two men who flanked him carried wide-bladed, long-hafted war axes.

'What they'll do,' I said, 'is try to hook my shield down with the axes so that Cnut can finish me. When they do it, you two can kill the axemen.'

Uhtred said nothing. He was shaking. He had never fought in the shield wall and perhaps would never fight in one again, but he was trying to look calm. His face was grim. I knew what he felt. I knew the fear. Finan was muttering in Irish, I assume it was a prayer. He carried a short-sword like mine.

The Danes were still shouting. We were women, we were boys, we were shit, we were cowards, we were dead men. They were scarce twenty paces away and they stopped there. They were summoning the courage for the rush uphill, for the killing. Two younger men stepped forward and called challenges to us, but Cnut snarled at them to get back in their ranks. He did not want any distractions. He wanted to kill us all. There were horsemen behind the deep ranks. If we broke and some of us fled westwards, which was the only direction where no Danes threatened, those horsemen would pursue and cut us down. Cnut did not just want to kill us, he wanted to annihilate us; he wanted his poets to sing of a battle where not one enemy survived, where Saxon blood made the ground sodden. His men shouted their insults, and we watched their faces, watched the blades, saw the shields lock and saw the spears fly. Spears and axes, hurled from the enemy's rearward ranks, and we crouched, shields locked, as the missiles struck. A spear thumped hard into my shield, but did not lodge there. Our own spears flew. They had small hope of piercing the shield wall, but a man whose shield is cumbered with a heavy spear or axe is at a disadvantage. Another blade crashed against my shield and then Cnut bellowed his order, 'Now!'

'God is with us!' Father Judas shouted.

'Brace yourselves!' Finan called.

And they came. A scream of war cries, faces disfigured by hate, shields raised, weapons ready, and perhaps we shouted too, and perhaps our faces were ugly with hate, and for certain our shields were locked and weapons ready, and they hit, and I went down on one knee as Cnut's shield slammed forward and crashed into mine. He thrust it low, hoping to slant the top away from my body so that his axemen could hook it with their blades and drag it down further, but I had anticipated him and the shields met plumb, and I was the heavier man so that Cnut recoiled, and Pyrlig's shield was above me as the twin axes slashed down, and I was moving.

Moving forward. Moving forward and rising. The axes struck Pyrlig's shield, which hit my helmet hard, but I hardly felt the blow because I was moving fast, snarling, and now it was my shield that was lower than Cnut's and I was driving his upwards. The axemen were trying to drag their weapons out of Pyrlig's shield, and Finan and Uhtred were screaming as they thrust at the pair, but all I saw was the inside of my shield as I thrust it up, still up, and Ice-Spite was too long to be used in this close embrace, but Wasp-Sting was short and she was stout and she was sharp, and I rammed my shield arm to the left, saw the bright mail beyond, and stabbed.

All my strength went into that stab. Years of sword-craft, of exercising, of training went into that lunge. I stood as I thrust. My shield had swept Cnut's aside, he was open, Ice-Spite was tangled in an axe-haft and my teeth were clenched and my hand death-tight around Wasp-Sting's hilt.

And she struck.

The blow jarred up my arm. Wasp-Sting's short blade struck Cnut hard, and I felt him recoil from the savage thrust, and still I pushed her, trying to gouge the guts from his belly, but then the man to Cnut's left chopped his shield down and the rim struck my forearm with such force that I was driven back down to my knees and Wasp-Sting was pulled back by the motion. The axe was raised, but stayed aloft as the strength went from the man's shield arm. A spear was in his chest, thrust by a man behind me, and I stabbed Wasp-Sting again, this time taking down the axeman, whose blood was already soaking his chest's mail. He went down. Uhtred had his seax in the dying man's face and pulled it free as I dragged my shield to cover myself and looked over the rim for Cnut.

285

And could not see him. He was gone. Had I killed him? That blow would have felled an ox, but I had not felt her pierce mail or break through skin and muscle. I had felt her strike with vicious force, a sword-thrust as heavy as Odin's thunder, and I knew I must have hurt him if not killed him, yet Cnut was nowhere to be seen. I could only see a man with a yellow beard and a silver neck ring coming to fill the place where Cnut had been standing and he was shouting at me as his shield crashed onto mine and we were shoving at each other. I probed with Wasp-Sting, found no gap. Pyrlig was bellowing about God, but keeping his shield high. A spear scraped against my left ankle, which meant a man was crouching low in the Danish second rank and I thrust my shield hard forward and the yellow-bearded man went backwards, tripped on the crouching spearman, and there was a gap and Finan was into the space faster than a mead-quickened weasel. His sword drank blood. The point was in the spearman's neck, not deep, but blood was rushing and bright, spurting and bright, and Finan twisted the blade as I slid Wasp-Sting into the man to my right, another hard blow, and I could feel pain in my forearm where the shield rim had struck it, but Wasp-Sting had found flesh and I fed her, I drove her between ribs, and my son brought his sword up from below so that the blade buried itself in the man's guts and he was lifted up as Uhtred ripped the sword still higher.

Guts and blood, shining coils, smelling of shit, spilling from a dying man's belly to be trampled into the mud, and men screaming and shields splintering, and we had only been fighting for a few heartbeats. I did not know what was happening on that low, smoke-wreathed ridge-top. I did not know which of my men were dying, or whether the enemy had broken our shield wall, because when the shield walls meet you only see what is there in front of you or just beside you. A blow struck my left shoulder and did no harm; I did not see who dealt it, I had stepped back and my shield was high and touching Finan's to my left and my son's to the right, and all I knew was that our part of the wall had held, that we had driven Cnut away, that the Danes were now impeded by their own dead, who made a low rampart in front of us. That made their job harder and made them easier to kill, yet still they came.

The Welshmen had stopped singing, which told me they were fighting, and I was dully aware of the sounds of battle behind me, the thunder of shields meeting shields, the clash of blades, but I dared not turn because an axeman was swinging his long-shafted axe to bring it down on my head and I stepped back, lifted the shield to let the axe strike, and Uhtred stepped over the dead man in front of me and took the axeman under the chin. One stab, quick and upwards, the blade going through the chin, the mouth, the tongue, up behind the nose and then he stepped away from the threat of a Danish sword-lunge, and the axeman was shaking like an aspen leaf, the axe forgotten in his suddenly weak hand as blood spilled from his mouth to run in wriggling rivulets down his beard, which was hung with dull iron rings.

A terrible scream sounded from my left and suddenly, above the stench of blood, ale and shit, I smelt roasting flesh. A man had been thrown into a burning cottage. 'We're holding them!' I shouted. 'We're holding them! Let the bastards come to us!' I did not want my men breaking ranks to pursue a wounded enemy. 'Hold hard!'

We had killed the enemy's front rank and hurt their second rank and now the Danes in front of me pulled back some two or three paces. To attack us now they had to clamber over their own dead and dying and they hesitated. 'Come to us!' I taunted them. 'Come and die!' And where was Cnut? I could not see him. Had I wounded him? Had he been carried down the slope to die where the big drums still thudded their battle-rhythm?

But if Cnut was missing, Sigurd Thorrson was there. Sigurd, who was Cnut's friend and whose son I had killed, bellowed at the Danes to give him room. 'I'll gut you!' he shouted at me. His eyes were red-rimmed and his mail thick and heavy and his sword a brutal long blade, and his neck was hung with gold and his arms were bright with metal as he charged up the slope, seeking me, but it was my son who stepped forward.

'Uhtred,' I shouted, but Uhtred ignored me, taking Sigurd's sword

287

blow on his shield and driving the seax forward with a young man's speed and strength. The seax glanced off the iron rim of Sigurd's shield and the big Dane tried to swing his sword at my son's waist, but the blow had no power because Sigurd was off balance. Then the two stepped apart, pausing to appraise each other.

'I'll kill your pup,' Sigurd snarled at me, 'then I'll kill you.' He gestured for his men to step back a pace, to give him space to fight, then he pointed his heavy sword at my son. 'Come on, little boy, come and die.'

Uhtred laughed. 'You're fat as a bishop,' he told Sigurd. 'You're like a Yule-fattened pig. You're a bloated piece of shit.'

'Pup,' Sigurd said and stepped forward, shield high, sword swinging from his right, and I remember thinking that my son was at a huge disadvantage because he was fighting with a seax and I thought to throw him Serpent-Breath, and then he went down.

He went down onto one knee, the shield held like a roof above him, and Sigurd's long-sword glanced off the shield, going nowhere, and my son was rising, the seax held firm, and he did all this so fast, so smoothly that he made it look easy as his brief blade punctured Sigurd's mail and buried itself in the heavy gut and Uhtred was still coming from his knees, all his body's strength behind that short blade that was deep inside his enemy's belly. 'That's for my father!' Uhtred shouted as he rose.

'Good boy,' Finan muttered.

'And for God the Father,' Uhtred said, ripping the seax upward, 'and God the Son,' he said with another jerk, pulling the blade higher, 'and God the Holy bloody Ghost,' and with that he stood fully upright and slit Sigurd's mail and flesh from the groin to the chest and he left the blade there, the hilt stuck in a gutted trunk and he used his free hand to rip Sigurd's sword away. He hammered the captured weapon on Sigurd's helmet, and the big man went down into the mess of entrails that had spilled around his boots, and then a group of Danes rushed to take revenge and I stepped forward to haul Uhtred back into the wall and he raised his shield to touch mine. He was laughing.

'You idiot,' I said.

He was still laughing as the shields hit, but the Danes were stumbling on dead men and slipping on guts, and we added to that carnage. Wasp-Sting went through mail and ribs again, sucking the life of a man who gasped the stench of sour ale into my face, then his bowels loosened and all I could smell were his turds, and I smashed the shield into the face of another man and flicked Wasp-Sting at his belly, but only broke a link of mail before he staggered backwards.

'God help us,' Pyrlig said in wonderment, 'but we're holding.'

'God is with you!' Father Judas shouted. 'The heathen are dying!'

'Not this heathen,' I snarled, and then I screamed at the Danes to come and die, I taunted them, I begged them to fight me.

I have tried to explain this to women, though few have understood. Gisela did, as did Æthelflaed, but most have looked at me as though I were something disgusting when I talked of the joy of battle. It is disgusting. It is wasteful. It is terrifying. It stinks. It makes misery. At battle's end there are dead friends and wounded men, and pain, and tears, and awful agony, and yet it is a joy. The Christians talk of a soul, though I have never seen, smelt, tasted or felt such a thing, but perhaps the soul is a man's spirit and in battle that spirit soars like a falcon in the wind. Battle takes a man to the edge of disaster, to a glimpse of the chaos that will end the world, and he must live in that chaos and on that edge and it is a joy. We weep and we exult. Sometimes, when the nights draw in and the cold days are short, we bring entertainers to the hall. They sing, they do tricks, they dance, and some juggle. I have seen a man tossing five sharp swords in a swirling, dazzling display, and you think he must be cut by one of the heavy blades as it falls, yet somehow he manages to snatch it from the air and the blade whirls upwards again. That is the edge of disaster. Do it right and you feel like a god, but get it wrong and it will be your guts being trampled underfoot.

We did it right. We had retreated to the ridge where we had made a circle of shields and that meant we could not be outflanked, and so the enemy's vast advantage of numbers counted for nothing. It would have counted in the end, of course. Even if we fought like fiends from the pit they would have worn us down and we would have died one by one, but Cnut's men were not given the time to destroy us. They fought, they struggled, they began to outweigh us, thrusting men forward by sheer force of numbers and I thought we must die, except suddenly the pressure of dying men holding shields that were being pushed by the men behind went away.

It was desperate for a while. The Danes crossed the line of dead and slammed shields against ours, and the men in the ranks behind heaved on the men in front, while men at the very back of the Danish ranks hurled more spears and axes. I killed the man facing me, I drove Wasp-Sting into his chest and felt the warm blood pour onto my gloved hand, and I saw the light go from his eyes and his head drop, but he did not fall. He was held upright by my blade and by the shield of the man behind him, and those men behind pushed and pushed so that the dead man was edging me backwards and there was nothing I could do except try to push him down with my shield, but a long-hafted axe was threatening me, and Pyrlig was trying to deflect it, and that meant he could not push against me and so we went back, step by step, and I knew the Danes must push us into a tight huddle that they could slaughter.

Then I managed to step back fast and so release the pressure and the dead man fell forward as I stepped onto his back and slid Wasp-Sting at the axeman. Something struck my helmet a ringing blow so that for a moment I saw nothing, just darkness riven with lightning, but I held onto the seax and stabbed it again and again, and then the pushing started again. A crash of shield on shield. An axe hammered onto my shield, driving it down and a spear came over the rim to pierce my left shoulder, striking bone, and I hauled the shield up, feeling a stabbing pain rip down my arm, and Wasp-Sting found flesh and I twisted her. My son Uhtred had dropped his shield that was little more than splinters of wood held together by cowhide, and he was using Sigurd's sword two-handed to thrust at the Danes. Finan was half crouched, darting his sword between shields, and the men behind us were trying to thrust spears into bearded faces, and no one was shouting any more. They grunted, they cursed, they moaned, they cursed again.

We were being pushed back. In a moment, I knew, we would be pushed past the fires of the burning houses and the Danes would see the gap and there would be a rush of men to fill it, to hack at our ranks from inside. This is the way I would die, I thought, and I gripped Wasp-Sting tight because I must hold her as I died so that I would go to Valhalla and drink and feast with my enemies.

Then suddenly the huge pressure vanished. Suddenly the Danes stepped back. They still fought. A snarling beast of a brute was hammering an axe at my shield, he split the boards, tried to rip the shield from my wounded arm, and Uhtred stepped in front of me and stabbed low so that the man dropped his shield and my son's stolen sword swept up, fast as a kingfisher's flight, to slash across the man's throat so that his brown beard turned dripping red. Uhtred stepped back, a Dane came for him and he contemptuously beat the man's sword aside and rammed his blade into the attacker's chest. That man fell backwards and there was no one behind to hold him upright and I realised that the Danes were now going backwards.

Because Edward of Wessex had arrived.

The poets sing of slaughter, though I have seen very few poets on a field of slaughter and those I have seen were usually whimpering at the back with their hands over their eyes, though that slaughter at Teotanheale was worthy of the greatest poet. Doubtless you have heard the songs that tell of King Edward's victory, how he cut down the Danish foemen, how he waded in pagan blood, and how God gave him a triumph that will be remembered as long as the world exists.

It was not quite like that. In truth Edward arrived when it was almost over, though he did fight and he fought bravely. It was Steapa, my friend, who panicked the Danes. Steapa Snotor he had been called, Steapa the Clever, which was a cruel joke because he was not a clever man. He was slow-thinking, but he was also loyal and terrible in battle. He had been born a slave, but had risen to become the leader of Alfred's household troops, and Edward had been clever enough to keep Steapa in his service. And Steapa now led horsemen in a fierce charge against the enemy's rear ranks.

It is a truth that men who do not feel the joy of battle, men who are frightened of the shield wall, will be at the rear. Some of them, perhaps most, will be drunk, because many men will use ale or mead to find the courage to fight. Those men are the worst troops and they were attacked by Steapa leading the king's household men and that was when the slaughter began, and when the slaughter begins, panic quickly follows.

The Danes broke.

The men at the back of the Danish ranks were in loose order, their shields were not touching, they expected no attack, and they broke apart before Steapa even reached them. They ran to find their horses and were ridden down by Saxon horsemen. More Saxons were making a new shield wall at the ford, and I saw that I had been looking in the wrong direction to find Edward's approach. I had thought he would come from the south, but instead he had followed the Roman roads from Tameworþig and so came from the east. The dragon banner of Wessex had been unfurled, and close to it was Æthelred's flag of the prancing horse, and I suddenly laughed aloud because there was a third flagstaff held high aloft at the centre of the rapidly forming shield wall, and this third staff had no banner. Instead a skeleton was tied to the long pole, a skeleton without a skull and with only one arm. Saint Oswald had come to fight for his people, and the bones were held high above an army of West Saxons and Mercians. The shield wall grew longer as Steapa's men herded the fleeing Danes like wolf-hounds chasing goats.

And someone checked the Danish panic. Their battle was still not lost. The men at the rear of the shield wall had broken and were being slain by Steapa's vengeful horsemen, but hundreds of others went east towards the ditch-like river where a man was bellowing at them to form a new shield wall. And they did make a new wall, and I remember thinking what magnificent warriors they were. They had been surprised and panicked, but still they had discipline enough to turn and stand. The man bellowing orders was on horseback. 'It's Cnut,' Finan said.

'I thought the bastard was dead.'

We were no longer fighting. The Danes had fled from us and we had stayed on the ridge surrounded by blood-laced bodies, by a rim of bodies, some still living.

'It's Cnut,' Finan said again.

It was Cnut. I could see him now, a figure in white amongst ranks of mail-grey men. He had found a horse and was riding beneath his big banner, constantly looking back to watch the West Saxons crossing the ford. He was plainly determined to rescue as much of his army as he could and his best hope was to go north. Edward and Æthelred's forces were blocking any escape southwards, Steapa's horsemen were rampaging to the west, but there were still those Danes to the north who, though they had failed to break the Welsh shield wall, had kept their discipline as they retreated down the hill. Cnut now led the remainder of his army towards them, using the strip of pasture between the river and the ridge. He had lost almost all his horses, and perhaps a quarter of his men were either dead, wounded or fleeing, but he still led a formidable army and he planned to lead it north till he found a place to make a stand.

Edward's shield wall was still forming, while Steapa's men would be helpless against Cnut's new shield wall. Horses can chase down fleeing men, but no horse will charge into a shield wall, which meant Cnut was safe for the moment. Safe and escaping, and I knew only one way to stop him.

I seized Æthelstan's horse and dragged the boy from the saddle. He yelped in protest, but I threw him aside, put my foot in the stirrup and hauled myself up. I took the reins and kicked the horse towards the river. The Welshmen on the east of the ridge parted to let me through and I spurred into a billow of pungent smoke that bellied from a dying fire, then was clear of the hill's crest and galloping down towards the Danes. 'Are you running, you coward?' I bellowed at Cnut. 'Have you got no belly for a fight, you slug-shit?'

He stopped and turned towards me. His men also stopped. One of them threw a spear at me, but the weapon fell short.

'Running away?' I jeered. 'Abandoning your son? I'll sell him to slavery, Cnut Turdson. I'll sell him to some fat Frank who likes small boys. Such men pay well for fresh meat.'

And Cnut took the bait. He spurred his horse free of the ranks and came towards me. He stopped a score of paces away, kicked his feet from the stirrups and slid down from the saddle. 'Just you and me,' he said, drawing Ice-Spite. He carried no shield. 'It's fate, Uhtred,' he said it almost mildly, as though we discussed the weather. 'The gods want it, they want you and me. They want to know who's the best.'

'You haven't much time,' I answered. Edward's shield wall was almost formed and I could hear his captains shouting, making certain the ranks were tight.

'I don't need time to finish your miserable life,' Cnut said. 'Now get off your horse and fight.'

I dismounted. I remember thinking how strange it was because just across the river two women were gleaning in a field of stubble, bent over to find the precious grain, apparently uninterested in the armies beyond the ditch. I still had my shield, but my shoulder and arm hurt. The pain felt like fire burning down the muscles, and when I tried to lift the shield there was a stab of agony that made me flinch.

And Cnut attacked. He ran at me, Ice-Spite in his right hand, coming high towards the left side of my head and I lifted the shield despite the pain and somehow, I never knew how, his sword was coming from my right, only it was lunging for my ribs and I remember being astonished at the skill and speed of that stroke, but Serpent-Breath knocked the quick blade aside and I tried to bring her up for a counter-stroke, but Cnut was already slicing the blade at my neck and I had to duck. I heard it clash and scrape on my helmet and I rammed the shield at him, using my greater weight to crush him, but he skipped aside, lunged again and Ice-Spite pierced mail to cut my belly. I went back fast, taking the sting from the blow as

I felt warm blood trickle down my skin, then at last I made a cut with Serpent-Breath, a backhanded stroke that scythed towards his shoulder and he was forced back, but came forward as soon as the blade passed him, lunging again, and I caught the tip of Ice-Spite on the lower rim of my shield and swung Serpent-Breath back to strike his helmet. The blade clashed loud on the side of his helmet, but he was moving away and there was no real power in the blow. It still shook him and I saw his teeth gritted, but he pulled Ice-Spite free of my shield and stabbed down at my left foot and I felt a lance of pain as I punched his face with Serpent-Breath's hilt to drive him back. He went back and I followed, swinging, but my wounded foot slipped in a patch of cow shit and I went down on my right knee, and Cnut, his nose bleeding, lunged his sword at me.

He was quick. He was like lightning, and the only way to slow him was to be close, to crowd him, and I drove myself forward from my knees, using the shield to deflect the lunge and try to hammer it onto his face. I was taller than he, I was heavier, I had to use that height and weight to overwhelm him, but he knew what I was doing. He grinned through the blood on his face and flicked Ice-Spite so that she tapped the side of my helmet, and he skipped back, hesitated, but the hesitation was a ruse for as soon as I stepped towards him the pale blade darted at my face, I flinched away and he tapped her on my helmet again. He laughed. 'You're not good enough, Uhtred.'

I paused, breathing heavily, watching him, but he knew that was my ruse. He just smiled and let Ice-Spite drop as if inviting me to strike. 'Strange to say,' he said, 'I like you.'

'I like you too,' I said. 'I thought I'd killed you on the ridge-top.'

He used his free hand to touch the thick iron buckle of his sword belt. 'You dented that,' he said, 'and took all the wind from me. It hurt, really hurt. I couldn't breathe for a while and my men dragged me away.'

I lifted Serpent-Breath and Ice-Spite flicked up. 'Next time it will be your throat,' I said.

'You're quicker than most,' he said, 'but not quick enough.' His men were watching from the hill's foot, as my men and their Welsh saviours were watching from the ridge's top. Even Edward's shield wall had stopped to watch. 'If they see you die,' Cnut said, twitching Ice-Spite's tip towards the West Saxon and Mercian army, 'they'll lose heart. That's why I have to kill you, but I'll make it fast.' He grinned. There was blood in his pale moustache and more trickled from his broken nose. 'It won't hurt much, I promise, so hold your sword tight, friend, and we'll meet in Valhalla.' He took a half-pace towards me. 'Ready?'

I glanced to my right, to where Edward's men had crossed the ford. 'They're marching again,' I said.

He looked southwards and I leaped. I sprang at him, and for a splinter of time he was looking at the West Saxons who were being urged forward, but he recovered fast and Ice-Spite darted up to my face and I felt her scrape on my cheekbone and catch between my skull and the helmet, and I did not know it but I was screaming a war shout as I slammed the shield onto him, thrusting it down to drive him to the ground, and he twisted like an eel, dragged his sword arm back and the blade cut my cheek, and the shield caught his right arm and all my weight and strength were in that blow, yet still he managed to dodge aside. I back-swung Serpent-Breath at him and he dodged and she went wide so that my arms were spread, the shield off to my left after its sweeping blow and Serpent-Breath to my right, and I saw him change hands, saw Ice-Spite in his left hand and saw her come at me like a stab of lightning and the blade struck me, she pierced the mail and broke the leather and she shattered a rib and pierced me and he was screaming his victory as I brought Serpent-Breath back in a last desperate swing and she crashed into his helmet and stunned him, and he went backwards, falling, and I was falling on him, my chest a furnace of pain, Ice-Spite inside me, and Serpent-Breath was across his throat and I remember sawing her and seeing her cut and the blood spraying into my face and my war cry became a scream of pain as we both fell on the meadow.

And then I remember nothing.

*　*　*

'Quiet,' the voice said, then said it louder, 'quiet!'

There was a fire burning. I sensed a lot of people in a small room. There was the stench of blood, of burned bread, of woodsmoke and of rotted floor rushes.

'He won't die,' another voice said, but not close to me.

'The spear broke his skull?'

'I lifted the bone back, now we must pray.'

'But I wasn't wounded in the skull,' I said, 'it's my chest. His sword went into my chest. Low down on my left side.'

They ignored me. I wondered why I could not see. I turned my head and there was a glow in the dark of my eyes.

'Lord Uhtred moved.' It was Æthelflaed's voice and I became aware that her small hand was holding my left hand.

'It was my chest,' I said, 'tell them it was my chest. It wasn't my skull.'

'The skull heals,' a man said, the same man who had talked about lifting the bone back.

'It was my chest, you idiot,' I said.

'I think he's trying to speak,' Æthelflaed said.

There was something in my right hand. I tightened my fingers and felt the familiar roughness of the leather bindings. Serpent-Breath. I felt a wash of relief go through me because whatever happened I had held onto her and my grip would carry me to Valhalla.

'Valhalla,' I said.

'I think he's just moaning,' a man said close by.

'He'll never know he killed Cnut,' another man said.

'He will know!' Æthelflaed said fiercely.

'My lady . . .'

'He will know!' she insisted, and her fingers tightened on mine.

'I do know,' I said. 'I cut his throat, of course I know.'

'Just moaning,' the man's voice said very close by. A cloth with rough weave was wiped across my lips, then there was a gust of colder air and the sound of people entering the room. A half-dozen people spoke at once, then someone was close by my head and a hand stroked my forehead.

297

'He's not dead, Finan,' Æthelflaed said softly.

Finan said nothing. 'I killed him,' I said to Finan. 'But he was fast. Even faster than you.'

'Sweet Jesus,' Finan said, 'I can't imagine life without him.' He sounded heartbroken.

'I'm not dead, you Irish bastard,' I said, 'we have battles yet to fight, you and I.'

'Is he speaking?' Finan asked.

'Just groaning,' a man's voice answered, and I was aware that more folk had come into the room. Finan's hand went away and another took its place.

'Father?' It was Uhtred.

'I'm sorry if I was cruel to you,' I said, 'but you're good. You killed Sigurd! Men will know you now.'

'Oh dear God,' Uhtred said, then his hand went away. 'Lord?' he said.

'How is he?' That was King Edward of Wessex. There was a rustle as men went to their knees.

'He can't last long,' a man's voice said.

'And Lord Æthelred?'

'The wound is grievous, lord, but I think he will live.'

'God be praised. What happened?'

There was a pause as if no one wanted to answer. 'I'm not dying,' I said, and no one took any notice.

'Lord Æthelred was attacked by a group of Danes, lord,' a man said, 'at the end of the battle. Most were surrendering. These tried to kill Lord Æthelred.'

'I see no wound,' the king said.

'The back of his skull, lord. The helmet took most of the blow, but the tip of the spear went through.'

The back of his skull, I thought, it would be the back of his skull. I laughed. It hurt. I stopped laughing.

'Is he dying?' a voice close by asked.

Æthelflaed's fingers gripped mine hard. 'He's just choking,' she said.

'Sister,' the king said.

'Be quiet, Edward!' she said fiercely.

'You should be at your husband's side,' Edward said sternly.

'You boring little fart,' I told him.

'I am where I wish to be,' Æthelflaed said in a tone I knew well. No one would win an argument with her now, and no one tried, though a voice muttered something about her behaviour being unseemly.

'They're rancid shit-wits,' I told her, and felt her hand stroke my forehead.

There was silence except for the crackle of the burning logs in the hearth. 'Has he been given the rites?' the king asked after a while.

'He doesn't want the rites,' Finan said.

'He must have them,' Edward insisted. 'Father Uhtred?'

'His name isn't Uhtred,' I snarled, 'he's called Father Judas. The bastard should have been a warrior!'

Yet to my surprise Father Judas was weeping. His hands shook as he touched me, as he prayed over me, as he administered the death rites. When he finished he left his fingers on my lips. 'He was a loving father,' he said.

'Of course I wasn't,' I said.

'A difficult man,' Edward said, though not unsympathetically.

'He was not difficult,' Æthelflaed said fiercely, 'but he was only happy when he was fighting. And you were all frightened of him, but in truth he was generous, kind and stubborn.' She was crying now.

'Oh, do stop it, woman,' I said, 'you know I can't bear weeping women.'

'Tomorrow we go south,' the king announced, 'and we shall give thanks for a great victory.'

'A victory Lord Uhtred gave you,' Æthelflaed said.

'That he gave us,' the king agreed, 'and that God allowed him to give us. And we shall build burhs in Mercia. There is God's work to do.'

'My father would want to be buried at Bebbanburg,' Father Judas said.

299

'I want to be buried with Gisela!' I said. 'But I'm not dying!'

I could not see, not even the glow of the fire. Or rather I could only see a great vault that was both dark and light at the same time, a cave shot through with strange lights, and somewhere in the far recesses of that glowing darkness were figures and I thought Gisela was one, and I gripped Serpent-Breath as the pain tore through me again so that I arched my back and that made the pain worse. Æthelflaed gasped and clung to my hand and another hand closed about the grip I had on Serpent-Breath, holding me tight to her.

'He's going,' Æthelflaed said.

'God take his soul.' It was Finan who was holding my hand to Serpent-Breath's hilt.

'I am not!' I said. 'I am not!' And the woman in the cave was alone now and it really was Gisela, lovely Gisela, and she was smiling at me, holding her hands towards me, and she was speaking though I could not hear her voice. 'Be quiet, all of you,' I said, 'I want to hear Gisela.'

'Any moment,' a voice said in a hushed tone.

A long pause. A hand touched my face. 'He still lives, God be praised,' Father Judas said uncertainly.

Then there was another silence. A long silence. Gisela had faded and my eyes stared at misted nothingness. I was aware of people around the bed. A horse neighed and out in the dark an owl called.

'Wyrd bið ful āræd,' I said, and no one answered, so I said it again.

Wyrd bið ful āræd.

Historical Note

AD 910. This year Frithestan took to the bishopric of Wintan-ceaster; and the same year King Edward sent an army both from Wessex and Mercia, which very much harassed the northern army by their attacks on men and property of every kind. They slew many of the Danes, and remained in the country five weeks. This year the Angles and the Danes fought at Teotanheale; and the Angles had the victory.

That was one of the entries in the Anglo-Saxon Chronicle for the year 910. Another recorded Æthelred's death, prematurely, though some historians believe Æthelred was wounded so gravely at Teotanheale that the injury brought on his death in 911.

Teotanheale is now Tettenhall, a pleasant suburb of Wolverhampton in the West Midlands. Readers familiar with the area might protest that the River Tame does not run near Tettenhall, but there is evidence that it did in the tenth century AD, long before it was diked, channelled and diverted to its present course.

We know there was a battle at Tettenhall in AD 910, and we know that it was fought by a combined army of Wessex and Mercia that decisively defeated the marauding Danes. The two Danish leaders were killed. Their names were Eowils and Healfdan, but rather than introduce two new names to the story and promptly kill them, I decided to use Cnut and Sigurd, who feature in some of the earlier novels about Uhtred's adventures. We know very little, indeed next to nothing, of what happened at Tettenhall.

There was a battle and the Danes lost, but why or how is a mystery. So the battle is not fiction, though my version is entirely invented. I doubt that the Danes precipitated the search for Saint Oswald's bones, though that too happened when Æthelred of Mercia sent an expedition into southern Northumbria to retrieve the bones. Oswald was a Northumbrian saint, and one theory holds that Æthelred was attempting to solicit the support of those Saxons living under Danish rule in Northumbria. The bones were discovered and taken back to Mercia where they were interred at Gloucester, all but for the skull, which remained in Durham (four other churches in Europe claim to possess the skull, but Durham seems the likeliest candidate), and the one arm that was at Bamburgh (Bebbanburg), though, centuries later, that was stolen by monks from Peterborough.

The first Latin quote in Chapter Eleven, *moribus et forma conciliandus amor*, which is incised on the Roman bowl that Uhtred reduces to hacksilver, is from Ovid; 'pleasant looks and good manners assist love', which is probably true, but was undoubtedly rare in Saxon Britain. The second quote, on the bridge at Tameworþig, is quoted from the magnificent Roman bridge at Alcántara in Spain: *pontem perpetui mansurum in saecula*, which means 'I have built a bridge which will last for ever.' The Saxons lived in the shadow of Roman Britain, surrounded by the ruins of their great monuments, using their roads, and doubtless wondering why such magnificence had decayed to oblivion.

The battle at Tettenhall has long been forgotten, yet it was an important event in the slow process that created England. In the ninth century it seemed as if Saxon culture was doomed and that the Danes would occupy all of southern Britain. There would probably have been no England, but a country called Daneland instead. Yet Alfred of Wessex stemmed the Danish advance and fought back to secure his country. His essential weapon was the burh, the series of fortified towns that sheltered the population and frustrated the Danes, who had no taste for sieges. Wessex then becomes the springboard for the campaigns that will reconquer the north and create a unified country of the English-speaking tribes: England. By

302

the time of Alfred's death in AD 899, the north, all but for impregnable Bebbanburg, is under Danish rule, while the centre of the country is split between Danes and Saxons. Yet slowly, inexorably, West Saxon armies advance northwards. That process was far from over in 910, but by winning the decisive victory at Tettenhall, the West Saxons drive the Danes out of the Midlands. New burhs in the conquered territory will consolidate the gains. Yet the Danes are far from beaten. They will invade again, and their hold on the north is still powerful, but from this point on they are mostly on the defensive. Edward, Alfred's son, and Æthelflaed, Alfred's daughter, are the driving forces behind this process, yet neither will live to see the final victory, which results, at last, in a country called England. That victory will be won by Æthelstan, Edward's son, and Uhtred will be there to witness it.

But that is another story.

Also by Bernard Cornwell

The WARRIOR Chronicles
The Last Kingdom
The Pale Horseman
The Lords of the North
Sword Song
The Burning Land
Death of Kings

Azincourt

The GRAIL QUEST Series
Harlequin
Vagabond
Heretic

1356

Stonehenge: a novel of 2000 BC

The Fort

The STARBUCK Chronicles
Rebel
Copperhead
Battle Flag
The Bloody Ground

The WARLORD Chronicles
The Winter King
The Enemy of God
Excalibur

Gallows Thief

By Bernard Cornwell and Susannah Kells

A Crowning Mercy
Fallen Angels

THE SHARPE SERIES
(IN CHRONOLOGICAL ORDER)

Sharpe's Tiger (1799)
Sharpe's Triumph (1803)
Sharpe's Fortress (1803)
Sharpe's Trafalgar (1805)
Sharpe's Prey (1807)
Sharpe's Rifles (1809)
Sharpe's Havoc (1809)
Sharpe's Eagle (1809)
Sharpe's Gold (1810)
Sharpe's Escape (1810)
Sharpe's Fury (1811)
Sharpe's Battle (1811)
Sharpe's Company (1812)
Sharpe's Sword (1812)
Sharpe's Enemy (1812)
Sharpe's Honour (1813)
Sharpe's Regiment (1813)
Sharpe's Siege (1814)
Sharpe's Revenge (1814)
Sharpe's Waterloo (1815)
Sharpe's Devil (1820–21)